Karate

Its History and Practice

Koyama Masashi

Wada Koji

Kadekaru Toru

Translated by Alexander Bennett

Translation and Editorial Conventions

Japanese words and expressions have been divided into their most logical components to assist with reading and pronunciation. Japanese terms, including most of the karate terminology used in this book, have been Romanised according to the Hepburn system and italicised. Japanese words found in most standard English dictionaries and most classical and modern budo disciplines (karate, karatejutsu, jujutsu etc.) are treated as Anglicised words or proper nouns. *Kata* names are capitalised and written with italics. Macrons have not been used to approximate long vowel sounds. Japanese names are listed in the conventional Japanese order with surname first. Organisations such as the Nippon Budokan and the Dai-Nippon Butokukai are commonly referred to as Budokan and Butokukai and are sometimes shortened as such in the text. All era dates in this book are quoted according to conventions used in the *Kodansha Encyclopedia of Japan*. Spelling is based on British conventions.

The translator is indebted to Bryan Peterson, Mako Inouye, Michael Ishimatsu-Prime, Hamish Robison, and Shishikura Masashi for their invaluable assistance preparing the English manuscript.

© Nippon Budokan Foundation
ISBN978–4–583–11401–9
All rights reserved by Nippon Budokan.
No part of this book may be used or reproduced without written permission, except for brief quotations in critical publications or reviews.

First edition published in July 2021
by Nippon Budokan
2-3 Kitanomaru Kōen, Chiyoda-ku, Tokyo, Japan

Written by KOYAMA Masashi, WADA Koji, KADEKARU Toru
Translated by Alexander Bennett
Design and Layout by Bunkasha International Corporation

Contents

Chapter 3   Kansai Region

Chapter 4   Postwar Period

RECOMMENDATION

Sasagawa Takashi
(Japan Karatedo Federation President)

— "The door has been opened to the techniques and history of karate"

Karate is a Japanese budo. It is a fusion of the ancient art of self-defence known as *Tii*, which was handed down through generations in the Ryukyu Kingdom of Okinawa, and Chinese fighting techniques known as *quanfa*, which was introduced by Ming Dynasty envoys. In the process of spreading the art, it developed into a Way inheriting the spirit of ancient Japanese martial arts. This is common knowledge for those involved in karate. The techniques and history of karate, and the way people thought and practised in the early days of karate, has never been fully explored until now.

Originally, this book was a series of articles that first appeared in the monthly *Gekkan Budo* magazine entitled "Karate: Its History and Practice" written by Koyama Masashi, Wada Koji, and Kadekaru Toru, and it was very well received. It brings me great joy to see that the articles have been collated into a single volume. It will surely become a must-read for all karate practitioners from now on.

FOREWORD

Mifuji Yoshio
Nippon Budokan (Executive Director and Secretary General)

Since 2010, the monthly Gekkan Budo magazine published by the Nippon Budokan has published a series of articles on the history and techniques of various budo disciplines. So far, we have completed series on kyudo, judo, sumo, and kendo. Eight years ago, we started planning the "Karate: Its History and Techniques" series and carefully considered what should be the overall concept, and who would write the articles.

Karate originated in Okinawa and is now taught mainly in Japan by the four major schools related to Shuri-te (Shotokan, Wado-ryu and Shito-ryu), and Naha-te (Goju-ryu). We consulted with Nagura Toshihisa, secretary general of the World Karate Federation who studies Shotokan, and Koyama Masashi of Goju-ryu, about how we could use the series to clarify the overall picture of karate rather than focus on a specific style.

Initially, we were thinking of asking Mr. Nagura and Mr. Koyama to write the articles. Mr. Nagura was at the forefront of the drive to get karate accepted as an official event for the Tokyo Olympics and did not have enough time to write. He recommended Wada Koji, winner of the 1st Karate World Championships, who happened to be his junior at Keio University. Mr. Koyama also suggested that we ask Kadekaru Toru, a karate researcher of renown in Okinawa, the birthplace of karate, to write about Okinawa. This would add a new dimension to the articles.

Thus, it was decided to start the series jointly written by these three authors. Most people know that karate originated in the Ryukyus (Okinawa) based on Chinese kempo, and spread to Japan later on where it developed into a Japanese budo. Nevertheless, until now there have been no reliable publications that explore the whole picture of how karate evolved.

Since both Mr. Wada and Mr. Koyama were both world champions in *kumite* and *kata* respectively, and as Mr. Kadekaru is both a researcher and a teacher of Okinawan karate, we decided to make some of the content based on their personal experiences.

The series started with a general commentary by Mr. Koyama, and then went through karate's evolution in chronological order. Mr. Kadekaru wrote about the developmental history of karate based on historical documents from Okinawa, and how it was transmitted to mainland Japan. Mr. Wada and Mr. Koyama wrote about training methods based on their own experiences, the history of *kumite* and *kata* competitions, activities of university students in the east and west of Japan and the internationalisation of karate.

Through their diligent work, I believe we were able to get a complete picture of the history and techniques of karate. The three authors decided on the various perspectives from which the history and techniques should be analysed and how to describe the processes involved in karate's development.

Mr. Wada also wrote of personal experiences at the 1st World Championships the people he interacted with. Mr. Koyama was able to share the results of more than 40 years of wide-ranging research on Miyagi Chojun, his personal career in karate, and accounts of his contact with world-famous athletes during his time as the All-Japan coach. Mr. Kadekaru wrote a valuable essay on the history of karate from the Ryukyu period based on the latest historical documents to be unearthed in Okinawa.

The diversity of karate, with its many schools and factions, can result in various problems that cannot be solved by any individual master. In the case of this co-authored book, the challenge was how to make the various historical viewpoints that exist consistent as a whole. We thought it would be useful to base the articles on three main trunks: Okinawa, Shuri-te in the Kanto region, and Naha-te in the Kansai region. The authors have direct experience in these different schools, so this ensured a balanced historical account. This is just the start. In the future I hope that these three trunks can be increased so that karate research becomes even broader and deeper, like a forest.

Karate has continued to change with the times and is scheduled to feature as an official sport at the upcoming Tokyo Olympic Games. It is my sincere hope that this book, Karate: Its History and Practice, will serve as the basis for the further research and development in karate, and as a reference for self-development and happiness among all practitioners. I would like to express my thanks to the authors, the book's editor, Nagasawa Katsunari of the Publications and Public Relations Section at the Nippon Budokan, and Alex Bennett for his hard work translating the book into English.

It is with great sadness that the Nippon Budokan announces the recent passing of Executive Director Mr. Mifuji Yoshio on June 11, 2021, just before this English translation was completed. He was always a dedicated servant to the promotion of budo culture.

CHAPTER 1

OKINAWA

Kadekaru Toru

The History of Karate and Okinawa

1. Historical Periods of Okinawa

Formerly known as the Ryukyu Kingdom, Okinawa is the birthplace of karate. The Kingdom lasted from the Muromachi period (1336–1573) through to the modern era. In the histography of Okinawa, the Kingdom's formative years are referred to as "Ko-Ryukyu" (Old Ryukyu), and a differentiation is made between period divisions in standard Japanese history.

The islands came under the control of the Satsuma domain samurai in 1609. With the dismantling of the feudal system in Japan in 1879, the Ryukyu Kingdom became Okinawa prefecture (*Ryukyu shobun*) and was subsequently administered by the newly established Meiji government based in Tokyo. The period extending from 1609 to 1879 is referred to as the Ryukyu's "early-modern era." The ensuing "modern era" encompasses the period from 1879 until 1945. Following Japan's defeat in the Second World War, however, Okinawa became an American protectorate according to conditions stipulated in the San Francisco Peace Treaty (1952) and was only returned to Japan in 1972.

2. The Origins of Karate

In 1372, King Chuzan O Satto of the Ryukyu Kingdom paid homage to the emperor in China, and the region became a tributary subordinate to the Ming Dynasty for the next 500 years. Chinese immigrants called *Binjin Sanjuroku-sei* ("36 families", a figurative number) established a settlement in Kumemura in Naha. Although often credited as being among the earliest Chinese settlers in Ryukyu, trade relations had long been in place by this stage, and immigrants from China were already spread throughout the islands. It is assumed that some of them were skilled in the martial arts.

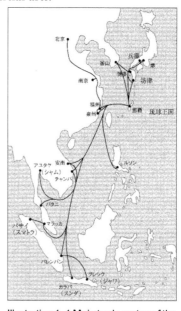

Illustration 1–1 Main trade routes of the Ryukyu Kingdom 14ᵗʰ–16ᵗʰ centuries.

The first consolidated Sho Kingdom was established in 1429 when Sho Hasshi unified the "Three Mountain" (Sanzan) polities of Hokuzan, Chuzan, and Nanzan. Taking advantage of its geographical location, the Ryukyu Kingdom actively engaged in maritime trade with East Asian countries such as Japan, Korea, Thailand, Vietnam, Malaysia, and Indonesia from the fourteenth through to the sixteenth centuries.

After unification of the three polities, Shuri Castle became the Ryukyu Kingdom's main centre for defence. A standing army was stationed there, and the castle was guarded by units of 100 men at any one time. Soldiers wore armour and helmets made of iron and carried two swords, one long and one short. The weapons were mostly the same as those in vogue in Japan at the time—bows, swords, and spears. A member of the royal family summoned all the soldiers once a year to lecture them on martial matters as the region was always on the precipice of conflict (*Okinawa Encyclopedia*, 1983).

	Year			Chinese Era	Ryukyu King	Chinese Envoy
1	1404		×	Yongle 2	Bunei	Shi Zhong
2	1415		×	Yongle 13	Taromai	Chen Xiuro
3	1425		First Sho Dynasty	Hongxi 1	Sho Hashi	Chai Shan
4	1443			Zhengtong 8	Sho Chu	Yu Bian
5	1448			Zhengtong 13	Sho Shitatsu	Che Chuan
6	1452	Ming Dynasty		Jingtai 3	Sho Kinpuku	Qiao Yi
7	1456			Jingtai 7	Sho Taikyu	Yan Cheng
8	1463			Tianshun 7	Sho Toku	Pang Rong
9	1472		Second Sho Dynasty	Chenghua 8	Sho En	Guang Rong
10	1479			Chenghua 15	Sho Shin	Dong Min
11	1534			Jiajing 13	Sho Sei	Chen Kan
12	1561			Jiajing 40	Sho Gen	Guo Rulin
13	1579			Wanli 7	Sho Ei	Xiao Chongye
14	1606			Wanli 34	Sho Nei	Xia Ziyang
15	1633			Chongzhen 6	Sho Ho	Du Sance
16	1663	Qing Dynasty		Kangxi 2	Sho Shitsu	Zhang Xueli
17	1683			Kangxi 22	Sho Tei	Wang Ji
18	1719			Kangxi 58	Sho Kei	Haibao
19	1756			Qianlong 21	Sho Boku	Quan Kui
20	1800			Jiaqing 5	Sho On	Zhao Wenkai
21	1808			Jiaqing 13	Sho Ko	Qikun
22	1838			Daoguang 18	Sho Iku	Lin Hongnian
23	1866			Tongzhi 5	Sho Tai	Zhao Xin

(Table 1-1 Ryukyu Kings and Chinese Emissaries)

A balustrade in front of Shuri Castle's main building was recorded in the text *Momo Urasoe Rankan no Mei* during the reign of King Sho Shin (r: 1477–1527) as being "stockpiled with swords, bows and arrows to protect the land... They had more weapons of war than any other region could amass." In 1500,

Sho Shin attacked the Ryukyuan chieftain Oyake Akahachi in the Yaeyama Islands, and a few years later he destroyed the Manikutaru Aji principality on Kumejima Island. It is clear from relics and records left by Chinese emissaries that both Japanese and Chinese weapons were used in these conflicts, but documentation pertaining to any actual style of unarmed combat has not been found to date.

3. Ryukyu Early-Modern Literary Sources

Historical sources related to the history of karate are extremely rare. The few modern Okinawan records and oral traditions that do exist have been accepted at face value without verification. The *Oshima Hikki* (1762), for example, was written after a Ryukyuan boat bound for Satsuma was blown off course and wrecked in a Tosa domain inlet (Oshima-ura) on the island of Shikoku. Tosa authorities sent their Confucian scholar Tobe Yoshihiro to interrogate the vessel's captain, Shiohira Pechin, and other crew members. A section of the text has been quoted frequently by historians and karate practitioners since the pre-war period as describing how Chinese hand-to-hand fighting techniques (*quanfa* or *kempo*) were conveyed to the Ryukyus.

It explains how Koshokun,[1] an expert in a peculiar style of grappling (*kumiai-jutsu*), and his entourage of followers demonstrated their art to their Ryukyuan hosts. With his right and left hands positioned in front of his chest, he struck out

---

1 公相君 There are various ways of writing this name in English. "Kusanku", "Kusankun", "Kushanku", "Kosanko", "Kwang Shang Fu". The karate *kata* named after him is usually expressed as "*Kushanku*" or "*Kusanku*". In Japan, the man himself is usually referred to as Koshokun.

with one fist and manoeuvred adroitly with curious shuffling footwork. Although he looked feeble, he was able to topple men of superior stature with relative ease (*Nihon Shomin Seikatsu Shiryo Shusei* Vol. 1, 1968).

There are several records of Ryukyuan vessels having been shipwrecked in Tosa. The *Oshima Hikki* is a rich compendium of material gleaned from these chance or accidental visitations, and introduces the systems, customs, literature, and geography of the Ryukyu Kingdom (*Rissho Daigaku Kokugo Kokubun* Vol. 46). Nevertheless, the original manuscript of *Oshima Hikki* is no longer in existence and the various reproduced copies that remain today are ridden with conflicting information. As such, the reliability of *Oshima Hikki* as a historical source is questionable for several reasons (*Seikatsu Bunka Kenkyujo Nenpo 12*, 1997).

For example, with the aforementioned demonstration by Koshokun and his men, the explanation of his style of grappling amounts to no more than several lines of text. Much is left to the imagination so it is not wise to believe all the assertions made in *Oshima Hikki*. With this in mind, let us de-construct the following four assumptions usually accepted as fact:

1. Chinese martial arts were introduced into the Ryukyu Kingdom by Koshokun
2. Koshokun's arrival in Ryukyu coincided with the 1756 Imperial Chinese mission led by the envoy Quan Kui
3. *Kempo* (C: *quanfa* = fist techniques) was called *kumiai-jutsu* (grappling techniques) in Ryukyu

4. The *kata* still known as *"Kus(h)anku"* was transmitted by its namesake Koshokun

First, it is commonly believed that Chinese *quanfa* spread in the Ryukyu Kingdom after Koshokun's arrival. It is recorded in *Oshima Hikki* that Koshokun demonstrated his martial art in front of officials, but Tobe and Shiohira make no mention of how it came to influence local martial arts. Other records from the same period also fail to corroborate the notion that Chinese *quanfa* spread from this time.

Second, it is usually inferred that Koshokun was a member of the 1757 diplomatic mission from China led by the envoy Quan Kui. Although this year falls closest to when *Oshima Hikki* (1762) was compiled, the phrase "last year" (*sennen*) which appears in reference to Koshokun's arrival is ambiguous and suggests a wider span of time than is typically thought. It could also be interpreted as "in years gone by". The passage of text before Koshokun in *Oshima Hikki* talks about Quan Kui, and even references one of his poems, but exactly when Koshokun arrived in the Kingdom is a point of conjecture.

Third, the Japanese term *kumiai-jutsu* mentioned in the text literally means the techniques of grappling. Perhaps Shiohira employed this appellation in a broad sense to facilitate Tobe's understanding of his notes. It is not clear whether Tobe already knew of Chinese *quanfa* through the text *Bubishi*, or if Shiohira explained the fighting system as *kumiai-jutsu* for Tobe's benefit, and he added *kempo* (fist techniques) as a later note. Irrespective, to date no historical sources have been found that prove a form of weapon-less Ryukyuan combat called *kumiai-jutsu* ever existed.

Fourth, the *kata* known as *Kus(h)anku* first appeared in an Okinawan education textbook called *Ryukyu Kyoiku* (1896).

> "Techniques of the fist unique to this prefecture are on par with sword fighting and spear techniques seen in other regions of Japan. In the system known as *todi* (Chinese hand) there are forms such as *Passai*, *Kusankun*, and *Naihanchin* that have been studied by Ryukyuans since ancient times."

Newspapers and educational publications wrote these terms with the phonetic system of *katakana* instead of using Chinese ideograms (*kanji*). It was not until 1922 when Funakoshi Gichin published *Ryukyu Kempo: Karate* when the name of the *kata Kusanku* was rendered into *kanji* using the same characters as the historical figure Koshokun (公相君). This was not simply a name change but was intended to associate the *kata* with a particular historical personage suggesting that the origins of Ryukyu *todi* can be attributed to Koshokun. This and other inconsistencies have simply been accepted as fact without satisfactory scrutiny.

When the Shimazu clan of the Satsuma domain invaded the Ryukyus (1609), the southern island of Amami Oshima located between Okinawa and Kyushu became separated from the Kingdom. In the *Nanto Zatsuwa* (1855), a collection of anecdotes from the southern islands written by Nagoya Sagenta, there is an illustration of a man strengthening his fists with the accompanying captions *tsukunesu* and *totsukuro*. It indicates that a bare-fisted style of martial art was practised on Amami Oshima, and the explanatory text provides clues as to how adepts trained in the system.

Illustration 1-2 Men strengthening their hands. (Nagai Ryuichi (ed.) *Nanto Zatsuwa*, 1933)

There are two methods of practice illustrated. The lower illustration shows an older man punching a solid object with his bare knuckles, and the other is someone striking a board wrapped in straw rope (*makiwara*). *Nanto Zatsuwa* consists of text and drawings by Satsuma samurai Nagoshi Sagenta, but the original work has been lost. The manuscript was reproduced many times and there are several copies in existence, all with slight differences in content. These drawings are from a copy which contains both (Illustration 1–2). The captions read *kempo-jutsu* (*tsukunesu*) and *totsukuro*. These depictions point to a connection between Ryukyuan training with *makiwara* and other methods still used to strengthen the hands today.

Ryukyu martial arts were conveyed mainly through the medium of *kata*. Techniques were learned through *kata*, and body strengthening exercises were incorporated into the forms. *Oshima Hikki* and *Nanto Zatsuwa* need to be compared with other relevant historical materials for a clearer picture of what unarmed combat was really like in the Ryukyus in the eighteenth and nineteenth centuries.

4. Clarifying Karate's History

Oshima Hikki and *Nanto Zatsuwa* are valuable resources for understanding unarmed combat in the Ryukyu Kingdom, but are not enough on their own. More questions arise than are answered. Being the roots of modern karate, it would be useful to know what the main characteristics of the Ryukyu's unarmed combat styles towards the end of the Ryukyu early-modern era were. What were the objectives and methods for training? Furthermore, in what way did the systems evolve into a distinctive indigenous Ryukyuan martial art? Perhaps some light can be shed on these queries by considering the historical experience of Okinawa.

SECTION 2

Three Aspects of Ryukyu Martial Arts

1. The Royal Government's Encouragement of Martial Arts

The Kingdom of Ryukyu was administered by Sho Shoken (Haneji Choshu, 1617–1675) in line with instructions stipulated in *Haneji Shioki* (Haneji Directives, 1666–73). Promulgated in 1667, these instructions formed the basis for education for officials in the Ryukyus at the time (*Majikina Anko Zenshu*, 1993).

Okinawan scholar Majikina Anko (1875–1933) wrote how the Haneji Directives were followed diligently by members of the elite ruling class. For example, knowing how to use the Japanese calendar, learning such traditional Japanese arts as poetry, tea ceremony, flower arranging, studies of classics, medicine, arithmetic, Chinese medicine, horse riding and so on were encouraged by the royal government for all its officials irrespective of position and standing. A man unable to excel in one area or skill was deemed to be of little use. It was upon Haneji's ideals that the royal government was reformed after the invasion of the Shimazu clan.

Horse riding included the different skills of *bajutsu* (horsemanship), *bai* (farrier), and *kyokuba-jutsu* (equestrianism). Ryukyuans visited Satsuma in Kyushu to learn these. It spread throughout the Ryukyus, and horse racing (*umazoroe*) became

	Year	Ryukyu King	Author	Publication
1	1667	Sho Shitsu	Haneji Choshu (Sho Shoken)	*Haneji Shioki*
2	1756	Sho Boku	Tobe Yoshiro	*Oshima Hikki*
3	1778	Sho On	Aka Pechin Chokushiki	*Aka Chokushiki Yuigonsho*
4	1801	Sho On	Retainer of Higo Domain	*Satsuyu-kiko*
5	1816	Sho Ko	Basil Hall	*Account of A Voyage of Discovery to The West Coast of Corea, and The Great Loo-Choo Island in The Japan Sea*
6	1855	Sho Tai	Nagoya Sagenta	*Nanto Zatsuwa*
7	1867	Sho Tai	Unknown	*TaaFaaKuu*
8	1867	Sho Tai	Unknown	*Nizam Waboku*

Table 1-2 (Historical sources related to early-modern Ryukyuan combat arts)

a popular pursuit for warriors. Moreover, Japanese and Chinese martial arts such as *bajutsu*, sword arts, spear, sword play, and so on were demonstrated at feasts to welcome Chinese envoys (*Majikina Anko Zenshu* Vol. 2, 1993).

2. The Martial Arts of Naha Shizoku Warriors

A century after the Haneji Directives were promulgated, a warrior of Naha by the name of Aka Pechin Chokushiki wrote a letter of advice to his son, Chokushu. The document is known as *Aka Chokushiki Yuigonsho*. Influenced by the Haneji Directives, this informative text explains how warriors approached their training in the martial arts.

The Aka clan were descendants of Ahagon Magura, a young general during the reign of King Shoshin when Yaeyama was subjugated (c. 1500). Chokushiki was the tenth-generation head of his family line, and he writes of his martial art studies which commenced from the age of 15 (*Higaonna Kanjun Zenshu*, 1978).

As an official in the royal administration, Chokushiki asserts that the most important skill a man could have is the ability to officiate ceremonies and work with documents in both Chinese and Japanese. Thus, he implores that "Learning how to write is of paramount importance", as was cultivating proficiency in other artistic pursuits such as "flower arranging, tea ceremony, the Jigen-ryu school of swordsmanship, *karamuto* (unarmed combat), and *yawara* (jujutsu)."

Chokushiki points out that the Aka clan were renowned as a martial arts family for many generations, and although swordsmanship was not considered so important in Ryukyu, his family studied the Jigen-ryu tradition to develop a strong martial spirit. If matters got out of hand in training and one was struck down and injured, however, this would be to the detriment of the other important pursuits such as Chinese and Japanese studies. As such, Chokushiki advised that training "be undertaken in a way that it does not interfere with other duties."

He also wrote, "My teacher in Jigen-ryu was Kuba Pechin Chito, and I trained under him for a long time. As our ancestors are time-honoured warriors, you must train [in the martial arts] along with the other arts when time permits." Chokushiki studied under Kuba Pechin Chito for many years, and given Kuba Pechin Chito's age, it can be surmised that Jigen-ryu had already become established in the Kingdom by the 1700s, to the extent that there were native Ryukyuan instructors teaching the tradition.

The Aka clan was also in possession of numerous Japanese weapons, military accoutrements, and scrolls. Chokushiki was born in 1721, but his great grandfather Chokko's weapons and scrolls remained in the Aka family as heirlooms. Chokko was clearly an avid martial artist and actively collected Japanese weapons and equipment. The following catalogue was written in 1667:

"Sword—Unnamed; two peg holes in the hilt. Passed down to my great grandfather Chokko—transmission scrolls of the Jigen-ryu, Ten-ryu spearmanship and *naginata* scrolls, three scrolls by Kusunoki Masashige, one *yari* (pike) made by Oku Izumi-no-Kami, a short sword 6-*sun* in length (made by Nobukuni), and other swords that he purchased (made by [Ogasawara] Ujioki), a *wakizashi* (no name), bows and arrows, and *kanate*. These are all family heirlooms bequeathed from Chokko's time to be passed on to our descendants."

3. Tile Smashing Fist

When did Ryukyuan-style unarmed combat become known to samurai of the Satsuma and other domains? Mizuhara Kumajiro, a Higo province samurai, wrote in the *Satsuyu-kiko* (1801) what he had heard from Satsuma warriors who were stationed in Ryukyu. Satsuma samurai were clearly familiar with the Ryukyuan martial arts, and warriors of the Higo domain were also showing interest.

"Ryukyuans are not particularly good at swordsmanship or jujutsu, but they are excellent at punching, and can smash or kill things with their bare hands. Satsuma samurai call it *tetsukumi*, and invited an expert to the domain's administration quarters in Naha. He piled seven tiles on top of each other and smashed through six with one blow. A punch to the face would be the same as cutting it."

How did practitioners improve their *tetsukumi* (punching) techniques? In the *Nanto Zatsuwa*'s illustrations of fist strengthening exercises, the man striking the *makiwara* looks to be young, whereas the other punching a box is sporting a beard and is older. The caption reads *tsukushisu, totsukuro*. Did the *tetsukumi* explained in the *Satsuyu-kiko* also make use of *makiwara* and other objects to toughen up the fists?

Fist strengthening involves repetitive and painful solo drills. Striking with the wrong part of the fist, or in the wrong way, can result in serious injury, not only to the hands, but also to other parts of the body. The man punching the *makiwara* has his left hand positioned on his hip and is thrusting with the right fist from the front. The man striking the solid object is using the back side of his fist. There must have been an established way of performing these drills.

4. Ryukyuan Stance

The British Amherst diplomatic mission visited the Ryukyu Kingdom 37 years before Commodore Matthew Perry arrived in Japan in 1853. Upon returning to Britain, the captain of the sloop, Basil Hall, published an account of his travels. He mentions an interesting exchange between royal officials and his sailors (*Account of a Voyage of Discovery to the West Coast of Corea and the Great Loo-Choo Island*, 1818).

"On returning to the cabin to tea, they were all in high spirits, and while amusing themselves with a sort of wrestling game [karate?], Ookooma (Okuma), who had seen us placing ourselves in the boxer's sparring attitudes, threw himself suddenly into the boxer's position of defence, assuming at the same time a fierceness of look which we had never before seen in any of them. The gentleman to whom he addressed himself, thinking

> that Ookooma wished to spar, prepared to indulge him;
> but Mádera's quick eye saw what was going on, and by
> a word or two made him instantly resume his wonted
> sedateness."

The aggressive stance that Okuma takes suggests that Ryukyu officials were actively engaged in martial art training.

5. Todi in Kingdom Ceremonies

As a part of the tribute system with China, The King of Ryukyu was given authority by investiture missions dispatched by the Chinese emperor. These visitations would come once in the life of a King and the ceremonies were grand affairs.

In 1719, King Shokei appointed Tamagusuku Chokun as the "*Odori Bugyo*" (Minister of Festivities) to choreograph *kumi-odori* theatre for entertaining Chinese envoys. *Kumi-odori* are a mixture of styles with roots in Okinawan, Chinese, and Japanese theatre, and the showcase court customs of the Ryukyu Kingdom.

In 1866, Shotai, the last Ryukyuan King, lavishly entertained a group of Chinese emissaries. The *Nizan Waboku* play was created for the occasion (*Kumiodori-shu*, 1867). The theatre is based in the Sanzan Period when the three polities of Hokuzan, Chuzan, and Nanzan co-existed. The Nanzan chieftain, Yoza Onushi, was taken prisoner by Hokuzan forces. The main theme of the dance centres on how his two sons demonstrated their filial duty by venturing to rescue him. Yoza Onushi was not allowed to return from Hokuzan, and his two boys were given to the care of Hokuzan concubines. Thinking about how things may take a violent turn in the future, Yoza Onushi taught them how to use the *kama* (sickle), *todi*, pike, *naginata* and various other martial arts. In the The *Nizan Waboku* became a very important play in government ceremonies after the administration adopted Confucianism. In its script, both Japanese and Chinese weapons are mentioned alongside *todi*.

6. Kumemura Martial Demonstration

In an early-modern source *Taafaakuu* there is a programme reproduced from a celebration held in Kumemura in 1867. The programme is titled *Sanruchu Narabi ni Shogei Bangumi* and outlines the events held in the village one year after the ceremony for the last King of Ryukyu, Sho Tai (*Shimabukuro Zempatsu Senju*, 1953). The celebration represented the essence of Kumemura culture with demonstrations of martial and other arts along with traditional Chinese drama. There were 47 performances of which ten were martial art displays.

Tinbee (shield)—Maezato Chikudu Pechin
Tesshaku and *Bo* (*sai* and staff)—Aragaki Tsuuji
Seisanho (*kata*)—Aragaki Tsuuji
Bo and *todi* (staff and hand-to-hand)—Maezato Chikudupechin, Arakaki Tsuuji Pechin
Chishokin (*kata*)—Arakaki Tsuuji Pechin
Tinbee and *Bo*—Tomimura Chikudu Pechin, Arakaki Tsuuji Pechin
Sai–Maezato Chiku Pechin
Koshu (*kumite*)—Maezato Chikudu Pechin, Arakaki Tsuuji Pechin
Shabo (farming tool for pounding grain)—Ikemiya Shusai
Suparinpei (*kata*)—Tomimura Chikudu Pechin

It is unknown exactly how the performances unfolded, but for Kumemura people to demonstrate traditional Chinese martial arts in front of the king was a matter of great pride and a splendid opportunity to exhibit their culture.

7. Three Aspects of Todi

It is believed that the unarmed style of Ryukyu *todi*[2] evolved through interaction between Ryukyuans and emissaries dispatched by the Chinese emperor. In other words, Chinese fighting techniques spread throughout the Ryukyus and adopted a local flavour. Furthermore, Japanese martial arts such as the classical school of swordsmanship Jigen-ryu, jujutsu, and *sojutsu* (spearmanship) also influenced how Ryukyuan martial arts took shape. In this sense, *todi* incorporates three overlapping aspects.

First, according to the Haneji Directives and the *Aka Chokushiki Yuigonsho*, it was recognised as a vehicle for nurturing the mental attitude and skills of self-defence befitting of an official in the royal government. Second, the martial aspects of *todi* are accentuated in the *Satsuyu-kiko*, *Nanto Zatsuwa* and *Chosen-Ryukyu Kokaiki*. The fists were fortified, tiles were broken with bare hands, and there is reference to a practitioner taking a special fighting stance against a foreign seaman. Third, the *Sanryuchu Narabi Shogei Bangumi* and the *Nizan Waboku* reveal that *todi* was performed at royal events, indicating that it was valued as being symbolic of warrior status.

---

2 *Todi* = 唐手. Other pronunciations include *todii*, *tode*, *tuudii*. It was the collective term for martial arts in Ryukyuan, and literally means "Tang + hand" or "China hand". *Todi* was used to the beginning of the 20th C.

SECTION 3

Karate after the 1879 Disposition of Ryukyu

1. Former Warriors after Abolition of the Domain System
When Japan emerged victorious in the first Sino-Japanese War in 1895, the relationship between Okinawa and China (Qing Dynasty) changed. In Okinawa, the so called *Fukkoku* Movement which advocated for the restoration of the Ryukyu Kingdom as a tributary of China became popular among noble warriors (*shizoku*) of Shuri, Naha, and Kume. Following the Disposition of the Ryukyu Kingdom, *shizoku* were stripped of their privileges, and were forced to eke out a living teaching arts in rural areas. The movement was short lived, however, as the Meiji government cracked down on Okinawans secretly travelling to China, and arrested them as *dasshin'nin* (refugees to Qing). Kumemura inhabitants' involvement in this movement was particularly notable. There were many there who played a central role in the advancement of trade between China and Ryukyu, they spoke Chinese, and were active in filing petitions (*Kumemura: Rekishi to Jinbutsu*, 1993). It is thought that many who made the perilous sea journey were practitioners of *todi* (*Ryukyu Kyukoku Undo*, 2010).

2. The "Stubborn Faction" and Children's Education
School attendance was sluggish when the independence movement was in full swing. However, after the Sino-Japanese War it rose to nearly half of the national average of about 65 per

cent. The following 1898 article reported that karate was being utilised in education. The content shows glimpses of what Okinawa was like at the turn of the century and its relationship with mainland Japan (*Ryukyu Shimpo*, June 13, 1898).

> "The *Gan-ha* (Stubborn Faction) are aware of the importance of education, and men of the same disposition conferred at Urasoe Chochu's house to teach the local youth. They gather children over the age of seven or eight, and instruct them in the Chinese classics, arithmetic, writing, and *todi* (something akin to Chinese-style jujutsu). There are 23 registered instructors, so there must be around 50 or 60 pupils in attendance."

The term *Gan-ha* or *Ganko-to* (Stubborn Faction) refers to a group of former warriors who were dogged loyalists of the royal administration and opposed annexation by Japan (Photo 1-1). An opposing clique was the pro-Japanese "enlightenment faction" called the *Kaika-to* or *Kaimei-ha* whose headquarters

Photo 1-1 Members of the Gan-ha who returned to Okinawa from China in 1896. (*Naha Hyaku-nen no Ayumi*, 1980)

were located next to the prefectural office of the Meiji Government. Urasoe Chochu lived in Qing China for ten years and ensconced himself in the independence movement. After Japan defeated China in the first Sino-Japanese War he returned to Okinawa and taught children of families that opposed government sanctioned education.

As the article states, Urasoe taught the "Four Books and Five Classics" (Classical Chinese texts), arithmetic, calligraphy, etc. and also instructed *todi*, which is referenced as something akin to "Chinese-style jujutsu". He also chaperoned students to cultural and athletic festivals, and on field trips. In the newspaper article, the teachers are described as being "horse-boned" as if to accentuate their robustness. The value of *todi* was not expressed per se, but given that it was included as a subject, there were obviously experts among the teachers, and they were clearly highly educated men. It is worth noting that as many as 60 children from the town around Shuri Castle were participating in these "Stubborn Faction" educational activities. It is not clear whether they were being taught in one place or several, but after the Russo-Japanese War (1904–5), the attendance rate at public schools in Okinawa rose rapidly, and many children who had been taught *todi* privately since childhood began formal education in the prefecture's government-backed institutions.

3. Tsunahiki Festival

One of the annual festivities in the castle town of Shuri was the Ayajo Tsunahiki Great Tug-of-War festival. As reported in the *Ryukyu Shimpo* (19 August 1898), "All the villages enjoyed great merriments after the festival where speeches were given, and much alcohol imbibed… For entertainment there was a heart-rending sword dance and a performance of impressive Chinese martial arts…" This was *todi*, and it was performed along with sword dances and the like at community gatherings. There must have been many local exponents as it seems people were accustomed to seeing such displays. The festivities conducted in other neighbourhoods (Akahira, Onaka, Yamakawa) likely had a similar line up of entertainment featuring *todi*.

4. Festival for a Bountiful Harvest

Todi was also demonstrated at an annual event in the Akata neighbourhood of Shuri. "On the 16th day of the 7th month of the old calendar, an annual ceremony for a bountiful harvest was convened with a special dance to honour Maitreya (*Miroku no Odori*). This year, performances of spear and *todi* were organised to encourage locals to immerse themselves in their chores." (*Ryukyu Shimpo*, August 19, 1899). This was the harvest festival of Akata held in honour of the Bodhisattva Maitreya. The programme was reported as being of great interest to the many onlookers.

Judging by the reports on education conducted in the Urasoe house in the Momohara area of Shuri and articles of festivals in the region, it seems that former samurai who had scattered throughout the villages and neighbourhoods of Naha and Shuri continued practising *todi* into the new era.

5. Reception for Returned Soldier

Conscription was introduced in Japan in 1873 but was not enacted in Okinawa until 1898. A party for a soldier from Tomari (Naha) who completed officer training in the army was reported in the *Ryukyu Shimpo* newspaper (October 21, 1899).

> "At the primary school, the county mayor was there along with over 30 middle school students, police officers, and active soldiers, as well as throngs of well-wishers totalling over 400 people. They all came to welcome the new sergeant major. Before long, Nashiro Masanari stood up to start the party. The sergeant major then addressed the crowd, and ever so politely informed them of events in the Sino-Japanese War. All present were moved by his account. Festivities commenced after his speech with the middle school pupils entertaining the gathering with displays of *gekiken* (kendo) and *kenbu* (sword dance). To the great delight of the sergeant major, there was also a demonstration of karate for which Tomari is known."

Such articles regarding karate appeared after 1898 in the *Ryukyu Shimpo*, a local newspaper first published in 1893. Unfortunately, most issues up to 1897 were destroyed by fire in the Battle of Okinawa at the end of the Second World War. In any case, from the articles seen thus far, displays of karate were enjoyed by people at various public and private events held in Shuri and Naha. Discoveries of any new historical documentation from the early days of Okinawa prefecture will facilitate a greater understanding of karate history. Until more sources are uncovered, however, we should be cautious in how the ones we do have are interpreted.

SECTION 4

The Introduction of Karate in Schools (1)

1. Karate Practitioners of Modern Okinawa

As we have seen, fist techniques (*quanfa*) introduced into the Ryukyu Kingdom from China were adopted and localised predominantly by the military class. In the 1860s, the now indigenous system of combat was referred to as *todi* and had three significant aspects: martial (for self-defence), educational (pursuit for warriors), performance art (at state banquets etc.).

What kind of instruction did *todi* practitioners born in the Ryukyu Kingdom receive? Yoshimura Chogi (1866–1945), a member of the Ryukyu royal family, chronicled his martial art training in the 1870s to the 90s in his autobiography, *Jiden Budo-ki* (1941). He was 74 years of age when he wrote about his boyhood experiences.

"I was initiated into the martial arts when I was 11 or 12. My master was Ishimine, an old man of around 60 years who oversaw financial and general affairs in the administration. Almost every day we would go through the forms of *Naifanchi* and *Passai* in the spacious courtyard. Of course, it was supplementary to writing and other topics of study, and I sometimes made excuses to get out of it. Still, I did plenty of training for two years. This was around the time when feudal domains (*han*) were abolished and replaced with a system of prefectures."

Yoshimura was probably referring to Ishimine Shinchi (1812–1892), a native of Torihori in Shuri.

"By the time I was 17 or 18 years old I had matured into a sturdy young man. From that time, I began training under Bushi Matsumura (Matsumura Sokon), and it became serious. I remember Master Matsumura was already advanced in years. He was a guard for the southern section of the palace. I met with him five or six times a month. My older brother, Choshin, and another lad called Tamagusuku also accompanied me. The main thing we practised was the *kata Gojushiho*, and we also learned *Kusanku*. It was from then that I really became aware of what budo really is, and was encouraged greatly by the master who took me under his wing. It wasn't long before my training showed in my manner and movement."

Matsumura Sokon (1809–1899) was responsible for instructing many of the great pioneers of modern karate such as Asato Anko (1828–1914) and Itosu Anko (1831–1915).

"From around the age of 22 or 23, I became a disciple of Master Higaonna. I went to Shuri to train with him about three times a month. He ran a business on the beach-front across from the Honganji Temple. For one whole year, come rain or strong wind, the master even came to my house in Shuri to instruct without ever taking a day off. The training time was from 6:00pm until 10:00pm. Different to now, in those days there was no means of transport except palanquins. Every evening somebody would escort the master home after training. It was a wonderful opportunity when I think about it. Master Higaonna taught mainly *Sanchin* and we also learned *Pechurin*. I wanted to study the deeper secrets of budo. I came to understand that movement of the limbs followed the forging of an indomitable mind and spirit."

This was Higaonna Kanryo (1853–1915). He taught karate at his home and at clubs at fishery, mercantile, and industrial schools in Okinawa. Having studied under Ishimine, then Matsumura, and finally Higaonna, Yoshimura reached a profound level of understanding of budo through arduous training (Photo 1–2).

Photo 1-2 Higaonna Kanryo c. 1912. (*Goju-ryu Kaisetsu-sho*, 2019)

Yoshimura began karate when Okinawa prefecture had just been established. His father, Yoshimura Chomei, was a central figure of the restoration movement. After the Sino-Japanese War (1894–95), Chomei travelled to Fuzhou in China where he died in 1898. Yoshimura was taught privately by great karate masters of the time. This shows that in a new era of modernity, high-ranking noble families like Yoshimura's were still engaged in the study of karate as a vehicle for personal development.

2. Karate's Introduction into Schools

Education statistics for Okinawa prefecture show that the enrolment rate of school-aged children after 1879 was only 4.1% compared to the national average of 41.2%. In 1896, after the Sino-Japanese War, the national average rose to 64.2%, while Okinawa still lagged at 31.2%. In 1906, following the Russo-Japanese War, the gap narrowed with Okinawa's enrolment rising to 90.1% compared to the national average of 96.1%.

Funakoshi Gichin wrote an article for the *Ryukyu Shimpo* titled "Karate is the 'bone marrow' of martial arts" (*Ryukyu Shimpo*, January 9, 1913). He says in the article that karate was introduced into middle and normal (teacher training) schools in Okinawa around 1901 as a subsidiary of physical education. Each year, the benefits gleaned from these classes were reported to the Ministry of Education. Thus, karate classes were conducted in some capacity at normal and middle schools as a part of callisthenics and military drills which were official curriculum subjects.

Funakoshi later wrote in *Ryukyu Kenpo Karate* (1922) that recruits in the military were judged by medics to be of excellent physical condition. This was attributed to the practice of karate, and is why, Funakoshi states, it was eventually deemed a suitable subject to be taught formally in schools. Furthermore, he informs us that a prefectural education official by the name of Ogawa Shintaro successfully petitioned the education board to get karate adopted by physical education departments at teacher training and middle schools.

Ogawa served as the principal of the Okinawa Prefectural Jinjo Normal School from June 1896 until June 1899. He was then appointed to the position of Okinawa prefecture education inspector. In October 1901, a newspaper covered a speech made by Ogawa at a meeting between regional chiefs and school principals at the Nakagami District Office regarding physical education. It is unclear whether he talked about the role of karate (*Ryukyu Shimpo*, October 23, 1901).

Miyagi Chojun wrote in *Ryukyu Kempo Karatedo Enkaku Gaiyo* (1936), an overview of the history of karate, that karate was introduced as a subject in the Department of Physical Education at Shuri Jinjo Primary School in April 1901. He contends that this denoted the beginning of karate instruction to large groups as opposed to the traditional one-on-one teaching method (Photo 1–3).

Photo 1-3 Shuri Jinjo Primary School in 1901. (*Meiji, Taisho, Showa Okina-wa-ken Gakko Shashin-cho*, 1987)

However, the official adoption of karate classes into primary and middle school education cannot be confirmed in newspapers or educational publications of the time. In addition, karate was not featured in the frequently held athletic festivals in Shuri and Naha during that era. The programme of an athletic meet held in Shuri and Naha on May 19, 1902 to mark the visit of the Taiwan Governor-General Kodama Gentaro was advertised in a local paper (Taiwan was made a colony of Japan in 1895).

1. *Kimigayo* (Japanese anthem) bugle
2. *Kimigayo* singing
3. *Kyosei-jutsu* (military drills)
4. *Kyosei-jutsu* (military drills)
5. Gymnastics
6. Dumbbells (callisthenics)
7. Bar-bell exercises
8. Military song
9. Flexibility exercises
10. Troop training
11. Flag-catching race
12. Flag-catching race
13. Hopping race
14. Running race, *gekiken* (kendo)
15. Games
16. Three cheers to the emperor, finishing bugle

Karate is not mentioned anywhere in the programme. A later article in the same newspaper reports that "The benefits of physical exercise were evident in the wonderful performance of *kyosei-jutsu* demonstrated by middle school students under the guidance of the Sergeant Hanashiro. The students were wonderfully disciplined and valorous." Sergeant Hanashiro, as he was affectionately known, was Hanashiro Chomo, a teacher of physical education at middle schools. There is no mention of karate at this meet either.

3. Karate—The Okinawan Treasure

Were Funakoshi and Miyagi mistaken in their understanding of when karate was adopted into the school system? Born in 1868, Funakoshi worked at a primary school in Naha. Miyagi was born in 1888 and began his studies under Higaonna Kanryo after graduating primary school. In March 1902, an article describing a graduation ceremony at the Okinawa Normal School appeared in their alumni journal *Ryutan* (Photo 1–4). The programme was organised as follows:

Graduation Ceremony Programme
1. Opening declaration
2. Speech
3. Song
4. Karate
5. Raffle
6. Primary school pupil chorus
7. Recital of poetry
8. Address
9. Staff and student party pieces
10. Auld Lang Syne (J: "Glimmer of a Firefly")

The ceremony was attended by the principal, staff members, and students. That a demonstration of karate was included in the

Photo 1-4 Okinawa Normal School in 1904. (*Ryutan Hyaku-nen*, 1987)

proceedings indicates the value already placed on it in education by this stage. The five demonstrators were all graduating students: Tomikawa Seiju (Shuri *shizoku*), Naka Kotoku (Naha *shizoku*), Nohara Naokichi (Shimajiri commoner), Toma Keitoku and Namizato Heihachi (Kunigami *shizoku*). The demonstration was conducted with the "ferocity of attacking beasts" and represented a powerful display of this "Okinawan treasure".

Another report in *Ryutan* gives details of a combined sports meet held in August for students of the Normal School in the northern part of the main island in Okinawa. Karate is designated as Mutekatsu-ryu (literally school for winning without holding anything). This is the first record of karate featuring at an athletic meet. A total of 81 students were invited to Okaneku Racetrack in what is now Nago City. There were dozens of guests including the administrator of district. The number of spectators is unknown, but it seems that the event was small in scale compared to athletic festivals held in

Naha and other places. Nevertheless, the area was reported as being crowded with people from the local community. The programme for the sports day consisted of various races, a baseball match, ten kendo matches, Okinawan sumo, and Mutekatsu-ryu.

Starting at around 9:00am the events lasted until the evening. From all accounts, it was a raging success with the following points of particular interest:

(1) It was the first time that karate (Mutekatsu-ryu) featured at an athletic festival
(2) Participants were teacher trainees from the normal school and other students from Kunigami district
(3) It seems that it was not the first time the spectators had witnessed karate
(4) There were no performances of gymnastics or other training exercises
(5) There were no formalities included in the programme
(6) The district administrator was among the special guests

The purpose of the sports festival was primarily to boost morale among students from the Kunigami area, but the positive influence on locals was also a consideration. The question that comes to mind is where did the students who demonstrated actually practice karate? Most records chronicling teaching activities of famous karate masters are centred around the vicinity of Shuri, Naha, Tomari, and Kume. It is unknown who taught karate in Kunigami, but clearly students were trained for this event at school.

Judging by the articles about the graduation ceremony and athletic events, karate had already become established in the normal schools from 1902. Karate was being taught to students and performances were enjoyed by the community at large in displays at local athletic events. It can also be assumed that karate experts were not restricted to teaching at the normal school in the Nago region.

Karate was featured yet again at the Okinawa Normal School's graduation ceremony the following year. The programme was reproduced in *Ryutan* (1903).

1. Opening address
2. Greetings from the head teacher
3. Greetings from graduate representative
4. Singing
5. Sword dance
6. Karate
7. *Joruri* (traditional puppetry)
8. Concert (*koto* and flute)
9. Auld Lang Syne (J: Glimmer of a Firefly)
10. Closing remarks

The author reported favourably that karate was performed as an art exclusive to the people of Okinawa prefecture and is something Okinawans could be rightfully proud of.

Although Funakoshi and Miyagi's claim that karate was officially introduced into the school curriculum in 1901 cannot be confirmed by official records of the time, local newspapers corroborate that it was celebrated by the people and officials of the prefecture as a unique culture to the area, and that it was indeed being taught in some capacity in some schools. Furthermore, Miyagi's assertion that karate was instructed to large groups from that time can be backed up by the demonstrations at sports meets. It stands to reason that group teaching was already underway to some extent at prefectural educational institutions for this to have taken place.

4. Exploring the Value of Karate

In May 1902, Yamada Yoshio, secretary general of the Dai-Nippon Butokukai (Greater Japan Society of Martial Virtue, hereafter "Butokukai") visited Okinawa to lecture on traditional Japanese martial arts. A branch of the prestigious Butokukai had yet to be established in Okinawa. The governor of Okinawa, Baron Narahara Shigeru, wrote an introductory message in local newspapers to celebrate Yamada's visit.

He explains how the Butokukai was launched as a society in 1895. The visit by Secretary General Yamada, he explained, was for the purpose of assessing the state of martial arts in Okinawa and offering support for further dissemination of budo in the prefecture. He announces that a branch will be established in Okinawa to "disseminate military virtue through bushido" and "inspire in the Okinawan people a heightened awareness of Japan's traditional martial spirit" (*Ryukyu Shimpo* May 9, 1902).

The governors of each prefecture in Japan were appointed as the Butokukai's prefectural branch representatives. Narahara took on this mantle of responsibility for Okinawa. Although karate had not yet been incorporated into the Butokukai as a recognised Japanese budo discipline, the prestige of the Butokukai and its objectives surely appealed to karate experts and other stakeholders. Karate was becoming increasingly influenced by the Japanese budo world, and having it legitimately connected with this broader family of combat traditions was viewed as an exciting prospect.

SECTION 5

The Introduction of Karate in Schools (2)

In December 1904, staff at the Okinawa Middle School launched a study group under the tutelage of a karate expert (*Okinawa Kyoiku* No. 31, 1908). The fruits of their research proved promising, and karate was acknowledged as having genuine educational value. The following school year commenced with formal karate classes as a part of the official curriculum. Although karate had featured at various education-related sports demonstrations and events, this was significant because it was now recognised as a regular course subject. By the following year, almost all normal schools had initiated karate classes as regular subjects in the curriculum (*Ryukyu Shimpo*, 27 June 1906).

The Russo-Japanese War accentuated karate's value as a way of nurturing martial spirit, and for promoting the popular catchphrase *Fukoku Kyohei* (Wealthy country, strong soldiers"). This marked the beginning of an era in which teaching the "spirit of budo" to youth was deemed indispensable for Japan's future prosperity. In 1911, the Ministry of Education revised the National Curriculum Guidelines for middle schools and permitted *gekiken* (kendo) and jujutsu to be adopted as regular physical education classes. The movement to embrace karate into middle school education in Okinawa preceded this national ordinance and was already operational in 1905. The frequent appearances of karate at community events and in the curriculum necessitated the modernisation of its teaching methodology.

1. The Modernisation of Karate in Okinawan Middle Schools

In 1904, karate was considered worthy of being included as a physical education subject at middle schools. This signified the start of a new era for the discipline. The *Ryukyu Shimpo* newspaper reported on this development and a demo class on February 5, 1905. "Although the instructor's explanation was vague and difficult to understand in some places, karate will surely become a valuable addition to school education in the future." Interestingly, the reporter noted the "current popularity of jujutsu in Europe" in the same article.

Around this time, karate instructors at middle schools included Hanashiro Chomo, and Yabu Kentsu and others who were teaching callisthenics at normal schools. Asato Anko and Higaonna Kanryo are also thought to have been involved with the Karate Research Society. Itosu Anko was the teacher of Hanashiro and Yabu. He was over seventy years old but was a central figure in middle school karate instruction. Itosu continued promoting karate until his death in March 1915.

2. Itosu Anko and "Karate Jukka-jo"

When Itosu passed away, Yabu celebrated his legacy in the *Ryukyu Shimpo* newspaper (March 13, 1915).

"The master was born in Shuri Yamakawa in 1832. He was fond of the martial arts from a young age. He learned *kempo* from the famous Master Matsumura, and from

Masters Sakiyama and Nagahama of Naha, Matsumora of Tomari, and Masters Makishi, Sakuma, Ishimine, and Asato. He studied diligently with these men and accessed the inner secrets of the art. He was a talented writer and worked as a scribe at the old government headquarters. Master Itosu had the righteous mind of a true gentleman and exuded the air of an old warrior. After the abolishment of feudal domains, he lamented the demise of such noble virtues among youth as they became evermore frivolous and effeminate. He summoned them and taught them to mend their ways, thereby improving their lives to no end."

Itosu studied under Matsumura Sokon and interacted with many practitioners. Amid the confusion following the abolition of the Ryukyu Kingdom, he brought young men together and enthusiastically taught them the art of karate. The so-called "Ten Precepts of Karate" (*Karate Jukka-jo*), written by Itosu Anko when karate was introduced into the school system in modern Okinawa, describes the origins of karate, the attitude required in practice, the forms (*kata*), and its educational value (*Karatedo Taikan*, 1938). The text offers guidelines on how and why karate is suitable for teaching in schools (Photo 1–5). Itosu's ideas influenced not only his direct students, but also subsequent karate leaders for generations to come.

The Ten Precepts of Karate are as follows. Some inconsistencies in the text and the incompleteness of some sections suggests that the following is one of his earlier drafts (See underlined sections).

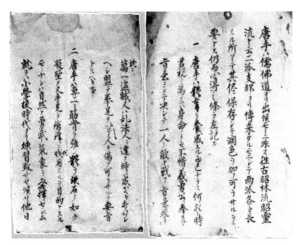

Photo 1-5 "*Karate Jukka-jo*". (*Karatedo Taikan*, 1938)

Karate does not derive from Buddhism or Confucianism. In olden times, the two styles of Shorin-ryu and Shorei-ryu came from China. Both have distinct advantages and it is necessary to preserve them and not colour them in any way. I leave the following articles with this in mind:

1. The aim of karate is to not only train one's body. Eventually you will gain the spirit to be able to sacrifice yourself for your ruler or nation. Never fight over insignificant matters; do not fight ruffians or villains. Avoid such people as much as possible. It is important to not inflict injury with your fists and feet.

2. The aim of karate is to forge muscles and bones as hard as iron and temper the hands and legs into spears so that one becomes naturally fearless in spirit. If a child were to start karate from primary school, he will be suitably prepared for military service and the practice of other martial arts. Hark back to the words of the Duke of Wellington following his defeat of Napoleon: "The Battle of Waterloo was won on the playing fields of our schools." This is a truly accurate aphorism.

3. Karate is not something that can be mastered quickly. Like the old saying about an ox that journeys slowly for the long distance of 1000-*ri*, it will reach the end of its journey. If one trains diligently for one or two hours each day, in three to four years one will have a physique superior to that of an ordinary person, and in many cases will come to conquer the deeper secrets of karate.

4. As karate requires the use of fists and feet, you should always practice with *makiwara*. <u>One must lower one's shoulders, open one's lungs up, remove any superfluous physical strength,</u> plant one's feet firmly on the floor while sinking one's energy in the lower abdomen (*tanden*). Practice this way one- to two-hundred times with each hand.

5. It is important in karate to assume one's stances with a straight back, <u>shoulders lowered with no tension,</u>

stand firmly with the legs, and focus energy (*ki*) in the lower abdomen (*tanden*), and have enough strength so that the upper and lower body are drawn together.

6. Practice the outward forms (*kata*) many times over. Study beforehand the meaning of each and how they should be applied. There are many oral teachings for the strikes, blocks, breaks, and *torite* (throwing) techniques.

7. Before practising an outward form (*kata*), determine whether it is suitable for cultivating the body or practical application, and train accordingly.

8. One should train in karate with the feeling of being on a battlefield. One's eyes should be open, shoulders lowered, and body braced. By always training with the intensity and mind to strike and block against a real opponent, the same attitude as being in actual battle will be cultivated naturally. One must always aspire to achieve this.

9. Take care not to utilise more strength than you should when training in karate. Otherwise your energy will rise to your upper body, your face and eyes will turn red and it will be damaging to your body. Be aware of this.

10. Countless karate masters from olden times have enjoyed long lives because training strengthens the

bones and muscles, and facilitates good digestion and blood circulation. Should karate be incorporated into the physical education curriculum in primary schools and be studied widely, <u>practitioners who become proficient will be able to conquer ten adversaries single-handedly.</u>

Students who study karate at normal and middle schools and abide by these ten precepts will be able to go forth to the outlying districts and expertly instruct children in primary schools after graduation. If taught correctly, karate will be disseminated not only in Okinawa but throughout Japan within ten years. This will be of immense benefit to our nation and its military forces. As such, I leave these words for your solemn consideration.

Itosu Anko, October 1908

In the preamble, Itosu states that karate did not originate from Confucianism, Buddhism or Taoism, but rather from the two ancient Chinese schools, Shorin-ryu and Shorei-ryu. As both schools have their own merits, he states, they should be inherited as they are and not be enriched or changed in any way.

The fundamental principles of karate according to the Ten Precepts can be found in Article 1: "The aim of karate is to not only to train one's body. Eventually you will gain the spirit to be able to sacrifice yourself for your ruler or nation."

Also, the notion that if children were to take up karate at a young age they would be prepared for military service and other martial arts is an important claim that aligned with the government's Imperial Rescript on Education and the Imperial Rescript to Soldiers and Sailors.

Articles 3 to 10 describe the attitude, practice methods, and fundamental postures required in karate. In addition, important training methods such as use of the *makiwara*, *kata* and *torite* (*kumite*) are also mentioned. By introducing karate into the school system, Itosu touted not only the benefits of the discipline as a form of physical education, but also believed that it could be effectively disseminated outside Okinawa. This would be a useful contribution to national military preparedness, and therefore beneficial to the country at large.

3. Tokuda Antei's "Karate"

Itosu taught a middle school student named Tokuda Antei. Tokuda wrote an article simply titled "Karate" which appeared in the school's alumni magazine *Kyuyo* (1909). Tokuda was born in Shuri in 1884 and entered the school in 1905 when karate had just been included as an official part of the curriculum. Tokuda's article came one year after Itosu publicised his Ten Precepts. He summarised the Ten Precepts and the style of instruction given by Itosu. He also included a poem that was composed by Asato Anko.

"Karate" by Fourth Year Student—Tokuda Antei

It is difficult for a man to always be safe, and sometimes one will be forced into a compromising situation. When

51

this happens, one who is unskilled in the art of fighting will regrettably end up in a sorry state. That is when knowledge of the martial arts is indispensable. Karate (Chinese hand) is a discipline in which one controls the adversary with *empty hands* without the need for small weapons. This martial art is peculiar to Okinawa and includes various aspects of combat but without the use of weaponry. The hands and feet are our weapons. People or space are not required to train. Be it indoors or out, it is possible to practise alone, even for a short time, within a confined area equivalent to six *tatami* mats. The following discourse is by karate master Itosu and will be of interest to people familiar with the martial arts.

Karate does not derive from Buddhism or Confucianism. In olden times, the two styles of Shorin-ryu (physical power) and Shorei-ryu (physical agility) came from China. Both have distinct advantages and it is necessary to preserve them and not colour them in any way. I leave the following articles with this in mind:

1. The aim of karate is to not only to train one's body. Eventually you will gain the spirit to be able to sacrifice yourself for your ruler or nation. Never fight over insignificant matters; do not fight ruffians or villains. Avoid such people as much as possible. It is important to not inflict injury with your fists and feet.

2. The aim of karate is to forge muscles and bones as hard as iron and temper the hands and legs into spears so

that one becomes naturally fearless in spirit. If a child were to start karate from primary school, he will be suitably prepared for military service and the practice of other martial arts. Hark back to the words of the Duke of Wellington following his defeat of Napoleon: "The Battle of Waterloo was won on the playing fields of our schools." This is a truly accurate aphorism.

3. Karate is not something that can be mastered quickly. Like the old saying about ox that journeys slowly for 1000-*ri* it will reach the end of its journey. If one trains diligently for one or two hours each day, in three to four years one will have a physique superior to that of an ordinary person, and in many cases will come to conquer the deeper secrets of karate.

4. As karate requires the use of fists and feet, you should always practice with *makiwara*. Plant your feet firmly on the floor while sinking one's energy in the lower abdomen (*tanden*). Practice this way one- to two-hundred times with each hand.

5. It is important in karate to assume one's stances with a straight back, shoulders lowered, chest out, stand firmly with the legs, and focus energy (*ki*) in the lower abdomen (*tanden*), and have enough rigidity so that the upper and lower body are drawn together.

6. Practice the outward forms (*kata*) many times over. Study the meaning of each and how they should be

applied beforehand. There are many oral teachings for the strikes, blocks, breaks, and *torite* (like throws in judo) techniques.

7. Before practising an outward form (*kata*), determine whether it is suitable for cultivating the body or practical application, and train accordingly.

8. One should train in karate with the feeling of being on a battlefield. One's shoulders should be lowered, and body braced. By always training with the intensity and mind to strike and block against a real opponent, the same attitude as being in actual battle will be cultivated naturally. One must always aspire to achieve this.

9. Take care not to utilise more strength than you should when training in karate. Otherwise your blood will rush to your head, your face and eyes will turn red and it will be damaging to your body, so be aware of this.

10. Countless masters of the Way of karate from olden times have enjoyed long lives because training strengthens the bones and muscles, and facilitates good digestion and blood circulation. Should karate be incorporated into the callisthenics curriculum in primary schools and is studied widely, not only will it be effective as physical education, the level of practitioners will improve drastically.

Poem by Master Asato

1. Karate makes the muscles and bones strong—The body becomes as hard as iron

2. Karate improves skill in punching and kicking—The hands and feet become like spear tips

3. Karate takes many years to master—One's frame is forged

4. Shoulders down, back straight—Strength is centred in the legs

5. In karate, energy is focussed down in the *tanden*—Take care to not let it float up

6. If the body is not forever forged, one will veer from the Way of karate

7. In karate, even if one is as swift as a swallow—If the punches are ineffective, there is no use

8. In karate, one practices the many techniques of the school—One must learn the purpose for each

9. There are no special techniques for winning—Victory is had through accessing the secret of strategy

10. In karate, if you do not know changes in strategy—Even with power, it will be to no avail

In the preamble, Tokuda declares that one can control an adversary with bare hands without the need for small weapons, and in a play on words, that "Chinese hand" is indeed "empty hand". He used the ideogram for empty in his text simply to indicate that combat in karate are bare-handed. He also points out that karate is peculiar to Okinawa, and although it has many factors in common with other combat arts, what sets it apart is that adepts do not carry weapons and that it is easy to train alone in a restricted space.

Asato was keen to promote karate into middle schools. No records have been found to date that confirm Asato's direct involvement in education, but he was clearly in agreement with the "Ten Precepts" laid down by Itosu. Several differences become apparent when comparing Tokuda's rendition of Itosu's "Ten Precepts" with the original.

1. Tokuda points out that Shorin-ryu emphasised "physical power", and the Shorei-ryu "physical agility".
2. In Article 4 where *makiwara* practice is mentioned, it states that the "lungs" should be open. Tokuda includes this in the next article on how to stand with the "chest out".
3. In Article 6, Tokuda clarifies that "holds" (*torite*) are "like throws in judo".
4. In Article 8, Tokuda omits "opening the eyes".
5. In Article 9, Tokuda expresses "*ki* rising to the upper body" as "blood rushes to the head".

These are just some minor differences in the text, but it is worth investigating the relationship between Itosu's Ten Precepts and Tokuda's essay more thoroughly. It is improbable that Tokuda took it upon himself to embellish Itosu's teachings in the essay. Rather, it is more likely that he wrote down what he was taught directly in training sessions. Whatever the case, the Ten Precepts show how karate could be modernised for the education system. The content continues to influence teachers and researchers regardless of *ryuha* affiliation. With Itosu leading the way, instructors worked hard to establish karate in schools. They succeeded, as it became popular among the general public and spread throughout Okinawa prefecture.

4. Hanashiro Chomo's "Karate Kumite"

In the 1938 publication *Karatedo Taikan*, there is a section titled *Kuushu Kumite* which contains Hanashiro Chomo's (1869–1945) early teaching materials (Photo 1–6). Hanashiro was a middle school callisthenics instructor and often led physical education demonstrations at athletic meets.

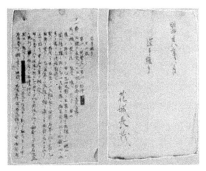

Photo 1-6 *Kuushu Kumite.* (*Karatedo Taikan*, 1938)

What do the ideograms for *kuushu* (空手= empty hand) indicate here? The *kanji* for *kuushu* can also be read as *karate*, which is a cause of confusion. The transition from Chinese hand to empty hand did not eventuate until the 1930s when different karate styles (*ryuha*) surfaced. As Tokuda stated, Chinese hand (唐手) is in fact done with the bare hands (空手).

In the same way, Hanashiro was not indicating a change in ideograms. Nor did he mean for the art to be called *karate* (empty hand) when he wrote *Kuushu Kumite* in 1905. Instead, he was emphasising the uniqueness of the Okinawan art compared to mainland budo in that it is weapon-less. It is unlikely that Hanashiro intended to change the meaning of the appellation of Chinese hand karate created by his teacher Itosu in the late nineteenth century. The important question is whether he did not mean fighting with bare hands, but actually intended to rename the art from *todi* to "empty hand" karate (空手). In this sense, Hanashiro's *Kuushu Kumite* is a valuable document in assessing the modernisation of karate in Okinawa (*Karate Kara Karate E*, 2011).

What was the purpose for creating *Kuushu Kumite*, and in what context was it taught? The outline is divided into "No. 1 Teaching" (*Dai-ikkyo*) and "No. 1 Section" (*Dai-ichibu*) followed by explanations of the processes and movements involved, and it was probably part of a more extensive instruction manual. It was handwritten and in draft form with words crossed out or changed, it is composed of a mixture of *kanji* and phonetic characters. There are explanations for set movements performed in pairs where both practitioners face each other and punch or block to the left or right in time with commands. In addition, the standing position, distance separating the practitioners, and thrusting and blocking methods are described.

In 1905, an athletic meet was held in Katabaru in Naha. Two kindergartens, seven primary schools, two middle schools, one normal school, and four specialist schools participated. There were 41 events demonstrated, and number 32 on the programme was a display of karate by middle school pupils. Hanashiro's notes for *Kuushu Kumite* may have been created by him for this festival.

A newspaper article was published soon after (*Ryukyu Shimpo*, November 13, 1905) in which the reporter writes his impressions of the good and bad aspects of demonstrating to verbal commands, and the difference between karate and physical education. After introduction in schools, traditional methods of teaching one-on-one were necessarily changed to group-based instruction, which further led to a modified way of performing it. Various opinions circulating about karate in schools influenced its modernisation and systematic organisation into a method of callisthenics.

In November 1906, a judo hall was built at Okinawa Middle School (Photo 1–7) with donations from staff and students. It was called Shobukan, or the "Hall of Martial Spirit". Five or six jujutsu matches along with karate and kendo demonstrations were held at the dojo opening (*Ryukyu Shimpo*, 2 November 1906).

Photo 1-7 Okinawa Prefectural Dai-ichi Middle School in the early 1920s. (*Meiji, Taisho, Showa Okinawa-ken Gakko Shashin-cho*, 1987)

SECTION 6

The Spread of Karate in Okinawa

1. Karate and Joint Athletic Meets

On March 8, 1905, former *daimyo* of the Sayama domain, Hojo Ujiyuki, visited Okinawa and an impromptu athletic meet was organised in Naha to welcome him. About 8,000 students from the normal, middle, and various specialist schools around Shuri and Naha participated in the event. Twenty-three different sports were featured, but all middle school students took part in the karate portion. It was reported as follows in the *Ryukyu Shimpo* (March 9, 1905).

"The most eye-catching spectacle for the public among the athletic displays were the *naginata* callisthenics demonstration performed by schoolgirls from Shuri, *yugi* (games) by students from Tenpi Primary School, the karate performance by middle school students, and races by the industrial school students. Esteemed guests included Hojo Ujiyuki and Governor Narahara as well as various officials. This is the first time in years that such a large event had been held, and even though the heavy rain made it difficult to reach the venue through the muddy roads, it was well attended by an enthusiastic crowd. The winners of each event were awarded prizes by Governor Narahara, Head of Police Mr. Wada, and Councillor Mr. Kishimoto."

As we have seen, from December the previous year, a karate course instructed by Itosu Anko, Hanashiro Chomo, Asato Anko and Higaonna Kanryo, among others, was started in which members of staff at middle schools attended. Students were taught the following year.

Evidently, they had completed enough training for a successful performance at the aforementioned athletic festival. It is estimated that the number of students who participated and spectators exceeded 10,000 people. Athletic meets in those days were large-scale events involving all inhabitants living in the region. In line with the times, athletic meets were intended to instil martial spirit in students and the locals, and enforcing imperialist and militarist ideals. Japan's victory in the Russo-Japanese War (1904–05), for example, was attributed to Japan's modernised military apparatus as well as the will to fight demonstrated by men in the armed forces. As such, the positive psychological effects of martial arts education were identified as an integral medium for strengthening the nation.

Originally from Okinawa, Naval Captain Kanna Kenwa wrote the preface for Funakoshi Gichin's first book *Ryukyu Kempo: Karate* (1922).

"If memory serves me correctly, it was around 1907 when Mr. Funakoshi pulled out all the stops to develop karate into a kind of callisthenics to be introduced in Okinawa's middle schools. It is thanks to his efforts that karate has in no small way contributed to rousing the spirit of today's youth."

2. Karate at Various Gatherings

A mere three years after its introduction into middle schools in 1905, karate had become a popular fixture at athletic festivals and various community events throughout Okinawa. According to numerous newspaper articles, karate featured in many school events, sports days, graduation ceremonies, cultural events, school induction ceremonies, dojo openings, education facility inspections, and was practised throughout the year in the physical education programme.

In addition, it was showcased in a range of community undertakings including youth association events, reunions, telegraph bureau opening ceremonies, and conferences. Newspapers show that school events were concentrated in Shuri and Naha. They were also held in islands such as Shimajiri in the south, Nakagami in central Okinawa, Kunigami in the north, and more isolated places such as Kumejima. It was also enjoyed as popular entertainment throughout Okinawa. Group demonstrations and teaching methods were devised to thrill onlookers, and this in turn also contributed to the modernisation of karate.

3. Okinawa Normal School "Karate Shorei Kai" (Karate Advancement Society)

In 1908, the Karate Shorei Kai was convened at the Okinawa Normal School. The following article shows how students were motivated to take up karate and improved their technical ability through advancements in group training and teaching methods (*Ryukyu Shimpo* February 10, 1908).

Date	Newspaper Article Title	Venue
5 February, 1905	Shuri Popular Discussion Meeting	Shuri
9 March, 1905	Naha Shuri Special Combined Sports Day	Naha
29 March, 1905	Girls Higher Normal School Award Ceremony	Shuri
15 May, 1905	Yoshu School Opening Ceremony	Shuri
19 August, 1905	Middle School Alumni Friendship Meeting	Shuri
1 December, 1905	Yoshu Middle School Combined Sports Day	Shuri
5 December, 1905	Kumejima Communications	Kumejima
12 December, 1905	Girls Higher Normal School Arts Festival	Shuri
12 March, 1906	Kenjutsu Tournament	Shuri
6 April, 1906	Shuri Memorial Service	Shuri
16 June, 1906	Normal School Opening Anniversary	Shuri
20 June, 1906	Ozato Memorial Service and Welcome Party	Shimajiri
22 June, 1906	Teacher Training College Foundation Anniversary	Shuri
6 October, 1906	Katabaru Area Schools Sports Day	Naha
28 October, 1906	Girls Higher Normal School Combined Sports Day	Naha
2 November, 1906	Middle High School Dojo Opening	Shuri
3 February, 1907	Affiliated Elementary Schools Arts Festival	Shuri
3 February, 1907	Hojo Chamberlain School Inspection Tour	Shuri
14 February, 1907	Kumejima Communications	Kumejima
27 March, 1907	Normal School Graduation Ceremony	Shuri
27 March, 1907	Ginowan School Graduation Ceremony	Nakagami
29 March, 1907	Yomiyama Telegraph Office Opening Ceremony	Nakagami
30 March, 1907	School Arts Festival	Kunigami
31 May, 1907	School Sports Day Report	Makabe
19 June, 1907	Teacher Training College Memorial Performance	Shimajiri
9 August, 1907	Kunigami-gun Youth Association – Sports Day Report	Kunigami
13 August, 1907	Middle School Alumni Meeting	Shuri
28 August, 1907	Nakagami-gun Youth Association	Naha
3 October, 1907	Kumejima Communications	Kumejima
19 October, 1907	Shimajiri-gun Youth General Assembly	Shimajiri
5 November, 1907	Headquarter School Arts Festival	Kunigami
25 November, 1907	Middle School Sports Day	Shuri
28 November, 1907	Record of Nisihara Primary School Sports Day	Nakagami
7 December, 1907	Nakagami-gun Youth Club	Nakagami

Table 1-3 *Ryukyu Shimpo* articles about community karate events in Okinawa

"The importance of karate in physical education has been recognised by the public. Since last year, the Okinawa Normal School has been studying karate in parallel with kendo, judo, and tennis. All students and staff, from the headmaster down to the secretary, participated in the Shorei Kai's activities. Three or four of them showed the skills they had developed over an extended period of training. Observations:

1. Last year they were too rigid and did not understand where to direct their strength. This time, they clearly knew what to do.

2. Nevertheless, eyes, hands and feet were not in synch with the mind, and more practice is required.

3. The reason for this is that they practise striking at imaginary targets without an actual object in front of them. It is important to train with the same spirit as if facing an enemy.

4. When two or more people are standing in a line, it is only natural that they are unable to form a single file as in callisthenics.

5. In short, relatively large strides have been made since last year."

Photo 1-8 (Yabu Kentsu teaching karate at the Okinawa Normal School in 1932. *Natsukashiki Okinawa*, 2000)

Demonstration Content
Naihanchi, Kusanku, Gojushiho, Passai, Pin'an, Ji'in,
Jitte, Chinto, Chinte, Rohai, Sanchin, Seisan, Wando, two
matches, closing & awards ceremony.

With Yabu Kentsu as its president, the Karate Shorei Kai
operated as an extracurricular club along with kendo, judo
and tennis from 1907 (Photo 1–8). Yabu commended students
for their improvement compared to a year before. There were
13 forms (*kata*) being practised, and although no details are
mentioned, it is also interesting to note that matches were
conducted this early on.

4. The Normal School "Karate Taikai"

At the normal school, a tournament (*taikai*) was held along
with research into teaching methods (*Ryukyu Shimpo*, January
25, 1911). No details of the organisers or participants of the
tournament are given. However, as the event was called the Karate
Tournament and awards were given to the top performers, it is
likely that dignitaries were also in attendance. The tournament
consisted of 80 pairs of student demonstrations, four pairs of
kumite, and five pairs of middle school students. In addition,
instructors gave model performances: Funakoshi Gichin
performed *Seisan*, Kiyuna did *Passai*, Itosu demonstrated
Naihanchin, and Yabu Kentsu *Gojushiho*. Thirteen types of
kata were performed at the Karate Shorei Kai meet, and fifteen
at the tournament (Table 1–4).

Of interest here is that *kumite* was also performed. The reporter
did not give details as to what the competition rules were. As

	Karate Shorei Kai	Karate Taikai
1	*Naihanchi*	*Naihanchi*(*n*) (Itokazu)
2	*Kusanku*	*Pin'an*
3	*Gojushiho*	*Chinto*
4	*Passai*	*Wansu*
5	*Pin'an*	*Passai* (Kiyuna)
6	*Jian*	*Ronsu*
7	*Jitte*	*Kusanku*
8	*Chinto*	*Rohai*
9	*Chinte*	*Gojushiho* (Yabu Kentsu)
10	*Rohai*	*Jitte*
11	*Sanchin*	*Nante*
12	*Seisan*	*Jii*
13	*Wando*	*Seisan* (Funakoshi Gichin)
14	-	*Wandau*
15	-	*Jiumu*
Total	13 types	15 types
Notes	Two matches Yabu Kentsu's "Shihan-te"	Karate 80 pairs Kumite 5 pairs Guest Middle School pupils 5 pairs Names in parentheses conducted demonstrations

Table 1-4 "Karate Shorei Kai" and "Karate Taikai" Kata and Demonstrations

such, it is impossible to know what relationship they had with Article 6 in Itosu Anko's "Ten Precepts" regarding the training method of *torite*, and Hanashiro Chomo's *kumite*. Apart from karate participation in schools, police, military, and in various locales around Okinawa, we are unsure of the nature of the *kata* and practice methods employed in the Meiji period.

5. Normal School Graduation Ceremony

At the graduation ceremony of the Normal School held in March 1911, graduation diplomas were awarded as well as various other certificates to members of the kendo, judo, tennis clubs. Graduating members of the karate club were given the grades of 1st Kyu to 4th Kyu. Details are not known about what kind of promotion system this was, but it is noteworthy that they were awarded as graduation certificates.

6. Demonstrations on the Mainland

In 1908, six middle school students who participated as Okinawa representatives for the judo and kendo matches at the 10th Grand Youth Embukai (demonstration event) hosted by the Dai-Nippon Butokukai, performed karate in front of Kano Jigoro, founder of the Kodokan, and other dignitaries. About 2,000 people were present in what was certainly a grand occasion. The karate demonstration was reported in a local newspaper as follows:

"During the Judo Club performance, a karate *kata* was performed by six students from Okinawa and Tamaki Taketa. This is a martial art unique to the region and rarely seen by mainlanders. They dazzled with their performance like *Nio*, the wrathful and muscular guardians of the Buddha. Their steely bodies, coalesced shouts and breathing were piercing and greeted with a great deal of excitement, and the applause continued unabated. The ensuing 250 judo matches finished at six o'clock in the evening. The day's events were watched by Dr. Koch and Dr. Kita Tsuneo of the Kyoto Medical Association, Mr. Kano, the head of the Kodokan, and other dignitaries. The venue was packed to capacity."

Karate was shown at the judo competition and was received enthusiastically by onlookers. Heinrich Koch, the famous German microbiologist was also there. Two days later, the same newspaper reported the story under the headline "Ryukyu's Mutekatsu-ryu". Clearly the reporter was enthralled with karate. There is no mention of the name of the *kata* performed, but it was most probably *Sanchin* based on the description of the powerful physicality and distinctive breathing. The author also wrote that Kano Jigoro appeared to be utterly engrossed in the performance and the peculiar but powerful breathing method.

Three years later in 1911, six students from Okinawa prefecture Normal School and a teacher were invited by Kano to visit the Kodokan. The students performed *tameshi-wari* (board-breaking techniques) in front of Kano and high-ranking judo practitioners. The students also took questions from Kano and answered them with much enthusiasm (*Ryutan*, 1911).

The performance by the Okinawan middle school pupils and the demonstration commissioned by Kano were invaluable experiences for the young men, but also proved to be pivotal events in the dissemination of karate in mainland Japan. The Butokuden in Kyoto and the Kodokan in Tokyo were perfect venues to showcase the uniqueness of Okinawa's karate (Photo 1–9).

7. Modernisation and Multilinear Development

After 1905, karate was encouraged through the guidance and support of the local government in Okinawa. At the forefront of its instruction at education institutions were Yabu Kentsu and Hanashiro Chomo, with Itosu Anko providing a leadership role. Itosu fostered apprentices who established their own styles of karate and can thus be credited as being the catalyst for karate's

Photo 1-9   Okinawa prefecture Middle School Budo Commemoration group photo. (*Okinawa Karate Kobudo Jiten*, 2008)

modernisation from the Meiji period. Many famous karate leaders such as Asato Anko, Higaonna Kanryo, Yabu Kentsu, Hanashiro Chomo, and Kyan Chotoku had a direct connection with him.

When karate was first introduced into the education system, it was referred to as "karate callisthenics" and "karate exercise". In only two or three years, karate demonstrations became an established fixture at official school and community events. At the Okinawa Normal School, the Karate Shorei Kai conducted trainings and tournaments, and research for teaching methodology into matches and *kumite*. A promotion system like that employed in judo and kendo was also introduced. Furthermore, Okinawan students who travelled to the mainland and performed karate demonstrations around this time were instrumental in promoting it to influential martial artists such as Kano Jigoro. The foundations were laid for multi-linear development across Okinawa and the mainland.

SECTION 7

SECTION 7

The Arrival of Modern Karate (1) Shifting from Chinese Kempo Origin Theories

Karate was posited as a Japanese budo after the establishment of several styles (*ryuha*). How did men like Itosu Anko, Funakoshi Gichin, Motobu Choki, Miyagi Chojun, Mabuni Kenwa, and Nakasone Genwa, who sought to establish karate as a Japanese budo art through publishing their research, discuss the theory of its roots in Chinese *kempo*? The transition of the Chinese *kempo* theory offers important clues into how the history of karate in Okinawa and Japan was constructed.

1. Questions Regarding the History of Karate

In modern Okinawa, the spread of karate in schools was promoted mainly by the administration which facilitated its modernisation. Funakoshi Gichin, who was at the forefront of the spread of full-fledged karate on the mainland, promoted modernisation largely through university clubs in the Kanto region.

Karate was considered a unique aspect of Okinawan culture and viewed with considerable pride. It was not deemed necessary to develop individual styles (*ryuha*) when it was introduced into Okinawan schools. On the other hand, for students of karate clubs on the mainland, and those who studied with karate instructors from Okinawa, the creation of *ryuha* was an inevitability following in the traditions of Japanese budo.

Different *ryuha* distinguish between methodology and philosophy and identify with particular lineages. Clarification of origins is an important factor in *ryuha* identity *vis-a-vis* other schools. For modern karate to become a Japanese budo, it was necessary for the school's source and origin to be specified by the founder (Table 1–5).

2. The Source of Karate

In the *Heibonsha World Encyclopaedia*, popular in Japan, the entry on karate's origins is as follows:

> "Sources pertaining to the roots of karate are scant and there is no established theory as to how it arose. However, considering that many of the forms (*kata*) have Chinese appellations, it is certain that karate was influenced by Chinese *kempo*. These techniques were absorbed into ancient martial systems of Okinawa and evolved into its present form. Chinese fist techniques date back to the Spring and Autumn Period [c. 771 to 476 BCE] in ancient China and were developed as self-defence by the monks of Shaolin and other temples in the Tang Dynasty."

Furthermore, "Influenced by Chinese fist techniques, Okinawa's distinctive system of karate matured in two eras in which open martial training was prohibited." This passage claims that Okinawa's existing indigenous martial arts absorbed Chinese influences, eventually giving rise to karate. It also states that karate's evolution was facilitated by two martial prohibition policies: one enforced by King Sho Shin, and a later one by the Satsuma domain.

Okinawa's martial arts were already known by Satsuma clansmen and warriors of the Higo domain in the early-modern period (at the latest in the 1700s). By this stage, Ryukyuans were also learning Japanese *bujutsu* such as swordsmanship (Jigen-ryu), grappling (*yawara*), archery (*kyujutsu*), horsemanship (*bajutsu*), and spearmanship (*sojutsu*), to the extent that they were even qualified to teach these arts.

In what way did the Ryukyuans integrate the Chinese forms into the indigenous martial arts? Moreover, how did Okinawan karate become "Japan-ised" into budo when it was disseminated on the mainland in the twentieth century? Answers to these questions provide essential insights into how the art ripened into the karate of today.

The Ryukyus engaged in vibrant exchanges with Fujian province of China during the Ming and Qing Dynasties. As such, it is natural to assume that the so-called Southern Fist genre of Fujian hand-to-hand combat styles greatly influenced the development of fighting arts in the Ryukyus, and subsequently the various styles of karate that became popular on mainland Japan. Moreover, as many recent studies have pointed out, the common belief that *todi* in the Ryukyu Kingdom arose because of the military prohibitions enforced by King Sho Shin and the Satsuma clan needs to be reviewed.

Why do these assumptions quoted from the *Heibonsha World Encyclopaedia* remain prevalent? In order to clarify the history of karate, it is necessary to re-examine the historical relationship between Ryukyu/Okinawa, Japan and China. Likewise, the

Date	Author	Publication Name	Notes
July 1908	Itosu Anko	*Karate Jukka-jo*	April 1905: Karate is introduced in Okinawan junior high schools
9 January, 1913	Shoto (Funakoshi Gichin)	*Karate wa Bugei no Kotsuzui Nari*	October 1912: Dai Nippon Butokukai creates the Dai Nippon Teikoku Kendo Kata
17-19 January, 1914	Asato Anko (Funakoshi Gichin)	*Okinawa no Bugi*	July 1913: "Military drill" is renamed "drill"
25 November, 1922	Funakoshi Gichin	*Ryukyu Kempo - Karate*	April-May 1922: 1st Exhibition of Sport and Physical Education Funakoshi goes to Tokyo
14 March, 1925	Funakoshi Gichin	*Rentan Goshin Karatejutsu*	October 1924: Keio University Karate Research Society inaugurated
5 May, 1926	Motobu Choki	*Okinawa Kempo Karatejutsu (Kumite)*	September 1925: "Human Bullet Karate vs. Boxing Match" in King magazine 1929: Mabuni goes to Osaka
29 August, 1932	Miyagi Chojun	*Goju-ryu Kempo*	November 1930: Shinzato Jin'an goes to Tokyo
23 March, 1934	Miyagi Chojun	*Ryukyu Kempo Karatedo no Enkaku Gaiyo*	1933: Karate is approved by the Dai Nippon Butokukai
5 March, 1934	Mabuni Kenwa	*Kobo Jisai Goshin-jutsu* *Karate Kempo*	April 1934: Miyagi goes to China 1934: Mabuni founds the Yoshukan
25 May, 1935	Funakoshi Gichin	*Karatedo Kyohan*	
28 October, 1935	Mabuni Kenwa Nakasone Genwa	*Kobo Jisai Goshin Kempo Karatedo Nyumon (Karate Dokushu no Tebiki)*	December 1935: Ritsumeikan University Karatedo Association established
20 September, 1941	Funakoshi Gichin	*Supplement:* *Karatedo Kyohan*	July 1937: Marco Polo Bridge Incident (second Sino-Japanese War) January 1939: Funakoshi establishes Shotokan December 1941: Attack on Pearl Harbor (Pacific War)
15 August, 1942	Miyagi Chojun	*Hogoju Donto*	March 1945: American and British forces land in Okinawa (Battle of Okinawa)

Table 1-5 Main sources in which the Chinese Kempo origin theory is discussed

reasons for the change of name from karate (Chinese hand) to karate (empty hand), the creation of karate *ryuha* from the 1930s onwards, and the development and succession of karate on the basis of these *ryuha* should also be reviewed.

3. Itosu Anko's Description of Karate's Roots

The oldest source outlining the roots of karate is Itosu Anko's *Karate Jukka-jo* (Ten Precepts) published in 1908.

> "Karate did not derive from Buddhism or Confucianism. In olden times, the two styles of Shorin-ryu and Shorei-ryu came from China. Both have distinct advantages and it is necessary to preserve them and not colour them in any way."

Itosu explains that the two schools of Shorin-ryu and Shorei-ryu were introduced from China, and that there was no religious affiliation. After the first Sino-Japanese War (1894–95), the Boxer Rebellion of 1900 was reported on widely in Okinawa. There was a degree of criticism that the martial arts used by the pseudo-religious Boxers (Militia United in Righteousness) was the same as karate, and that teaching such culture in Okinawan schools warranted caution. Itosu's denial of the religious nature of karate reflected the social situation in Okinawa and Japan after the Russo-Japanese War (1904–1905) as Japan's political hegemony in Asia was solidifying.

4. Historical Research—Funakoshi Gichin

In 1913, Funakoshi published an article in the *Ryukyu Shimpo* newspaper titled "Karate represents the marrow of martial arts".

As did Itosu, Funakoshi also advocated that karate derived from the two Chinese schools of Shorei-ryu and Shorin-ryu. He also discussed, for the first time, the theory that karate was facilitated by the two martial prohibition policies enforced by King Sho Shin and the Satsuma domain.

He asserts that, in the Ryukyu Kingdom, there were the three styles of Shuri-te, Naha-te and Tomari-te, but that their predecessors were the

Photo 1-10 Preamble for Itosu Anko's *Karate Jukka-jo*. (*Karatedo Taikan*, 1938)

two aforementioned Chinese schools; Naha-te was influenced by Shorei-ryu, Shuri-te by Shorin-ryu, and Tomari-te by both. He also made the distinction that the Shorei-ryu emphasised training the body, and the Shorin-ryu was more centred on technique. In addition, *Kamite* and *Meekata* (performance arts) were also mentioned in inscriptions.

The following year, Funakoshi published in the same newspaper a transcript of discussions with his teacher, Asato Anko, titled "Okinawan Martial Techniques" in three instalments. The beginnings of karate are discussed in more detail here.

In the Asato discussions, mention is made of Sakugawa Kanga (*todi* Sakugawa), the person responsible for popularising the term "karate" (Chinese hand). Detail is also given of Chinese emissaries who came to the Ryukyu Kingdom and Chinese masters from Fujian province who taught the Ryukyuans their system, and of Ryukyuans who travelled to China to study.

In 1922, Funakoshi went to Tokyo to attend the Exhibition of Sport and Physical Education sponsored by the Ministry of Education. It was there that he introduced Okinawa's martial arts. In the same year Funakoshi published *Ryukyu Kempo: Karate*. *Oshima Hikki* (1762) was introduced in his book, as was the idea that a Chinese named Kushanku (Kwang Shang Fu) brought with him many apprentices to Ryukyu who then taught locals.

Regarding the designation karate, he explains that Ryukyuans who practised Chinese boxing incorporated the teachings into their indigenous systems and adopted the ideogram indicating "China" (唐) to mark this development. *Te* (*tii*), he argues, came from traditional *Meekata* dances found throughout the Ryukyu islands.

In 1925, Funakoshi corrected and added to *Ryukyu Kempo Karate* by replacing the illustrations with photographs, and republished it as *Rentan Goshin Karatejutsu*. The content regarding karate's history and the transmission of Chinese fist fighting is basically the same. However, he does change the ideograms used for Shorin-ryu in previous writings from 昭林流 to 少林流, the latter of which designates the Shaolin Temple.

In 1926, Motobu Choki also published *Okinawa Kempo Karatejutsu Kumite-hen*. He too explains that the culture of karate came from Ryukyu's long-standing relationship with China. Ryukyuans were able to receive teaching from Chinese martial art experts and then it spread widely through the kingdom.

5. Goju-ryu Karate Kempo

In November 1930, Miyagi Chojun's apprentice, Shinzato Jin'an, demonstrated at the Meiji Jingu Budo Tournament. Shinzato was at a loss when asked what school of karate he represented. He talked to Miyagi about this conundrum. Miyagi apparently named their style Goju-ryu, inspired by the essential teaching *Ho goju donto* (the way of inhaling and exhaling is hardness and softness) contained in the classical Chinese martial art text *Wubei Zhi* (J: *Bubishi*). This name is first seen in print in Miyagi's book *Goju-ryu Kempo* (1932) where he states that Ryukyu inherited the lineage of the Chinese boxing from the southern Fujian sect in 1828, and this is what eventually developed into Goju-ryu Karate Kempo.

Miyagi went to Hawaii in May 1934 at the invitation of Okinawans who had migrated there. He gave lectures and demonstrations of karate. In *Karatedo Gaisetsu* (1934) he espouses that karate derived from Chinese *kempo*, and that there were three main theories as to how it was transmitted to and evolved in the Ryukyus. Miyagi maintains that the most convincing theory is that Chinese and Ryukyuan systems amalgamated and matured into its current form.

6. Okinawa-te

The same year that Miyagi announced his school as Goju-ryu, Mabuni Kenwa published *Kobo Jizai Goshin-jutsu: Karate Kempo* (1934). A section in his book, "Karate and its Evolution", explains how Bodhidharma, a monk in the Shaolin Temple in Henan, created prototypical forms (*kata*) of Chinese *quanfa* which later spread and divided into the Southern kempo (*nanquan*) and Northern kempo (*beiquan*) streams. It was these techniques, he claims, that were transmitted to the Ryukyus. Goju-ryu *kempo* was a derivative of the Fujian method taught by Higaonna Kanryo (his and Miyagi's teacher), and thus traces its origins to the Southern line. Miyagi travelled to China on two occasions to further his studies in the system and continued developing it in Japan.

Funakoshi wrote *Karatedo Kyohan* in 1935. He explains that modern karate was the result of many Ryukyuan warriors learning fist techniques in China, and from Chinese who settled in the Ryukyus. Further, he points out that Okinawan *kempo* was the product of the unification of Okinawan *Te* and Chinese *quanfa*, and this was combined to become karate. The reason for changing the designation from Chinese hand to empty hand karate was due, Funakoshi reasons, to the fact that Okinawan martial arts had already become Japanese budo, and a change in *kanji* was necessary to differentiate Japanese karate from Chinese martial arts. He also points out that Shaolin Temple *quanfa* was founded on Bodhidharma's text *Yijin Jing* (literally: Muscle/Tendon Change Classic). This was communicated to the Ryukyus and later became Okinawa *te* (*ti* or *tii* in the Ryukyuan language).

7. Empty Hand Karate's Origins

Mabuni Kenwa co-authored a book with Nakasone Genwa called *Kobo Jizai Goshin Kempo Karatedo Nyumon* (also called *Karate Dokushu no Tebiki*) (1935).

> "This book contains explanations of the karate *kata* of master Mabuni Kenwa's Seiden Itosu-ha [Correct transmission of the Itosu stream]. As I [Nakasone Genwa] am co-author, I have written down and added to the information passed on to me."

This indicates that Nakasone probably wrote most of the text. Chapter 6 is titled "Reflections on the Origins of Karate". The author expresses his doubts about Funakoshi's claims that karate came from the Shaolin Temple. He asserts that boxing was much older than this, and in fact, unarmed martial arts represent mankind's oldest form of combat. Unarmed fighting methods exist, he asserts, everywhere. As such, he argues, Okinawan *todi* has always been in Okinawa, but Chinese methods introduced later blended with existent indigenous methods and evolved into karate.

He compared Funakoshi's books *Ryukyu Kempo Karate*, *Rentan Goshin Karatejutsu*, and *Karate Kyohan*, and concluded dismissively that the Bodhidharma Shaolin origin theory and the subsequent fragmentation of streams from this original source are groundless.

In a monthly Okinawan publication called *Gekkan Bunka Okinawa* (1941), Mabuni wrote an article titled "Establishing karate as an offshoot of Japanese Bushido". He acknowledges the fusion of indigenous Okinawan martial arts with Chinese elements but proclaims that karate is a Japanese budo imbued with the very same spirit. He even connects karate with jujutsu and the legendary progenitor of sumo, Nomino Sukune, as described in the ancient Japanese text *Nihon Shoki* (720). He supports the idea that karate was refined by necessity under the martial art prohibition policy enforced by the Satsuma domain.

Funakoshi published a revised edition of *Karatedo Kyohan* in 1941 but did not make any changes to the text regarding karate's origins.

8. The Okinawa-Mainland Gap

In *Gekkan Bunka Okinawa* (1942), Miyagi Chojun published "*Ho-goju-donto karate zatsuwara*". He argues that the roots of karate are undoubtedly found in Chinese *quanfa*, but that these methods were in fact adapted and improved in Okinawa. Moreover, karate developed in accordance with the situation and environment in each region and ultimately became a "true Japanese art" (hence, empty hand) when it was inducted into the pantheon of other Japanese budo by the Dai-Nippon Butokukai.

9. Japanese Budo and the Chinese Quanfa Origin Theory

The origin theory of karate having derived from *quanfa* saw various iterations after Itosu. Karate's historical research began with the goal of making the value of its existence as the Ryukyus culture known to mainlanders. In order to introduce karate into the school curriculum in Okinawa, it was essential to clarify its potential to encourage personal development, and elucidate how it was a popular pursuit among the Ryukyu Kingdom's military elite and was often performed at important state ceremonies. Efforts were made to construct an interpretation of karate as a Japanese budo but one that still retained its Okinawan roots.

As it spread to the mainland, however, with few sources available it proved to be no easy task to construct a historical narrative of karate so that it could be accepted as a genuine Japanese budo. Various discussions took place between masters who established their own *ryuha*, such as Miyagi Chojun, Funakoshi Gichin, Mabuni Kenwa, Motobu Choki, Nakasone Genwa, newly emerging mainland instructors, and students at university karate clubs.

Prominent Okinawans such as Iha Fuyu, Higaonna Kanjun, Majikina Anko, martial artists, historians, military men, politicians, administrators, and others sought assistance from mainland martial artists and educators such as Kano Jigoro in order to establish karate as a recognised Japanese budo art.

Significant efforts were made to forward the various manifestations of the Chinese *quanfa* origin theory. Although the expressions vary, constructing a historical narrative reflects an important part of the modernisation process. Karate narratives then focussed on issues highlighted in Japanese budo: physical, martial and spiritual values. In this respect, the karate in Okinawa and that introduced to the Japanese mainland were heading in the same direction.

Since the modern era, Okinawa and the mainland have coexisted within the framework of a unified Japan, but they are geographically separated and different historically and socially. This influenced the evaluation of the Ryukyuan-isation of Chinese martial arts, and the perceived ideal direction karate should take as a Japanese budo unfolded. From the 1930s, Japan's relationship with China deteriorated enormously, which encouraged the change in *kanji* characters from Chinese to empty hand. The transition seen in the Chinese *quanfa* origin theory is still relevant and requires consideration as we continue to plot the future of karate.

SECTION 8

The Arrival of Modern Karate (2) Standardisation of New Kata

The formation of new *kata* forms had a remarkable effect on the modernisation of karate. It was the creation of the *Pin'an* (*Heian*) *kata* by Itosu Anko that led the way in this respect. *Pin'an* became one of the most established and fundamental of all karate *kata,* not only in Okinawa, but also on the Japanese mainland and overseas. Traditional *kata* were reconstituted and modified depending on the instruction policies of individual masters, and were also influenced by *kata* in mainstream Japanese budo. *Kata* designations were prefixed with the names of charismatic masters or regions in Okinawa where the art was particularly popular. Variations in technical interpretations in newly established *ryuha* also led to the development of new *kata*, and forms have been continually evolving from the modern era.

1. The Formulation of the Pin'an Kata

In the preamble of Itosu's "Ten Precepts", which he wrote to promote the introduction of karate in Okinawan schools, he states that karate should be preserved in its original form without "adding any colour". At the old Okinawa Prefectural Middle School (now Shuri High School), where Itosu was a commissioned karate teacher, local practitioners and staff studied teaching methods from the end of 1904, and from April of the following year karate was taught as a kind of callisthenic exercise in regular classes.

The *Pin'an kata* (*Shodan–Godan*) created by Itosu and some collaborators were designed as educational forms and accepted as such. In addition to Itosu, others known to have been involved in this research included middle school PE teacher Hanashiro Chomo, Asato Anko, and Higaonna Kanryo. In middle schools, the *Pin'an* form became mainstream, but some students who learned directly from Itosu also frequented Higaonna's dojo after school. At this time there were no *ryuha* per se, so students would learn forms from various masters simultaneously.

In August 1909, at the 11th Youth Grand Embu Tournament held at the Butokuden dojo in Kyoto, a special display of karate was performed by middle school students. The *kata* they did were *Kusanku* (*Dai & Sho*) and *Sanchin*. Traditional forms such as *Kusanku* and *Sanchin*, and new teaching forms such as *Pin'an* created by Itosu were being taken up in schools confirming that students were also learning from local instructors outside school.

Given what Itosu expresses in the preamble to his "Ten Precepts", this development may seem contradictory. Perhaps it can be reconciled by the fact that he was tasked with developing *kata* to be taught in schools but which were still imbued with the essence and principles of traditional forms. Itosu describes *kata* as being the exterior art of karate. A direct student of Hanashiro, Kinjo Hiroshi from Shuri, explained that he trained in the educationally oriented *Pin'an* to learn the techniques and movements found in other forms, and that the finer technical details and deeper principles of traditional karate were passed on orally by the master.

After that, *Pin'an* was not only taught in schools, but also became a fundamental *kata* in the various *ryuha* that sprung up in the future. After the promotion of teaching materials by Itosu, karate instructors and students participated together in karate promotion meetings and competitions held at the Normal School, and the traditional one-on-one instruction via oral transmission was replaced by the verbalisation of *kata* and group instruction so that everyone could understand, and the path of training was clearly laid out.

Nakasone Genwa, who was a middle school student when Itosu was teaching, said that *Pin'an* was initially called "*Chan'nan*", and although there were some differences, the name and the content of the *kata* were fixed by Itosu. Kinjo also argues that, from the point of view of *kata* technique, *Pin'an* is modelled on the old forms of *Passai* and *Kusanku* and can therefore be regarded as an introduction to both (*Karate Kara Karate E*, 2011).

2. Karate Zadankai

In 1931, the Japanese military sparked the Manchurian Incident. The following year, Prime Minister Inukai Tsuyoshi was assassinated by a young army officer in what is known as the "May 15 Incident". In February 1933, Japan left the League of Nations and rapidly descended into a militaristic regime. In December the same year, karate was recognised as Japanese budo by the Dai-Nippon Butokukai. Until this recognition, karate was posited as a subsidiary of judo. Three years before, in November 1930, the Okinawa Prefectural Athletic Association launched a dedicated "Karate Division" which was headed by Miyagi Chojun, a permanent councillor of the Dai-Nippon

Butokukai Okinawa prefecture Branch. Oshiro Chojo, Shinzato Jin'an, and Tokuda Antei were also appointed as officials in the division.

Amidst this time of social upheaval, on October 25, 1936, a Karate Roundtable (*Karate Zadankai*) was hosted by the *Ryukyu Shimposha* newspaper. There were 19 participants including eight karate masters: Hanashiro Chomo, Kyan Chotoku, Motobu Choki, Miyagi Chojun, Kyoda Juhatsu, Chibana Choshin, Shiroma Shimpan, and Oroku Chotei.

Also taking part were karate researcher Nakasone Genwa, director if education Sato Koichi, prefectural library director Shimabukuro Zempatsu, company district command vice commander Fukushima Kitsuma, director of the police department Kita Eizo, head of security Goeku Chosho, sports director Furukawa Yoshisaburo, writer Ando Sakan, president of *Ryukyu Shimpo* Ota Chobu, editor-in-chief Matayoshi Kowa, Yamaguchi Zensoku and others. The content of the discussion was transcribed and published in the newspaper in 12 issues.

The following headline graced the front page the next day: "The designation 'Karate' [empty hand] is to become standard and a promotion association to be launched! Prefectural masters gather for discussions!"

- October 27 (Tuesday)
  Part 1: "Karate's [Chinese hand] unsuitability for students—A right hand strike to karate [empty hand]"
- October 28 (Wednesday)

Part 2: "All participants agree to name change—Butokukai is also investigating"

- October 30 (Friday)
  Part 3: "The ideograph for karate [Chinese hand] is an Okinawan invention—Positive martial art 'karate' [empty hand]"

- October 31 (Saturday)
  Part 4: Standardising *kata* for dissemination—Two forms of traditional and fundamental"

- November 1 (Sunday)
  Part 5: "Agreement to launch the Karate Promotion Society (Karate Shinkokai)—*Ryuha* to be differentiated by teaching methodology"

- November 2 (Monday)
  Part 6: "Teach primary school children first—Dan ranking system to be nationalised"

- November 6 (Friday)
  Part 7: "My heroics are not true—Master Miyagi dismisses false rumours"

- November 7 (Saturday)
  Part 8: "The unidentified mysterious master! Encourage young men with spirit"

- November 8 (Sunday)
  Final Part 9: "Matsumura's ingenuity saves the day—Warriors know warriors"

- November 9 (Monday)

- Part 1: "Warrior master Motobu Choki talks about fighting! Roundtable session held by young karate exponents"

- November 10 (Tuesday)
  Part 2: "Warrior master Motobu Choki talks about fighting!

Roundtable session held by young karate exponents"
- November 12 (Wednesday)
  Part 3: "Warrior master Motobu Choki talks about fighting!
  Roundtable session held by young karate exponents"

Discussions concerning the name change of karate featured three times. After that, various other issues related to karate were discussed by the team of experts such as the standardisation of *kata* forms, the establishment of an association to promote karate, the introduction of karate in primary schools, instigating a consistent ranking system, and the establishment of common technical terms for teaching. There are also sections dedicated to the exploits of individual masters. The main points raised concerning *kata* are as follows:

Physical education supervisor Yoshikawa spoke of kendo as an example when advocating for the creation of a *Dai-Nippon Teikoku Karatedo Kata*. He also asserted that the title should be in standard Japanese (not Okinawan dialect).

Miyagi Chojun suggested that the original *kata* forms should be left as is, and new forms created for national dissemination to suit the various age groups in schools.

3. Formulation of the Karatedo Kihon Kata 12-Dan

Following the roundtable discussion, the Okinawa prefecture Karatedo Promotion Society was launched in November 1936. In March the following year, the society's Instruction Division formulated *Karatedo Kihon Kata 12-Dan* (Twelve-Step Karatedo Fundamental Forms). In this way, the two objectives of creating a promotional society and standardising forms for national dissemination were realised four months after the discussions.

The eight instructors included Yabu Kentsu as division chief, Hanashiro Chomo, Kyan Chotoku, Chibana Choshin, Shiroma Shimpan as secretaries, and Maeshiro Choryo as secretary, and secretary of the promotion division Nakasone Genwa. Kyoda Juhatsu and others in the roundtable sessions were absent due to public duties.

As for the significance of the Twelve-Step *kata*, Nakasone later wrote in *Karatedo Taikan* (1938) that they were "formulated by consensus of the Karatedo Promotion Society" (1938). This was a momentous event in the modern history of karate. The following is an outline of the six main characteristics of the Twelve-Steps:

1. It is possible to adjust the teaching content to suit developmental needs of boys and girls of all ages
2. It is easy to teach the purpose of karate
3. It is useful for remembering [the forms] and training
4. It is useful for accurately learning the various movements for traditional *kata*
5. As physical exercise, each part of the body can be strengthened uniformly
6. It enables the unification of movement and spirit

Twelve-Steps was considered a self-study method for learning fundamental techniques that superseded differences in *ryuha*, and which also provided the basis for studying classical forms. In addition, in Notes for Practice, it explains the order and frequency of practising the Twelve Steps, how to prepare, the importance of continuous training, and the effectiveness of the techniques in self-defence and for promoting health. Nakasone argues that it is easier to learn and improve by practising in order from the first step.

In particular, emphasis was placed on etiquette, on training seriously with the mindset of attacking and defending against the enemy, and on the spiritual significance of the karate *kata*, which, unlike standard gymnastic exercises, reflected the practicality and spirituality expected of budo at the time.

The forms were designed to teach specifically designated techniques, stances, points of focus with the eyes, vital points for attack, and precise methods and parameters in the line of movement (*embusen*) for performance. The Twelve-Steps included punches, (*jodan-tsuki, chudan-tsuki*); blocks (*jodan[age]-uke, chudan[yoko]-uke, gedan[barai]-uke*); kicks (*jodan-geri, chudan-geri, gedan-geri*); shifting (*tenshin* – forward, back, and on the spot); stances (*hachiji-dachi* [natural stance], *nekoashi-dachi* [cat foot stance], *zenkutsu-dachi* [front stance]); and the *embusen*.

There is a definition for each technique. For example, the following explanation is provided for punching and shifting. There are two ways of thrusting: high (*jodan-tsuki*) and to the middle level (*chudan-tsuki*). The former is for punching the opponent in the face, and the latter for striking the solar plexus or the chest. A direct thrust (*choku-tsuki*) requires the fists to be extended directly in front and aiming for the higher or lower target directly from the stance. The back of the fist is turned up during the thrust.

Shifting the body (*tenshin*) involves moving forward, back, or pivoting on the spot. When turning, the right foot points to the north and is used as the pivot point, or the left foot serves as the pivot while being pointed to the east. In all cases the front of the foot slides across the floor while the heel is raised in the turn.

The purpose is stated briefly but clearly in the explanations for each step. Illustrations are included in each

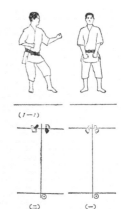

右 拳 構 脇。 着 眼 北 方。

北 方 へ 左 拳 中 段 横 受。 左 猫 足。

第一動 (第二圖)

に 構 へ、 顎 を 引 き 着 眼 東 方。 膝 を

伸 ば し 肩 を 下 げ 力 を 丹 田 に 取 る。

外 八 字 立。 両 拳 腰 の 付 け 根 の 處

構 へ 方 (第一圖)

Illustration 1-3 Explanation of *Dai-ichi Dan no Kamae* and *Dai-ichi Do.*

section with foot movements drawn over the *embusen* lines (Illustration 1–3). The purpose for each step is outlined in Table 1–6.

Technically, it is possible to combine various techniques described and practise them in different directions, thereby increasing the difficulty incrementally.

Kata Name	Training Objectives
1. Dai-Ichidan	The first stage of the basic *kata* focuses on practising the *chudan yoko-uke* and the *chudan choku-tsuki* techniques.
2. Dai-Nidan	The main focus of the second stage is to practise *jodan choku-tsuki*. The target height is the opponent's face.
3. Dai-Sandan	The third stage is a combination of the first stage and *gedan-geri*. *Gedan-geri* is a kick to the knee.
4. Dai-Yondan	The fourth stage is a version of the first stage with *jodan-geri*. *Jodan-geri* is aimed at the solar-plexus.
5. Dai-Godan	The fifth stage is a combination of the second stage and *chudan-geri*. *Chudan-geri* is aimed between the testicles and the lower abdomen.
6. Dai-Rokudan	The second stage has *jodan-geri* in mind. It is a combination of *chudan yoko-uke, jodan choku-tsuki*, and *jodan-geri*.
7. Dai-Nanadan	The seventh stage combines a *gedan barai-uke, chudan yoko-uke*, and *chudan choku-tsuki*.
8. Dai-Hachidan	The eighth stage combines of *gedan barai-uke, chudan yoko-uke*, and *chudan choku-tsuki*. There is also *jodan choku-tsuki*.
9. Dai Kyudan	The ninth stage combines *gedan barai-uke, chudan yoko-uke, chudan-geri*, and *jodan choku-tsuki*.
10. Dai-Judan	The tenth stage combines *chudan yoko-uke, jodan age-uke* and *chudan choku-tsuki*.
11. Dai-Juichidan	The eleventh stage combines *chudan yoko-uke, jodan age-uke, chudan-geri*, and *chudan choku-tsuki*.
12. Dai-Junidan	The twelfth stage combines *chudan yoko-uke, jodan age-uke, chudan-geri*, and *jodan choku-tsuki*.

Table 1-6 Training objective for *Kihon Kata 12 Dan*

At the end of the manual for the Twelve-Steps there is an explanation why all of the forms begin with *nekoashi-dachi* (cat foot) stance and then progress in a *gedan-barai* lower block and into the *zenkutsu-dachi* (front) stance.

With *zenkutsu-dachi*, when changing to a *chudan yoko-uke* (middle-side block) from the *gedan barai-uke* (lower sweep block), it is necessary to pull the front foot back slightly without moving the rear foot, while at the same time extending both knees into the *chudan yoko-uke* position. This means that the forward-bending posture is, in a sense, an unavoidable sacrificial posture leaving one momentarily vulnerable. Thus, it is important to re-establish a stable posture quickly without making lots of defensive changes. In other words, *zenkutsu-dachi* is a stance taken as an extension of *nekoashi-dachi* and should be practised and understood as such.

4. The Creation of Gekisai 1 and Gekisai 2

Miyagi Chojun created the forms *Gekisai* 1 and 2 around 1940, but details of the creation process and the *kata* have since been forgotten. Miyagi was elected as the head the Okinawa Prefectural Athletic Association Karate Division. He worked throughout the prefecture as an instructor at institutions such as the Police Academy and the Naha School of Commerce. After Yabu Kentsu died in 1938, Miyagi took over his role as the head instructor at the Okinawa prefecture Normal School and was considered one of the most prominent masters in the region. He advocated at the roundtable discussions the value of developing standard forms for teaching beginners at all school levels. To this end, he devised *Gekisai* 1 and 2.

Gekisai 1 consists of around 30 basic attacks executed in all directions: to the left and right, back and forward, and on a cross-shaped *embusen* line.

From the bow and the stance in which both open hands are positioned in front of the groin (and then moved to the sides), the practitioner then demonstrates various techniques including *jodan-tsuki*, *chudan-tsuki*, *jodan-uke* and *chudan-uke* (*harai*), *mae-geri*, *hiji-ate*, *ura-ken*, *ashi-barai*, *shuto*, *morote-tsuki*, and various thrusts. The stances include *musubi-dachi*, *heiko-dachi*, *shiko-dachi*, *zenkutsu-dachi*, *hachiji-dachi*, and so on.

Gekisai 2 is composed of almost the same techniques as *Gekisai* 1. Instead of a rare *chudan-uke* and *morote-tsuki* two-handed thrusts to the front, the movements incorporate open-handed *chudan kake-uke* and *nekoashi-dachi* two-handed *shuto mawashi-uke* (hand-sword roundhouse block) with a *shotei-tsuki* (*toraguchi*) thrust with the bottom of the hand. These two techniques are included in many Goju-ryu *kata*. In particular, *toraguchi* is seen in the *Suparimpei* (*Pechurin*) form which is considered to be the highest level of *kata* in Goju-ryu. Thus, although *Gekisai* forms were created with beginners in mind, the techniques corresponded with the budo ideal that the fundamentals also encompass the highest level of the art.

5. Creation of Fukyu Kata 1 and Fukyu Kata 2

In 1941, Okinawa prefecture Governor Hayakawa Hajime helped launch the Karatedo Specialist Committee and advocated that before learning the classic forms, beginners should practise techniques that are easier to learn. Committee members included Chairman Ishihara Masanao (Butokukai Okinawa Branch Director), Miyagi Chojun (Naha-te), Kamiya Jinsei (Naha-te), Shinzato Jin'an (Naha-te), Miyazato Koji (Naha-te), Tokuda Anbun (Shuri-te), Kinjo Kensho (Shuri-te),

Kyan Shin'ei (Shuri-te), and Nagamine Shoshin (Shuri-te).

The *kata* that they created were called *Fukyu Kata* 1 and 2. *Fukyu* means dissemination. *Fukyu Kata* 1 was devised by Nagamine, and *Fukyu Kata* 2 was based on *Gekisai* 1 created by Miyagi.

Fukyu 1 consisted of about 25 basic movements to the left, right, front, back, and moving to the diagonal as techniques are executed on a *kome* (米) *embusen*. It is unknown what relationship the *Fukyu kata* had with the Twelve-Step forms, or how successfully they spread.

Fukyu 1 was executed after a bow from a stance in which the open hands guard the groin. From there, practitioners thrust to the upper and middle target areas and execute upper and lower defensive blocks. The stances include *musubi-dachi* (heels together), *shizen-dachi* (natural stance), and *zenkutsu-dachi*. No kicks are performed in the *kata*. When comparing the techniques and stances between the two forms, clearly *Fukyu* 2 is more advanced than 1.

6. Dai-Nihon Karatedo Ten-no-Kata

Funakoshi Gichin published *Zoho Karatedo Kyohan* in September 1941. *Dai-Nihon Karatedo Ten-no-Kata* forms can be found in the appendix printed on one large sheet of paper. It is also called "Body, mind, and spirit training national self-defence" (*Shinshin Tanren Kokumin Goshin-jutsu*) and says that it was established by Dai-Nippon Karatedo Shotokan. At that time, the chairman of Shotokan was Funakoshi, and his deputy was his third son, Gigo. In the book are six types of *kata* performed by Egami Shigeru, and in the back are photographs of each of the etiquette protocols and six types of *kumite* performed by Gigo and Egami with accompanying explanations.

On the front page of the book, there is a section titled "Ten Rules for Demonstrations". In the first paragraph, the intention behind the establishment of *Ten-no-Kata* is stated as follows. "*Dai-Nippon Karatedo Ten-no-Kata* is a selection of forms suitable for beginners, and for use in group demonstrations. Of course, it is also effective for individual physical and mental training. It does not require much space, time or equipment to practise, and we hope that it will become a popular form of exercise for busy modern people."

The techniques consist of three parts: (1) Basic *tsuki* (4 types), (2) *Chudan-uke*, *tsuki* and *nuki* (3 types), and (3) *Jodan-uke*, *tsuki* (3 types). There are four types of punches: *gyaku-tsuki* and *oi-tsuki*; and two types of attack points, *chudan* and *jodan*. The stances include *hachiji-dachi*, *kokutsu-dachi*, *zenkutsu-dachi*, and *fudo-dachi*, and offensive and defensive techniques are *gedan barai-tsuki*, *chudan-uke* or *tsuki*, and three types of *nuki*, *jodan-uke* or *tsuki*. There are 10 types of *kata* in total. Photographs are taken from the front and sides and are accompanied by explanations.

Regarding offensive and defensive techniques, when practising *uke* and *tsuki*, it is advised to break them down into two movements as shown by the numbers in the diagram, and to master each movement individually. As for the frequency of practice, it is stated that each of the ten *kata* be executed twice. That is, each technique can be performed on the left then the right side. As a rule of thumb, students were encouraged to always assume that the enemy is right in front of them, and should never let their guard down.

On the back of the book, there is an explanation of how to bow. The six *kumite kata* are organised in eight steps, with a photograph of each movement for attack and defence. The first section of the book, "Notes for Demonstrations", states that *Ura-Roppon* is a combination of the six *Omote kata* from the fifth to the tenth, practised by two people, and is referred to as *kumite*.

The text also states where the position of the thrusting hand should be, and that the attacker should always look the opponent in the eye when striking. Also, energy should be focussed in the lower abdomen (*tanden*) the moment of impact. During demonstrations, the text advises both the thrusting hand and the blocking hand should be resolute and powerful.

The *Dai-Nippon Karatedo Ten-no-Kata* was established by adopting Shotokan training methods for the purpose of teaching beginners and for group demonstrations. It was designed to further promote the spread of karate.

7. The Arrival of Modern Karate
The creation of new *kata* and their reconfiguration and modification was aimed at spreading karate in accordance

with the needs of the times. Forms passed down by Ryukyuan warriors were re-evaluated for their educational value and transformed into teaching materials for school education. In the modern era, the roundtable discussion held in Okinawa was also an opportunity reassess the status quo and take new steps to reformulate karate for popularisation on the mainland.

Although karate spread and developed in a multi-linear way in Okinawa and on the mainland, the ravages of the Second World War had a major impact on its progress. A study of the evolution of its techniques and their significance in modern times is an important task for the future of karate.

1904 (December)	*Pin'an (Heian), shodan~Godan*
1937 (March)	*Kihon Kata 12 Dan*
1940–	*Gekisai 1, Gekisai 2*
1941–	*Fukyu Kata 1, Fukyu Kata 2*
1941 (September)	*Dai-Nihon Karatedo Ten-no-Kata*

Table 1-7 Creation of the main *kata* in modern karate

8. The Battle of Okinawa

On 26 March 1945, at the end of the Pacific War, American troops landed on the Kerama Islands in Okinawa, resulting in a fierce ground war between Allied and Japanese forces. The Battle of Okinawa resulted in heavy losses. Among the approximately 200,000 casualties, about 2,000 young students were mobilised to fight, with about half of them losing their lives.

The Battle of Okinawa resulted in a great deal of human suffering and loss of life, as well as the burning to ashes of valuable cultural heritage and historical records. In the midst of harsh social conditions during and after the war, karate leaders such as Motobu Choki, Kyan Chotoku, Hanashiro Chomo, Miyagi Chojun, Tokuda Ambun, Shinzato Jin'an, Yoshimura Chogi and Chinen Sanra all passed away.

CHAPTER 2
KANTO REGION
Wada Koji

INTRODUCTION

The Significance of Competition Karate

It was decided at the IOC Board Meeting convened in Rio de Janeiro on August 3, 2016, that karatedo would be included as an official event at the 2020 Tokyo Olympic Games (The Games were postponed to 2021 due to the COVID-19 Pandemic.)

Karate has come a long way from its early days in the Ryukyu Kingdom where it developed independently over many centuries from *quanfa* as a system of self-defence. After being introduced to the Japanese mainland by Funakoshi Gichin (1868–1957) at the 1st Exhibition of Sport and Physical Education almost a century ago in 1922, it was disseminated as Japanese budo. In the aftermath of the Second World War, American military personnel stationed in Japan, and students of Japanese instructors who had been dispatched around the world to teach, contributed to its rapid international growth culminating in the 1st World Championships in Japan in 1970. Now contested at the Olympic Games, it has been a remarkable journey and I am truly honoured to have been involved in some small way.

This chapter concerns the period extending from Funakoshi's introduction of karate to mainland Japan through to the staging of the 1st KWC. I will outline the series of events leading up to this point while also including some pertinent episodes in my own karate career. Competitive karate today is different from the style that Funakoshi introduced into Japan. Many karate practitioners hold negative views toward the modern sporting version. Before delving into the history of karatedo in the twentieth century, I would like to outline my own ideas on the significance of competitive karate.

Karate is thought to have around a hundred-million practitioners worldwide. It is thought that karate's incredible growth is due in great part to its "sportification". I would like to stress here, however, that competition is merely a part of karate, and does not represent karate itself.

Funakoshi was opposed to competitive karate. The fear of diluting its essence by making it a sport must have been a major factor. This is understandable. When karate is made into a contest, certain rules are put in place out of necessity. The most effective competition-oriented techniques are developed within those rules, but there are also times when traditional karate techniques are inevitably dropped or compromised in order to win.

The sportification of karate was facilitated by *kumite* (sparring). As *kumite* became more popular, practitioners started losing interest in *kata*, and fewer people were able to demonstrate the forms correctly. If *kata* was to disappear then authentic karate itself would exist no more. *Kata* forms differ between each style of karate. Respecting the values instilled in the various *kata*, the forms were also turned into a competitive event using the same evaluation system as gymnastics. This helped to instil a sense of enthusiasm toward *kata*, thereby preventing its demise. However, with the adoption of *kata* as a tournament event, competitors developed strategies designed to appeal to the judges' sensibilities. In other words, movements were introduced into *kata* performances that are far removed from karate's original form. Rules have since been amended to discourage embellishments such as superfluous sounds and manoeuvres contrived to create a more powerful impression in the judges' eyes. In this way, efforts are continually being made to ensure karate's techniques retain their authenticity.

In both *kumite* and *kata*, rules and regulations will no doubt continue to be amended to ensure that the inherent beauty and appeal of karate is maintained, but there is no perfect fix. One of the main characteristics of karate was that it was originally designed as a system of self-defence where a person of small stature could overcome a bigger adversary. Many techniques such as *nukite* (spear-hand) and *ippon-ken* (one-knuckle fist) and others are meant to cause damage by blinding the opponent, pulling their hair, kicking the groin, and so on.

These techniques, of course, are prohibited in the rules of *kumite*. Although there are many techniques for grabbing and throwing the opponent, regulations have been revised to focus on striking to distinguish it from judo and other grappling sports. However, with the introduction of weight categories as well as the prohibition of certain *waza*, there are still concerns that karate techniques are being lost.

In today's karate, the attitude you need to win, says a mental trainer for sports, "is to focus only on maintaining a positive image of winning, not the negative image of not losing." In the "Twenty Principles" (*Nijuka-jo*) Funakoshi states, "Do not think of winning. Just think of not losing." The prevalent attitude nowadays is testament to how competitive karate has really become as a sport in which fine-tuning the mind and body for victory in competitions is what consumes many practitioners.

It is significant, however, that the number of karate practitioners in Japan and abroad has exploded since it became a competitive sport. Even if it differs somewhat from original karate, the energy, physical and mental strength, and technical ability obtained through participation are valuable attributes in modern society. Aspects of traditional karate, such as the *waza* and mindset for self-defence, which cannot be learned adequately in sports karate can be studied separately. The important thing is to not think of competitive karate as the be-all and end-all.

The founder of Goju-ryu, Miyagi Chojun, advised that the following mindset is important in karate. "Do not be struck by others. Do not strike others. Do not let things happen to you." "One spends a lifetime polishing techniques that one will never use." "It is not a matter of defeating others, but about bettering the self of yesterday." This is the point of studying karate. When competing, then winning is of course an important objective. It is natural to want to win, but I would like to stress that a lifetime of karate is much more than just winning or losing tournaments.

SECTION 1

The Foundations Set by Funakoshi

1. Introduction to the Mainland

On May 6, 1921, the Crown Prince (later to become Emperor Showa), stopped off in Naha on his way to Europe. As a part of the welcoming ceremony, a group of children performed karate in front of the main hall of Shuri Castle. The man giving the commands at this demonstration was Funakoshi Gichin.

A few years earlier in 1910, Admiral Yashiro Rokuro of the Japanese Imperial Navy called at the port of Naha and showed a keen interest in Okinawan karate. Yabu Kentsu (1866 –1937) of the Okinawa prefecture Normal School was then asked to teach the *Naihanchi* form to seamen. The Japanese Imperial Navy maintained a close connection with Okinawan karate from that time. Moreover, the captain of the Crown Prince's ship "Katori", Kanna Kenwa, was born in Okinawa. Following the karate performance, Funakoshi was encouraged by him to spread the art as far as the mainland. To make good on this request, Funakoshi headed for Japan the following year. He was 54 years of age at the time.

Funakoshi was the president of the Okinawa Shobukai, an organisation dedicated to the promotion of martial arts. He received an invitation from the prefectural board of education to represent Okinawa for one month in Tokyo from April 30, 1922 at the Exhibition of Sport and Physical Education. He penned an introductory text titled "The History of Karate" as an short explanation for mainlanders and included photos of *kata* and other karate scenes in three scrolls to supplement his explanations to interested onlookers.

Upon arriving in Tokyo, Funakoshi immediately visited the dormitory Meishojuku located in Koishikawa ward for Okinawan students. He met with a third-year student, Gima Shinkin (1896–1989), who was studying at the Tokyo University of Commerce (now Hitotsubashi University). Gima agreed to assist Funakoshi in his quest to spread karate.

Gima had studied karate under Itosu Anko (1831–1915) for ten years. Although Funakoshi was old enough to be his father, he was Gima's junior in this respect. It seems that Gima was even better at performing *Naihanchi* than Funakoshi.

2. Meeting Kano Jigoro
Even though a karate demonstration was held at the 1st Exhibition of Sport and Physical Education, interest among the public was not high and the response was lukewarm. The so-called Okinawa Karatejutsu Introduction Demonstration held later at Kano Jigoro's Kodokan, however, was a marked success and was met with much enthusiasm.

On May 17, 1922, Kano Jigoro, who was the rector of the prestigious Tokyo Higher Normal School as well as the president of the Kodokan, invited Funakoshi and Gima to the Kodokan dojo in Tomisaka-cho (Tokyo). The person who introduced Funakoshi to Kano was either Kinjo Saburo from Okinawa (professor at the Tokyo Higher Normal School), or

Baron Ie Chochoku (fifth son of King Sho Ko of the Ryukyu Kingdom), who was also a disciple of Matsumura Sokon.

Many governmental officials, military men, police, and students gathered in the spacious 207-*tatami* mat Kodokan training hall to witness the karate demonstration. Newspaper and magazine reporters also turned out in force. Notable judo luminaries Nagaoka Shuichi (10th Dan) and Saigo Shiro (6th Dan and model for the popular novel *Sugata Sanshiro*) were also present. Funakoshi demonstrated *Kushanku* and Gima performed *Naihanchi*. They also ran through predetermined sparring techniques (*yakusoku kumite*).

Although there are striking techniques in jujutsu, the thumb is usually encased inside the fingers when the fist is clenched. In the case of karate, the thumb placed on the outside of the clenched fingers, which seems to have been quite a revelation to onlookers. Kano and others were curious about leaving the arm extended after executing a punch. They believed that leaving one's arm out would provide the opponent with an opportunity take hold and execute a counterattack. In actual fighting, it was explained, returning the arm immediately after making the strike is fundamental. The arm is left suspended in the course of practice as a way for checking stability and effectiveness of the technique, and to receive instruction from the teacher.

There were many other probing questions, but Funakoshi responded clearly and calmly to the satisfaction of Kano. The event caused quite a sensation when it was reported in the newspaper.

Kano made a promise to Funakoshi: "Okinawan karatejutsu is indeed a wonderful combat system. If you are thinking of promoting it here on the mainland, I will do all I can to help you. Whatever it is that you need, please do not hesitate to ask." Kano also requested Funakoshi to teach Kodokan students some of the karate forms. When Kano developed Kodokan judo from jujutsu he reluctantly excluded striking techniques (*atemi*). The prevalence of strikes in karate was clearly attractive to him.

Not long after Funakoshi started teaching karate at the Kodokan, Kano left the country on a trip to China for an extended period. Although Funakoshi was scheduled to return to Okinawa after the sports exposition, he decided to stay in Tokyo and await Kano's return. During this time, influential men such as Admiral Yashiro Rokuro (former Minister of the Navy), who read about karate in the newspaper, sent requests to Funakoshi for instruction. With interest in karate burgeoning, Funakoshi once again delayed his return to Okinawa for a few weeks and continued promoting karate around Tokyo.

Although there was an offer to include karate as a branch of judo, Funakoshi declined as he wanted to advance it as an independent martial art. Nevertheless, when karate was later inducted into the pantheon of Japanese budo under the auspices of the Dai-Nippon Butokukai, its affiliation was registered as a "division of judo".

Funakoshi ultimately succeeded in spreading Okinawan karate to the mainland but felt indebted to Kano Jigoro. On his way to and from the dojo, he always stopped in front of the Imperial Palace and the Kodokan, removed his hat and bowed as a sign of respect.

3. The First Karate Gi

In Okinawa there was no such thing as a standard dress code for karate training. Most people wore short trousers with nothing covering the upper body. It was not considered appropriate, however, to demonstrate karate bare-chested in such a hallowed hall as the Kodokan. Gima intended to wear his judo *gi* in the demonstration. Funakoshi purchased some white cotton linen from a store in the neighbourhood and made his own uniform resembling that used in judo. He also made one for Gima and instructed him to wear that instead. It was comfortable enough but was not suitable for a typical arduous training session because it quickly became saturated with sweat and clung to the skin. The *obi* he used seems to have been a judo belt. Many of early practitioners in the mainland wore their *judo-gi* initially, but the uniform tailored by Funakoshi's hand became the prototype for what karateka wear today.

4. Meishojuku

Even though Funakoshi kept busy presenting karate every day during his stay in Tokyo, the honoraria he received for his efforts were barely enough to live on. In the first week of August, Funakoshi checked out of the inn he was staying and moved his belongings to the Meishojuku student dormitory . The building was named after the two periods that its construction straddled—the Meiji era and the Taisho era. Funakoshi moved into a small three-*tatami* mat room beside the entrance and earned his keep by sorting mail and cleaning the building.

His first disciple was a painter named Kosugi Hoan who had became interested in karate when he ventured to Okinawa. As there were no instructors in Tokyo until Funakoshi's arrival, and there were no books from which he could learn, Kosugi was quick to seek instruction. Funakoshi agreed and travelled several times a week to teach him at the Tabata Poplar Club for artists. It was at this time, according to a passage in his book *Karatedo Ichiro*, that Funakoshi decided to remain in Tokyo long term.

From the beginning of September, requests for Funakoshi to demonstrate karate started to dwindle. He began using the Meishojuku's 20-mat auditorium located on the first floor as a base for training. Apart from Kodokan members, others who frequented these sessions included Kasuya Shinyo (professor of German at Keio University and founder of the Keio Gijuku University Karate Kenkyu Kai), followed by Otsuka Hironori (osteopath and founder of the Wado-ryu), and Matsuda Katsuichi (Tokyo Imperial University School of Medicine student and founder of Tokyo Imperial University Karate Kenkyu Kai).

There were also two or three others from the local area who worked in shops, the railway, and the post office but they did not continue for long. The number who participated in weekday trainings was around five or six, but this doubled to 12 or 13 people during the weekends. Funakoshi received a nominal instruction fee from students, but it was never enough to live on. He even had trouble settling the bill for his room and meals at the dormitory.

5. Issuing of Dan Grades

In April 12, 1924, Funakoshi issued Dan grades for the first time under authorisation of the "Karate Kenkyu Kai". The first recipients numbered around seven students, but all records pertaining to this event were lost in fires during the Second World War. What we do know is that Gima (then a teacher at Maebashi Commercial School), Kasuya, Otsuka, and Konishi Yasuhiro (instructor of kendo at Keio) were promoted. According to Gima, Shimizu Toshiyuki (judoka), Shimoda Takeshi (Nen-ryu *bujutsu*), and others were awarded Dan ranks in 1928.

Funakoshi's students came up with the idea of establishing a promotion system to alleviate Funakoshi's financial woes. Still, the Kodokan's influence here is obvious. Subsequent instructors also adopted the Dan system and it became a standard part of karate thereafter.

6. Change in Training Venues

The auditorium in the Meishojuku became unusable due to damage from the Great Kanto Earthquake of 1923. Through an introduction by his student Konishi, Funakoshi was able to continue teaching at kendo master Nakayama Hiromichi's Yushinkan Dojo (Shindo Munen-ryu) until the spring of 1931. After this, he rented a small house in Masago-cho where he laid down wooden planks in the front yard and conducted training in a space equivalent to about ten *tatami* mats. It was not an ideal environment for training. A widow named Yoshiyama Masuko moved into a large two-storey house next door. In the autumn of 1932, Funakoshi rented three six-*tatami* mat rooms from her in the ground floor of the house. This became known as the Masago-cho Dojo. He taught there until March 1, 1938 (spring of 1936 according to Gima) when he opened the "Shotokan Dojo" in Zoshigaya, Toshima-ku. Incidentally, Yoshiyama became his first female student.

7. The Birth of University Karate Research Societies

Kasuya Shinyo, the professor of German at Keio Gijuku University who became Funakoshi's student in the Meishojuku in 1922, had long been interested in martial arts such as kendo and judo, and was keen to take up any budo should he have an opportunity. His meeting with Funakoshi Gichin gave him the chance he was after.

He was attracted to the combative forms of karate, and after being awarded 1st Dan (*shodan*) in April 1924, Kasuya was motivated to promote it among Keio students. To this end he established the Karate Kenkyu Kai (Karate Research Society) on campus on October 15 that year.

Following his initiative other such societies were established at the University of Tokyo (1925), Takushoku University (1930), Waseda University (1931), Nihon Medical University, Hosei University (1934), Dai-ichi Higher School, Tokyo University of Agriculture, Tokyo University of Commerce, and various other institutions of higher education.

In accordance with Keio's "Half study, half teaching" motto espoused by its founder Fukuzawa Yukichi to encourage teachers and students to learn off each other, his young charges were not afraid to bombard Funakoshi with questions. Keio's Karate Kenkyu Kai published a newsletter called *Kobushi* (fist), the first of which was issued in November 1930. In the inaugural edition there is an article describing how one student, Shimokawa Goro, audaciously grilled master Funakoshi about his teachings.

The content concerns the ninth fist movement in the *kata* "*Heian Sandan*". The premise for this movement is to break free from the enemy's hold, and as it is still performed today. Funakoshi rotated the right hand inside the left, then pivoted his body to the left while striking the opponent's midriff with the left hand. Shimokawa, however, questioned the validity of this movement. "Just the other day, you said that the hand is moved around to the right, just as in *Kankudai*."

Funakoshi explained that he opted to incorporate a movement different from *Kankudai* to increase the repertoire of skills. Funakoshi made it clear that although his mentor, Itosu Anko, created the *kata* in the first place, nothing was absolute.

Notwithstanding, Funakoshi was certainly not advocating that it was okay to neglect correct form. In Funakoshi's "Twenty Principles" (Table 2-1), he states that *kata* must always be performed precisely although actual application in a fight may differ. In other words, to become skilled at the techniques expressed in *kata* forms, it is necessary to practise them diligently. Several techniques are hidden within the forms. As such, they must not be reinterpreted or changed at will (Table 2-1).

1. Karate begins and ends with *rei*.
2. There is no first strike in karate.
3. Karate stands on the side of justice.
4. First know yourself, then know others.
5. Mentality over technique.
6. The heart must be set free.
7. Calamity springs from carelessness.
8. Karate goes beyond the dojo.
9. Karate is a lifelong pursuit.
10. Apply the way of karate to all things. Therein lies its beauty.
11. Karate is like boiling water; without heat, it returns to its tepid state.
12. Do not think of winning. Rather, think of not losing.
13. Make adjustments according to your opponent.
14. The outcome of a battle depends on how one handles emptiness and fullness (weakness and strength).
15. Think of one's hands and feet as swords.
16. When you step beyond your own gate, you face a million enemies.
17. Formal stances are for beginners; later, one stands naturally.
18. Perform prescribed sets of techniques exactly; actual combat is another matter.
19. Do not forget the employment or withdrawal of power, the extension or contraction of the body, the swift or slow application of technique.
20. Be constantly resourceful in your pursuit of higher principles.

(Table 2-1, Funakoshi Gichin's "Twenty Principles" —*Niju-kun*)

The fact that karate's dissemination on the mainland occurred mainly in universities shaped the way it progressed. As students at the highest level of education, they were instrumental in turning a potentially dangerous art into a spiritual budo discipline and sport. On the other hand, instructors were stuck with the dilemma that four years was hardly enough time to train students adequately, and they needed to devise unconventional teaching methods to get the most out of their charges in their short time at university.

Funakoshi's third son, Gigo (1906–45), came to Tokyo from Okinawa at the age of 17. He helped his father teach at university karate clubs such as Keio and Waseda. To improve their level as quickly as possible, Gigo taught students to lower and widen their stance to augment their lower body strength. Funakoshi's own stance was quite narrow and upright, but he did not object to his son's teaching method (Photos 2–1 and 2–2).

Students analysed techniques scientifically and approached their training from the perspective of modern theories in physical education and movement. This resulted in an inevitable rejection of some outdated training methods. Importantly, this in turn led to inadequate execution of some traditional techniques.

Photo 2-2 Funakoshi Gigo. (Nihon Karatedo Shotokai)

Photo 2-1 Funakoshi Gichin showing Shuto-uke. (Mita Karate Kai)

Wada Essay 1

Wayward Pride
Wada Koji

My father worked for Keio Gijuku University and my brother was a student at the university's affiliated junior high school. Through this connection to Keio, my family moved into the university housing complex near the Hiyoshi Campus when I was ten years old. Our house was located directly in front of the athletic ground. It really was a wonderful wilderness in the old days. We could hear owls hooting at night. We even used to catch snakes in the garden and used to bake them over an open flame to eat.

I started karate because of my brother. He was four years my senior. My brother joined Keio High School's karate club when I was in the sixth grade of primary school. I figured that I would be no match for my brother if I didn't do something as well. Every morning, I walked to school after running five laps on the 400m track in the athletic stadium. I also did 200 practice swings with my bamboo sword, and my brother started teaching me karate techniques and *kata*. Most junior high schools in mainland Japan did not have karate clubs at the time, so Keio was exceptional in this sense. The captain then was Nagura Toshihisa, the current secretary general of the World Karate Federation (WKF).

I strongly desired to join the junior high school club and studied hard to somehow gain entrance into the school. When I had time, I accompanied my brother to a karate dojo in Mamushidani to watch him train. His peers praised me when I performed the *Heian shodan kata.* This made me even more determined.

I successfully passed the entrance examination for Keio Junior High School and joined the karate club straight away. By the time I was in my third year I was awarded the rank of 1st Kyu. Nobody had ever attained this grade in the club before. I was terribly excited. High school and university clubs also had the rank, but it considered a higher level than junior high school Kyu grades. When I continued through to high school, I assumed that I would continue to hold the same grade. Nagura graduated three years before with 2nd Kyu and his rank was recognised when he joined the high school club. I figured that my 1st Kyu grade would also be acknowledged.

When I was awarded 1st Kyu, my brother was in his sophomore year at university and held the 'lower' rank of 2nd Kyu. Foolishly, I told my brother that I must be stronger than him. He called me out and decided to teach me a lesson. Of course, there was no way a mere junior high school pupil would be able to match the superior skills and experience of a university student. He proceeded to punch and kick me in the guts at will. I was winded badly and blood was gushing from my nose. Holding back my tears I refused to submit, thinking, "Karate is one blow, so I will be triumphant in the end." I knew I couldn't win, but my stubbornness took over. I was not going to stop, even if it meant getting killed in the process. I retook my stance and was ready to continue, but my brother offered a concession by calling it a draw. Knowing that this was my last chance I replied, "If that's what you want, a draw is fine. But I will win if we continue." "Okay, okay" he said, letting me off the hook. He was proud of my fighting spirit, and I really appreciated his kindness. I never fought my brother again after this.

Incidentally, in the almost century-old history of the Keio Gijuku University Athletic Association Karate Club, I am only one of three members who graduated with the grade of 4th Dan. The others were Ito Shuntaro (class of 1940) and Takagi Fusajiro (1943). However, when I transferred to high school, I was not allowed to keep my grade of 1st Kyu. I was not even 4th Kyu. Instead, I was made provisional 4th Kyu and was only returned to 1st Kyu when I graduated. I managed to pass *shodan* when I entered university thanks to the hard training I endured in high school. There is a saying, "Inscrutable are the ways of heaven." I was just lucky.

SECTION 2

Karate Takes Root

1. From Todi to Karate, and then to Karatedo

Karate's origins are found in Chinese *quanfa*. In the Ryukyus, however, it was originally just called *ti* (or *te* = hand). It developed independently in the island kingdom for over five centuries but continued to value its Chinese connection. Therefore, the logograms "Chinese + hand" (唐手) read *todi* or *karate* were used initially. In the turmoil of first half of the twentieth century, Sino-Japanese relations worsened, prompting Funakoshi to Japanise the designations for the *Pin'an kata* to *Heian*, and *Kushanku* to *Kankudai*.

This was not limited to the names of *kata*. To emphasise karate as a Japanese budo, Funakoshi changed the *kanji* for Chinese hand with the homophone empty hand (空手). He also changed the *kanji* for his own name (富名腰 ⇒ 船越) after this.

In 1929, Keio's Karate Club celebrated its fifth anniversary. Funakoshi asked a member of the club, Shimokawa Goro, to consult with his friend Furukawa Gyodo (head priest of Kamakura's Engakuji Temple) about a suitable *kanji* for karate. Furukawa suggested that in Mahayana Buddhism's "Heart Sutra" (written as *han'ya shingyo* = 般若心経 in Japanese) is the famous statement "Form is empty, emptiness is form" (*shiki-soku-ze-kuu* = 色即是空). This corresponds with the karate teaching *Kenzen itchi* (the fist and Zen as one). Furthermore, as karate is essentially empty-handed, the logogram for empty (read as *kuu* or *kara* = 空) was indeed a suitable homophone. Funakoshi was satisfied with this reasoning and substituted in the *kanji* for "empty hand".

There is a theory that empty hand karate was already being used in Okinawa before this, and that therefore its true origins were there. At a demonstration, Hanashiro Chomo, wrote 空手組手 using the logogram for empty in the programme. However, this was referring to the fact that the demonstration was of empty-handed techniques, as opposed to weapon-based techniques such as those for the staff and *sai*, and was not meant as an alternative homophone for Chinese hand. It was in not meant to represent an ideal, and as such, Hanashiro should not be credited with the eventual change from Chinese hand to empty hand. Hanashiro himself never claimed that this was his doing.

Photo 2-3 Stone memorial located inside the precincts of the En-gakuji Temple. (Mita Karate Kai)

With this connection to the Engakuji Temple, the custodian of the temple, Asahina Sogen, wrote the calligraphy for Funakoshi's motto "*karate ni sente nashi*" (there is no first strike in karate) in 1968. This was engraved on a memorial stone which was placed inside the temple grounds (Photo 2–3). In April 29, 1968 (Showa Emperor's birthday), representatives of Funakoshi's Shotokan-ryu gathered for the unveiling ceremony (Photo 2–4).

Photo 2-4 Group photograph from the first Shotosai. (Mita Karate Kai)

Every year thereafter, Shotokan members continued to gather at the Engakuji Temple on April 29 (Showa Day) to hold the Shotosai (ceremony) in memory of Funakoshi's passing (April 26). A karate performance is traditionally held in front of the stone monument at the beginning of the ceremony. I was honoured to perform *Kankudai* as the captain of the Keio Gijuku University Karate Club in 1971.

After changing from Chinese hand to empty hand, new ideals of karate being a Way (*michi* or *do*) for character development and self-perfection were promoted. The suffix -*do* was added to emphasise educational motivations, and karatedo became the commonly accepted appellation irrespective of *ryuha* affiliation. Still, many collegiate clubs that have existed since from the pre-war days, such as Keio, continue referring to themselves simply as karate clubs.

2. Shotokan Dojo

In 1935, a group of Funakoshi's disciples established a "Dojo Construction Committee" and started seeking donations from karate enthusiasts throughout Japan. Before long, enough funds were collected to commence construction. In March of 1938 (some say 1936), the dojo was completed in Toshima-ku in Tokyo. An impressive signboard adorned with "Shotokan" was placed in the entranceway. "Shoto" (waving pine) was the pen name Funakoshi used when he wrote poetry in his youth. Funakoshi wrote in *Karatedo Ichiro* of how incredibly moved he was at the construction of the Shotokan dojo.

The dojo's construction coincided with karate's application to join the Dai-Nippon Butokukai. Standardised regulations for Kyu and Dan ranks were formulated, and teaching methodology and content was also improved. Sadly, the Shotokan dojo was destroyed in an air raid on March 9, 1945. It had only been in use for seven years.

3. Systemic Organisation of Karate

As we have seen, following the Exhibition of Sport and Physical Education in 1922, Funakoshi designed karate uniforms modelled after those used in judo, and also introduced a prototype Dan promotion system. There were no established training uniforms worn in Okinawa. Moreover, there seems to have been no system for measuring technical progress. In Funakoshi's Karate Kenkyu Kai, ranks were issued to students who attained a certain level of proficiency, but there were no detailed criteria for promotion. When his Shotokan style was registered in 1935 with the Butokukai, a unified teaching methodology was formulated which contained all the fundamental aspects of karate starting with stances, handwork, footwork, *kata*, *kumite*, and so on.

The systemisation of instructional methodology and content made it possible to quantify the improvement of students. College clubs which came under the umbrella of the Shotokan *ryuha* were authorised to award Dan and Kyu grades to members. Anybody who was awarded the grade of 1st Kyu qualified to attempt *shodan* issued by the Karate Kenkyu Kai (Honbu). Instructors from various *ryuha* and factions adopted this system and issued Dan and Kyu grades respectively.

4. Changes in Training Methodology

College students on the mainland were inquisitive about theories that underpinned the techniques. They asked Funakoshi to explain the meaning behind the various *kata* he taught. Funakoshi's specialty *kata* was *Kushanku*, but he mainly taught the five *Pin'an* forms created by his teacher Itosu Anko. Because of this, his students labelled him *Pin'an Sensei*. Incidentally, it was Funakoshi who devised the terms *Nidan* (Stage-2) and *Sandan* (Stage-3) for *Pin'an*. When Funakoshi Japanised *Pin'an* to *Heian*, he decreed that *Heian Shodan* (Stage-1) is the simplest of the forms for novices. Itosu's naming was probably in the order he created the forms.

When Funakoshi was in his twilight years, his third son, Gigo, often taught in his father's place. Obviously being much younger, Gigo was more energetic and dynamic than his father. He also had a splendid physique, making him a popular instructor among college students.

The way Gigo taught was to take a wider stance with lowered hips, and he encouraged active movement. He also taught *bunkai kumite* where fighting techniques were extracted from *kata* and practised in pairs. He incorporated *kihon gohon kumite* (fundamental 5-step sparring) which he may have devised after learning the continuous striking drill practised in kendo called *kirikaeshi*. In short, his pedagogical approach to mainland students was different to how karate was taught in Okinawa.

5. Training at Keio

Allow me to explain what kind of training regime I underwent in Keio Gijuku University's club. I assume what we did was basically the same at other university clubs.

When public interest in karate heightened, there were times when as many as 100 freshmen wanted to join the club. Most of them were unable to keep up with the intense training and by their fourth year there were usually only 30 members left in that cohort. There was no official match system or tournament rules for karate until the late 1950s. Even when a match system was implemented, emphasis was always placed on individual discipline rather than winning tournaments. It was not until the late 1960s that matches (*shiai kumite*) were convened regularly.

No warm-ups were conducted at the Keio club. The training was based on the assumption that you never knew when you would have to fight. We were instructed to be ready to move at any time, because who knew when you would be attacked? What we were doing was definitely more of a "martial art" than a run-of-the-mill sport.

The first drill involved pairing up with a partner who weighed approximately the same and piggybacking them from end to end of the 10-metre-long dojo for two or three round trips. Going one direction, we would do a length leaning forwards, and then we would return leaning backwards while carrying our partner. Seniors would kick us in the back of the knees to check the stability of our stances and to strengthen our legs. Skin would rip off our toes and our feet would get soaked in blood. If we fell when kicked, both of us would crash into the floorboards, so our passengers always had to be alert too. Sometimes we had to hop on one foot (Photo 2–5).

Photo 2-5 Keio training July, 1959. (Mita Karate Kai)

Next was body movement drills. We repeatedly practised blocks, *jun-tsuki* and *gyaku-tsuki* punches while seniors kept kicking the back of our legs. If there was no tension in the leg, the knee would drop to the floor, twisting the upper body and putting pressure on the lower back. Many students ended up injuring their backs during this exercise. Trainings seemed to go on forever. Although Funakoshi did not teach it, we copied the Okinawan practice method in which the teacher beats the student's body to tighten and temper it. This is still practised in styles such as Uechi-ryu. One of my seniors, the famous TV presenter Sugita Shigemichi, used the phrase "*muyo no yo*" (a necessary evil) with regard to the fruits of this rigorous training method for forging stamina. In other words, it was not practical, but had significant peripheral benefits. Nevertheless, no universities incorporate it in training today as it contravenes basic principles of exercise physiology, and is potentially very harmful.

In addition, we did endless repetitions of thrusts and front kicks for fundamental training. The best techniques are executed when you reach the point of exhaustion, so we would punch the air and kick alternatively with the left and right 1000-times. After this, half of the club members would remain in the dojo to practise *kata* and the rest would go outside to continue *makiwara* training. *Kata* was performed in stages and repeated from 2–30 times. We would punch *makiwara* boards 300 times with the left and right hands each day. The *makiwara* were handmade. We collected straw from a local farmer, and club members would weave it into cords to be wrapped around the boards. The cord itself was so hard the surface would not fray even if beaten with a stick. Each *makiwara* was coloured by the blood that splattered from our fists. Nobody gave a thought to the dangers of infectious diseases in those days!

Then we would move into *gohon kumite* and *yakusoku-ippon kumite* against opponents. We punched as hard as we could and had to block just as hard. Not to do so would result in powerful blows to the guts and face. Bloodshed was copious and inevitable. Our mantra was "*ichigeki hisatsu*" (annihilate with one blow) and "*uke sunawachi kogeki*" (blocking is attacking). To strengthen our arms, we faced off against partners and smashed our forearms together. It hurt more if you tried to take it easy, so we hit as hard as we could. Looking back, I am surprised that we didn't break our bones.

We also ran outside barefoot. Returning to the dojo we washed our feet in buckets of water left in front of the entrance and wiped our feet off before entering. When the floorboards dried, there was always a thin film of mud covering the surface.

Training finished in *kiba-dachi* (low stance) with a partner perched on our shoulders. Senior students would stand on either side and kick our knees with the outer edges of their feet (*sokuto*) as we desperately tried to hold our partner up. It is was gruelling and cruel. The point was to cultivate mental toughness more than improving physical strength. Each training lasted for two to two-and-a-half hours in total, but it felt much longer. It was through attrition that 100 members dropped to about 30 by graduation.

I rarely found karate to be enjoyable when I was a student. I endured the excruciating trainings of my college days with single-minded determination to get stronger. In a sense, it was simply the feeling of self-satisfaction and achievement of survival that kept me going. That was what got me hooked on karate, and has kept me going throughout my life.

Among the various annual events that we participated in, one particularly memorable occasion was called the "night march". This was conducted throughout the night on the last training day in December. I remember walking around the Miura peninsula in my third year at high school. It was a 60km trek. We gathered in front of Isogo Station in the pouring rain before departure. It was supposed to be cancelled in the case of rain, but the new captain of the university team, Nagura Toshihisa, was having none of it. Fourth-year students in the university club who had recently retired kept watch over us from the comfort of cars in case of an emergency. It was the end of December, so the freezing rain and hail really dampened our spirits. At first, we took short breaks under the eaves of buildings, but we were already drenched, and nobody even bothered with umbrellas. Wet clothes drained our body heat and it was unbelievably cold. By ten o'clock, the rain finally stopped, and we barely managed to complete the course. It was hellish, but finishing gave me an immense sense of confidence.

It must be said, it was close to a miracle that no accident occurred. In the old days they used to walk 100km from the Mita campus to Odawara in the dark nights of midwinter. It apparently took 20-hours without a break. One senior before my time commented, "This experience actually saved my life." When he was interned in Siberia after the war and forced to walk great distances in the falling snow, the fellow countrymen beside him fell one by one, but the experience of this night march kept his spirits up and he was able to see it through. That man was Takeuchi Shuichi, a graduate of 1946. I cannot forget his words, "I am eternally grateful to the karate club."

‖‖

Wada Essay 2

The Unreasonable "Vaccine"
Wada Koji

These days, bullying and hazing are viewed by society as unacceptable. In my younger days, however, even the most unreasonable intimidation was the norm. I think learning to tolerate unreasonable treatment does cultivate resilience to adversity. In a sense, being treated harshly during college was a kind of vaccine. Nevertheless, the dosage this vaccine is administered is a tricky issue. Too much medicine makes people sick. In this essay, I will outline my experiences of what would now be condemned as harassment.

During the last spring break in my third-year of high school, I was invited by a university student to participate in a college training camp to be held in Izu Nagaoka. It was the first time a high school student had been asked to join, and I simply thought I would be treated as a guest. At the first meal of the training camp, I sat at the table with a T-shirt on and was reprimanded for not wearing a shirt with a collar when eating. Alas, I did not pack a shirt with a collar so a student in his second year of college said he would lend me his. As I thanked him for his generosity, the club captain interjected saying that borrowing from others was unacceptable. "Does this mean that I am not allowed to eat?" I asked. The captain replied, "What about the clothes that you wore on the way here?" When I pointed out that it was my school uniform, he snapped at me. "School uniforms have collars, don't they?" He ordered me to wear my uniform at mealtimes. I changed into my stuffy school uniform three times a day for the next seven days just to eat.

I did not know why it was "unacceptable" to borrow a shirt, and thought it was simply a case of the captain throwing his weight around. Nowadays it would not be an issue. About 12 years ago, a doctor and writer by the name of Watanabe Jun'ichi, wrote a book in which he talked of the "power of insensitivity". In retrospect, the captain's ultimatum, in a sense, was making me less sensitive.

I got into trouble with the vice-captain at another training camp held in Lake Yamanaka during the summer that year. During *sanbon kumite* training, I unleashed three *jodan-oitsuki* punches, but my opponent managed to get me with a *chudan-tsuki*. I thought he scored, and as soon as I let my guard down, he landed a decisive punch. I didn't even have time to lament my lack of vigilance. My opponent jumped on top of me, grabbed my hair, and smashed my head into the floor three times. It was my fault that I copped a punch because I let my guard down, but smashing my head into the floor was uncalled for!

Even though he was my senior, I could barely control my rage. In the second round, the instant I blocked his incoming attack, my opponent followed through to grapple. I grabbed his lapel and forced him to the edge of the dojo with the intention of pushing him through the open lower window. It was certainly not appropriate behaviour for a first-year student against a senior, but I let my anger get the better of me. Other members intervened and stopped me from following through, and the *kumite* training was stopped there. Everything seemingly returned to normal after that, but I didn't talk with him again throughout the training camp.

I thought his actions constituted unreasonable treatment at the time, but thinking back on it now, the shock of having my hair grabbed and my head bounced off the floor taught me to never drop my guard in training or matches. The fact that I have never been injured over decades of training in karate shows that this "vaccine" provided effective immunity thereafter.

SECTION 3

The Spread of Karate in Japan

1. The Keio Gijuku University Karate Research Society

Around the 1920s, karate had already been introduced into the middle school curriculum in Okinawa. The military was looking at introducing karate training as a course at the Imperial Japanese Army Toyama School thanks to the courageous exploits of karateka Yabu Kentsu during the Sino-Japanese War (1894–95). Funakoshi was invited by the principal of the Toyama School to teach and he took his students to demonstrate some techniques. Although it helped greatly in their understanding of karate, it was ultimately not adopted by the school. People around him urged Funakoshi to return to Okinawa, but he decided to try and introduce karate to the Tokyo Metropolitan Police Department. The police also decided not to embrace karate despite Funakoshi's efforts. Funakoshi continued to promote karate with the assistance of the Kodokan. Although he did amass some enthusiastic students, due to a series of unfortunate events, including the Great Kanto Earthquake of September 1, 1923, it was proving very hard for him to establish an organised karate movement.

The first college karate club was formed at Keio Gijuku University in the autumn of 1924, two years after Funakoshi arrived in Tokyo. I have a letter written by one of the founding members, Asahara Yasuyoshi, a graduate of 1929. It explains many hardships the university club faced in the early days. The following is an outline of its content.

Following karate's rejection as a regular course by the Toyama School and the Metropolitan Police Department, Kasuya Shinyo (German language professor at Keio), who could be described as Funakoshi's number one apprentice, invited his master to the second floor of his home in Shibuya in 1923, and devised a plan to generate Funakoshi a means for living.

Kasuya first came up with the idea of formally starting karate at Keio, and it was he who set about recruiting members. First, he asked one of his first-year students, Asahara, to help find interested people, but this bore no fruit. He then decided to appoint three student leaders in the A, B, and C cohorts that he taught in the Law Faculty as promoters, and arranged a demonstration to be held in one of the small halls on campus.

The three "promoters" immediately set about devising ways to let students know of the event, but realised that the amount of space allotted on the school notice board would not be sufficient for their needs. They hoped to hand out leaflets, but the university refused to grant permission. Even the student newspaper *Mita Shimbun* which Asahara belonged to was not interested in running an article to publicise the event. With few options left, the promoters came up with a last-ditch plan to get the word out. They wrote in big black letters on nine large pieces of paper *Rentan Goshin no Jutsu* (The art of strengthening character and self-defence). They placed the signs on the lawn in front of the library for all to see.

The tactic worked and the demonstration was a resounding success. Unfortunately, there are no records detailing who did what in the display. But there was a bigger problem. Inspired by the performance, more than ten students took it upon themselves to imitate the techniques and attack their friends. Nosebleeds, broken windows, and damage to desks and walls resulted. The first aid room was inundated with injured students leading university authorities to forbid the holding of such events in the future. Nevertheless, Asahara somehow managed to convince the *Mita Shimbun* to support establishing karate in the university. Their sponsorship led to permission for a one-year workshop.

Kasuya was not satisfied with introducing karate just as a "Ryukyuan martial art". He devised a plan to promote karate as a Japanese budo discipline which could become a permanent fixture at the university. He purchased many books on martial arts at second-hand stores in Kanda. He, Funakoshi, and Asahara met several times in Funakoshi's room at the Meishojuku and talked at length on the best way to proceed.

In the end, however, they concluded that even though karate was an "art" (*jutsu*), it was not a "Way" (*do*) in the budo sense, and wound down their efforts in less than a year. It was a 1927 graduate by the name of Nakano, along with Akasaka (who did not graduate) and some others, who resurrected these talks. They started karate after witnessing the demonstration at Keio, and figured that if kyudo (archery) could be counted as budo, then so too could karate. They studied kyudo's format, and in less than a year they successfully constructed an outline of karate as a budo discipline that impressed Funakoshi.

In other words, they advanced the peaceful ideals of *karate ni sente nashi* and *gosen-no-sen* to gain the university's understanding that karate was a genuine budo and should be acknowledged in the same light as the Athletic Association's kendo and judo clubs. Keio's Karate Kenkyu Kai was authorised by the university in 1924, and the group became an Athletic Association club in 1932. Although this was supposed to help Funakoshi somehow eke out a living, the club had few resources. The best they could do was pay for Funakoshi's train fare to come and teach them. Obata Isao (class of 1929), Yamamoto Takashi, Akashi Akira, Ohshima Keiji, Kogure Kiyokatsu (class of 1932), and others kept the group running, and helped develop it into the prominent club it is today.

Establishment of the Karate Kenkyu Kai was certainly not achieved overnight. It took considerable effort by students who saw the appeal of karate. They continued to plug away at promoting it on campus the best they could. After graduating, Obata continued to assist Funakoshi in demonstrations of *kumite* and *kata* at various venues (Photo 2–6). In 1972, he was appointed the second *Shihan* of the Keio Gijuku University Athletic Association Karate Club. Before starting karate, Obata was a kyu-

Photo 2-6 Funakoshi Gichin (R) performing *kumite* with Obata Isao. (Mita Karate Kai)

do practitioner of considerable skill, and one of the best in Japan at national tournament level.

Obata joined the Karate Kenkyu Kai about the same time that it was launched. The initial membership was around 73. Trainings were held twice a week during the one-hour lunch break. Training content consisted of imitating Funakoshi's movements and constant repetition of the *Heian shodan kata*. His teaching method adhered to the traditional way in which students would copy everything their master did. Obata would question Funakoshi on this or that move until he was satisfied. He also consulted with his clubmates and erected a *makiwara* so that they could practise during recess. Apparently, this is also when they started devising *sanbon kumite* and *ippon kumite*.

In addition to the three founding committee members, Obata was appointed by Kasuya as manager of the Karate Kenkyu Kai at the end of 1924 in recognition of his hard work. However, before long one of the members lost interest and left the club. Others followed, and by the middle of the following year the club was in crisis. Even when Funakoshi came to the university, only two or three students would turn up. Club finances were also critical and Kasuya resorted to funding activities out of his own pocket. One of the founders even suggested they dissolve the group.

In April 1926, there was a sudden increase in membership, and some of them even supplemented their sessions at Keio by going to train at the Meishojuku Honbu Dojo. The university group started picking up momentum. In October of that year, five students, Nakano (graduated in 1927), Gomi (1927), Akasaka, Obata, and Kogure, were awarded *shodan* at a promotion test convened at Keio. In autumn the following year, Keio's Karate Kenkyu Kai held its first public *embukai* (demonstration) to show other students how effective karate was for self-defence. Because the practitioners usually only performed *kata*, some students would mock it as resembling Ryukyuan dancing. This demonstration was different. Kogure attacked without holding back and Obata deflected and countered with his bare hands. It was an energetic display showing karate's explosiveness, and onlookers were suitably impressed. Following the demonstration, training methodology was adapted and the Karate Kenkyu Kai sessions reached a new level of intensity hitherto unseen in the workshop sessions. In 1933, Tsujioka Hideo (class of 1933) became an instructor at the Honbu Dojo Meishojuku, and the university began to produce people of real ability.

As an aside, club activities were suspended before the end of the Second World War, and the university gave Funakoshi severance pay to thank him for his service as the *Shihan*. Funakoshi donated the entire amount to the Asahi Shimbun Airplane Donation Fund. He was not wealthy by any means and led a frugal lifestyle, so this selfless act is an indication of his character.

Funakoshi taught 15 *kata* to the Keio students: *Heian Shodan-Godan, Tekki Shodan-Sandan, Bassai (Dai), Jitte, Empi, Hangetsu, Gankaku, Kanku (Dai)*, and *Jion*. There are 11 other Shotokan-ryu *kata* registered in the current "Karate Competition Regulations". These are the *kata* that Funakoshi taught to his direct students, and some forms conveyed by other karate masters under Funakoshi's guidance that have also been incorporated into the Shotokan style.

The basic notion that Karate has no schools was stringently advocated by Funakoshi. Before going to Tokyo, Funakoshi created a study group called Shobukai in 1917 with Mabuni and Miyagi. Funakoshi served as the chairman. They conducted research, devised teaching methods, and interacted with other practitioners to gain a common understanding of the strengths and weaknesses of each.

Funakoshi studied under the Shuri-te masters Itosu Anko and Asato Anko. In 1929 Funakoshi taught his students the Naha-te forms *Sanchin*, *Suparinpei*, *Tensho*, and so on, but not *Seienchin*. Moreover, in 1935 he called on Mabuni to come and instruct his students in the *Seienchin* form. In this way, Funakoshi was attempted to unify karate, but because the fundamentals of Shotokan had already been established, some differences in the way the *kata* were performed was inevitable. For example, *shiko-dachi* (square stance) was changed to *kiba-dachi* (horse rider stance). He was ultimately unsuccessful in realising his aspiration to standardise the *kata* regardless of style. Currently, Shotokan, Goju-ryu, Shito-ryu and Wado-ryu are considered the four mainstream schools in the Japan Karatedo Federation. There is overlap, but also differences in their *modus operandi*.

2. The Founding of Shotokan

Although Funakoshi championed the idea that there are "no schools in karate", Miyagi, Mabuni, and later, students such as

Otsuka, broke away and created their own styles anyway. As they operated independently, they deemed it necessary create specific school names.

Funakoshi was a primary school teacher who enjoyed composing poetry under the pen name "Shoto". When he built his dojo in 1936, he called it Shotokan, the "Hall of Shoto". His students persuaded Funakoshi to use this as the name of his school and teachings. Nevertheless, to the very end Funakoshi was reluctant to do so.

Funakoshi emphasised fundamental movements so that everyone could participate in karate. The *kata* he taught were executed with big, purposeful movements and were not necessarily practical from a fighting perspective. Rather, he taught them for educational purposes, and as a way for maintaining health and well-being. Analysing Okinawan karate from a rational and scientific perspective, his pedagogy abided by the principles of physical education. Some detractors pointed out that his style seemed more like a form of callisthenics, but as Funakoshi states in his "Twenty Principles", "Perform prescribed sets of techniques (*kata*) exactly; actual combat is another matter." In other words, not all the movements in *kata* are necessarily combative.

As mentioned before, when Funakoshi's third son, Gigo, started helping his father, he taught students to take a wider stance with their hips lowered. This became the basic stance in Shotokan-ryu. The *kata Naihanchi* was changed in name to *Tekki* and was performed from a newly-created dropped stance (*kiba-dachi*) for strengthening the lower body.

Shiko-dachi (square or straddle stance) is not seen in Shotokan, but similarly *kiba-dachi* is not found in other schools. Perhaps this has something to do with students in the Keio club who were unconvinced of the point of *shiko-dachi* when it left the groin open for attack. On the other hand, with *kiba-dachi* it is possible to twist the sole of the foot into the floor and turn the toes to the front to reinforce protection of the groin. This is possibly why they opted to adopt this stance instead. *Kiba-dachi* is not often encountered in Okinawan karate. As Funakoshi states in the Twenty Principles, "Be constantly mindful, diligent, and resourceful, in your pursuit of the Way." The fact that even though Mabuni directly taught Funakoshi's Keio students *Seienchin*, they adapted it to perform from *kiba-dachi* rather than *shiko-dachi* is testament to this ideal. At that time the only kind of paired training was *kihon kumite* (basics) and *yakusoku kumite* (pre-arranged combinations). *Shiai kumite* (competitive sparring) was prohibited.

Incidentally, in the *Waseda Daigaku Karate-bu 70-Nenshi*, a commemorative book celebrating the 70th anniversary of the Waseda University Karate Club, there is a section related to a discussion held in April 1949 by a number of active students and alumni about unifying the Shotokan *kata*. By this stage, there were already differences in interpretation of stances and technical details among groups affiliated to the Shotokan. Different teachers in the same school taught *kata* in different ways.

3. Creation of the Wado-ryu

As with Goju-ryu, Wado-ryu was recognised by the Dai-Nippon Butokukai in 1939. The previous year, an application was made under the name "Shinshu Wado-ryu Karatejutsu".

The founder, Otsuka Hironori (1892–1982), studied Shinto Yoshin-ryu jujutsu as a child and received a teaching license (*menkyo kaiden*) in the tradition on his twenty-ninth birthday in 1921. He began studying karate under Funakoshi at the Meishojuku in 1922. He was a banker at the time, but was unhappy with his job and quit to become a bodywork therapist, making use of his knowledge of jujutsu. He helped develop the profession by creating a scheme in which unemployed jujutsu practitioners could make a living. He later received instruction from Mabuni and Motobu Choki (Tomari-te). He combined their teachings with the Shuri-te style he learned from Funakoshi and traditional jujutsu to create Wado-ryu in 1934. *Wa* means Japan, and he chose this name to highlight the connection with traditional Japanese jujutsu.

Already a licensed jujutsu expert, Otsuka was not content with Funakoshi's basics-oriented teaching method. He was more interested in competitive *shiai kumite*. This difference in opinion led to his eventual excommunication. On two occasions, Obata Isao of Keio mediated between the two, but Otsuka was unwilling to relent, so he left Funakoshi's school of his own accord. Wado-ryu aimed at being a practical style of karate based on principles of *ten'i* (moving off the line of attack), *tentai* (turning the body to minimise exposure), and *tengi* (allowing the opponent's attack to go past while counterattacking). The actions are rapid, and the stance is high to enable ease of movement. There are some similarities but also important differences with Funakoshi's Shotokan-ryu, which is predominantly centred on strengthening the body through fundamental techniques.

In addition, the University of Tokyo started utilising protective armour to engage in freestyle bouts even though Funakoshi expressly prohibited it. Funakoshi ceased teaching at the university after December 1929. In September 1935, the University of Tokyo Karate Club invited Otsuka to be their third *Shihan* as they saw commonalities with his style of teaching and changed from Shotokan-ryu to Wado-ryu.

4. Motobu Choki and Konishi Yasuhiro

When discussing the spread of karate on the mainland, other than the founders of the four mainstream schools, there are two more pioneers who deserve mention: Motobu Choki (1870–1941) and Konishi Yasuhiro (1893–1983).

Motobu was two years younger than Funakoshi. He rose to fame when he knocked out a professional boxer in a prize fight in Kyoto. Many judo and sumo practitioners had challenged the boxer in the hope of winning prize money, but none were successful until Motobu who, to the absolute delight of the Japanese spectators, floored the huge Russian pugilist with a decisive punch. This famous bout happened in November 1922 when Motobu was 52 years of age. The affair was featured in the popular *King* magazine in 1925, consequently contributing to widespread recognition of karate's effectiveness. Motobu's name became known throughout the country because of it, but the photo of the karate master in the magazine was, to his dismay, mistakenly that of Funakoshi.

Motobu was a descendant of the Ryukyu royal family. From the age of 12, he and his older brother Choyu learned Shuri-te under Itosu Anko. Not wanting to be outdone by his brother, Motobu also studied Tomari-te under the famous master Matsumora Kosaku. He earned quite a reputation in Okinawa for beating on thugs in street fights. He was a formidable fighter who did not know the taste of defeat.

Motobu moved to Osaka in 1921 and started teaching karate at the Mikage Normal School and Mikage Police Department. He visited Funakoshi in 1926 and decided to move to Tokyo. Although two years Funakoshi's junior, his family pedigree was higher, and he was not particularly friendly. Funakoshi the affable educator found it very difficult to deal with Motobu's haughty demeanour.

Funakoshi was nowhere to be found when Motobu visited his dojo for the first time. It is rumoured that Motobu began taunting Funakoshi's students as they practised. Thinking it was a case of "*dojo yaburi*" where a challenger commandeers the dojo signboard upon defeating all its members, one of Funakoshi's students called Motobu out. The student was Konishi, and he was quickly kicked into submission. It seems that Konishi became quite a devotee of Motobu's after this (Photo 2–7). Konishi introduced Motobu to Otsuka, and both of them provided financial backing for Motobu's activities. Konishi brought a member of Toyo University's judo club named Murakami to engage in a bout against Motobu. Murakami was also soundly defeated, and instantly appreciated the value of karate as a fighting art. He set up a karate group within the judo club and requested that Motobu come to instruct. About two years later, in 1927, an official karate club was established at Toyo University, and Motobu was appointed its *Shihan*. This is a good example of how the student's network of connections contributed to the spread of karate in Japan.

Photo 2-7 Motobu Choki (R) engaging Konishi Yasuhiro in *kumite*, September 1935.

In 1934, Motobu, with the assistance of Konishi and Otsuka, opened a dojo called "Daidokan" in Tokyo. Among the dojo's students, world champion boxer "Piston Horiguchi" also studied karate for a while under Motobu and Konishi. Everyone recognised Motobu's prowess as a fighting man. He taught man-to-man in his thick Okinawan accent and apparently had difficulty communicating in standard Japanese. He was not interested in spreading karate widely, so never amassed the same number of students that Funakoshi did. With war on the horizon, Motobu eventually closed the Daidokan and returned to Okinawa in 1941.

Konishi had been the captain of the Keio Gijuku University Athletic Association Kendo Club. After graduation, he joined kendo master Nakayama Hiromichi's Yushinkan Dojo while continuing to instruct kendo at his alma mater. It was Konishi who negotiated Funakoshi's use of the Yushinkan when he had trouble finding a venue. Konishi had long been interested in Okinawan fighting arts and immediately became Funakoshi's student. Konishi was one of the seven students to whom Funakoshi first awarded the grade of *shodan*.

A weak child physically, Konishi began kendo with the hope of building up his constitution. He demonstrated a natural talent in the martial arts and was even awarded a provisional teaching licence in the Shindo Munen-ryu during his second year at university. He was enamoured with karate the moment he saw it and instantly became Funakoshi's student. In addition to looking after Motobu, he was later also appointed as an assistant to Mabuni and Miyagi when they visited Tokyo. He devoted himself to mastering the art of karate.

Funakoshi was tolerant of Konishi learning from other skilled exponents of karate. Back in Okinawa, studying under several masters was commonplace, and Funakoshi was not particular about differences in styles. Konishi continued jujutsu and the new martial art of aikido, and established a comprehensive fighting system he called Shindo Jinen-ryu Kuushu-jutsu. In addition to self-defence, he touted karate as having a wide range of health and beauty benefits, and proactively promoted it among women.

According to Konishi's eldest son, also called Yasuhiro, his father was greatly troubled by the bad blood between Funakoshi and Motobu. Although Konishi was a Funakoshi devotee, he was also captivated by the practical style of karate taught by Motobu. As a result, members of Keio Karate Kenkyu Kai, such as Obata, were not particularly fond of Konishi. Although his alma mater was Keio, he kept his distance from the karate club there.

Funakoshi and other instructors found success by focussing their activities in university clubs. This led to an extensive network between the various clubs. There are no examples of karate being taught as a curricular subject, and there was never any guarantee that an instructor could make a living through teaching it as an extracurricular activity. Funakoshi's frugal lifestyle was well-known, but others such as Otsuka Hironori were forced to sell assets that had been handed down in his family for generations in order to continue promoting karate. Konishi came from a wealthy family and had the wherewithal to look after visiting masters such as Motobu, Miyagi, and Mabuni. Funakoshi also frequently visited Konishi's family home.

What would prompt a practitioner of jujutsu (Otsuka) and kendo (Konishi) to take up karate? Clearly there was an intense attraction for them to devote themselves to the art when it was far from being a profitable or prestigious undertaking.

5. Schools Introduced in *Kempo Gaisetsu*
In January 1930, a member of the University of Tokyo Karate Kenkyu Kai named Miki Jisaburo published a book titled *Kempo Gaisetsu* (An Outline of Kempo) with Takada Mizuho. Takada was the club's manger. A staff member at the universi-

ty, he was also a graduate of Keio's karate club. Both received direct instruction from Funakoshi but were not content to settle just for his teachings. They wanted to conduct more thorough research into the roots of karate. To this end they visited Okinawa to interview such well-known masters as Yabu Kentsu, Kyan Chotoku, Oshiro Chojo, Miyagi Chojun, and Yabiku Moden.

The first chapter of the book starts with the heading "What is Karate?" The following four chapters provide an overview of all aspects of karate: "The Schools of Karate", "Kata Names", "The Mindset for Practising Kata", "The Value of Karate". The eight sections in Chapter 1 include "How to Make a Fist", "How to Stand", "*Empi*", "Cultivating Attacking Power", "Illustration of Body's Vital Points", "Methods of Attack and Defence in Karate", "Components and Explanation of *Kata*", and "*Kumite*". The ten *kata* explained in the book include *Bassai* (*Sho*), *Kushanku* (*Sho*), *Chintei*, *Niseishi*, *Gojushiho*, Kyan Chotoku's version of *Bassai*, Itosu's *Passai*, Oshiro's *Seishan*, Kyan's *Chinto*, and Yabu's *Gojushiho*. In addition to various methods of *kumite*, there are also 19 patterns introduced for countering adversaries wielding bladed weapons. The book concludes with three chapters titled "Three Fists of Life, Four Prohibitions, and Five Essentials", "Zen and Karate", "Objectives, Karate as Budo, Karate for the Times".

Although not published for sale, it is a beautifully bound volume of 184 pages with easy-to-understand illustrations. It was an impressive book for being put together in a mere six months. Miki and Takada clearly had an unbridled enthusiasm for karate. It contains the following information regarding different schools of karate.

> "Schools became distinguished by the names of the later masters. In essence, however, there were only the two styles of Shorei-ryu and Shorin-ryu. Currently in Ryukyu, the former tradition is taught mainly around Naha by master Miyagi Chojun, and the latter in Shuri by Yabu Kentsu, Kyan Chotoku, and Yabiku Kumoden… Shorei-ryu focuses on the callisthenic of karate. The various exercises developed by Miyagi Chojun prove this… However, Shorin-ryu aims to be more practical. The practice of thrusting, kicking, blocking and so on demonstrate a combat mindset. As for *Bassai*, even if the name of the *kata* is the same, there are various ways of executing it. For example, Kyan Chotoku's *Bassai* is different to that taught by other masters. This is because each has differing perspectives on combat and continues to develop their knowledge and methods through ongoing research. The masters take only a small number of *kata* and develop them thoroughly with a mind to practical application. They eschew the shallow acquisition of numerous techniques. For over 20 years, master Yabu Kentsu has only studied the two forms of *Gojushiho* and *Kushanku*. He says that he knows no other *kata*…"

Thus, even though there are two schools of karate, Shorei-ryu and Shorin-ryu, from Miki's point of view the only difference seems to be whether they were systematised by Miyagi Chojun or not. To him, all forms of karate have the same roots.

In addition, Miki mentioned a criticism he received from Yabiku Moden regarding how he approached *kata*. "Your *Bassai* and *Naihanchi* is not karate. It is a dance." Perhaps this can be construed as a gibe at the level of karate that was being taught on the mainland predominantly among students.

Although the details are unclear, in the book *Kindai Karatedo no Rekishi wo Kataru* (Talking about the History of Modern Karate), Gima Shinkin (1896–1989) references something Takada talked about when he and Miki visited Okinawa. Apparently, Funakoshi took umbrage at Takada's comments, which resulted in him cutting ties with the University of Tokyo. In addition, the club had created a system for conducting matches and had been experimenting with protective armour in flagrant disregard of Funakoshi's express wishes.

Date Koji joined the University of Tokyo's club in 1961, and later started a karate club at the Tokyo Metropolitan Police Department. In his personal correspondence, Date mentioned to me that as Takada had been Funakoshi's deputy, he was made the second *Shihan* of the university's club after Funakoshi stepped down. For some reason, however, this fact has all but been erased from the club's history.

There is an interesting story relayed in *Keio Gijuku Taiikukai Karate-bu 75-Nenshi*, a publication celebrating the 75th anniversary of Keio's karate club. In the summer of 1941, club members Matsuzaki, Ogata, and Mukaida went to Okinawa with the intention of somehow unifying the styles of karate being practised at universities. In the spring of that year, the All Japan

Student Karate Embu Tournament was held in commemoration of Meiji University Karate Club's official launch. Representatives from 14 universities in Kanto and Kansai gathered at the Meiji University Memorial Hall. The four mainstream schools were taught at the following colleges: Wado-ryu—Meiji, University of Tokyo, Rikkyo, Tokyo University of Agriculture, Jikei University, Nihon University; Goju-ryu—Ritsumeikan and Doshisha in Kyoto; Shito-ryu—Kansai University and Kwansei Gakuin University; Shotokan—Keio, Waseda, Takushoku, and Hosei universities.

There was consensus that to further develop karate in Japan it was necessary to bring together the styles of karate being taught at universities. It was also agreed that Keio, due to its history and high level of karate, should be entrusted with the responsibility of overseeing this unification process. The goal was not to unify techniques per se, but to establish a standardised system for grades, and establish a central body to manage university karate activities. Funakoshi and Mabuni were in favour of the idea, so it was decided that a visit to Okinawa was in order to seek further support. Goju-ryu teachers Miyagi, Hanashiro, and Chibana met with the representatives and expressed their agreement. With the outbreak of war not long after, however, the plans were put on permanent hiatus.

Before this, the Greater-Japan Students Karatedo Federation was formed in 1936 by colleges or related schools where Funakoshi was *Shihan*. Saigo Kichinosuke was appointed president, and the six college club directors Kasuya Shinyo (Keio), Ishikawa Mitsuharu (First Higher School), Ohama Nobumoto (Waseda),

Itani Zen'ichi (Tokyo University of Commerce), Egashira Masaharu (Takushoku), Irie Naosuke (Hosei) were chosen as advisors. The body engaged in combined demonstrations and exchanges. This organisation was later to become the All Japan Student Karate Federation, which still administers student club activities transcending style to this day.

6. Publication of *Karatedo Shusei*

To commemorate its 10th anniversary, the Keio Gijuku Athletic Association Karate Club published *Karatedo Shusei* (Compilation of Karatedo Historical Materials) in February 1936. This was six years after the publication of *Kempo Gaisetsu*. Materials were collated by Keio students under the editorial guidance of Funakoshi. The resulting book is an impressive volume with 350 pages.

7. A Study of the Styles

The four mainstream schools that make up the Japan Karatedo Federation have only been around for eight or nine decades. Notable differences can be seen between Naha-te and Shuri-te styles developed in Okinawa, but going back further in time it is thought that transmission of skills and knowledge was exclusive and secretive as there is no existing framework from that era. Naha-te and Shuri-te differences are primarily due to the environment where they were practised. In other words, hilly areas with poor footing versus flat ground. As self-defence, the essence of karate is the same.

The teacher of Funakoshi Gichin's masters (Itosu Anko, Asato Anko) was Matsumura Sokon, an adept of the Jigen-ryu tradition of swordsmanship. The influence of this school can still be seen in Shotokan. One of the central teachings of Jigen-ryu is "Three thousand strikes in the morning, three-thousand in the evening, to a standing tree". Adherents of the tradition train their bodies and spirit to cultivate destructive power to overwhelm enemies with brute force. At the end of the Edo period, a member of the pro-Bakufu Shinsengumi was killed by an imperial loyalist of the Satsuma domain. So devastating was the cut from above by this Jigen-ryu swordsman, that the Shinsengumi member's attempted block with his own sword was futile. His body was found with a cross pattern impressed on his head. The leader of the Shinsengumi, Kondo Isami, advised his men that blocking the Satsuma samurais' attacks was pointless. Instead, they should seek to dodge the first blow at all costs. The power of Jigen-ryu swordsmen was peerless.

Similarly in Shotokan karate, students are also taught to stand firm as if the feet were tree roots, and to use the trunk of the body to administer powerful thrusts and kicks. According to Takushoku University Karate Club Alumni Association president Yoshida Moto'o (1955), training at Takushoku in those days involved relentlessly smashing nine *makiwara* erected beside the dojo. "Every day, we hit the *makiwara* 1000 times on both the left and right sides. Everybody's fists were ripped to shreds, and there were bits of flesh and blood everywhere." The intensiveness of this frenetic training was the same as that undertaken by Jigen-ryu swordsmen. As with the Jigen-ryu, only the first blow counted. There was no second. After competition rules were established in karate, the idea that a "second blow was not needed" fell by the wayside.

Of course, there are some notable exceptions. Eriguchi Eiichi, a University of Tokyo alumnus once made the following observation about his Tokyo University of Agriculture contemporary, Kihara Shujiro. "He had a sportsmanlike physique but was slim with no extraneous muscle. He was a handsome lad with an oval face. Once he put on his *keiko-gi* and stood in the dojo, however, he transformed. He moved with lightning speed and danced like a butterfly, dazzling his opponents with his effortless manoeuvring. But, with the motto of 'One blow, certain death', he attacked like a ferocious tiger when the opportunity presented itself. He was a hard karate man with brutal intent that did not match his usually kind manner." His reputation is reminiscent of Wado-ryu's founder, Otsuka Hironori.

Schools and their distinctive methodologies are created according to the needs of the time. Priority is placed on strengthening muscles and acquiring technical ability, but progress depends on individual differences such as experience, physical power, and aptitude. However, in order to teach a group of people, it is necessary to have a common set of guidelines. The school's guiding principles are a tool for the unified teaching of its members. For example with a middle inward block (*soto-uke*) with the front arm, in Shotokan, the tip of the index finger is placed next to the wrist on the other hand, while in Goju-ryu it is placed at the elbow, and in Shito-ryu it is placed next to the fist. None of these methods can be declared superior to the other. First and foremost, what is necessary is for the receiver to be prepared to take the brunt of the attack while being ready to follow through from the middle block to counter. In order to master this defence-attack amalgamation, practitioners repeat the movements over and over so that the axis for execution is stabilised and techniques can be performed rapidly.

Just as Otsuka, formerly a student of Funakoshi, established the Wado-ryu, practitioners develop their own opinions and interpretations of the teachings they receive. This in turn leads to the establishment of yet more schools of thought. Paradoxically, the specificity of schools in karate is only a matter of extremely fine details. There may be any number of trailheads for climbing the mountain of karate, but it is a fact that the trailheads of the four mainstream styles are now well established. I think that the only real differences between them all now are found in the details of the *kata* conveyed in each one.

Although Funakoshi's students referred to his school as Shotokan-ryu, he never relinquished his attitude that karate has no schools. This is in line with the idea "don't think that your karate is the only karate." In the Twenty Principles, Funakoshi wrote as one of the dictums, "Be constantly mindful, diligent, and resourceful, in your pursuit of the Way." This means that there is always more depth to karate techniques no matter how proficient one may become. Most of the students Funakoshi taught at universities were novices. He emphasised the fundamentals and building up core strength.

Internationally renowned martial artist Tokitsu Kenji is a graduate of Hitotsubashi University Karate Club. He is two years my senior in terms of university year group. I recall him once stating, "As a student of Shotokan, I was of the belief that it was the strongest karate. I know that to be wrong now." Not only Shotokan, all styles are simply a gateway into the "Way" of karate. That is why Funakoshi continued with his mantra that there are "no schools". Regardless of style, teaching that one school's technique is stronger than another's is pointless. No techniques are effective unless you have trained your heart out. It is not about where you train.

Wada Essay 3

A 100% Just Fight
Wada Koji

Karate is for self-defence. You train as hard as you can to polish your techniques in the hope that you never have to use them. Nevertheless, being only human we may succumb to the urge to try the techniques for real. If you are going to use your fists, it must be in a situation that is 100% just to do so. There is a saying "To know right and fail to act is to be without courage". In other words, there is no shame in using your fists to help others if the need is truly there and justified, but such situations are rare.

When I was in my senior year at college, two friends and I were walking in Shibuya one night. Three salarymen approached us. One was extremely drunk. "Are you assholes students?" We were wearing our university uniforms. I replied, "Have you had a lot to drink?" My response irritated the drunkard. "You cheeky little bastards!", he screamed as he grabbed an empty whiskey bottle lying on the pavement and smashed it on a concrete wall. He faced off against us with weapon in hand and prepared to attack. "Now's my chance" I thought. After all, he was the one in the wrong. We had justice on our side, 100 percent. Without changing my complexion, I said to him, "Are you going to make the first move?" The three of them seemed unsettled and asked us if we trained in something. "Nothing in particular", I replied. They apologised profusely and stumbled away into the dark.

Soon after I graduated and entered the workforce, I was walking along an almost empty street. A stylish looking fellow in his thirties was approaching from the opposite direction. The street was fairly wide, but we both kept to our course and it looked as though we were on a collision course. I pulled my shoulder back to avoid bumping into him, but contact was still made. After walking a few more steps, I turned around to see him looking back at me. We stared at each other for a while, and then he approached me. "Why did you bump into me?" he asked. I could not deny a degree of culpability which meant that "100% justice" was not on my side. "We both bumped into each other, didn't we?", I replied. "You turned and glared at me!" he said. "So did you!" "Stop taking the piss!" he snarled while preparing to fight. I assumed he was about to let his fists fly so I said to him, "Yeah, you're right." If I had continued arguing it would most certainly have escalated into a brawl. I spoke in a calm tone and with a sense of normalcy, which seemed to bring him back to his senses as well.

I have had other experiences in which, although I was not in the wrong, it could have ended up in a violent tussle. All these situations were defused midstream and I have gone throughout my life never having been in a real fight. Karate has given me a sense of confidence and the ability to act with equanimity in a confrontation. There really is no such thing as a 100% justified fight. The best kind of life is one without conflict.

llllllllllllllllllllllllllllllllllllllllllllllllllllllllllllllllllllllllllllllllllllllllllllllllllllllllllllllllllllllllllllllllllllllllllllllllllll

CHAPTER 3

KANSAI REGION

Koyama Masashi

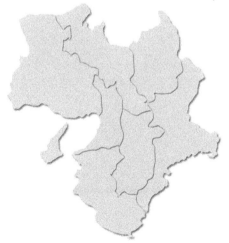

SECTION 1

Kano Jigoro and Karate

Before he had ever seen karate, Kano Jigoro was already a leader in the development of budo in education, and was a giant in the Japanese sports world. We already introduced Kano's involvement in promoting karate in Chapter 2. What was it about karate that intrigued Kano so much? Most people believe he first came across it in 1922 when he met Funakoshi, but in fact it was before this. There is an interesting article in the August 9, 1908, edition of the *Osaka Jiji Shimpo* newspaper.

> "Preceding the judo matches held at the Kyoto Butokukai Youth Bujutsu Demonstration, locals were enthralled as they witnessed forms of the new and only martial art from the Ryukyus, karate, performed by students from Okinawa Middle School… Dr. Kano could also be seen watching the spectacle in awe."

This was over a decade before what is widely assumed to be Kano's introduction to karate. Furthermore, three years after this event, Kano invited students from Okinawa who were in Tokyo on an excursion to the Kodokan for what was remembered as a pleasant exchange. A publication titled *Ryutan*, issued by the Okinawa Prefectural Normal School Alumni Association published a commemorative issue to celebrate the 40th anniversary of its founding. Dated June 1, 1911, there is a report by authored by Yamauchi Seisan and Moromizato Choho. The following is quoted from the introduction: "In April, third-year students were able to visit the founder of judo, Kano Jigoro, during their jaunt to Tokyo proved to be an enjoyable encounter for the old master." Titled "Karate Club Chronicle", the article goes into detail about the exchange between Kano and the six students, and how they perceived this famous man of judo. The boisterous students were clearly undaunted meeting such a notable figure, and it is easy to imagine how this encounter convinced Kano to help karate gain a foothold in Japan several years later. The following summary of the article is taken from Kadekaru Toru's presentation and subsequent paper published in issues 14 and 15 of the journal *Karatedo Kenkyu*.

1. Kano Jigoro and the Okinawa Normal School Students

In April 1911, students of the Normal School embarked on a trip to Tokyo. They were joined by Professor Nakamura soon after their arrival, after which they set off for their appointment at Kano Jigoro's residence. Getting off the train at the Edogawa-bashi terminal at 13:30 on April 18, they waited until everybody had gathered and walked to the Kano house at 14:00. The area one kilometre away from the train stop looked completely deserted. "Is this really Tokyo? The students were a little disappointed. The people and the buildings were so rustic that the scene was no different from any small countryside town."

The party arrived at Kano's house at 15:00. There they waited for another 30 minutes until a distinguished looking gentleman arrived in a rickshaw.

"He ushered us into the Kodokan dojo. The size of the dojo was almost twice as big as our lecture hall. The master's seat was situated high up in the middle of the dojo and a portrait of the founder of judo, Kano-sensei, hung above it… Before long, the master dressed all in cotton entered with a smile, followed by his wife and apprentices. We were asked about karate, so we gave an account of the history and situation of karate, followed by a demonstration of techniques performed by the six of us…"

The Kodokan was attached to Kano's home. "The master was extremely satisfied. He fired many questions at us, which we answered to the best of our ability. He started to imitate our various karate moves." "How do you do this?" "What about this?" He kept asking the students questions and confirmed his understanding by moving his hands and body in accordance with their explanations.

Kano was 51 at the time and was clearly enjoying this intellectual sparring session with the students. "As the master was so enthusiastic, we tried to explain that karate was in fact superior to judo." "No, it's not" Kano retorted, but the students became even bolder in their claims. "What do you do in judo when somebody twists your arm?" Kano replied, "Just because someone locks your arm does that mean that you submit?" Kano stood up and offered his arm to be twisted. One student attempted to grab hold of the arm, but before he could do anything Kano pressed him into the ground.

This report may give the impression that Kano was behaving somewhat immaturely, but he was interacting with these young practitioners in what was a lively and agreeable exchange. The first student, Yamauchi Seisan said, "What about me?" He was then pushed down in a heap to everybody's great amusement. Next, "Hirata Kishin looked as if he was about to break down and cry in pain. This made everyone laugh even harder." Kano started speaking with more enthusiasm on the merits of judo. Nevertheless, the young visitors were still not ready to relent.

The chronicler of the event, Moromizato, boasted that "Ryukyu fists are so tough that smashing a column is a piece of cake!" Kano threw the challenge back. "I don't mind if you break this pillar. Go ahead and show me. If you can, it will be here forever as a testament to your feat." The brave Kinjo Rikuryo jumped to his feet and whipped his hand into the ready position to strike the post. Everybody stared in anticipation, but he stepped back claiming that if he broke the pillar as requested, the whole building would collapse. Of course, it was an impossible ask. Moromizato exclaimed that their teacher would be able to break it no problem. They were not going to back down so easily. As a show of strength, Kinjo smashed through a wooden board. One more student, Ireimon, smashed another with little trouble.

Kano then suggested the students break his very sturdy *go* table. They protested that it would be a waste of such a beautiful piece of furniture used for playing the traditional strategy game. Kano responded with a teasing smile "Go ahead and break it. People get lazy when they see a *go* table."

The exchange between Kano and the Okinawan students was a memorable affair and they returned to Okinawa in high spirits. Moromizato concluded the article with the following statement. "Rejoice! Our karate club has been introduced in the capital to the east, the heart of the empire, and has received the praise of the King of Sports, Kano-sensei. We look forward to working together to improve, and to a time in the near future when karate will be introduced to the world as a global sporting discipline." This affirmation of karate by the so-called father of sports in Japan took place in 1911.

In July 1912, Japan entered what is known as the Taisho era (1912–1926) after the passing of Emperor Meiji. The Taisho period is considered the embryonic period of karate's dissemination on the mainland. Various happenings of consequence occurred in the world of Okinawan karate, leading to the auspicious meeting between Funakoshi Gichin and Kano Jigoro.

Of primary significance were the deaths of Asato Anko, Itosu Anko, and Higaonna Kanryo around 1915 and 1916. The pioneers of karate's modern development in the Meiji period were gone. It was from that point onwards that the next generation of leaders following Yabu and Hanashiro came to the fore: Funakoshi Gichin, Miyagi Chojun, and others dedicated themselves to furthering karate's cause. Funakoshi took his knowledge to the capital, while Miyagi continued exploring the path set by Higaonna in Okinawa.

In addition, Motobu Choyu, Motobu Choki, Kyan Chotoku, Chibana Choshin, Oshiro Chojo and others also contributed to the future growth of karate. When Kano met Funakoshi, he gave him confidence and support to spread karate. Kano's words of advice to Funakoshi were a major step forward in the history of karatedo.

In January 1927, Kano visited Naha at the invitation of the Okinawa Judo Yudansha Kai. A karate demonstration was held as a part of the welcoming event, and Kano was able to meet with members of the Okinawa Karate Club. Among them were two men who would later become founders of their own schools: Miyagi Chojun and Mabuni Kenwa.

Taking advantage of this opportunity, Miyagi and Mabuni would later move to the mainland and promote karate in the Kansai region. Without this encounter with Kano, the future of karate in Japan would have been very different. Kano also adopted some of the techniques from his interactions with karate into the judo *kata Seiryoku Zen'yo Kokumin Taiiku*. I will delve into this in more detail later on in the chapter.

2. Kano Jigoro and the Okinawa Karate Club

The encyclopaedia *Okinawa Karate Kobudo Jiten* (2008) states that Funakoshi Gichin, Hanashiro Chomo, Tokuda Anbun, Chibana Choshin, Oshiro Chojo, Mabuni Kenwa, and Shiroma Shimpan met at Mabuni's house in 1917 or 18, and launched the Karate Kenkyu Kai (Karate Research Society).

Miyagi Chojun started the Karate Kenkyu (Kai) Club around 1925. Practitioners such as Kyoda Juhatsu, Shinzato Jin'an, Madanbashi Keiyo, Shiroma Koki, and Kyan Chotoku were also in and out of the club. According to an entry in the encyclopaedia, "Both of these clubs were more like informal gatherings, and it is uncertain if they engaged in official organisational activities."[1] Details concerning their undertakings in the 1920s are unknown.

Together they represented the first such organisation in the history of Okinawan karate, and they combined to become the Okinawa Karate Club (here referred to as the "Club"). The Club later became the Karate Division of the Okinawa Prefectural Athletic Association after it was formed, and was later affiliated with the Dai-Nippon Butokukai. Quoting the encyclopaedia again, "[Affiliation with the Butokukai] was a momentous event in Okinawan karatedo. This occasion marks its formal acknowledgement as a Japanese budo discipline."

The first time I heard of the Club was in the autumn of 1977, from Tazaki Kogyu, an early disciple of Miyagi Chojun. Tazaki became an apprentice of Miyagi's in 1923 and was subsequently taught by him at the Club, which opened in March 1926. Tazaki also received guidance from other teachers who instructed on different days of the week. Tazaki was 15 years old at the time, and his junior by one year, Kina Seiko, was put in charge of the Club's general affairs.

"The purpose [of the Club] was to gradually unify karate so that Shuri-te and Naha-te could stand shoulder to shoulder with judo and kendo. The instructors were Miyagi Chojun, Motobu Choyu (Choki's older brother), Mabuni Kenwa, and Oshiro Chojo (according to Uehara Seikichi of Motobu-ryu, Hanashiro Chomo, Yabu Kentsu, Kyan Chotoku, Teruya Kamesuke,

Tomoyose, and Motobu Choki were also at the Club). These instructors set up a dojo near Naminoue and shared teaching duties from Monday to Saturday."

Students were taught the strengths of both Shuri-te and Naha-te with the intention of spreading karate far and wide. In *Goju-ryu Karatedo-shi* (A History of Goju-ryu), it states that, "The Club's *Shihan* (head instructors) in addition to Master Chojun... were masters Hanashiro Chomo, Motobu Choyu, and Mabuni Kenwa. Each one of them decided on a different day of the week to teach and focused their efforts on popularising karate. Many other instructors also visited the Club, but these four were the official teachers."

In addition, "As Motobu Choyu was the oldest, he resided on the Club's premises as the caretaker. It was agreed that the students of each instructor all train there and pay a monthly fee to the Club... The building was 66 m², and the earthen-floored dojo where practices were conducted was 165 m². *Makiwara* were placed in the dojo, and other equipment was also purchased to assist in training." Kina Seiko wrote, "I was encouraged by Master Chojun to study Shuri-te, so I learned under Master Motobu (Choyu), who taught me the *Unsu kata*. Even now, I practise that *kata* and teach it to my students."

Tazaki Kogyu observed the following:

"At that time, there was no rank system[2] in place and there was nothing to prove the ability of the students. When I went to Tokyo to enter the Tokyo School of

Callisthenics, I received a certificate inscribed with the words 'The holder of this diploma is hereby certified as having studied intensively for five years at this club. Karate Kenkyu Kai Representative Miyagi Chojun'. I had never seen such a diploma before, so I assume it was prepared especially for me upon my departure to Tokyo…

At this time during the Taisho period, Shuri and Naha masters joined forces and set up an organisation to teach the younger generation. They built a dojo and devised a daily teaching program to pass on their knowledge. The Club was modified into the 'Karate Club' on the death of the president Motobu Choyu and with the founding of the Okinawa Prefectural Athletic Association. As such, the stated purpose at the time of its establishment was not accomplished. However, it was an endeavour in which one senses the high motivation of Okinawan karate practitioners before the rise of *ryuha* schools."

According to the encyclopaedia, Hanashiro Chomo, Kyan Chotoku, Kuba Kosaku, Miyagi Chojun and Mabuni Kenwa performed karate at the demonstration to welcome Kano Jigoro to Okinawa. Miyagi and Mabuni were tasked with explaining karate and looking after Kano. In his first book, *Kobo-jizai Goshin-jutsu Karate Kempo*, Mabuni wrote the following about the event.

"In January 1927, Dr. Kano Jigoro, Director of the Kodokan, visited Okinawa. Over two days, Miyagi

Chojun and I showed him karate *kata* and explained the content. Dr. Kano was very impressed and suggested that we teach our forms of attack and defence to the whole country."

Regarding Miyagi,

"In 1927, the founder of judo, Dr. Kano Jigoro, visited Okinawa at the invitation of the local Judo Yudansha Kai... After the demonstration, Master Chojun performed throwing and ground *waza*, and explained how each is decided with breathing technique. Dr. Kano was apparently surprised by the advanced level of the techniques shown... In 1927, following a demonstration of judo performed in the dojo constructed on the school grounds, Kano watched an impromptu karate demonstration by Miyagi and his students, and was seemingly captivated."

Sakiyama (formerly Senaha) Tattoku, a student of Miyagi, wrote the following of their interaction:

"Dr. Kano Jigoro came to Okinawa with his top student Nagaoka Shuichi, and his assistant Yokomoto Isekichi. It seems that he mentioned to Master Miyagi how he'd very much like to see karate. It just happened to be class time, but the principal ordered the classes to stop and we went to the Okinawa Ryokan Inn. Already at the inn were local dignitaries such as the mayor of Naha Mr. Kishimoto and deputy mayor Ose Kokei. After Master Miyagi explained karate, Azama (who is now known as Nanjo), Nakaima Genkai, and I performed all the basic techniques in front of him."

This meeting was epochal in the history of Japanese karatedo. After this, Miyagi Chojun (who learned Naha-te from Higaonna Kanryo) and Mabuni Kenwa (who studied both Shuri-te and Naha-te) settled down in the Kansai region, and their teachings became prominent not only in Japan, but also around the world. In this way, through his meetings with Funakoshi, Miyagi, and others, Kano Jigoro left an indelible mark on karate's promotion on the mainland. His contribution cannot be overstated in the process that transformed *todi* into karate, which changed subsequently into karatedo (a Japanese budo) and ultimately into an Olympic sport.

It is useful to reassess what Kano meant to karatedo, and what can still be learned from him. To put Kano's contribution into context, we will now look at his martial arts career and the *Seiryoku Zen'yo Kokumin Taiiku kata* (Maximum-Efficiency National Physical Education Kata) that he created. This *kata* is particularly pertinent as it contains some karate techniques.

3. From Jutsu to Do
—Kano Jigoro and Seiryoku Zen'yo Kokumin Taiiku
① Judo and Jujutsu to Kano

Kano was born the son of a *sake* brewer in Mikage-cho, Hyogo prefecture, in 1860. He began living with his father in Tokyo at the age of 10. In 1873, he entered the foreign language school Ikuei Gijuku and began his academic career.

"Kano Jigoro, whose childhood name was Shinnosuke, was a child prodigy. He was not a sickly child, but he was extremely frail and physically inferior to most of his peers. For this reason, he was often looked down upon by other children, and although he was confident in his academic ability, he was often teased... He heard of an ancient <u>Japanese martial art called jujutsu in which even weak men could defeat stronger adversaries. This motivated him to learn the art."</u> (Underlined by author)

Soon after entering the Faculty of Letters at Tokyo Imperial University in 1877, Kano began studying the Tenjin Shin'yo-ryu tradition of jujutsu under Fukuda Hachinosuke. After Fukuda's sudden death, he continued under Iso Masatomo. Iso also passed away, so Kano began learning the Kito-ryu tradition of jujutsu under Iikubo Tsunetoshi.

While learning these two traditions, Kano continued researching the history and principles of jujutsu in general. Five years later in 1882, Kano founded his own school which he called Kodokan Judo. Kano once wrote about the state of jujutsu at that time:

"At the beginning of the Meiji era, jujutsu was considered a physically dangerous pursuit and of little benefit to learn. Moreover, in olden times, those who entered a school of jujutsu were not allowed to instruct until they received a teaching license. This is not the case now. Those who are not yet technically proficient are quick to pass on their knowledge in what cannot be called genuine jujutsu. <u>People belittle jujutsu even though they do not know what the real thing is...</u> In addition, some people turned jujutsu into a spectacle, charging spectators for demonstrating sumo or fancy techniques at entertainment venues. <u>More and more people have come to see jujutsu as a lowly art."</u> (Underlined by author)

Jujutsu, a combat method enabling a weaker man to defeat a powerful one, was a system of self-defence that empowered Kano. Nevertheless, he realised that traditional teaching methods required considerable modification to suit the modern era. Kano also did not want his school to be associated with the unfavourable attitudes surrounding jujutsu at the time. He adopted the word *judo*—the Gentle Way—to designate his new style of jujutsu.

"There is a fundamental Way that lies at the root of jujutsu, and the techniques (*jutsu*) are the application of this. It is appropriate to teach the 'Way' first and then techniques as an application of this. I named the place where judo is taught as Kodokan (Hall where the Way is taught). This is to make clear that it is not simply fighting techniques that are conveyed. I called it Kodokan so that people uninitiated in the Way can learn about what it is. The purpose of studying judo is to learn about physical education, competition, and to cultivate the spirit."

Kano was an avid promoter of the benefits that could be gleaned from judo.

"I was once very short-tempered and excitable. As my physical health improved through jujutsu training, my mental state calmed down, and my powers of self-control became stronger. Moreover, I believed that the theory of jujutsu was relevant to many other aspects of society. Intellectual capacity nurtured to prevail in jujutsu matches was valuable wisdom that could be applied to anything. I did not think that jujutsu taught the traditional way was effective. With a degree of innovation, however, I knew it would be useful not only as a martial art, but also as a vehicle for intellectual, physical, and moral education."

Kano was a professional educator. Starting his career as a lecturer at Gakushuin University, he then became a professor of political economy at Komaba Agricultural School. He was later appointed as professor at Gakushuin University, and in 1893 after studying in Europe, he became rector at the Tokyo Higher Normal School at the young age of 33.

Balancing his studies and furthering his career. Kano continued to run the Kodokan and promote judo by taking advantage of his position as an educator and his sway in the Ministry of Education. As president, he established a callisthenics course at the Tokyo Higher Normal School and the majors of *gekiken* (kendo) and judo. He later made both martial arts compulsory subjects for students there.

Kano was appointed as the first Asian director of the IOC in 1909. He also established the Japan Amateur Athletic Association in 1911 and became the organisation's first president. Kano is recognised as a central figure behind the elevation of budo as an official subject in schools, the beginning of Japan's Olympic movement, and also the facilitation of karate's spread across Japan. Kano first met with Funakoshi Gichin, and then Miyagi Chojun and Mabuni Kenwa in the late 1920s, when he assisted them in their quest to disseminate karate. What Kano discovered in karate greatly influenced his creation of the *Seiryoku Zen'yo Kokumin Taiiku no Kata* (literally Maximum Efficiency National Physical Education Forms, hereafter referred to as SZKTK).

② Kano Jigoro, Karate and SZKTK

Seiryoku zen'yo (maximum efficient use of energy) and *jita-kyoei* (mutual prosperity for self and others) are the cornerstone ideals of judo espoused by Kano. The two principles were, in Kano's mind, key to the survival and prosperity of society.

As a member of the IOC, he explored sporting relations with other countries and thought deeply about physical education designed specifically for Japanese. He was determined to find a way to create a national sports program that would "promote physical excellence in the Japanese people."

In 1931 he publicised his ideas in the booklet *Seiryoku Zen'yo Kokumin Taiiku*. In the first section he introduces the forms as the ideal physical education:

1. To develop muscles and organs of the body uniformly, and as safely as possible.

2. Each exercise is meaningful, and as one becomes more adept they can be utilised in other areas of one's life.

3. The exercises can be done alone or in groups and are suitable for young and old alike.

4. A large space is not required for the exercises, and only the simplest equipment and clothing is needed.

5. The exercises can be performed at a set time during the day or whenever is convenient, depending on one's circumstances."

"Ideal Physical Education" written by Kano nearly a century ago had been laid out by Funakoshi beforehand. Moreover, these were the very same benefits touted for karate when budo was made a compulsory subject in Japanese junior high schools in 2012. The inspiration for Kano's "National Physical Education" came from his encounters with Funakoshi in 1922 and Miyagi in 1927. Kano was impressed by karate's effectiveness as a means for self-defence. At the same time, he recognised the potential of karate techniques as a medium for physical education.

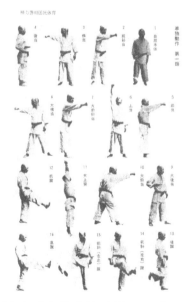

Photo 3-1 "Individual Movements—First Category". (*Kano Jigoro Taikei* Vol. 8 p. 155)

Todo Yoshiaki wrote in *Judo Sono Rekishi to Giho* that "The techniques employed in the 'individual movement' section in SZKTK include many *waza* from karate including strikes, thrusts, and kicks. Kano's meeting with Funakoshi and the fact that he wanted Funakoshi to stay in Tokyo suggest that karate's impact on him was significant."

- First Category (Individual Movements): *Goho-ate* (hit in five directions); *Dai-goho-ate* (hit in five directions with the addition of a step); *Goho-geri* (kick in five directions).
- Second Category (Partner Exercises): *Kagami-migaki* (polishing of a mirror with two hands); *Sayu-uchi* (hit left and right); *Zengo-tsuki* (punch forward, elbow back); *Ryote-ue-tsuki* (two-handed upward punch); *Dai-ryote-ue-tsuki* (two-handed upward punch with a jump); *Sayu-kogo-shita-tsuki* (alternating downward punches); *Ryote-shita-tsuki* (two-handed downward punch with a squat); *Naname-ue-uchi* (knifehand strikes diagonally up); *Naname-shita-uchi* (knifehand strikes diagonally down); *Dai-naname-ue-uchi* (knifehand strikes diagonally up with the addition of a step to the side); *Ushiro-sumi-tsuki* (downward punches across the body behind the opposite hip); *Ushiro-uchi* (backstroke-like strike); *Ushiro-tsuki-mae-shita-tsuki* two-handed punch behind the head leaning back, and two handed punch to the ground leaning forward).

Professor Shishida Fumiaki, formerly of Waseda University, also observed that, "Apart from one technique in the individual training category, all are *atemi* techniques (punches). The series of *waza* for practising in pairs contain many similarities with the Kodokan's *Kime-no-kata* devised in 1906 (*Kime-no-kata* was in turn developed from the *Shinken Shobu-no-kata* which had been created shortly after the Kodokan's inception.) Shishida asked the question why more than half of the *waza* employed in Kano's SZKTK *kata* were striking techniques.

"The characteristics of the individual training could be expressed as karate-type callisthenics. Kano was obviously influenced by martial traditions other than jujutsu—in other words, karate. Greatly impressed by the demonstration of karate *kata* by Funakoshi Gichin in 1922… One cannot help but notice the profound influence it had on his thinking."

		Total	Throws	Holds	Strikes	Unknown
Individual	1st Category	**15**	0	0	15	0
Movements	2nd Category	**13**	0	0	12	1
Partnered	1st Category	**10**	0	4	4	3
Movements	2nd Category	**10**	4	0	0	6

Table 3-1 SZKTK Technical Breakdown (Shishida Fumiaki, "*Kano Jigoro no Judo-kan to Sono Hatten*", Master's thesis, Tsukuba University, 1979)

Both Shishida and Todo interpreted the influence of karate as coming from Funakoshi. In addition, I believe that Kano was also greatly inspired by the technical knowledge imparted to him through exchanges with Miyagi Chojun and others in Okinawa. I would like to draw the reader's attention to testimony by Miyagi's second daughter, Kojo Yasuko. Born in 1912, Kojo Yasuko was 15 years old when she first met Kano.

"I remember when Master Kano came to Okinawa. He was a small man who seemed very affable. I served him tea when my father was showing karate forms at Naha Jinjo Primary School. He smiled when I gave him the cup… I know that they got on well together. They exchanged letters many times after that. My father was fond of books and had many in his collection. There were 16 baskets full, but they were destroyed in the war, as were all the letters [from Kano].

Jun was born that year (1927)… He died as a member of the *Tekketsu Kinnotai**, but Dr. Kano was his godfather. It was extremely sad. Of the family' four sons, Jun was the most dedicated to karate. I hear that Dr. Kano wrote something about karate after he left." (Interview recorded on November 5–12, 1977. Koyama Masashi, "Waga Miyagi Chojun", *Gekkan Karatedo*.)

(*The Imperial Blood and Iron Student Corps (*Tekketsu Kinnotai*) were a military unit of middle and normal schoolboys who fought in the Battle of Okinawa. Out of the 1779 of members, 890 were killed in combat.)

This exchange took place in 1927. Little is known of what Miyagi and the others performed at the demonstration and at the private gathering held on a different day. It can be inferred by Kano's descriptions that *Sanchin* and *Yobi-undo* (preparatory exercises) etc., which would be incorporated into Goju-ryu's curriculum later, were explained to him. Kano notes, "Make a fist with the right hand; lift the fist up close to the body just under the right breast. Thrust out at an angle of about 45 degrees with the back

Photo 3-2 Kyan Chotoku instructing students. (*Okinawa Karate Kobudo Jiten*, p. 599)

of the hand to the left diagonal, up to shoulder height. The gaze is directed to the striking target (front diagonal)". The fist is drawn back but to slightly varying positions depending in the karate school. In Funakoshi's Shuri-te line, the fist is usually pulled back to the hip. Take note of the hand positions as taught by instructors Kyan Chotoku (Photo 3-2) and Shiroma Shimpan (Photo 3-3) in the group demonstration photos taken in front of Shuri Castle in 1937.

In comparison, the pulled hand position in Miyagi's Goju-ryu is the same as that recorded by Kano after his visit (Photo 3-4). Kikukawa's left hand position was probably taught to him by Miyagi. More clues are found in Kano's eighth article of a series of 13 titled "Let's start by improving our daily lives" in *Sakko* (Feb. 1924–Dec. 1935 in *Kano Jigoro Taikei*, Vol. 9).

"Even if we are busy all day, exercising does not take up much time and is enjoyable. It really is easy to do. Still,

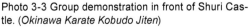

Photo 3-3 Group demonstration in front of Shuri Castle. (*Okinawa Karate Kobudo Jiten*)

Photo 3-4 Go-ju-ryu *Sanchin.* (JKF Goju Kai, *Goju-ryu Karate-do*, p. 69)

there are occasions when there is no time during the day. On such days, I make sure to exercise on the floor in the evening, and work on my joints. I start by bending and stretching my toes, ankles, knees, then hands from the fingers to the wrists and elbow joints, and finally my neck and chest."

Interestingly, this series of exercises described by Kano is almost identical to what Miyagi outlined for *Yobi-undo* after receiving advice from a physician. Kano mentions before this passage, "I made SZKTK and practise it every day," as if he devised the exercises as a part of his system. I suspect that the explanation he received from Miyagi on *Yobi-undo* eight years before stuck with him. Seeing it as a simple means for enhancing health in daily life, it fitted perfectly with his intentions in creating

SZKTK. The position of pulling the hand back and the sequence of preparatory exercises (*Yobi-undo*) he employed in SZKTK were clearly inspired by Naha-te karate.

Miyagi's influence on Kano is evident, however, SZKTK was not a martial art *kata* per se. It was a series of exercises pieced together by Kano to promote physical well-being among the Japanese people. "Attack and defence form the basis of the exercises, but it is not a pure martial art. It was organised in light of conditions for ideal physical education." Kano rated karate highly and, just as Funakoshi had, Miyagi and Mabuni greatly respected Kano. The influence and respect went both ways.

As an aside, it was not widely known that Kano and Miyagi engaged in frequent letter exchanges after their meeting, or that Kano was the godfather of Miyagi's third son. As mentioned in Miyagi's daughter's testimony, all the letters and books were destroyed in the war, and the only remaining evidence of this close relationship is the interview recorded with her in 1978.[3]

Notes

(1) Takamiyagi Shigeru, Shinzato Katsuhiko, Nakamoto Masahiro (eds.) *Okinawa Karate Kobudo Jiten*, Kashiwa Shobo, 2008. The timeline says that the Okinawa Karate Kenkyu Club was launched in 1925, which is at odds with the date quoted in the text.

(2) As Kadekaru mentions in the previous chapter, the Tokyo Higher Normal School introduced a promotion system. Funakoshi adopted this Dan system when he was in Tokyo.

(3) Koyama, "*Waga Miyagi Chojun*", *Gekkan Karatedo*, 1981 (November Edition). Although I have listened to the tape recording of the interview with Miyagi's daughter Kojo Yasuko, I was unable to verify the section in which she said Kano was Jun's godfather.

SECTION 2

The Dai-Nippon Butokukai and Karate

The Dai-Nippon Butokukai (Greater Japan Society of Martial Virtue) was a private organisation created in 1895. As its membership and influence grew at a remarkable pace in the following decades, the society became the representative body of Japanese martial arts in the pre-war period. Budo experts who were awarded the Butokukai title of *Hanshi* (Grandmaster) received a pension. Martial artists in all disciplines hoped to acquire the lower titles of *Renshi* then *Kyoshi* to open a path to the highest title of *Hanshi*. The annual Butokukai Embu Festival (*Butokusai*) held in Kyoto was a prestigious event in which all budo experts desired to participate. The Butokuden hall, the venue for the *Butokusai*'s promotion exam, was considered hallowed ground.

Mainland karate practitioners who learned under the Okinawans Funakoshi, Motobu, Miyagi, and Mabuni also started participating in the *Butokusai*. This was accompanied by both the switch of the *kanji* from Chinese hand to empty hand and the change of the appellation from karatejutsu to karatedo (Way of the empty hand). The following section will map out this gradual process.

1. Kyoto 1928—Miyagi Chojun goes to Kyoto

Kadekaru discovered in an article published in the Kyoto Imperial University Newspaper that Miyagi Chojun visited

Kyoto to teach at the university. The article was titled "Karatejutsu Seminar" and was published on November 1, 1928 (Photo 3–5). The following is an excerpt from the article.

Photo 3-5 *Kyoto Teikoku Daigaku Shimbun* article. (Kyoto University archives, November 1, 1928)

"There is no first attack in karate. Teacher and students soaking in sweat. Karatejutsu Seminar. Hoping for a big turnout!

A karatejutsu seminar has been held every day from the 25th at the old dojo in the dormitory. The instructor, Miyagi-sensei, travelled all the way to Kyoto from Okinawa. A man of robust stature, he took 30 perspiring students through their paces. They all did their best to survive the rigorous training sessions. A public display was held at the Butokuden in Okazaki (Kyoto) on the 24th. Karatejutsu has its roots in Chinese fist-fighting and looks rough, but the training methodology is well ordered and much like Japanese budo. Miyagi-sensei is the number one instructor of karatejutsu and has many students at his dojo in Okinawa. He emphasises that 'there is no first attack in karate'. The point is self-defence only. Perhaps this is because so many people misunderstand karate and think of it as an inferior discipline compared to judo and kendo. People who learn karatejutsu have a character which seeks to quell violent tendencies. But once they do attack, they have the courage to slay even the wildest beast."

The point of karate is explained in simple terms. It introduces the roots and current situation, and concludes with a quote from Miyagi.

"'The participating students are very eager to learn, and I am pleased that it proved to be a valuable experience for them. I think it was particularly meaningful that ranked judo practitioners came along, and it will be meaningful for them to study the crossover between karate and judo.' From the judo club, two 4th Dan practitioners Aoki and Dogane, and many others trained diligently as they tried to master each attack and movement. As the seminar still has another week, the organisers are happy to have members from the general public attend in addition to students."

It is not explained how Miyagi was invited by the judo club to hold this seminar at Kyoto Imperial University. With regards to the workshop, Yamaguchi Gogen, founder of Ritsumeikan

University's Karatedo Club, and later instructor for mainland Goju-ryu, said,

> "When Miyagi-sensei came to the mainland for the first time, it was at the invitation of Kyoto Imperial University's judo club. At the time, Mr. Ono Kumao of the Butokukai was the Dean of Student Affairs. Sakai Katsumi was a lawyer from Saga, and I was his clerk... As Sakai-sensei's secretary, I was able to watch Miyagi-sensei's seminar at Kyoto University... There were between 40 and 50 people who took the course. A person named Yoshida Shigenari later said he was actually the one who invited Mr. Miyagi."

I was able to confirm the existence of the judo 4th Dans Aoki and Dogane mentioned in the article. There was a later article in Kyoto Imperial University's newspaper covering the annual judo competition with Tokyo Imperial University, in which Dogane defeated Tokyo University's Kitayama 3rd Dan with *Yoko Shiho-gatame* to win the match without Aoki 4th Dan needing to fight.

Yamaguchi names Ono Kumao as the Dean of Student Affairs, who is also referred to as the Newspaper Office Manager by the *Kyoto Teikoku Daigaku Shimbun* (Kyoto Imperial University Newspaper). As for Aoki, Dogane and Ono are all listed in the Kyoto University Judo Club Alumni Directory. Aoki and Dogane were admitted into the university 1926, while Ono matriculated in 1914 and 1917 (he graduated from both the Faculty of Law and the Faculty of Economics).

One wonders if there was any mention in the letters between Miyagi and Kano of this demonstration at the Butokuden and the seminar at Kyoto Imperial University. Unfortunately, the performance on October 24 at the Butokuden cannot be confirmed, but Miyagi's first trip to Kyoto certainly took place.

2. Kansai in 1929
—The *Butokusai* and Mabuni Kenwa's Move to Osaka

1929 was an important year for karate in the Kansai region. One reason is that the three people who were awarded the rank of Butokukai *Kyoshi* demonstrated at the *Butokusai* that year. Another significant happening was that Mabuni Kenwa, who later founded Shito-ryu, moved to Osaka.

Name	Dai-Nippon Butokukai (Greater-Japan Society of Martial Virtue)
Establishment	April 17, 1895
Activities	Building and maintaining the Butokuden Hall, organising the *Butokusai* Festival, building and operating educational institutions and facilities, awarding certificates of excellence (or rewarding excellence), preserving traditions, compiling historical and educational materials, and publishing bulletins.
Organisation	The Imperial Princes Komatsunomiya, Fushiminomiya, Kuninomiya, and Nashimotonomiya were all appointed as superintendents, and the local government officers and officials from the Ministry of the Interior, such as the police, were given positions in the society. Branches were established in each of the prefectures of Japan to grow the membership. The head of each prefectural branch was the governor of the prefecture, and the head of municipal branches were mayors.
Membership	In 1909 membership reached 1.51 million. By 1942, it had grown to 2.24 million.

Achievements	Establishment of awards and titles for martial artists—*Seirensho* (certificate of mastery). Established the titles of *Hanshi* and *Kyoshi* in 1903. Standardised *kata* established (by Kano and others)—In 1906, the *Dai-Nippon Teikoku Kenjutsu Kata* was established (revised in 1912). Also, the *Dai-Nippon Butokukai Jujutsu Kata* was established under the leadership of Kano Jigoro. Match and refereeing rules established (by Kano and others)—1899 Match referee regulations for both jujutsu and kenjutsu established (later revised). Establishment of the Budo Vocational School—1905 Bujutsu Teacher Training Institute, 1912 Bujutsu Vocational School, 1919 Renamed Budo Vocational School (Busen). Bujutsu terminology changed to budo (Nishikubo Hiromichi)—Kenjutsu (Gekiken)→Kendo, Kyujutsu→Kyudo, Jujutsu→Judo.
Dissolution	In 1946, GHQ ordered the dissolution of the Butokukai. This took place on November 9, and those involved were banned from public office.

Table 3-2 History and Outline of the Dai-Nippon Butokukai (Koyama)

① The 1929 *Butokusai*

Since its inception, participation in the Dai-Nippon Butokukai's annual *Butokusai* festival became a goal for martial artists all over the country. (Refer to Table 3-2 for an outline of the Butokukai and its activities.) As for performances of karate at the Butokuden, we have already introduced the one performed by students from the Okinawa Prefectural Middle School and led by Funakoshi Gichin in 1916. How did karate become affiliated with the Butokukai? Who was involved, and what did they do to achieve this goal?

Not long after the Butokukai was founded in 1895, a rewards system was instigated in 1902 to recognise those individuals making genuine contributions to the promotion of Japan's traditional martial culture. Those awarded the title of *Hanshi* were selected on the basis of character and the fruits of their studies, and contribution to the Butokukai with over 40 years of training experience. Those awarded *Kyoshi* had equivalent qualifications, and also held the title of *Seirensho*.

Seirensho was later renamed *Renshi*, and *Kyoshi* was changed to *Tasshi* during the war, but the authority commanded by holders in the world of budo remained the same. Three early karate practitioners were also awarded the title of *Kyoshi*. First, let us look at Konishi Yasuhiro.

Among the names of the many people who started karate after Funakoshi opened his school in Tokyo is Konishi Yasuhiro (1893–1983). Konishi's name appears in the foreword of Mabuni Kenwa's 1934 book *Kobo-jizai Goshin-jutsu Karate Kempo* with the title Karatejutsu Promotion Hombu Chief. On November 8, 1977, I visited Konishi at his home and asked him about why he started karate, and also about the Butokukai and what karate's affiliation to the society entailed.

When Konishi was a member of the Keio Gijuku University Kendo Club, he was intrigued one day by the strange ha-f-naked dance-like movements his junior Aragaki Tsuneshige performed at a drinking party. It was the first time Konishi had ever seen karate. He told Aragaki that he wanted to learn it too and got him to teach the *kata*. Konishi studied Takenouchi-ryu jujutsu when attending Kagawa Prefectural Takamatsu Higher Commercial School. In the Takenouchi style, he also practised punching and kicking cushions attached to pillars, and strung a ball from the ceiling to practise striking a moving target.

After graduating from university, Konishi became the instructor at the Keio High School Kendo Club. It was then that he became acquainted with Funakoshi, who was using the same practice hall. He heard that this old gentleman from Okinawa had even published a book on karate. It turned out that it was the same martial art that his junior Aragaki had shown him before. Konishi was well-versed in jujutsu and asked Funakoshi to teach him some of the *kata* introduced in his book. From then, Konishi and other kendo people also joined the Meishojuku.

Since his jujutsu days, Konishi often accompanied his master to the *Butokusai*, and already knew a lot about the organisation. He was even good enough in kendo to have been awarded the title of *Seirensho* sometime in the early 1920s and had participated in *Butokusai* matches himself. Konishi Yasuhiro of Tokyo was to become one of the three men awarded karate *Kyoshi*.

The second recipient was Ueshima Sannosuke. I could only find his name in the journal of the Dai-Nippon Butokukai, *Butokushi*, covering the 34th *Butokusai* in 1930. "Karatejutsu: Osaka – Ueshima Kiyotada". I found a record of Konishi, Ueshima and Miyagi performing in the same place in 1929. It was in a photograph collection of Matsuzaki Horyu, a member of the Kushin-ryu Karatedo connected with Ueshima

Sannosuke. It probably belonged to Ueshima and fortunately survived the air raids on Osaka in March 1945. It is a valuable historical document.

It is a list from the 33rd *Butokusai* Grand Demonstration Programme. On the front cover it states, "This programme is valid for the duration of the festival and will not be reissued, so please take care not to lose it". "The 33rd *Butokusai* Grand Demonstration Programme for May 1929, Part 1: Judo (9th and 10th), Dai-Nippon Butokukai Headquarters".

On page 24, the following schools of jujutsu are listed: Musoryu, Daito-ryu, and Yagyu-ryu. Skipping one group, there is a reference to "Karatejutsu: Osaka—*Kyoshi* Ueshima Sannosuke Kiyotada", followed by "Karatedo *kata*: Okinawa—Miyagi Chojun", and then "Nihon Kempo Karatejutsu: Tokyo—*Renshi* Konishi Yasuhiro." There is a further note: "Kushin-ryu: Osaka—*Kyoshi* Ueshima Sannosuke Kiyotada, Yano Seiichi, Ueshima Mikiko." Ueshima Mikiko was Ueshima Sannosuke Kiyotada's daughter. In 1935, she and her father were commended in the *Kyoto Hinode Newspaper* for their performance.[1]

Ueshima was born in Ako, Hyogo prefecture, in 1893. He studied Konshin-ryu jujutsu and karate under Motobu Choki before founding Kushin-ryu in 1932. In the programme from the same exhibition, there are four names including Konshin-ryu: Osaka—*Renshi* Tazura Kasaburo, Kanaya Senkichi. This was listed as jujutsu, but what was the connection with Kushin-ryu? There are many things we do not know about Ueshima because he was not very active after the war.

The third *Kyoshi* was Miyagi Chojun, but the entry in the 1929 programme list raises several issues:

(a) How should one read Ueshima's 空手術 and Konishi's Nihon Kempo 空手術? An alternative reading to karate-jutsu for the *kanji* could possibly be *kuushu-jutsu*.

(b) Miyagi Chojun's art is written as karatedo (唐手道), but he is not listed as having the title of *Kyoshi* or *Renshi*.

As for (a), Keio Gijuku University changed its club *kanji* from 唐 (Chinese) to 空 (empty) in October of that year. The authors of this book came to the following conclusion. These two arts should be read as *kuushu* rather than *karate*. This is because Konishi advertised Shindo Jinen-ryu Kuushu-jutsu, clearly indicating the reading of the *kanji* was not *karate* but *kuushu* (Photo 3–6). It was not until later that the reading of karate became established after a debate ensued in Okinawa in 1936.[2]

Regarding (b), Miyagi's karatedo (唐手道) has several meanings. As noted above, even though Ueshima and Konishi used the *kanji* for empty hand but pronounced it *kuushu* instead of karate, at this juncture Miyagi added -*do* (Way) as a suffix to Chinese hand. What did he mean by this? Miyagi's enthusiasm for research was universally acknowledged, and Konishi informed me that when Miyagi visited Tokyo, he always frequented bookshops in Kanda. It is possible that Miyagi, who had been searching for the ideal form of karate before meeting Kano Jigoro, identified that the path karate should follow was one as a budo.

The three were later awarded the title of *Kyoshi*, but there are many unanswered questions about how this transpired. First, in Konishi's case, according to the *Budo Hanshi Kyoshi Meikan*, a catalogue of rank holders published by the Dai-Nippon Butokukai in 1937, he apparently received his *Seirensho* certificate for kendo in August 1924. According to the 1929 *Butokusai* Programme he was he was listed as Nippon Kempo Kuushu-jutsu *Renshi*. Did he

Photo 3-6 Promotion leaflet for Konishi's Shindo Jinen-ryu Kuushu-jutsu. (Courtesy of his son)

really obtain the *Renshi* rank in Kuushu-jutsu? In the programme of 1941, he is listed as Shindo Jinen-ryu Karatejutsu *Kyoshi*.

According to the programme listings of 1929, Ueshima Sannosuke was already *Kyoshi* in both Kuushu-jutsu and Kushin-ryu. However, according to the *Budo Hanshi Kyoshi Meikan*, he was awarded a *Seirensho*"title for judo in 1930, and "Judo *Kyoshi*" in 1933. The disparity between the programme list of the Dai-Nippon Butokukai exhibition and the *Budo Hanshi Kyoshi Meikan* is puzzling. In addition, Ueshima's *Kyoshi* certificate for "Kuushu-jutsu" awarded in 1939 still exists, so when did he get the prior title of *Renshi*? Could it be that his judo title was for Kuushu-jutsu? Ueshima also participated in judo demonstrations, which further confuses the issue.

Incidentally, in the *Budo Hanshi Kyoshi Meikan*, the name Inagaki Torakichi can be seen in the "Kuushu-jutsu *Renshi*" list in 1936. In the 1941 exhibition programme, there is a description of what could be *kumite* with Konishi. This means that Inagaki could have been a student of Konishi's Shindo Jinen-ryu.

As for Miyagi Chojun, his name does not appear in the *Renshi* list of *Budo Hanshi Kyoshi Meikan* issued in March 1937. However, according to Miyagi's curriculum vitae, his *Kyoshi* title was granted in May 1937, so it is clear he was not yet *Kyoshi* when the directory was published. Why then is his name not in the *Renshi* section? Konishi also confirmed that Miyagi was *Kyoshi*, so it is odd that he was not listed as *Renshi*, which was a prerequisite for *Kyoshi*. It seems that the 1902 Butokukai regulations for the awarding of *Shogo* titles were revised in 1934:

Kyoshi
1. *Must have received the title of Renshi.*
2. *Must have attained the rank of 5th Dan or above.*
3. *Must have a good knowledge of budo.*

However, at that time there was no Dan system in Okinawa. Therefore, Miyagi did not have a rank. Regarding *Renshi*, Article 19 in the regulations stipulates, "Those who are recognised as having the skill to take the *Renshi* examination (in the case of budo disciplines that do not have ranks) shall be issued an examination voucher." Article 24 says, "Ranks can be granted through examination or by recognition without examination, but ranks without examination ranks shall be granted only for kendo and judo." Although it is rather convoluted, it stipulates that the candidate must hold the rank of 5th Dan or above. At that time, however, there was no Dan system in Okinawa, so Miyagi did not have the required rank. So, according to Article 19, Miyagi may have been given a special dispensation in recognition of his skill. Nevertheless, it also states that such consideration was only afforded to kendo or judo practitioners. Karate was demonstrated in the judo section, where judges included famous *judoka* such as Isogai Hajime and Nagaoka Shuichi. This is probably how he was awarded his title. Later, there was a debate within the Butokukai as to whether karate was "closer to judo or kendo".

In any case, Miyagi continued appearing at the *Butokusai* demonstrations many times after. Isogai commented that "Okinawan karate is as magnificent as the *yawara* of old", and it seems that Miyagi was considered by *judoka* to be the "Kano of karate". Miyagi had taught karate as an instructor for the Butokukai in Okinawa during the Taisho period, and in 1934 he became an officer of the Okinawa branch of the Butokukai, so I believe the bestowal of *Kyoshi* was in recognition of his undeniable skill and contributions.

Much remains unknown about the three karate *Kyoshi*. Hopefully more information will eventually be discovered in *Butokushi* magazines, programme listings, directories of high-ranked martial artists, and other sources. Notwithstanding, the year 1937 was when karate was affiliated with the Butokukai, and the three *Kyoshi* qualified to become judges (examiners). From the following year, 1938, more and more karate practitioners began actively performing at the *Butokusai*. Of note here is the exclusion of Funakoshi. I will discuss this later in the chapter.

② Mabuni Kenwa Comes to Osaka

According to *Yukyu no Ken* (November 1995) published by the Japan Karatedo Federation's Shitokai, Mabuni Kenwa retired from his job as a karate instructor at various schools in April 1929 at the age of 41, and moved from Okinawa to Osaka. He opened a dojo in Tsurumibashi, Nishinari-ku, and began promoting karate there (pp. 116–117). Ken'ei, Mabuni's eldest son, explains how this came to pass.

> "First, my father went to Osaka alone. Okinawa was a long way from everywhere back then. He had to go via Kagoshima by ferry. Later, when I was in the middle of my sixth year at primary school, the whole family moved to Osaka.[4] Only a few students and lawyers wanted to learn karate. It was very difficult financially. When my father opened his dojo in Nishinari, no one came at first. Eventually a man named Sawayama Masaru came. He was a member of the judo club at Kansai University and later founded Nippon Kempo. We practised in a six-mat Japanese-style room. The *tatami* became so tattered we had to put thin mats on top of them."

What prompted Mabuni to relocate to Osaka from Okinawa? Even if he was encouraged by Kano, why Osaka instead of Tokyo? Furthermore, Motobu Choki moved to Osaka in 1921, and his famous bout with the boxer in Kyoto took place in

1922. Motobu lived in Osaka until the beginning of the Showa era, and then he moved to Tokyo. According to Kushin-ryu records, it was during this time in Osaka that Motobu taught Ueshima Sannosuke. Uechi Kambun of Uechi-ryu was living in nearby Wakayama at this time. His son and successor, Kan'ei, began training under his father in Wakayama from 1927. Why was it that so many of karate's future leading instructors lived in the Kansai region?

History shows that economic depression[5] forced many Okinawans to look for work outside the prefecture and move to Kansai, especially Osaka, where there were job opportunities in the textile industry.[6] Even today, Taisho Ward in Osaka City is known as Little Okinawa, and one quarter of its residents, including second and third generation descendants, have their roots in Okinawa.

Funakoshi's activities in Tokyo and Motobu's celebrity status in magazines drew public attention to karate and Okinawa. Mabuni's visit to Osaka was also in part due to burgeoning Okinawan pride and enthusiasm for spreading karate beyond the islands.

In October 1929 in the Kanto region, the Keio Gijuku University Karate Kenkyu Kai held a tournament to commemorate the fifth anniversary of the changing of the *kanji* for karate from Chinese hand to empty hand. Miki Jisaburo, a student at Tokyo Imperial University, visited Okinawa during his summer holidays and recorded the teachings of various instructors he interviewed in his book *Kempo Gaisetsu* (1930). This was the same year Mabuni went to Osaka.

3. Butokusai Festival

Konishi made a name for himself in the karate world through his activities with the Butokukai. In his words:

> "After starting karate, I had the opportunity to demonstrate in front of the famous *judoka* Isogai Hajime and Nagaoka Shuichi. They advised me to 'show *kumite*, as it is easy to understand'... One year, Hongo Fusataro, then chairman of the Butokukai, stopped the proceedings and called me to his seat to ask me about the name of the *kata*. He told me, 'This is a wonderful exercise. Please do your best to spread karate from now.' This strengthened my resolve and I decided to devote myself to the task of popularising karate."[(3)]

With regards to Funakoshi being snubbed by the Butokukai for promotion, Konishi relayed the following:

> "After karate teachers received Butokukai titles (*Kyoshi*), it was mainly myself, Ueshima, and three *judoka* who served as judges. Miyagi lived too far away in Okinawa, so he was never asked... Mabuni Kenwa, Otsuka Hiroki, Nagamine Shoshin, Yagi Meitoku, Higa Seko and others came from Okinawa. Funakoshi also sat the exam together with his students. Although it was thought that he would get the same *Kyoshi* title as Miyagi, he was only awarded *Renshi*. This was partly because of Butokukai regulations stating that the first examination must be from *Renshi*, and partly because *judoka* in Kyoto were not fully aware of Funakoshi's name and career."

After that, Funakoshi refused to go to Kyoto again. Konishi lobbied the Butokukai and Funakoshi was eventually awarded the title *Tasshi* (equivalent to *Kyoshi*). Ueno Jitsuro, an alumnus of both Tokyo University and Kyoto University, wrote the following which corroborates Konishi's statement.

"The requirement to perform in the *Butokusai* was the rank of 3rd Dan or above. If you passed a practical and oral examination, the Butokukai would award the titles of *Renshi* or *Kyoshi*. This was equivalent to a doctoral degree. The title of Butokukai *Renshi* held a great deal of prestige and authority. That is why martial artists from all over Japan gathered in Kyoto each year in May. Today it is called karatedo, but before the war it was called *karatejutsu*. The martial arts with the suffix '-*jutsu*' included *juken-jutsu* (bayonet), *bo-jutsu* (staff), and *iai-jutsu* (sword drawing). There were few in the -*jutsu* arts who were awarded *Renshi* and *Kyoshi*. It was debated whether *karatejutsu* resembled kendo or judo. The highest grade in *karatejutsu* was *Kyoshi* and Konishi Yasuhiro was the examiner. I took my oral examination from him…

Otsuka-sensei also appeared in 1938 and became a *Renshi* in *karatejutsu*. Fortunately, Konishi was a friend of Otsuka's. Otsuka-sensei first recommended two of his students, Eto Takehiko of Meiji University (originally from Kumamoto), and Kihara Hidejiro of Tokyo Agricultural University (died in the war). They both passed successfully. That was in 1939. Of course, practitioners of the Kyoto University Karate Club also performed... In 1939, Master Funakoshi Gichin appeared with his students from Waseda, Keio, and other schools. The students numbered around 50 in total. Funakoshi expected that as such a well-known master in Tokyo, the Butokukai would present him with *Kyoshi* as a matter of course. However, the result of the examination was the same as Otsuka-sensei—*Renshi*. Dissatisfied with the result, Funakoshi-sensei did not appear at the *Butokusai* after that. According to Butokukai leaders, it was customary for everyone to start with *Renshi*. In 1942, however, he was awarded the title of *Tasshi*. This was to encourage promotion of budo during the war."

A pioneer in the world of mainland karate, it must have been a bitter blow for Funakoshi that his labours were not recognised by the Butokukai. Considering the development of karatedo after the war, Funakoshi's status and contribution is incontrovertible, irrespective of whether he was rewarded with the titles of *Renshi* or *Kyoshi* from the Butokukai or not.

Ueno Jitsuro describes what the examinations were like and the joy of Otsuka's disciples when they received *Renshi*. The following depicts the examination scene in Kyoto before the war.

"Half of Butokuden was a kendo hall with a wooden floor, and the other half was a judo hall with *tatami* mats. The width of the hall was about 36 metres. With 60 of Otsuka's students lined up to perform, it was technically difficult to move forward and backward in the space available. Karate demonstrations were held in the kendo hall... The judges were professors from Busen, as well as *Hanshi* and *Kyoshi* masters. With binoculars in hand, they paid close attention to the knotting of fists and the manipulation of the fingers. The results of the examination were announced on the evening of May 6. Otsuka-sensei was worried, and kept asking me about Konishi-sensei's questions. The questioning took place in a corner of the judo hall. First, he had me re-enact the *kata* I performed on May 5, and then he asked me about the principles of budo. In particular, he asked if I combine my studies with budo. I replied that they must go hand in hand, like two wheels of a car... The announcement was made that night at the Budo Vocational College. The gates were closed. Otsuka-sensei and I climbed over a low wall and entered the school where we found many of our colleagues standing around. We lit candles to see, and Otsuka-sensei congratulated us on passing the exam, shouting excitedly 'there's your name on the list!'"

Notes

(1) *Kyoto Hinode Shimbun*, May 5, 1935. "Ueshima Mikiko performs Kushin-ryu brilliantly with her father, Sannosuke, and was admired by the audience."

(2) *Kuushu*. Similar usage can be found in Okinawa in a book called *Kuushu Goshin Jutsu* (1921) by Buyoken Kensai.

(3) The name Hongo Fusataro can be confirmed in Matsuzaki Horyu's *Jinsei wo Shobu Suru - Kushin-ryu Karatedo Gokui*.

(4) Circa 1930.

(5) Known as *"sotetsu jigoku"*, the 1920s saw economic depression and food shortages in Okinawa. Many people left Okinawa to emigrate overseas or work on the mainland.

(6) There were purportedly 30,000 Okinawans living in Kansai in 1925.

SECTION 3

The Creation of Ryuha

"The Way (*michi*) is pervasive and infinite, and free on all sides. Everything forms around the *michi* and is dependent on it. However, *michi* does not turn them away. It inspires you to have boundless imagination. The level of inspiration the *michi* affords is deep and ineffable, but the *michi* itself never dwells on that." (Suzuki Daisetz, *Toyo no Kokoro*, 1965)

There were hundreds of schools (*ryuha*) of kenjutsu and jujutsu throughout history. From each sprung more stream schools. In the age of the Ryukyu Kingdom, *todi* was handed down from father to son, or from master to disciple. After Okinawa became a prefecture of Japan, karate acquired a new status. The rise of the Butokukai also marked the beginning of the process in which a clear pedagogy and philosophy was implemented for karate as a Japanese budo. This in turn led to karate adopting the traditional Japanese martial art notions of *ryuha*. In 1930, Miyagi Chojun's student, Shinzato Jin'an, was asked what the name of his school was. It was a simple question, but one that had profound consequences.

1. 1930—Shinzato Jin'an Performs Karatejutsu at the Meiji Jingu Budo Dedication Embu

Shinzato Jin'an was born in Kume, Naha in 1901. After graduating from Naha Municipal Commercial School, he worked as a bank clerk and then as a teacher. In 1923 at the age of 21, he entered the tutelage of Miyagi, then became a police officer upon his mentor's recommendation.

Miyagi started teaching at the Okinawa Prefectural Police Academy in 1924. Before becoming Miyagi's student, Jin'an was not particularly strong and had little athletic experience. As a police officer he worked hard at karate and judo, and his poor physique was transformed by the rigorous training he underwent. He was recognised as one of the most talented students in the academy. His earnest character was evident in the way he trained, and in the humble way he taught younger students. He would ask his juniors to repeat a technique if they were good at it so that they could learn from each other.

He sometimes refused his teacher's advice when Miyagi directed him to move on to the next *kata*, saying, "I'll wait until I've mastered *Seisan*." It was precisely this attitude to refine his techniques to perfection, his enthusiasm for research, and his inquisitive mind that earned him the undying trust of Miyagi. Miyagi sent Jin'an to the prestigious Meiji Shrine Budo Embu in 1930 as his representative. It is likely that Miyagi considered Jin'an to be his successor. The following is an article from an Okinawa newspaper about the Meiji Shrine demonstration.

"The power of karate impresses crowd. Shinzato returns from the Meiji Shrine Budo Dedication Embu
… Naha police sergeant Shinzato Jin'an (30), who performed at the Meiji Shrine Budo Dedication Embu, returned to his post yesterday. On the second day of the

tournament, he appeared on stage wearing only a pair of shorts to perform his karate demonstration. The organiser initially requested that he perform fully clothed, but he was finally given permission after insisting that he had to do it unclothed to show the true essence of his art."

After his demonstration, Jin'an was asked by a martial artist from the mainland, "What school do you belong to?" Jin'an thought, "All the representatives were martial artists who belonged to established schools. If I could not provide an answer, they would assume that I was only an amateur."[1] It is said that Jin'an replied on the spur of the moment, "It's Hanko-ryu." On his return to Okinawa he reported back to Miyagi. He decided that, "It is necessary to have a name for our style in order for karate to develop as a Japanese budo, and to encourage exchanges with other budo *ryuha*." Perhaps drawing from *Kempo Taiyo Hakku* (The Eight Precepts of Combat) in the *Bubishi*,[2] he adopted the phrase *Ho Goju Donto* (inhaling and exhaling with strength and softness is the Way) as the basis for his school's new name. The "Eight Precepts of Combat" are:

1. The mind is one with heaven and earth[3]
2. The circulatory rhythm of the body is similar to the cycle of the sun and the moon
3. The way of inhaling and exhaling is hardness and softness
4. Act in accordance with time and change
5. Techniques will occur in the absence of conscious thought
6. The feet must advance and retreat, separate and meet
7. The eyes do not miss even the slightest change

8. The ears listen well in all eight directions

Miyagi is said to have named his style Goju-ryu after the third precept.

It was the *kata Sanchin* that Jin'an insisted be performed with the upper body exposed. This was the same *kata* that impressed Kano Jigoro and was also taught by Miyagi at Kyoto University in 1928. Going back even further, Kadekaru found that it was also probably performed by the middle school student Tamaki Kenta at the Butokuden in 1908. It was this powerful *kata* that "impressed the whole audience" and enabled "karate to earn the respect of mainland martial artists."[4]

Miyagi wrote in *Karatedo Gaisetsu* (1934), "In the 11th year of the Bunsei era (1828), there was a man who inherited the teachings of the Fujian White Crane lineage in China and it was this that was to become Goju-ryu Karatedo." *Sanchin* is the basic *kata* that Miyagi's teacher, Higaonna Kanryo, learned from his master, Ryu Ryu Ko (also called Ru Ru Ko), in Fuzhou, Fujian province during the Qing Dynasty. Although it is unclear on what exactly Miyagi based the Goju-ryu starting point as 1828 on, if we take this as the beginning, then the style would be a century old by the time Shinzato Jin'an was training. The connection between Ryu Ryu Ko, Higaonna Kanryo, Miyagi Chojun and Shinzato Jin'an lies in *Sanchin*. In the following section I will focus on *Sanchin* to highlight the transmission of techniques.

2. The Sanchin of Higaonna Kanryo

Just before Kanryo's death, Miyagi visited Fuzhou in Fujian Province, the place where his master studied. He wanted to trace the footsteps of Kanryo's teacher, Ryu Ryu Ko, and seek teachings from anybody affiliated with his family. Through an introduction by Nakamoto Eisho, Miyagi was able to meet with some of Master Ryu's old students. However, China was embroiled in a period of turmoil with the Xinhai Revolution and the transition from the Qing Dynasty to the Republic of China. As such, many of the old master's students had dispersed and could not be located. Miyagi showed the old disciples that he did meet his rendition of *Sanchin*. He probably also showed them other forms and confirmed the correct appellations. He stayed for two months and visited the temple site where the young Ryu Ryu Ko once trained. Nevertheless, due to the unfavourable timing of the trip, he was unable to fulfil his original intentions before returning to Japan.

Kanryo died a few months later. Miyagi visited Fuzhou again in July 1917 with Go Kenki (C: Wú Xián Guì).[5] They walked around Fuzhou in search of historical materials related to their martial art. Again, due to the political situation and anti-Japanese sentiment, they were unable to achieve the results they had hoped for.

① Kinjo Saburo's "Higaonna Sensei no Koto"

There is a valuable testimony describing Higaonna Kanryo's condition just before his death in an article by Kinjo Saburo titled "*Higaonna Sensei no Koto*" (*Gekkan Karatedo*, published by Kinjo Hiroshi).[6] Kinjo Saburo was the man who inspired

Funakoshi Gichin to come to Tokyo for the MOE's Exhibition of Sport and Physical Education.[7] Kinjo's article appears on pages 58–59 of the second issue of the monthly magazine *Gekkan Karatedo*.[8] It is a memoir of Kinjo's childhood days in Naha when he studied with Higaonna. As perhaps the first-ever description of Higaonna in mainland Japan, the text has been quoted many times.

"The Dojo: My impressions of Higaonna-sensei are hazy now as they are based on memories of when I was only 12 or 13. Even so, we were aware of Higaonna-sensei's fame. Fortunately, we lived near his dojo, so we sometimes went there to look in on him.

Higaonna-sensei's dojo was located on Tondo Miegusuku street. That is, across the Yamakawa Bridge from Nishi-Honmachi, or to the right after crossing the Saikai Bridge from Nishi-Shincho, opposite the *Okinawa Shimbunsha* newspaper office. I do not remember the size of the dojo exactly, but I think it was small and narrow. It was about 2.7 metres wide and around 5.4 metres long. It kind of resembled a so-called 'eel's burrow.'

There was an article about Itosu Anko in the inaugural issue of the *Gekkan Karatedo* magazine. It referred to him as Itosu Tanmei (Grandfather Itosu). The same honorific was also applied to Higaonna Kanryo, and he was called Higaonna Tanmei or Bushi Tanmei. The reason we went to Sensei's dojo was to watch him in all his glory doing karate. Nevertheless, we hardly saw him.

Instead, we mainly saw his students practising *Sanchin*. It was not often that we caught the master in the dojo. My faint recollection of him is that he was of medium height (to a child's eye, he looked rather feeble). Still, we were eager to see that old gentleman doing karate. Unfortunately, however, we never had the chance to see him in action.

Sanchin, as we all know, is a basic karate form in which the performer is naked and moves back and forth, exhaling and inhaling. With the teacher at your back, move back and forth, while he slaps your shoulders with both hands to adjust your posture with each step. I remember being amazed at how difficult karate must be when I saw them training by holding two-foot jars filled with sand with both arms extended horizontally as they moved back and forth."

This article is referring to Higaonna Kanryo's home dojo around 1912–13. The heavy jars that Kinjo mentions were used by Miyagi to train Jin'an, and are still used in Okinawa to this day (Photo 3–7).

両手指先で提げて持ち、三 一歩進み、肩を落とす。 左右に上げ、脇を締め止める。
戦の呼吸法で行う。

Photo 3-7 *Nigiri-game* jars filled with sand. (*Goju-ryu Karatedo*)

I should mention a little about Higaonna Kanryo's career. At the end of the section there is some information that is usually quoted as a standard part of any biography of Higaonna.

"Higaonna Kanryo was born in Naha City in 1852 and died in December 1915 at the age of 63. When he was 17 or 18, he travelled to Fujian in China to study the martial arts. He returned to Japan at the age of 35."

According to the family document *Shinsei-kafu* (*Shin* is the Chinese surname of Higaonna), the year of his birth is stated as 1853.[9] The month of his death was October, not December. There are several theories about his travels to China at the age of 17 or 18 and his return to Japan when he was 35. Some say he was 14 or 15 years old, and others claim he was 22 or 23. With regard to how long he spent in China, some sources suggest that it was for three years, others for more than ten years, and some say that he travelled there three times instead of one extended period of stay.

There is also a theory that there was another master named Maya Ara Kachi (meaning "like a cat") (Arakaki Seisho) before Ryu Ryu Ko. I have tried researching Ryu Ryu Ko through a number of channels, but to no avail.[10]

Reliable information about his life was provided by Miyagi An'ichi, who sat with Miyagi Chojun almost every night around 1952 or 53, and listened as he reminisced about the old days. This information was passed on to Higaonna Morio and then to me. Having been passed on orally, there are many discrepancies in the dates and in the veracity of various episodes talked about, but it is still more trustworthy than other sources.

② Higaonna Kanryo's Sanchin

Kanryo's training in Fuzhou is described in *Goju-ryu Karatedo-shi* as follows. "Auxiliary exercises and *Sanchin* continued every day. I practised *Sanchin* every single day for the first five years." At the end of the book there is a section titled "*Sanchin* in Detail".

> "For the first two weeks only practise footwork. From the second month, use the sand jars to strengthen the grip and footwork. From the third month, the student is taught breathing and the precise technical movements. The form consists of three steps forward, a turn then three steps forward, another turn, one step forward and one step back. The training method is not only three steps forward, but can also be done with five or ten steps forward, or from wall to wall in the dojo, turning and moving forward again, and so on for as long as one's strength lasts."[11]

This is a similar training method to that described by Kinjo Saburo. In *Karatedo Gaisetsu*, Miyagi wrote about the purpose of *Sanchin* and other *kata*: "*Sanchin*, *Tensho* and *Naifanchi* are all basic forms of karate. Their purpose is to develop a solid physique and nurture a martial spirit by holding the body in a prescribed posture, and harmonising breathing and physical power." *Naifanchi* was the basic *kata* performed in the Shuri-te system, and is the form in which Itosu Anko excelled. Gima Shinkin performed it in front of Kano Jigoro. These fundamental *kata* are said to integrate breathing and the tensing and relaxing of physical strength.

The techniques and breathing methods that Higaonna Kanryo learnt from his teacher Ryu Ryu Ko are somewhat different to the way modern Goju-ryu practitioners perform it.

> "In the *Sanchin* Master Kanryo learned from Master Ryu Ryu Ko, he was told to thrust out the hand quickly in time with the breathing... The thumb should be bent tightly and all four fingers extended together... The tips of the fingers should be as sharp as a spear... Breathe out with a 'whooshing' sound in time with the movement."

For some time after his return to Japan, Kanryo taught *Sanchin* as he had been taught in China. Naturally, Miyagi and his students were initially taught it this way. "Later on, Kanryo Sensei improved *Sanchin* according to local customs, the environment and the times. He changed the fast breathing to slow breathing, and the open-palm thrust to a clenched-fist thrust." Kanryo's improvements in *Sanchin* were passed on to Miyagi.

3. Miyagi Chojun's Sanchin
Miyagi was drafted into military service in December 1908. He was discharged from the army in November 1910. After returning to Okinawa, he invited Kanryo to his home and received special instruction from him.

"Each day we went over *Sanchin* dozens of times with training tools such as the *nigiri-game* jars, *chishi*, *ishisashi* and *makiwara*. We went over every detail of the *kata* movements repeatedly. The *kata* was practised very slowly to acquire the correct movements. After learning the *kata* actions the speed and intensity was increased. The next step was to place the soles of the feet firmly on the ground, and while breathing from the lower abdomen (*tanden*), I performed *uke* (blocks) with whip-like *muchimi*. The master taught it to be aware of where to apply the power in each movement, including blocks, strikes, thrusts, kicks, footwork, and posture. He taught me secret techniques as we de-constructed the *kata*. I was given daily homework to study how to apply the techniques."[12]

When Kanryo fell ill, Miyagi took him into his home to nurse him. He received further instruction including knowledge in the oral traditions. A few years after Kinjo Saburo's article, Higaonna Kanryo passed away in October 1915. Miyagi no longer had a teacher who would take him through his paces. He ruminated on Kanryo's teachings and explored karate theory in books and documents such as the Okinawan *Bubishi*.

"I beat myself with two sandbags to tighten my body. I did *Sanchin* neck-deep in the sea and forged a spirited *kiai* not to be defeated by the sound of the waves. I also decided to try *Sanchin* while fasting... In the mornings I did flexibility exercises and thrusts against a mosquito net. Before going to bed at night I extinguished candles with *shokken-tsuki* (punches)... I did respiratory exercises and shouts, and trained the sharpness of my eyes at the beach."

Miyagi married at the age of 20. By this time, he already had four daughters. His eldest son, Kei, was born in 1919. The following anecdote shows his commitment to furthering the martial arts he learned from Kanryo. He asked his wife to "Open and close the door many times in the morning so to see which was faster: the light coming into the room, or the sound of the door being opened." "When she woke me up, she poked me with a long thin bamboo stick as it was too dangerous to touch me with her hands." Apparently, she knew that he would reflexively lunge out with his hands and feet![13]

I was once advised rather cryptically by a senior member of the Miyazato dojo in Naha named Kanari that one should study *Sanchin* and *ninjutsu* in a seated position. Later, I heard from various sources that Miyagi always taught methods of self-protection that involved sensing danger. He urged his students to walk on the dark side of streets at night, to always look out for umbrellas and other possible weapons when people pass one by, to pay attention as to whether the person walking behind is a woman or a man, how much they weigh, whether they are right- or left-handed, and so on.

Detecting light and sound as the door was opened and closed was meant to sharpen the senses, and lashing out with hands and feet was to prepare the body and mind to react instantly even when asleep. I believe that these were direct teachings from Kanryo from his experience sailing across the East China Sea.[14]

Miyagi's research was both consolidation and further development of Kanryo's teachings. Miyagi's *Sanchin* employed slower breathing than Kanryo's, and he added "back and forth (*zenshin*) *Sanchin*" to "turning (*kaiten*) *Sanchin*". He invented the *Tensho kata* (rolling palms) from the form *Rokkishu* in the *Bubishi* that he acquired in Fuzhou.[15] Conferring with a doctor friend, he also devised the *Yobi-undo* preparatory exercises (Photo 3–8).

Chojun was responsible for the systematisation and rationalisation of Kanryo's Naha-te. It was in the Taisho era, after the death of Kanryo, that *Yobi-undo* and *Tensho* were devised by Miyagi. In 1932, after the naming of Goju-ryu, Chojun wrote a little booklet entitled *Goju-ryu Kempo*, which he presented to his student Senaha (Sakiyama) Tattoku, describing in detail the essentials of *Sanchin* techniques. It begins as follows:

> "In the first movement, the left upper limb should be opened as if the palm were turned, and the knuckle should be attached to the root of the first part of the phalanges joint (the joint between the phalanges and the palm bone)…"

It was a gift to his disciples, and is a valuable document in which Chojun writes about *Sanchin* at length for the first time. Nevertheless, it is very technical and the terminology is not used in modern anatomy, making it difficult to follow in places. In 1942, Chojun wrote the following:

> "*Heishu kata* [with closed hands] is the fundamental *kata*. Before entering the Way, you must build strength

in your body and train your mind. In Goju-ryu, this is achieved through *Sanchin*. To be precise, when you stand up, stomp your feet, ready your hands, tense your body and breathe, you are already in the fixed form of *Sanchin*—a beautiful state with an unshakable soul and a spirit that is unafraid of death. When you move from

四指を反らす
Bend the other toes

アキレス腱の伸張
Extend the Achilles tendons

手指関節の運動
Exercise of the hand joints
胸の前で押し合う
Push the hands together in front of the chest

横押しの準備
Prepare side pushing

横押し
Side pushing
体側屈（息を吐く）
Bend the body to side (Breathe out)

天突きの準備（片手）
Prepare Tentsuki (one hand)

波状の腕立て伏せ
Wavelike push-up

波状の腕立て伏せ
Wavelike push-up

波状の腕立て伏せ
Wavelike push-up
あごを出して前方をみる（息を吐く）
Push out the jaw and look ahead (Breathe out)

後ろ跳び
Ushiro-Tobi

後ろ跳びの着地
Landing after Ushiro-Tobi
（息を吐く）
(Breathe out)

膝当て
Hiza-Ate

膝当て
Hiza-Ate

Photo 3-8 *Yobi-undo* "preparatory exercises". (*Goju-ryu Karatedo*)

217

the static position to the dynamic position, it is called *happuren* (a movement in *Sanchin* where the feet make a ハ shape). Usually, however, the static and dynamic types are described together as *Sanchin*. The focal points for the mind's power are below the navel (*tanden*), back of the head, and the buttocks. To put it simply, pull the chin back, stand the back of the head up, lower the solar plexus to accumulate the power that is not put into the *tanden*, and tighten the buttocks. These three concentric forces are not separated but are inseparably related."

Sanchin is still the most important *kata* in Goju-ryu. The transmission of *Sanchin* lies at the core of Goju-ryu's tradition and lineage.

4. The Naming of Goju-ryu and the Emergence of Various Schools

① The Intention in Naming Goju-ryu

What was Miyagi Chojun's intention in naming his school Goju-ryu? In *Karatedo Gaisetsu*,[16] Chojun wrote the following:

"There are various theories about the Ryukyu schools of karatedo, but none of them have been proven. Most theories are based on nothing more than vague speculations. The most popular theory claims that karate derives from the two schools of Shorin-ryu and Shorei-ryu. The former was suitable for those with a larger-than-normal constitution and a big frame, and the latter for those of wispy stature and lesser strength."

Chojun clearly indicates that the Shorin-ryu and Shorei-ryu origin theory lacks credibility. It is true that *todi* traditions in Ryukyu and Okinawa were traditionally labelled as Shuri-te, Naha-te, Tomari-te after the regions in which they prospered, but not as schools in the sense of the word "*ryuha*". Shuri-te and Naha-te were, as I mentioned before, passed down from master to trusted disciple, and those who learned were instructed to absorb as much from the other traditions as possible to make them "practical". It is safe to say that there was no *ryuha* system like that seen in traditional Japanese martial arts.

When he became involved with the Butokukai, Chojun realised that having a name for his school would give it an identity. He was confident that what he had created in the Taisho period was sufficient to live up to being called an individual *ryuha*.

When Chojun named his school Goju-ryu, he said, "Only one time in ten could I match Kanryo-sensei's *Sanchin*... Difficulty knows no bounds." Keenly aware of the profound secrets of the martial arts, we can see Chojun's sense of mission to clarify the teachings he inherited and to convey to the world the wonderful Okinawan culture of karate.

He did not accept tuition fees from those he taught. He was happy devoting himself to training the bodies and minds of young men in the art of combat. Once a disciple entered his school, he was made to weed the garden, carry stones and generally take care of the master's needs. This way the new disciple could learn about human nature and develop his character through training. He did not tolerate irreverence but taught "humility and self-defence". This was Miyagi Chojun's unchanging guiding principle.

Following the designation of Goju-ryu, many other schools of karate arose—*ryuha* that were very different to the intentions and ideals espoused by Miyagi. Chibana Choshin's Shorin-ryu, Uechi Kambun's Pangai Noon-ryu (later Uechi-ryu), Otsuka Hironori's Wado-ryu, his junior Mabuni initially called his school Goju-ryu, but later changed his style to Shito-ryu. Each took responsibility for and pride in their own *ryuha*, and this is how the various schools of karatedo were born in Japan.

② From Butokukai Embu Demonstration Records

Records of demonstrations at the *Butokusai* mentioned in the previous section, especially those from 1941, contain some interesting information. Although Funakoshi did not condone his students calling themselves members of a school, they still participated under the name Shotokan-ryu. According to the program list of the 45th *Butokusai* Grand Embu Demonstration:

1. Shotokan-ryu—(Toyama: *Renshi* Shimizu Toshiyuki, Asahi, Sugai, Tatekawa, Takemori, Tamura)
2. Wado-ryu—(Tokyo: Eriguchi Eiichi; Kyoto: Ueno Jitsuo, Nakamura, Ikoma, Sonoda, Kato, Takada, *Renshi* Otsuka Hironori–*Renshi* Kihara Hidejiro, Otsuka–Hirakawa, Otsuka–Kozuma, Otsuka–Shimizu)
3. Kushin-ryu (空眞流)—(Osaka: Itokazu Yoshio–Sakihama Seijiro, Shirota)
4. Shito-ryu—(Osaka: *Renshi* Mabuni Kenwa, Kouda, Ieuma, Uechi, Yoneda, Hioka, Nishida–Takahashi,

Morimoto, Adachi, Murata, Ogata, Sakagami)

5. Wado-ryu—(Ohara–Kurosu, Koshikawa–Morimoto, Suzuki–Kikuchi, Nakashima–Tanaka, Takayasu–Yabuki, 13 pairs)

6. Ken'yu-ryu—(Tomoyori Ryusei, Watanabe Masaru, Koja, Higa Iwao, Higa Yoshinari, Sakihama, Nakamura, Kinjo)

7. Nippon Kempo Kuushu-jutsu—(*Renshi* Inagaki Gohei, Wada, Nozawa–Inagaki)

8. Goju-ryu—(Okinawa: Miyazato Koji, *Renshi* Higa Seko (Miyazato also demonstrated weapons)

9. Kushin-ryu (空心流)—(Osaka: *Kyoshi* Ueshima Sannosuke–*Renshi* Kinjo Kanemori, four in a row, Ueshima–Kinjo–Itokazu–Sakihama)

10. Shindo Jinen-ryu Kuushu-jutsu—(Tokyo: *Renshi* Sodeyama Hosaku, Sodeyama–Namiki, Namiki Chutaro, *Renshi* Inagaki Torakichi–Konishi Yasuhiro; Tokyo: *Kyoshi* Konishi Yasuhiro) [17]

Seven schools featured in the festival. As well as appearances by the founders such as Konishi Yasuhiro, Mabuni Kenwa, Otsuka Hironori and Ueshima Sannosuke, we also see Eriguchi Eiichi (who would become a leader of the JKF), and Higa Seko (a major figure in Okinawa Goju-ryu). There is also reference to Ken'yu-ryu, which became closely associated with Kansai University. Sakihama Seijiro of Jugo Jinen-ryu demonstrated under the banner of Kushin-ryu. Miyazato Koji from Goju-ryu is listed as demonstrating with *nunchaku* and the *kata Saifa*, but the *kanji* in the programme are difficult to decipher.

Summary—Ryuha and Students

In his article "The Dan System in Budo",[18] Nakabayashi Shinji once stated that the conditions for the establishment of a school were: first, the emergence of a genius fighter; second, his techniques must be at an advanced level; and third, because the techniques are advanced, there must be a system and course of instruction to pass on the knowledge.

Nakabayashi states, "For a school to become established, maintained and further developed, the founder needed to be a man of immense talent. When a brilliant disciple joined the founder, this ensured the continuation of the school." This was the relationship between Higaonna Kanryo and Miyagi Chojun. Kanryo was most certainly a genius.

Kanryo did not call his teachings Goju-ryu. In the history of Japanese karatedo he is regarded as *Naha-te Chuko no So*—the reviver of Naha-te. However, there is no doubt that he was a prodigious master of advanced technical ability, and it was he who nurtured the talented Miyagi. It is clear that Miyagi Chojun was the brilliant disciple of the genius. Goju-ryu represents the systematic organisation of techniques and methods that Chojun inherited from Kanryo.

In the early years of the Showa period, Chojun headed the karate department at the Okinawa Sports Association and was a member of the Okinawan branch of the Butokukai. Most recognised him as the leading figure in the Okinawan karate world. The naming of Goju-ryu was the culmination of his research. Chojun believed that by clarifying the characteristics of

Shuri-te, Naha-te and Tomari-te collectively as Okinawa karate, the streams would be able to cooperate and further enhance karatedo as an Okinawan asset. To this end, he continued his promotional activities by visiting Hawaii in 1934, Shanghai in 1936, and by teaching university students on the mainland. It was his hope that this would contribute to favourable perceptions and the rising status of karate as a budo recognisable for its great intrinsic value.

Of the seven schools mentioned above, four were destined to become the major schools on the mainland after the war. The path each *ryuha* took led to becoming associated with different universities. In the early post-war period, enterprising college students continued training in karate and advancing it through trial and error. The post-war history of karatedo was very much shaped by the labours of students.

Notes
(1) M.T., "*Goju-ryu ni tsuite* (2)", *Shin-Karatedo*, No. 6, June 25, 1969 (*Shin Karatedo* was a magazine dedicated to karate. I have been unable to confirm the identity of the author M.T.)
(2) *Bubishi* refers to a text transmitted in Okinawa, as opposed to another classic Chinese text on strategy and tactics of the same name compiled in the Ming Dynasty by Mao Yuanyi. In modern times it is referred to as "*Okinawa-Den Bubishi*" to avoid confusion. There are several different versions of the *Okinawa-Den Bubishi* due to discrepancies when copies were handwritten. Modern publications of the text include works by Otsuka Tadahiko, Tokashiki Iken and others.
(3) The first part of the phrase *jinshin* (人心 = human mind) is sometimes written with different *kanji* (人身) which means "human body". There are several theories as to its origin. It could mean, "The human body and mind are a small universe, and the two energies of yin and yang flow through the body. The essence of the martial arts is to find soft in hard, and hard in soft. Hands and feet coalesce to strike at openings in the opponent. We must use our eyes, ears and whole body to detect and respond to changes." This phrase is open to interpretation.

(4) Did Jin'an only perform *Sanchin*? The expression "letting his mollusc shell fists fly" suggests that he may have also performed *Seisan*. The same phrase was used when Motobu Choki featured in the magazine *King* for his famous fight with the boxer.

(5) Go Kenki (1886–1940) emigrated from Fuzhou in Fujian Province in the early Taisho era, and ran the Eiko Tea House in Naha. He was a businessman by day and taught the White Crane Fist system (Tsuru no Te) by night. He interacted with and influenced Miyagi, Mabuni and others. *Okinawa Karate Kobudo Jiten*, p. 429

(6) Kinjo Hiroshi authored *Karate Kara Karate E* (Nippon Budokan, 2011). He is not related to Kinjo Saburo.

(7) Kinjo Hiroshi, *Karate Kara Karate E* (p. 371) introduces him as a Professor at Tokyo Higher Normal School. His job was recorded in *Gekkan Karatedo* as an employee of the company Nippon Shoji.

(8) There was another magazine also called *Gekkan Karatedo* published by Fukushodo in the 1970s. The earlier *Gekkan Karatedo* was first published in 1956 and is a valuable source of information of the era before a match system was introduced into karate.

(9) In the *Shinsei-kafu*, a family history of the Higaonna clan, it says: "Tenth generation Kanryo was born on the 10th day of the 3rd month in the third year of Kaiei (1853)."

(10) Tokashiki Iken, Higaonna Morio, Kizaki Tomoharu and others have conducted research since the 1980s when reforms made it possible to obtain the cooperation of Fujian Province and Fuzhou City. Kinjo Akio developed his own hypothesis based on his own research before this. Tokashiki's theory was published in the *Okinawa Times* in a series of articles and caused quite a stir. Kinjo's other postulations on Ryu Ryu Ko are also very stimulating. I published my own theories on Higaonna's lineage in the journal *Karatedo Kenkyu*.

(11) Higaonna Morio, Miyagi An'ichi (supervisors), *Goju-ryu Karatedo-shi*, p. 166. Miyagi An'ichi was born in 1931 and became a disciple of Miyagi Chojun in 1948 at the age of 17. While receiving instruction from Chojun in the twilight years of his life until his death in 1953, An'ichi took care of his teacher's needs and engaged with him in nightly conversations about Kanryo, about Chojun's own life, and about the *Bubishi*. *Goju-ryu Karatedo-shi* is rich in valuable information and is considered to be the most reliable source for understanding both Kanryo and Chojun. There are still many things about their lives that need verification.

(12) A summary of page 35 in Higaonna Morio, Miyagi An'ichi (supervisors), *Goju-ryu Karatedo-shi*. This is how he instructed his trusted disciples. "This is the way it is done in the *kata*, but this is how to apply it for real."

(13) A family anecdote. Kojo Yasuko allowed me to touch a dent in her forehead. A friend of hers who was curious about karate practice once

peeked into the dojo and started to chuckle. Chojun opened the sliding screen and struck Yasuko on the forehead with the one-knuckled fist *Ippon-ken* (*Keiko-ken* in Goju-ryu). The mark remained on her forehead for the rest of her life. No wonder his wife was afraid to wake him up.

(14) Kanryo's wife could not wake him up with her hands because it was too dangerous to touch him. I wonder if these teachings were handed down by Kanryo as a way of protecting himself when he sailed across the East China Sea in a ship crewed by dangerous men.

(15) *Tensho*. Like *Sanchin*, this has a forward and backward movement from the *sanchin-dachi* stance, but it is a unique *kata* using internal and external rotations of the wrists. It is said that Miyagi performed this *kata* often in his later years.

(16) There are two editions of *Karatedo Gaisetsu*. The first was published 1934 and the other in 1936. The section introducing karate outside Okinawa prefecture was revised.

(17) Names connected with "—" probably means that they performed *Kumite*.

(18) Nakabayashi Shinji, *"Budo ni Okeru Menkyo Dan'i-sei"*, *Taiyo*, September 1980, Heibonsha. The late Nakabayashi's contribution to the understanding of budo theory cannot be overstated. His work is still considered the starting point for budo studies (Professor Sakai Toshinobu, University of Tsukuba website).

SECTION 4

College Students in the Kansai Region

1. Universities in Kansai (1)
—Kansai University and Kyoto Imperial University

In *Karatedo Gaisetsu*, Miyagi Chojun wrote, "A karatedo club in Osaka was established at Kansai University in May of 1930. Another club was established at the same university's vocational department in December of that year."

Karate at Kansai University started when Mabuni Kenwa came to Osaka. Kenwa's eldest son Ken'ei recollected, "When my father opened a dojo in Nishinari, a member of Kansai University's judo club called Sawayama Masaru, later the founder of Nippon Kempo, came to visit."

Regarding Sawayama's introduction to karate, Kaku Kozo wrote the following:

"Sawayama was suddenly taken with Okinawan karate. This, he thought, was the real deal. A first-class product. It was Mabuni Kenwa, an orthodox master of karate, who first showed it to him. Mabuni studied under Itosu Anko (Shuri-te) and Higaonna Kanryo (Naha-te) and was a key member of the first karate research group in Japan, the Okinawa Karate Kenkyu Kai (later the Karate Kenkyu Kai Club). He is still highly respected to this day, along with Funakoshi Gichin, Miyagi Chojun, Yabu Kentsu, and Hanashiro Chomo, all of whom brought karate to the mainland. Many people remember Mabuni as the founder of Shito-ryu."

Kaku states that the exact time of their fateful meeting is a mystery. Ken'ei confirms that Sawayama certainly paid Mabuni a visit and asked for instruction. Sawayama himself later wrote, "The founding of Nippon Kempo began with my search to learn fist techniques, which happened to be in decline in Japan at the time." He did not, however, mention his encounter with Mabuni. In *Karatedo Gaisetsu* where he discusses karate's situation outside Okinawa, Miyagi mentions Sawayama Masaru's name after writing about Mabuni Kenwa's contributions.

Miyagi states that the Kansai University Karate Kenkyu Kai was formed in 1930 when Sawayama proudly displayed the sign "Karate Kenkyu Kai" at the university on May 5, 1930. Kaku records this day as being on June 15, 1930. To add to the confusion, in September 2017, the General Assembly of the Japanese Academy of Budo was held at Kansai University. In his welcoming address, President Shibai Keiji introduced the university by saying that its karate club started in 1932. In *Kobo Jizai Goshin-jutsu Karate Kempo* there is a photograph of a karate course being taught by Miyagi Chojun at Kansai University in June 1932, showing Miyagi and Mabuni together (Photo 3–9). Could this be the basis for the 1932 date mentioned by Shibai? The workshop in question seems to have been conducted by Miyagi at the request of Mabuni.

In *Karate Kenkyu Dai 1-Shu* (first edition in 1934), there are scenes of students practising *Sanchin*, *yakusoku kumite*, and some with stone barbells on the rooftop (Photo 3–10). It can be assumed that these are the members of the Karate Kenkyu Kai which was led by Sawayama at the time. It is probable that karate was indeed being practised at Kansai University in 1932. However, Sawayama is known for departing from traditional methods of *kata* training, and sought a new kind of fighting with free use of the fists and feet. He said that he secretly refined new techniques in the precincts of the Tarumi Shrine.

The new style he created involved the formulation of competition rules, the use of protective gear, throwing techniques, and groundwork. He was looking to create a sporting form of karate. After graduating from Kansai University in 1932, Sawayama set up an organisation called "Dai-Nippon Kempo" and developed his own art which was to become known widely as "Nippon Kempo" after the war.

He was not the only one with these aspirations. Experimentation with protective gear started with Miki Nizaburo, a member of the Tokyo Imperial University's karate club. Miyagi and Mabuni followed later with their own trials. This took some time, and protective equipment did not immediately lead to competition. In short, the development of modern karate passed through several overlapping stages: affiliation with the Butokukai, the rise of the different schools, the development of teaching systems, and the change from "Chinese-hand" to "empty-hand". Then, there was a new generation of mainland practitioners who dared to test the traditional protocols.

Kansai University, June, Showa 7 (1932) on the occasion of Chojun Miyagi (seated in the front row 5th from left) teaching a seminar at the university. Seated to his immediate right is Kenwa Mabuni.

Photo 3-9 Kansai University in June, 1932. (*Karate Hassho-no-Chi Okinawa*)

Photo 3-10 Karate training at Kansai University.

In any case, the Kansai University Karatedo Club does not consider 1930 to be the year of its foundation. In *Yakushin*, the 60th anniversary commemorative booklet of the Kansai Student Karatedo Federation, Kansai University Karatedo Club states that it was actually founded in 1938, and that the first *Shihan* was Mabuni Kenwa. This is probably referring to when the university officially recognised the club.

Sawayama's creation of Nippon Kempo was inspired by the Ryukyu kempo karate which he initially learned from Mabuni. Ultimately, though, he chose a different path from that of karatedo. After the war, the club at Kansai University continued its activities under Mabuni. Later on, Tomoyori Ryuichiro (eldest son of Ken'yu-ryu's founder, Tomoyori Ryusei) took over, and Kansai University became the leading university for Ken'yu-ryu for many years.

The full title for Miyagi Chojun's *Karatedo Gaisetsu* is *Ryukyu Kempo Karatedo Enkaku Gaiyo* ("Outline of the History of Ryukyu Kempo Karatedo"). Sawayama utilised Nippon (Japan) in the name of his school instead of Ryukyu. Konishi Yasuhiro called his school Nippon Kempo Kuushu-jutsu in 1929. After the war, Konishi and others stopped including "Nippon" and "Kempo" and just referred to the name of their school. It is important to note that using designations such as Nippon (or Nihon) and *kempo* were common in the early days before the terms of karate and karatedo had been popularised.

What was the case at Kyoto Imperial University, the venue for Miyagi Chojun's workshop in 1928? This was the real start of efforts to spread karate in Kansai, but the inauguration of an actual karate club at Kyoto Imperial University would have to wait until 1938, ten years after Miyagi's first visit.

After graduating from Tokyo Imperial University, Ueno Jitsuro then came to Kyoto Imperial University and sowed the seeds for Wado-ryu karate. A book celebrating the 80th anniversary of Kyoto University's karate club contains the following passage.

"In April, after graduating from the Department of Oriental History in the Faculty of Letters at Tokyo Imperial University, Ueno Jitsuro matriculated at Kyoto Imperial University and immediately began taking a karate class with a group of like-minded students in the Botany Department.

In September of 1938, to make karate known throughout the university, the group moved to the Seibu Konai Dojo in the west of the campus (now known as Seibu Kodo). At the time, Azusawa Takeshi (the first to join the club), Takada Tetsuo, Seki Hiroshi, Kato Masahide and others also became members. The Kyoto Imperial University Karate Kai (predecessor of the Kyoto University Karatedo Club) was officially established, and Professor Koriba Kwan of the Faculty of Science's Department of Botany was appointed chairman. A commemorative towel (*tenugui*) was made with Professor Koriba's inscription "*Musho Futsu*" (no place is impassable) by the chairman of the association. We also welcomed Otsuka Hironori, *Soke* of Wado Ryu, as our first *Shihan*."

The Kyoto University Karatedo Club was affiliated with Wado-ryu until the end of the war. In 1955, when Master Otsuka was too busy to conduct the promotion examinations, Tani Chojiro, who lived in Kobe, was appointed as the university's second *Shihan*. Tani met Mabuni at Doshisha University (Kyoto) and later became *Soke* of Tani-ha Shito-ryu. Following Tani's death, the karate club remained an important constituent of the Shito-ryu Shukokai, which continues in Tani's footsteps to this day.

2. Universities in Kansai (2)
—Ritsumeikan University and Doshisha University

According to Yamaguchi Gogen, the karatedo club at Ritsumeikan University was established in 1931. Yamaguchi was a leader of Goju-ryu in Tokyo after the war and exerted considerable influence on the Japanese karatedo world. After the war, Goju-ryu was the only one of the "four main schools" that still existed both on the mainland and in Okinawa. A graduate of Ritsumeikan, Yamaguchi was the main advocate of this style on the mainland.

When he first me Miyagi Chojun, Yamaguchi had So Neichu and Ujita Shozo as his juniors. After the war, Yamaguchi established the Goju Kai and played a major role in the establishment of the Japan Karatedo Federation. So Neichu had a student named Oyama Masutatsu. After the war, Oyama founded an organisation called Kyokushin Kaikan, which is separate from the Japan Karatedo Federation, but is still very active in Japan and abroad.

Yamaguchi was the founder of Ritsumeikan's karate club and claims 1931 as its year of foundation. Miyagi's *Karatedo*

Gaisetsu, however, states that official date of the club's inauguration was December, 1935. The club today concurs with this date.. Perhaps the discrepancy is due to the lack of verifiable information on how Yamaguchi went about setting up the club and their activities during the early 1930s.

I discovered that the relationship between Ritsumeikan and Miyagi Chojun started when a student called Yogi Jitsuei enrolled at the university in 1934. Yogi was born in 1912 and became Miyagi's disciple when he entered Okinawa Prefectural Second Middle School. He also received instruction in karate at Miyagi's home. In a book published in celebration of Ritsumeikan University Karatedo Club's 60th anniversary, there is a section in which Yogi answers questions posed by his junior, Goto Muken, about his time at Ritsumeikan efforts in helping Yamaguchi with karate.

> "Goto: Please tell me about what it was like back in the day when the club was first launched and karate was written as Chinese-hand.
> Yogi: At that time, I had an opportunity to get to know Yamaguchi Gogen. He was a very active fellow in many ways back then.
> Goto: He was also the head of the Cheering Squad, wasn't he?
> Yogi: Yes, he was. I talked about Okinawan karate with him, and he decided to do that as well."

Yogi graduated and went on to work for the Osaka Prefectural Police. Kizaki Tomoharu (a Ritsumeikan alumnus who later led the Kansai Student Karate Federation) asked Yogi to teach him karate. He even spoke frankly about his opinion of Yamaguchi in the interview. Yamaguchi took over the leadership of the club when Yogi left, and he was in turn succeeded by So Neichu and Ujita Shozo (who is now the former mayor of Wakayama City).

Yamaguchi may have established a small informal gathering for karate in 1931, but it was not yet affiliated with the university's Athletic Association, so would not be considered an official club. Goju-ryu was bestowed on the group by Miyagi Chojun, who was in Okinawa at the time. This encounter with Miyagi's direct disciple Yogi was a fateful event for Yamaguchi, for Ritsumeikan, and indeed for the Japanese karate world.

Doshisha University's club was founded in 1937. It states in the publication marking the 80th anniversary of the club's foundation:

"Our club was started by Tanabe (captain), Shirai (vice-captain), and Saito (treasurer). *Shihan* was Miyagi Chojun, founder of Goju-ryu... In 1939, members of the Doshisha and Ritsumeikan clubs went to Okinawa to train with Miyagi-sensei for over two months... In 1942, Miyagi Chojun-sensei came to Kyoto for the last time, and spent three months at Ritsumeikan. After that, Mabuni Kenwa was asked by Miyagi-sensei to look after our club as the main instructor."

In the club's 60th anniversary publication, Fujimoto Hiroshi (former president of the alumni association) wrote "The members of the club trained in Goju-ryu karatedo under the guidance of Miyagi Chojun and Mabuni Kenwa. After the war, we studied theory and technique under Sakihama Seijiro-sensei (founder of Jugo Jinen-ryu) and Toma Shinko from the same style." It was in 1942 that responsibilities for the club were passed from Miyagi to Mabuni. Until 1942, the two universities of Ritsumeikan and Doshisha, located respectively to the north and east of the Imperial Palace in Kyoto, maintained a relationship of friendly rivalry. They trained together at the Gihokai Dojo.

Many of these students were destined to go to war. Ritsumeikan alumnus Kimura Konosuke, who became a reporter for the *Yomiuri Shimbun* newspaper after his military service, wrote the following:

"From February to November 1941, we rented a two-storey private house in Hyakumanben for a 'long training camp' (to be precise, it was simply communal living). Those there included So Neichu (senior), Ujita Shozo, Nakamura Taisuke, Kizaki Tomoharu, Katano Kinkichi, Kimura Konosuke…15 in total, plus 2 civilians including a cook were present. From the end of February through to March 1941, a week-long joint camp was held there by Ritsumeikan and Doshisha (40–50 students). Before each training, we ran to Kamigamo and then went for a dip in the Kamo River near Shimogamo while it was snowing. At the end of trainings, we swam in a canal near Ginkakuji at 5 o'clock."

3. The Foundations of Ritsumeikan University

To recap, Miyagi's first connection with Kyoto Imperial University brought him to the city in 1928, and from the first Butokuden Embu Demonstration (October 24, 1928) he became a frequent visitor to Kyoto. In 1928 *karatejutsu* was officially recognised as a Butokukai discipline, albeit as an auxiliary of judo. Miyagi Chojun, along with Konishi and Ueshima, were awarded the Butokukai title of *Kyoshi*. He also taught for an extended period in Hawaii from April 1934 to February of the following year. This was when Yogi enrolled at Ritsumeikan.

After Chojun's return to Japan in 1935, Yogi accompanied him to the demonstration at the Butokuden as his student, and was his partner in the *yakusoku kumite* performance. According to the *Okinawa Karate Kobudo Jiten*, Chojun performed *Sanchin* and *Seisan*. Yogi once told me that "Chojun-sensei was very fond of *Seisan*. He was guaranteed to do it at demonstrations."

At Ritsumeikan, Yamaguchi, who was three years Yogi's senior in age, led the group's organisational activities and managed to get it accepted as an official university club. After Yogi's graduation in 1937, Yamaguchi invited people with experience in other martial arts and disciplines, such as Okamura Mitsuyasu and So Neichu to join the club. This is how he built up membership. He rented Fukushima Seizaburo's (Butokukai *judoka*) Gihokai dojo near the Shinsengumi tomb in Mibu, and devised ways to improve training. The type of training back then was outlined in *Ichigeki*, Ritsumeikan's 60th anniversary publication. Suzusho Toshihiro, who matriculated in 1937, wrote as follows:

> "The term '*choppaa*' is probably Okinawan dialect.[1] The attacker is free to punch and kick at the opponent's vital points without making contact (*sundome jiyu kumite*)... The defender blocks and receives just as he would in a match with protective gear. This is why we always practise stopping within a few centimetres of the target. In the event of an accidental collision, the resolve not to follow through ensures that the impact is not serious."

Choppaa was the word used for *sundome jiyu kumite* (non-contact freestyle sparring) at Ritsumeikan. They used this experience to devastating effect when cross training with other universities. Suzusho was a student coach in 1939, and he wrote in detail about their training at the time.

> "Basic movements—1) *Seiken* (*shomen-uchi*), *yoko-uchi*, *yokomen-uchi*, *tonkachi-uchi*; 2) *Soto-geri*, *uchi-geri*, *mae-geri*, *yoko-geri*, *kin-keri*, *nidan-geri* (there was no *mawashi-geri* in the old days); 3) *Hiji-uchi* (*mae, yoko, shita, ue, ato-uchi*); 4) Frontal strike (*mae*) with recoil of the arm, *yoko-uchi*; 5) *Shuto, suihei-uchi, yokomen-uchi*; 6) *Ippon-ken, nihon-ken* (one or two-fingered thrust aiming at the eye, scooping up from below);[2] 7) *Hiza-uchi, atama-uchi* (strikes with the head, front and back); 8) Stances—*chokuritsu-dachi, heiko-dachi, sotohachiji-dachi, uchihachiji-dachi, nekoashi-dachi, shiko-dachi*... Kata—*Sanchin, Tensho, Saifa, Sanseru, Seiunchin, Kururunfa*, etc."

There are also references to training exchanges with other universities: "In 1939... I was invited to Sakai Ohama Beach in Osaka for a match between Kansai University and Kwansei Gakuin University."[3] Uchiage Kenzo, who enrolled at the university that year, wrote of the experience:

"Trainings were held at judo professor of the Butokukai Fukushima Seisaburo's Gihokai dojo in Kyoto, and on the university grounds. Practice lasted for about two hours, and consisted mainly of preparatory exercises, *kata*, *tegumi* (sparring), and *ishiage* (lifting barbells). Against the background of the times, there was a tendency to try and boost the morale of youth and ready them for battle at a moment's notice. The members of the karatedo club, too, were required to arrive early to practice with this thought in mind."

In another section, Uchiage writes,

"From around 1937–38, Ritsumeikan was the first to introduce *tegumi* (free *kumite*). Other universities followed suit.[4] In the early days of Japanese karatedo, exchange training was held between schools to improve the techniques in *tegumi*, and this developed into the grand championships we have today."

Today, more than 50% of the population aged 18 in Japan go to university. In the Meiji period (1868–1912), only 1% of the population enrolled at university. In the Taisho period (1912–1926), the rate increased to 2–5%. This shows why university students in pre-war Japan were considered the elite of Japanese society.[5] As such, students were afforded conscription deferrals. As a result of Japan's war with China and withdrawal from the League of Nations, the state of the world would soon dictate that students also be mobilised for war. Authorities tried to inspire youth to ready themselves in mind and body for the inevitable. Members of college karate clubs trained actively for this purpose.

It was an age when people learned martial arts to prepare themselves for the battlefield. This mood engulfed the entire country. In Kyoto, Ritsumeikan and Doshisha students were at the forefront of karate's development, and they put themselves through combined trainings to forge strong bodies and equip them with resolve to fulfil their duty to the nation.

Notes

(1) Yamaguchi Gogen also used the term "*choppaa*" (*Gekkan Karatedo*, June 2001). The origin of this term is still unknown.

(2) In the *Seisan kata*, the fingers are turned three times in front of the opponent as if to blind him. Taught by Yogi-sensei, I used this technique when I competed in the National Sports Meet (*Kokutai*).

(3) As it is described as a "*kempo* match", it was probably organised by Sawayama. The Kwansei Gakuin Karatedo Club was founded in 1948, and it is thought that the Kansai University vs. Kwansei Gakuin match at this stage was connected with Nippon Kempo.

(4) Page 108. So Neichu, who instructed Suzusho and Uchiage, led the *tegumi* and *ishiage* barbell training.

(5) University entrance rates for people aged 18: 1945-57 = 7-10%, 1963-5 = 12-13%, 1970 = 17-18% 1989 = 24.7%, 1995 = 32%, 2002 = 40%.

Koyama Essay 1

Kyoto Budo History—The Gihokai Dojo

Koyama Masashi

The Gihokai's dojo, where Ritsumeikan and Doshisha students practised starting from 1937, was built by Fukushima Seizaburo in October 1936, when he was 46 years old. It was located in the Sakyo ward of Kyoto City. The building was situated to the north of the Budo Vocational School where Fukushima worked as a professor, near the Eizan Electric Railway's Mototanaka Station.

The dojo was 80-*tatami* mats in size. It had a dining room, three other rooms, and an osteopathic clinic attached to it. Fukushima opened his dojo for children in the neighbourhood and it was a popular facility where everybody was welcome.

Fukushima is standing next to him in the last photo of Miyagi Chojun teaching on the mainland in 1942 (Photo 3-11). Yamaguchi and his group were practising nearby in Mibu. Kono, who had come from Doshisha, introduced Yamaguchi to Fukushima. The two men of Kyushu hit it off immediately (Fukushima was from Kumamoto and Yamaguchi from Kagoshima), and Ritsumeikan students were permitted thereafter to utilise the splendid Gihokai dojo for their trainings.

Fukushima built a dormitory called "Kyowajuku" next to Gihokai's dojo. He appointed So Neichu of Ritsumeikan's club as the head of the dorm. So Neichu originally came to Kyoto University from Korea because of his interest in Marxist ideals. He became disillusioned after the Takigawa Incident and decided to pursue another avenue of study. He found what he was looking for when he met Yamaguchi and Fukushima. So Neichu said of Fukushima, "The focus of the Gihokai was the formation of character, and chairman Fukushima's fairness and selflessness based on merit do not discriminate against ethnic groups. This made him a father figure to me."

Fukushima was once a devout follower of Japanese Imperial Army General Ishiwara Kanji, who often visited Kyoto. He became involved in the East Asia Alliance Movement advocated by Ishiwara. Regarding Ishiwara, So Neichu said the following:

> "When I first met him, he suddenly said that Korea should be an autonomous government. I was surprised, and thought it was strange for a soldier to say such a thing. I didn't believe him at first. Even so, I always went to Ishiwara's lectures. Even though he was eventually suppressed by the extreme right and the military, he never changed his opinion. That's why I trusted him in the end."

Ishiwara was indeed an interesting fellow. In 1931, at the age of 44, he was responsible for the Mukden Incident that took place in Manchuria in 1931. At the age of 48, he became Chief of Operations of the Imperial Japanese Army General Staff. In 1936, he was appointed Operations Officer of the Martial Law Headquarters for handling the February 26 Incident. In 1937, he became a Major General Vice Chief of Staff of the Kwantung Army. In 1938, he criticised General Tojo Hideki, commander-in-chief of the Kwantung Army, for his policy of colonial occupation and non-expansion in Manchuria.

Photo 3-11 Miyagi Chojun (centre of the second row). Taken in November, 1942. (*Ritsumeikan Daigaku Karatedo-bu Enkaku-shi*, p. 203)

An embarrassment to his superiors, he was dismissed from his post in December that year and transferred to a local Army base in Maizuru, on the coast near Kyoto. In August 1939, he was appointed commander

of the 16th Division in Fushimi, Kyoto. Eventually, however, due to his outspoken criticism of the Army and Tojo, he was forced into retirement. In April 1941, he became a professor at Ritsumeikan University and director of the Institute of National Defence Studies. He was forced to abdicate that post in September and returned to Yamagata at the age of 53. From the exchange of letters between Fukushima and So Neichu, it is clear that they were extremely fond of Ishiwara and his ideals.

Some great martial artists were affiliated with the Gihokai. Namely, Ushijima Tatsukuma, Kimura Masahiko, and Oyama Masutatsu.

Ushijima was Fukushima's junior from Kumamoto. Kimura was Ushijima's student, and the young Oyama, after he smuggled himself into Japan from Korea, was taken care of by So Neichu in the Kyowajuku dormitory. This is when he started karate. Some say that Kimura met Oyama at the Gihokai. Another theory is that So Neichu was a classmate of the famous wrestler Rikidozan's brother. It is possible that the great 1950s wrestling rivalry between Rikidozan and Kimura started here. Also, although not directly related to the Gihokai, it is said that the famous Japanese-American pro-wrestler Oki Shikina was in Hawaii when Miyagi Chojun visited in 1934, and that it was Oki who taught Rikidozan the "karate chop", his signature move.

In any case, in many ways the fighters who congregated at the Gihokai dojo in Kyoto shaped the history of Japanese karate, judo and professional wrestling during and after the war. Fukushima, Ishiwara, Ushijima, Kimura, Yamaguchi, So Neichu, Oyama, and Ritsumeikan's Ujita Shozo, Kizaki and Uchiage were just some of the greats who forged their skills in Kyoto.

SECTION 5

Ties Between Universities in East and West Japan

Successful development of karate *ryuha* on the mainland was largely due to students who belonged to university clubs. When the early initiates graduated and entered the workforce, many maintained their involvement in karate and supported their juniors in keeping it alive. Passing on the techniques and spirit of karate in the limited span of four years was no easy task. The transmission from master to pupil was always important in traditional karate, but in modern karate the transfer from seniors and juniors at universities became the vital connection for the continuation of its traditions. As war loomed, however, karate took on an even more important role for students.

1. Activities of Kanto Universities in the Early Days

According to an article written by Fukui Isao (then vice president of the Kanto Student Karatedo Federation) in Toyo University's 70th anniversary booklet, creation of college karate clubs at the beginning of the Showa era unfolded as follows:

1927—Toyo University (First *Shihan* Motobu Choki)
1930—Takushoku University (First *Shihan* Funakoshi Gichin)
1931— Waseda University (First *Shihan* Funakoshi Gichin)
1934— Tokyo University of Agriculture (First *Shihan* Otsuka Hironori)

1934—Hosei University (First *Shihan* Funakoshi Gichin)
1935—Ritsumeikan University (First *Shihan* Miyagi Chojun)
1936—Meiji University (First *Shihan* Otsuka Hironori)
1936—Rikkyo University (First *Shihan* Otsuka Hironori)

Other universities included: Tokyo University of Commerce, Showa Medical University, Showa Pharmaceutical University, Nippon Dental University, Akita Mining College, Yokohama Vocational School, First Higher School.

At the time of the founding of Toyo University's club, the *Shihan* was Motobu Choki. In the university's 70th anniversary booklet, it states that the second *Shihan* was Toyama Kanken, followed by Mabuni Kenwa. Since then, it became a Shito-ryu university despite being located in the Kanto region.

Yoshida Motoo, president of Takushoku University's Takkukai Alumni Association, wrote the following about the founding of the club at the university:

"In October 1930, at the suggestion of Takagi, who was then in his third-year in the technical department, the first 'Karate Club' was established and new members were invited to join. There were ten of us: very strong third-years Hioki and Murakami, and first-years Kugimiya, Suzuki and Okuda, myself and others... In those days there was no rational method for training as we know it today. Nine *makiwara* were set up beside the dojo, and every day we hit them a thousand times with each hand.

Our fists were covered with blood as the skin was torn off…"

According to the Waseda University's 50th anniversary booklet, an inauguration ceremony for the Waseda University Dai-ichi High School karate club was held on September 27, 1931. A congratulatory speech was delivered by president Ohama Nobumoto and the *Shihan* of the club, Funakoshi Gichin, and demonstrations were performed by both Keio and Takushoku students.

Tokyo University of Agriculture's (Nodai) club was founded at the same time as Hosei University's. Eriguchi Eiichi, an alumnus of Tokyo University, wrote an article for Nodai's 50th anniversary publication.

"In the early days of the school, from 1936 to 1938, Mr. Kihara Shujiro [of Nodai] used to come all the way from the Tokiwamatsu Campus in Shibuya to the Tokyo Imperial University's Yamagami Dojo in Hongo. He would train with us, and we were able to improve greatly thanks to his excellent teaching ability. He was a handsome man with an egg-shaped face, but once he put on his training gear and entered the dojo, he was light and agile, with body movements like that of a butterfly. He could toy with his opponent freely. At the last moment, he would unleash his aggression like a fierce tiger with his motto of 'One strike, one kill'. In essence, he was a karate man with an extremely hard character that seemed at odds with his normally gentle demeanour…

There is not a single person in the world who has been able to raise *kata* and *kumite* to the aesthetic beauty demonstrated by him. Kihara Shujiro's brilliant young life was extinguished on the Chinese front."

The founder of Meiji's club, Tanaka Tokuya, enrolled in Meiji University's preparatory course in 1935. In May that year he established the "Meiji University Preparatory Course Karate Kenkyu Kai". Tanaka had been a student of Funakoshi's after moving to Tokyo from Saga. He initially asked Funakoshi to be the teacher. However, due to various reasons this never came to pass so he asked Yabiku Moden, who was living in Sasazuka at the time, to be the instructor instead.[1]

Like Funakoshi, Yabiku had studied under Itosu Anko of Shuri-te, and he was skilled in the art of the staff and *sai*. Yabiku's name is also mentioned in Miki's *Kempo Gaisetsu*. After Yabiku, Otsuka became the university's *Shihan* from May 1937. (Author's note: That is why Fukui's aforementioned text is mistaken. It should refer to the Meiji club's founding as 1935 with the first *Shihan* being Yabiku Moden.)

2. Students Visit Okinawa

Miki Jisaburo, a student at Tokyo Imperial University, visited the Okinawan masters and later published his experiences in *Kempo Gaisetsu* (1930). As far as I can establish, there are only records of student visits to Okinawa in the pre-war years from Ritsumeikan, Doshisha, Keio, and Takushoku. If we add post-war visits before Okinawa's reversion to Japan, Waseda brings the total to five universities. These were sincere attempts to find out what karate really was, and what it should be.

① *Kempo Gaisetsu*

An interesting anecdote about Miki Jisaburo's visit was passed on to me by Miyagi Chojun's daughter.

> "I remember it very well. He came to Okinawa in mountain-climbing clothes because he thought it was a very steep place with lots of poisonous *habu* snakes slithering everywhere. He had his rucksack, leggings and a pilgrim's staff... I wondered why he dressed like this. He said he was afraid of getting bitten by snakes. When he arrived at the port, he said he was surprised to see it more crowded than he expected. He stayed in an old inn for two or three months to learn karate, and then he up and left...
>
> He had a plump face and was about the height of our Ken (Chojun's fourth son, about 165cm). I remember him very well. He came to our house and said he would do anything to help if he could stay. My father told him we had a lot of girls in our large family and didn't need any more help. He introduced him to one of his apprentices who ran an inn, and Miki stayed there. Trainings were very early in the morning, but he was always so enthusiastic. I still remember his name. Even though it was 50 years ago..."

Kempo Gaisetsu was the first book on karate written by a mainlander and was a landmark publication. Takada, who co-authored the book, later published *Karate Kempo* under the pseudonym Mutsu Mizuho (1933, University of Tokyo Karate Kenkyu Kai). Due to some friction between him and the university club when Takada decided to run for election to the Diet, his name all but disappeared from karate. Miki worked in the medical field as a radiographer but died in 1952.

② Ritsumeikan and Doshisha

Ten years after Miki's visit, five students from Ritsumeikan and Doshisha, who were students of Miyagi Chojun, also went to Okinawa to study. One of the students, Ujita Shozo (later mayor of Wakayama), wrote of the trip:

"In July 1939, when I was in my second year of preparatory studies, I went to Okinawa to visit Miyagi Chojun, the founder of Goju-ryu. The party consisted of five of my classmates, Nakamura Taisuke, Ioku Tetsuya, Taniguchi Yuzuru, Tanabe, the captain of Doshisha, and myself. In those days there were no flights to Okinawa, so we had to travel by boat. Okinawan manners, customs, everything I saw and heard seemed so foreign. The women were beautiful, and the trip still remains in my heart as one of the great memories of my youth. It is a great pity that four members of our group of five were killed in the war. I would like to take this opportunity to offer my sincere condolences to their families.

It was a very special experience for me to study directly with Miyagi Chojun and his apprentice Shinzato during our two-month stay in Naha. Mr. Miyagi was an incredibly strong, robust looking man, while Mr.

Shinzato was strong, but very smart in appearance. Moreover, Mr. Shinzato's movements were quick and soft, just like a cat.

I was surprised at how different Shinzato-sensei's techniques were from ours, even though we were from the same school. He told me that he had only studied Miyagi-sensei's secret techniques because he was so small in stature. The *kata* we learned back home were riddled with mistakes. He corrected them all during the two months we were there."

Ujita's junior colleague Uchiage Kenzo and others wanted to visit Okinawa in 1941 to receive guidance from Miyagi. However, they were not allowed to travel and had to abandon their plans.

③ Keio Gijuku University

The following episode was recorded in the 75th anniversary publication of Keio's karate club.

"In 1941, Meiji's club held a demonstration to commemorate the anniversary of its founding. Many people from Keio also attended. At the after party, it was agreed that for the future well-being of karatedo, some kind of organisation should be formed to unify the various schools. Differences between the schools could be kept as they are, but something was needed to promote more interaction between the schools and to make promotion examinations and the like more balanced. It was decided that Keio should be responsible

for the establishment of such an organisation."
To obtain permission, they first consulted with Funakoshi, who was quick to grant his approval. "Matsuzaki, Ogata and Mukoda visited Mabuni-sensei in Kyoto, and then they travelled to Okinawa to consult with masters Miyagi, Hanashiro, and others."

④ Takushoku University
In the July/August 1956 issue of Kinjo's *Gekkan Karatedo*, there is an article regarding the Takushoku expedition to Okinawa.

"In 1941, after completing their training camp, the seven members of Takushoku led by Fukui embarked on an expedition to Okinawa, the home of karate. This was the first such trip in the student karate world. In Okinawa, the group became acquainted with *Shihan* Miyagi, the successor of *Shihan* Funakoshi. He taught us many things."

⑤ Waseda After the War
In 1960, the Waseda University Karate Club, led by Oshima Tsutomu (an alumnus of the club), travelled to Okinawa. It had been separated from the mainland since the end of the war. The group consisted of coach Kamibayashi, captain Naito Takenobu, manager Kasao Kyoji, vice-captain Shirai Kiyoshi, and Honda Sadaharu. For 15 days they practised together with the University of the Ryukyus' karate club and at other dojos. Their trip was reported on daily in local newspapers and on television. Kasao, who is now active as a researcher of Chinese martial arts, wrote about this event in his book *Chugoku*

Bujutsu-shi Taikan (Historical View of Chinese Martial Arts). I had an opportunity to talk directly with Kasao about this trip to Okinawa and what he learned there. This turned out to be a starting point for my own research.

3. Exchange and Associations
① Student exchanges between Kanto and Kansai

In 1936, Keio, the First Higher School, Waseda, Tokyo University of Commerce (now Hitotsubashi University), Takushoku, and Hosei, all of which had been taught by Funakoshi, formed an organisation called the Dai-Nippon Gakusei Karatedo Renmei (Greater Japan Student Karatedo Federation). Through this, students under Funakoshi's tutelage came together to promote exchange. The following explanation can be found in Keio Karate Club's 75th anniversary publication:

> "In the past few years, exchange trainings with other schools have taken place, and there has been a shift from *kata* in favour of *kumite*. There was a tendency among some of the middle and lower ranks, who were not satisfied with the refined training of the master, to be attracted to the youthfulness and intensity of Gigo (Funakoshi's son). Students at Waseda, Takushoku and other universities started to worship Gigo and his methods. His harsh training was in complete contrast to *Shihan*'s, but it certainly attracted a lot of young people to karate."

Regarding the transition from *kata* to *kumite*, Nakayama Masatoshi (former chief instructor of the JKA and 1937 graduate of Takushoku University) wrote in the 50th anniversary book of Waseda's karate club about how *kumite* training was devised.

"The Waseda and Takushoku karate clubs were established almost at the same time... Both universities requested that Shimoda-sensei come to instruct as *Shihan*'s representative. He was very enthusiastic when teaching us... At the suggestion of *Shihan*, *gohon kumite* was introduced as our basic practice menu. The way he practised, with all his strength, his determination, arm against arm, was very different from the way O-Sensei practised, which was more centred on *kata*. This somewhat rough training was greatly appreciated by the members of both universities, who are known for their rebelliousness and toughness.

In order to overwhelm your opponent in *gohon kumite*, you have to train your fists on the *makiwara* and beat your arms against the *makiwara* to toughen them up and gain confidence in your *jodan-age uke* and *chudan-ude uke*. This is why we had to develop a 'strong friendship' with the *makiwara* every morning and evening...

The following year (1935), after consultation with Mr. Noguchi, Mr. Funakoshi Gigo, who was a medical technician at the Ministry of Health and Welfare, was invited to join the karate clubs of both schools from the new term. After that, training between the two schools became more intense in *gohon kumite* and *jiyu ippon kumite*.[2] This was due to Gigo's fierce temperament and strict training."

The promotion of exchange also led to violence. In the 75th anniversary booklet for Keio, the following passage explains how students interacted.

> "A third exchange training was held but there was little gained by both sides. Although a sense of rivalry could not be helped, the more we trained together the worse things got, and there was a tendency to neglect *kata* in favour of *kumite*... However, once it had started it could never be reversed as long as exchange trainings continued. Whether this could be called development of karate or not is a matter of opinion, but the reality is that it changed. However, it is also true that karate then was very different from the current system of competitive karate."

In the early days of karate, trial and error by students essentially wrote the history of the sport. In addition to this, there are records of heated exchange training sessions between Keio and Waseda in 1938 and 1940. These old rivalries exist to this day.

How did Otsuka Hironori's group, which would later become Wado-Ryu, form? According to the 50th anniversary of Wadokai commemorative book, in May 1938, the "Imperial University Karate Federation" was established, and the following year in May 1939, the "Kanto Student Karate Federation" was formed by nine schools including Tokyo Imperial University, Chuo University, Tokyo University of Agriculture, Rikkyo University, Meiji University, Jikei Medical College, Japan Dental College,

Nippon Medical School, and Yokohama College.

In Kansai, we have already mentioned Ueno Jitsuro, a member of the Tokyo Imperial University Karate Club who later entered Kyoto Imperial University and founded the karate club there. Ueno was instrumental in forming the Kansai Student Karatedo Federation while he was at Kyoto University.

Appointed officers were honorary advisor Miyagi Chojun, advisors Mabuni Kenwa, Yamaguchi Gogen, Otsuka Hironori, student committee chairman Ueno Jitsuro. Schools affiliated to the federation were Kyoto Imperial University, Ritsumeikan, Doshisha, and Doshisha Commercial. However, as this federation is not mentioned in the history of Ritsumeikan and other universities, it is speculated that there was little actual activity. Photo 3–12 shows Otsuka, Mabuni, Konishi, Ueshima, Yamaguchi, So Neichu and others gathering at the *Butokusai* on May 5, 1938. It is difficult to say if there was any kind of federation in motion at the time, but it is conceivable that they had made an agreement around this time.

In the following year, Yamaguchi Gogen, who had already been to Manchuria in 1939, returned to Japan with a delegation to participate in the East Asia Budo Tournament in Tokyo (Photo 3–13). There is no record of students from the Kanto region having participated in this demonstration, but in 1938 there was an exchange with Otsuka and others, so it is possible that universities in the east and west of Japan were starting to collaborate.

Photo 3-12 Karate masters gathered for the *Butokusai*. Second from the left in the front row is Otsuka, followed by Konishi, Ueshima, and Mabuni. Fourth from the left in the second row is Yamaguchi. To the back on the right is So Neichu. (Matsuzaki Horyu, *Jinsei wo Shobu Suru*)

In any case, in Tokyo, the Greater Japan Student Karatedo Federation under Funakoshi, and the Kanto Student Karatedo Federation under Otsuka co-existed. This should not be confused with student federations today. Although the names of the federations are similar, it is more appropriate to think of the pre-war versions as unions of the founders' students at Tokyo universities.

② Kanto Students and Ritsumeikan

In 1939, Kugimiya and Yoshida of Takushoku University visited Ritsumeikan after demonstrating at the Butokuden with Funakoshi and others. This was a training exchange between Shotokan and Goju-ryu.

Photo 3-13 East Asia Budo Delegation and students from Ritsumeikan University Karate Club. Yamaguchi Gogen is in the centre.

"At the end of the day, Kugimiya and I, accompanied by some of our club members, visited Ritsumeikan without an appointment. Ritsumeikan was the headquarters for Goju-ryu in the Kansai region. We immediately engaged in training together. We learned from the others but gained more and more confidence in our practice. Miyata's kicks were so powerful that the Ritsumeikan students were gob-smacked."[3]

In addition, Sato Yasoo of Meiji had the following to say regarding a joint training between Meiji, Ritsumeikan and some other institutions:

"In 1940, at the instigation of our second captain Takehara, our club decided to hold regular annual joint training sessions (*jiyu kumite*) with Ritsumeikan... Our ideal was always that students should be able to compete with each other in the art of karate in a relaxed manner, transcending differences between schools."

As mentioned above, Meiji University's Sato wrote that he had agreed to regular exchange trainings with Ritsumeikan in Kansai.[4] At Ritsumeikan, too, around this time Kimura Konosuke recorded in the 40th anniversary commemorative booklet, "It was around 1940 that Ujita-sensei began exchanges with Meiji and other universities in Tokyo... The expeditions of 1941 and 1942 were particularly successful." He also wrote, "In the summer of 1943, a group of about 10 members travelled to Tokyo and had trainings with Meiji, Keio, and Takushoku." This was facilitated by the demonstration at Butokuden in Kyoto, and the joint demonstration described in the next section.

4. Kanto-Kansai Joint Demonstration

From the mid-1920s through to the end of the Showa era, many university karate clubs were founded in both the Kanto and Kansai regions. Early students were trained by the founders of their *ryuha* of affiliation. While they followed their teachings, they also came up with their own ideas.

At first, exchanges took place between universities that belonged to the same *ryuha*. Then it developed into joint trainings regardless of affiliation. Students were stimulated by these exchanges and developed a strong sense of rivalry. This encouraged them to find ways of improving further. One of the most notable activities of the pre-war period were the gatherings of students from different regions and schools to hold *embukai* (demonstration meets). One such event was held to commemorate the official inauguration of Meiji University's club in 1941. Fukui Isao wrote of the proceedings.

"The number of colleges with karate clubs had been increasing. There was no competition system in those days, so there were few opportunities to get together with other schools. In 1941 an epochal event was held with the All Japan Student Karatedo Demonstration in commemoration of the Meiji club's foundation...

The venue was the Meiji University Memorial Hall, and 14 schools from the Kanto and Kansai regions participated. Major universities belonging to the so-called four major schools of Shotokan-ryu, Wado-ryu, Goju-ryu, and Shito-ryu were there in force. They competed and showed their skills in a friendly atmosphere. The gathering was noteworthy as it was one of the first student events to transcend the differences between schools."

Sato Yasoo of Meiji University writes,

"The first thing that needs mentioning in the history of the club over the past 40 years is that in April 1941, we were officially recognised as an Athletic Association entity. Under the leadership of captain Wada, as a commemorative event, a demonstration tournament was held the same year...

A national student karatedo demonstration tournament was held at the Meiji University Memorial Auditorium. Many famous schools from the Kanto and Kansai regions came to participate. This event was a momentous occasion in the history of student karatedo. The only regret is that Waseda University Karate Club objected to the name of the tournament, so we had to decline their participation."

Waseda's objection was probably due to the name of the tournament being the All Japan Student Karatedo Demonstration. This is somewhat different to the friction that arose later when the first All Japan University Championships was held in 1957, but differing opinions and objections are inevitable when something new is attempted.

In the Meiji University 40th anniversary special publication Sato Yasoo recollects:

"At the time, the karate world was filled with different styles, but there was little interaction. Student karate was in a similar position. There were only a few gatherings at major university *embu* tournaments. In 1940, our captain Takehara arranged for us to be involved in joint training (open demonstrations of *kata*, *kihon kumite*, and *jiyu kumite* by 30 to 40 pairs at a time) at Shotokan related universities. Since that year, we have regularly held exchange trainings (*jiyu kumite*) with Ritsumeikan. Unofficially, Horiguchi and I also visited the dojo at Keio. This kind of interaction was virtually unheard of then."

The schools that took part in the big All Japan Student Karatedo Demonstration Tournament were the Nippon Dental University, Tokyo Imperial University, Doshisha,

Rikkyo, Ritsumeikan, Waseda, Hosei, Kwansei Gakuin, Kansai University, Takushoku, Keio, Tokyo Nodai, and Jikei University. Present at the event were Funakoshi Gichin, Mabuni Kenwa, Konishi Yasuhiro, and karate clubs affiliated with Goju-ryu. It was an unprecedented gathering of karate instructors and their karate clubs. The Memorial Hall was filled to capacity, and the event was widely covered by the mass media.

At the beginning of the tournament programme, the words "Bow to the Emperor" and "Moment of silence for the spirits of the war dead" were included. These words indicate that the opening ceremony was a solemn occasion held on the eve of the outbreak of war. Each of the events in the programme was highly anticipated, including performances of top-level students and the founders themselves.

① What of the non-participation of Waseda University mentioned by Wada, the captain of Meiji University? The name of Hosokawa Ryuichiro (Waseda), a famous political commentator after the war, is listed in the programme in the weapons demonstration. As Waseda University refused to participate because of their objection to the name of the tournament, it is likely that Hosokawa did not attend.

② Participating schools according to the official programme, included Kwansei Gakuin University and Kansai University. Mabuni Kenwa, *Shihan* of both universities, was listed in the *tameshi-wari* display (board breaking), but oddly, no students from either university demonstrated in any of the divisions. One wonders if they were even at the event. The Kansai University club was founded in 1938, so it was possible that their members were at least present. The Kwansei Gakuin club, however, was founded in 1948. If they were there, it is possible that the members of the club at that time were students connected to Sawayama.

③ What was *shin kumite* that was mentioned in the programme? It is conceivable that it was *choppaa* style of Ritsumeikan's free *kumite* described in the previous section. The fact that it was held between students from the same clubs rather than opposing universities suggests that the competition did not escalate out of control.

This demonstration event was held on September 19, 1941, three months before the attack on Pearl Harbour. Many of those who took part in the event were destined for the front.

Notes

(1) In Meiji University Karate Club's 40th anniversary publication (1977), Tokuyama Shigetoshi wrote that this change was due to the sudden death of Yabiku. However, the *Okinawa Karate Kobudo Jiten* states that Yabiku Moden died in 1941, so it is difficult to confirm which is correct. In the encyclopaedia, the name of the club founded by Yabiku is stated as "Ryukyu Kobujutsu Kenkyu Kai".

(2) In *gohon kumite*, the attacker repeats the *jodan-tsuki* five times, and the receiver blocks with *jodan-uke* and counterattacks with a single strike at the end. Then the roles are reversed. This is basic *kumite* designed to learn distancing and timing, and blocking for *chudan-tsuki* and *chudan mae-geri*. In *jiyu ippon kumite*, the attacker chooses any of the following techniques: *jodan-* or *chudan- tsuki* or *keri*. The receiver responds with a counterattack.

(3) In "Takushoku Daigaku Karate-bu Monogatari Part 3" (p. 44), Yoshida stated that Funakoshi's demonstration was in 1940, but it was actually 1939.

(4) This regular tournament has continued to the present day, and may be the oldest university exchange for Kanto-Kansai universities.

CHAPTER 4

POSTWAR PERIOD

Wada Koji
Koyama Masashi
Kadekaru Toru

SECTION 1

Introduction
(Wada Koji)

1. The Development of Karatedo

After starting lessons at Keio Gijuku University, Funakoshi Gichin also began teaching at Tokyo Imperial University, Takushoku University, Waseda University, and Hosei University. Toyo University invited Motobu Choki as their head instructor. Kansai University appointed Mabuni Kenwa. Ritsumeikan invited Miyagi Chojun. Otsuka Hironori established karate clubs at Tokyo University of Agriculture, Meiji University, Rikkyo University, Jikei Medical University, Nippon Medical School, and many other institutions of higher education. In this way, karate became popular throughout the country, especially at university clubs.

The destructive power of karate was so well recognised in Okinawa, a famous saying dictates that no one is allowed to teach before making a "vow of non-violence" before one's master to a Shinto or Buddhist altar. Even if the goal was to spread karate on the mainland, it was not possible to teach it to just anyone. Fortunately, it was university students who first took an interest in karate, and they followed Funakoshi's teachings obediently. This set the foundation for its effective development and dissemination thereafter.

After Japan was defeated in 1945, GHQ issued a blanket ban on all budo. This put a stop to the practise of karate, kendo, judo and other martial arts. At that time, Ohama Nobumoto (later the president of Waseda University) negotiated with GHQ and the Ministry of Education on karate's behalf, and succeeded in gaining permission to resurrect karate as a "gentleman's sport" the following year.

Photo 4-1 Funakoshi Gichin introducing karate to an American officer at Keio University's Mita Dojo (Obata Isao is on the right side of the American. Takagi Fusajiro (left) and Murata Kazuo (right). (Courtesy of Mita Karate Kai)

The number of students learning karate swelled during the war years. Those lucky enough to return from war went back to their university karate dojos to train. At a time when supplies were extremely scarce, karate was a way for people to keep their bodies and minds active. They could practise anywhere without the need for equipment. Karate training in this era focused mainly on punching *makiwara* and *kumite*, but not so much on *kata*.

American and Allied military personnel who took an interest in karate asked members of the Keio, Takushoku and Waseda karate clubs to teach them. They showed their Japanese teachers respect, and after returning to their home countries they too became karate instructors, thereby contributing to its international dissemination.

2. Organisation

Karate spread mainly through universities, but the administration of karate based on specific styles (*ryuha*) began in 1949. The Japan Karate Association (Shotokan), the All Japan Karate Federation (Wado-ryu), and the Karatedo Goju-ryu Shinkokai (Goju-ryu) were all formed by the individual schools.

After the Second World War, some of Funakoshi's top disciples who had served in the military, including Kamata Hiroshi of Waseda, continued practising karate. Funakoshi's financial situation was difficult, so he called on his students to help him find a way to make a living. In 1948 he founded the Japan Karate Association (Nihon Karate Kyokai). Recommended by Keio graduate Ito Shuntaro, the first president of the Japan Karate Association was Diet member Saigo Kichinosuke. In addition to Kamata, the actual coaching was carried out by Obata Isao from Keio, and Nakayama Masatoshi from Takushoku. This was how the forerunner to the current JKA began its activities.

Ito Shuntaro looked after returned servicemen with karate experience who could not find work. A number of university karate club alumni, especially from Takushoku, were unemployed and slept on the first floor of the Ito Shoten company office. The building had sustained serious damage during air raids over Tokyo and times were tough for the demobbed *karateka*. Before long, Ito Shoten employees began to complain about this makeshift arrangement. Being one of the founders of the JKA, Ito decided to put them to work teaching karate. He rented a film warehouse in Yotsuya and converted it into a small dojo for them to instruct at.

After Funakoshi's death in 1957, Keio withdrew from the JKA and it became a group mainly run by Takushoku graduates. In 1958, when Nakayama Masatoshi became *Shihan* of the JKA, he refined teaching guidelines, reworked the basic stances, unified coaching methods, and introduced an instructor accreditation system. These measures to improve efficiency led to a gradual increase in the number of people who took up karate.

While college students of a particular *ryuha* were united even if their universities were different, they desired an organisation that would connect them with their counterparts in other *ryuha*. The All Japan Student Karate Federation was launched in 1950. Due to media reports of misconduct (violence) by some wayward karate students in 1955, the president of Waseda University, Ohama Nobumoto, was tasked by the Ministry of Education to clean up collegiate karate and improve its management. The result was the formation of the All Japan Student Karatedo Federation and holding of the 1st All Japan Student Karatedo Tournament in 1957.

At that time in Japan there were no joint *ryuha* organisations other than the student federation. In Europe, however, a degree of unity had been achieved through the activities of Japanese instructors who were sent there to teach. In 1963, the European Karate Federation was formed, and following their lead, in 1964, the year of the first Tokyo Olympics, the Japan Karatedo Federation (JKF) was launched. The JKF was registered as an incorporated foundation in 1969, and the first All Japan Karatedo Tournament was held at the Nippon Budokan to commemorate this.

In 1970, the World Union of Karatedo Organisations (WUKO) was formed and the 1st Karate World Championships were held in Japan on October 10 at the Nippon Budokan (teams), and October 13 at the Osaka Prefectural Gymnasium (individuals). Japan won both the team and individual competitions, but the level of other countries was not to be underestimated. Two years later in Paris, both the team and individual championships were lost by the Japanese.

Practitioners increased dramatically with the development of karate as a competitive sport. Karate clubs sprung up in companies, high schools, junior high schools, and primary schools. Competition events including regional and national tournaments were held at all levels.

3. Introducing a Match System

In the early days when karate was introduced as a method of self-defence, training mainly consisted of repeating basic techniques, *kata*, and *yakusoku kumite*. There were no competitive bouts, even in intercollegiate joint trainings. It is human nature, however, to want to establish superiority in contests of strength. Without proper judging protocols in place to decide the outcome of bouts, joint training was becoming an excuse for competitive expression. Some practitioners started wearing protective gear to engage in matches. Others experimented with a system of match regulations that prohibited making contact to enable competitive bouts without the risk of injury.

Tokyo Imperial University was the first to try it out. In 1929, Miki Jisaburo and Takada Mizuho published rules in a booklet titled "Todai-style Karate Kempo Matches". Competitors wore kendo armour to allow full contact strikes, and bouts were adjudicated by a referee. Mabuni, who was also trying to devise protective equipment, came to Tokyo and helped organise competitions. This method did not spread, however, because the armour proved to be too restrictive. It also encouraged bad posture due to an obsession with trying to hit the opponent quickly. Funakoshi was opposed to the whole idea from the outset, and resigned from Tokyo Imperial University as a result. He was replaced as *Shihan* by Otsuka Hironori—a proponent of *kumite*, and the Tokyo Imperial University Karate Club henceforth changed to Wado-ryu.

Rules for stopping strikes before making contact with a vital point (*sundome*) were also pondered, but many were opposed, thinking that the idea was impractical. Nevertheless, if karate was to be promoted successfully, it was necessary to establish a coordinated system for matches based on a standard set of rules.

According to the website of the All Japan Student Karatedo Federation, a league match was held in October 1955 at Meiji University's karate dojo by 10 representatives from each of Takushoku, Keio, and Meiji. The bouts were conducted under what were called the "Takkukai Tournament Rules". Members from karate clubs at other universities attended the tournament, and it was shown that with the right regulations in place, karate could indeed be contested as a competitive sport.

Three years before this tournament, in 1952, Waseda's captain Ohshima Tsutomu (now head of the SKA in the USA), accompanied by Komori Shoji and others, visited Keio to propose a match arrangement. They suggested having *Shushin* (referee) and *Fukushin* (judges) in each corner of the court to confirm techniques and ensure safety. The proposal was accepted by the Keio captain, Yamamoto Ichiro. He then requested Takushoku alumni Nakayama Ma-

Photo 4-2 Ohshima Tsutomu.
(*Gekkan Budo*, April, 2003)

satoshi and Fukui Isao to serve as referees. It is recorded in Keio's 75th anniversary commemoration book that this was the first properly adjudicated karate match in history. After that, refereeing skills improved through trial and error, and a league competition was set up between Takushoku, Keio, and Meiji. The rules adopted at this time became the official regulations for the All Japan Student Karatedo Championship held in 1957 (This was when the All Japan Student Karate Federation was changed in name to All Japan Student Karate-do Federation.) These guidelines form the basis of the current JKF and WKF rules today. It is thus important to remember that this constituted the starting point for the development of competitive karatedo as we know it.

Waseda students formulated the blueprint for the current match regulations. The president of Waseda and the head of its karate club, Ohama Nobumoto, advocated for introducing a competitive face to karate. Nevertheless, other Waseda stakeholders were sympathetic to Funakoshi's concerns that the very essence of karate could be compromised should competitive karate become the norm. For a long time, Waseda did not participate in the All Japan Student Karatedo Federation tournaments, or the league matches between Takushoku, Keio and Meiji. Waseda alumni led by Hironishi Motonobu remained vehemently against the initiative.

In those days, matches were two minutes in duration, and the first to score one full point (*ippon*) was the winner. The only scores were *waza-ari* or *ippon*, as is still the case in the Japan Karate Association. There were only two types of penalties—

hansoku chui (foul warning) and *hansoku* (foul)—if a thrust or kick made contact. Stepping out of bounds or avoiding confrontation was not penalised. Matches tended to be tense affairs as a single strike could decide the outcome. Even the slightest careless move could end in defeat.

As no protective gear was worn, tension between the fighters attacking with their bare hands was intense. Still, from a spectator's perspective, there was little movement, and it was not particularly interesting to watch. Karate prizes victory with a single blow, so popular techniques to win matches included *oi-tsuki* or *gyaku-tsuki*, and *chudan-maegeri*. *Mawashi-geri* (roundhouse kick) and kicks to the upper body were not used very often because they resulted in an unbalanced posture during execution. The referees did not reward *kizami-tsuki* (jab) because the technique was not deemed to be strong enough. The techniques *ura-mawashi-geri* and *sasori-geri* did not even exist then.

The current system varies between tournaments, but most matches are decided by the first competitor to accumulate 6-points, or to reach a 6 to 8-point margin. Even if a competitor is down by a few points, he or she can still close the gap by executing their best techniques, making it more interesting for spectators. The use of gloves and head protectors has reduced the chance of injury. On the other hand, the equipment has also led to a decline in ability to defend against and control offensive techniques. There also seems to be more fouls committed now than in the early days.

In the past, tournaments were held in venues with wooden floorboards, or *tatami* mats adorned with canvas covers secured at each corner of the match area. The high frequency of sprained ankles and other injuries facilitated the advancement of safer mats. With cooperation from the Sports Mechanics Research Institute at Tsukuba University, Japan Oil Seal Industries created a new type of mat in 1987 and provided 200 free of charge to the Kanto Student Karatedo Federation to try out. These are still used today to provide a safe arena. As competitive karate became more popular, facilities and equipment improved at a remarkable rate.

Wada Essay 4

Mita Karate Kai Thursday Club —Funakoshi *Shihan*'s Kata

Wada Koji

Founded on October 15, 1924, Keio has the oldest college karate club in mainland Japan. The club was originally instructed by Funakoshi Gichin. Mabuni Kenwa later taught Keio members *Seienchin*. It was well-known in the old days that if you wanted to know anything about *kata*, you just needed to ask a Keio student. Nakayama Masatoshi (former Japan Karate Association president) used to visit the Keio club to check technical details.

Eventually a system for *kumite* competition was established. I was able to win the All Japan Student Individual Tournament twice in a row in 1970 and 1971, and came first in the World Championships. Keio student Maehara Hiroshi made it to the semi-finals of the All Japan Student Individual Tournament in 1972. He also won the East Japan University Championship Team Event in 1974 (captained by Matsumoto Manabu). With these successes, Keio club members became ever more keen on *kumite* over *kata*.

Akashi Akira (graduated 1932) and Nakamura Sadao (1935) sat on a promotion committee at Keio in 1977. Seeing the sad state of the *kata* performed by candidates, they felt it necessary to ensure the preservation of correct *kata*. To this end, they convened a special training session at the Mita Karate Kai (Keio alumni group). The first training session was held on April 1, 1977, at the karate dojo in the Faculty of Medicine. The participants were Fujita Takemasa (1934), Hata Fujiki (1934) and Noguchi Tetsuro (1940), all of whom had received direct instruction from Funakoshi. Other graduates were encouraged to join and help save the integrity of kata.

Photo 4-3 Commemorative photo at the exchange demonstration (Mr. Iwamoto is on the left in the middle of the front row. At the right end of the front row is Kadekaru Toru, co-author of this book. The seventh person from the left in the back row is Wada Koji. (Courtesy of Mita Karate Kai)

Initially held on the first and third Saturdays of the month, the *kata* session became mostly a weekly affair from 1979. From 1980 it was held every Thursday. In 1982, the official name of the group was changed to "Mokuyo Kai" (Thursday Club). By continuing to practise all 33 *kata* traditionally studied at Keio University, the group strives to preserve the essence and form of the *kata*.

Forty-one years have passed since its foundation, and over 2000 trainings have been held over the years. There are usually more than 20 participants each time. After practice, we drink beer and talk about karate for about an hour. There are now only two people left who were taught directly by Funakoshi *Shihan*: Iwamoto Akiyoshi (1951) and Mashimo Kin'ichi (1955). Considering that most people tend to stop karate practice after graduation, the importance of these activities to pass on correct *kata* cannot be overstated. As an active member, I am proud to say that we as a group truly cherish "lifelong karate".

When the magazine *Gekkan Karatedo* published a special feature article about our activities, it caused quite a reaction in Okinawa. On December 21, 2010, Takamiyagi Shigeru brought a group of

Photo 4-4 At the opening ceremony of the Okinawa Karate Kaikan (2017). The author is fifth from the right, Mashimo is seventh, Iwamoto is ninth. Nagura is sixth from the left. (Courtesy of Mita Karate Kai)

masters representing Uechi-ryu, Shohei-ryu, Shorin-ryu, and Goju-ryu from Okinawa to Tokyo. We all trained together at the Mokuyo Kai. A demonstration followed at Keio's judo dojo in Mita. About 40 people from Keio and 20 from Okinawa attended the gathering. At the following reception, a lively exchange of opinions ensued about the karate that Funakoshi introduced to the mainland, and the methods that have been handed down over the generations in Okinawa.

The relationship between the various styles of karate in Okinawa has not always been amicable, but they came together to visit our Mokuyo Kai. The event helped strengthen bonds between Okinawa and the mainland, and also served to unite the karate communities in Okinawa. In March 2017, the Governor of Okinawa prefecture invited 16 Keio alumni to participate in the opening ceremony of the Okinawa Karate Kaikan, which was built with government support to promote Okinawa and its martial arts to the world.

Other people from all walks of life have visited the Mokuyo Kai. Mr. B, who studied karate in Spain, wanted to see the Meishojuku, where Funakoshi *Shihan had* once lived. He also wanted to visit the site where the Shotokan Dojo was before it was destroyed by fire in the Second World War. Nagura Toshihisa (WKF secretary general) together with the president of the Mita Karate Kai, took him to where the sites were once located.

They met an old lady who lived near the Shotokan Dojo. She was able to point out where the buildings were, and the kind of training that was held there. Without this Spanish fellow's request, we may have never learned where the Meishojuku and Shotokan once stood. Learning from others in this way is precisely the kind of education advocated by Fukuzawa Yukichi, the founder of Keio. Mr. S, a Frenchman, worked as a journalist for a karate magazine. He became acquainted with members of the Mokuyo Kai during his coverage of the Shoto Festival held every year on April 29 at the Engakuji Temple in Kamakura. He also began attending our trainings. He produced a DVD of *kata* performed by members of the Mokuyo Kai and sold it as the standard for promotion and Dan examinations conducted in France. Impressed by the way many elderly practitioners continued on their lifelong karate path, he went and got "Mita Karate Kai" and "Mokuyo Kai" tattooed on his arm! Keio alumni have no such tattoos. It opened my eyes to various cultural differences between countries.

Recently, a girl came from France on exchange to Keio Girls' High School for nine months in 2018–19. Having studied International Shotokan in France, she trained hard in the high school club, and practised diligently every Thursday at the Mokuyo Kai. She learned Keio's traditional *Suparinpei* form, and the Mita Karate Kai awarded her *shodan* on her return to France.

Until recently, Suga Masayuki (1942) took part in the various events held throughout the year by the Mokuyo Kai. Now that he has passed away, our oldest member is Iwamoto Akiyoshi. He is 90 years of age. Our younger members include university students and their coaches. We also welcome alumni from other universities. For example, we have people from Meiji Pharmaceutical University who were trained by Obata Isao, *Shihan* of Keio's karate club, as well as former students from Showa Women's University, and even those who have never studied karate before.

Specifically, we practise 31 *kata* out of 33 (no *bo kata*). We cannot do all the *kata* each session and choose one each month to do thoroughly each week. Practising this way takes around three years to complete a cycle. That means we relearn each *kata* intensively every three years. In order to take the Dan promotion test of the JKF, I practise the designated (*shitei*) *kata* of Shotokan with a mind to slight differences between them and the older forms. Although the Mokuyo Kai is only a small group of like-minded people, there are several high-ranking members, including three 7th Dan, six 6th Dan, and three 5th Dan participants, and one 8th Dan.

Since 2015, on the fourth week of every month we train by checking a photo book, *Ippon Kumite*, left by Ito Shuntaro (graduated 1940). He was a legendary figure in university karate. In this way, while the focus is to pass on the *kata* taught by Funakoshi *Shihan* correctly, we do not deny the importance of competitive karate. We just enjoy exploring techniques and practising together as a lifelong pursuit with men and women of all ages.

SECTION 2

International Diffusion: Technical Changes Through Kumite

(Wada Koji)

1. Changes in Waza Due to Kumite Competition

From here, I will illustrate how karate has changed due to the competition system. Keio won for the first time at the 8th Kanto University Championships held in 1965 by defeating Takushoku in the quarter-final, Toyo University in the semi-final, and Tokyo University of Marine Science and Technology in the final.

There were nearly 20 fourth-year students in the club, but none of them had any karate experience in high school. The captain of the team, Maruoka Katsuhiko, had already attained the rank of *shodan*, but he only started karate after entering university. There was only one other black belt, and the overall strength of the team was rather low compared to previous years. Special training was conducted under the guidance of head coach Murata Kazuo and Mashimo Kin'ichi. They trained students to perfect the technique *kizami-tsuki* (jab punch), which hitherto had not been favoured by referees. At the time, only *oi-tsuki* (lunge punch) and *gyaku-tsuki* (reverse) punches were usually awarded.

The Keio team managed to perform *kizami-tsuki* with speed and power never seen before, so the referees were compelled to award points. Our opponents, on the other hand, had difficulty dealing with such a simple technique which seemed to come out of nowhere. The basic principle of self-defence is to deal with an opponent by using techniques that cannot be easily anticipated. With the introduction of the match system, techniques seen in matches were starting to become predictable, so this created quite a stir.

After this tournament *kizami-tsuki* became popular in other schools, and is now a common *waza* used in *kumite* matches. In a sense, this event changed the way karate was practised thereafter. In the following years, various competitors started to score points with techniques that were rarely if ever seen in the past, and these also became popular among schools. In terms of encouraging openness, this is one of the good aspects of "competitive karate" compared to the secretive or exclusive

Photo 4-5 Group photo at the match venue (Maruoka is on the left in the front row, Nagura Toshihisa (current WKF Secretary General, who was a first-year university student at the time) is to his right in the second row). (Courtesy of Mita Karate Kai)

kind passed down from one generation to the next. Anyone with the ability to execute a given technique could do so. Nothing could be patented by an individual or a school.

Also, in karate as a form of self-defence, kicking to the upper body (*jodan-geri*) was not common as it is a risky technique to attempt. If safety is ensured by the rules, however, you can unleash techniques without having to worry about the consequences should the attack go awry. As it is prohibited to grab and throw in karate matches, and as *jodan-geri* is worth three times the points of a standard *tsuki* punch, it is only natural that competitors prefer to attempt it more now.

As a side note, Maruoka (Photo 4–5) was a gymnast in high school and possessed excellent athletic ability. His speed for thrusting and kicking was sublime, and his performance of *Hangetsu* during the lunch break of the All Japan Student Championships that year was spectacular. At that time there were no *kata* matches, so demonstrations were held during breaks. His punches were sharp and powerful. The height of his hips did not change in the slightest when he let fly with *mae-geri*, and the speed of his kicks made his leg look as if it was extending an extra 10 cm from the knee. It was the only time I have ever heard a loud gasp of astonishment from the audience at the Nippon Budokan during a demonstration. Maruoka passed away in 1997. People in the karate world still talk about his *kata* performance more than five decades later, which is testament to his greatness.

2. Steps Towards Internationalisation

A succession of karate instructors came from Okinawa to the mainland following Funakoshi's efforts to popularise karate starting from 1922. After the end of the war, karate spread throughout Japan mainly among students and also caught the attention of Allied military personnel. Karate lessons commenced at the Kodokan for US Air Force physical education instructors in 1950 (Photo 4-6). Their instructors were Obata Isao (Keio), Kamata Toshio (Waseda University), and Nishiyama Hidetaka (Takushoku University)—all members of the Japan Karate Association at the time.

In 1953, at the invitation of the US Air Force, these young instructors travelled to various bases in the USA, including some in Hawaii, where they taught servicemen for about three months. They were even transported to each base in the US Secretary of the Air Force's private aircraft.

Photo 4-6 Karate instruction by Funakoshi Gichin at the Kodokan. (Courtesy of Mita Karate Kai)

College students also frequented bases in Japan to demonstrate *kata*, *kumite* and self-defence to American military personnel. These included Keio's Iwamoto Akiyoshi and Mashimo Kin'ichi, Waseda's Egami Shigeru and Ohshima Tsutomu, and Takushoku's Nishiyama Hidetaka, Kanazawa Hirokazu and Enoeda Keinosuke. In addition to *kata* and *kumite*, they also engaged in multi-disciplinary matches against American soldiers and visited bases with famous Japanese celebrities such as Misora Hibari and Eri Chiemi. Some of the military personnel who participated in these sessions continued to practise karate after returning home.

Obata Isao and other students instructed at military bases until 1963. My brother, who is four years older than me, also went to the Zama base as a high school student and had the opportunity to do *kumite* with Americans. Whenever personnel of the Occupation Forces changed, Obata received new requests to come and introduce karate.

In the same way that Funakoshi left Okinawa for the mainland, Japanese instructors were also leaving Japan to take karate to the world. After graduating from Waseda University in 1953, Ohshima went to the United States in 1955 to study at the University of Southern California Graduate School. In 1956, he founded the first overseas karate organisation, the Southern California Karate Club. In 1957 he launched the first overseas university karate club at the California Institute of Technology. After that, he established Shotokan in France in 1964, and in more than ten countries in Europe, America, Asia, Africa, and South America. Ohshima translated Funakoshi's book *Karate-*

do Kyohan into English.

Kase Yasuaki from Senshu University, and Kanazawa Hirokazu and Enoeda Keinosuke from Takushoku were dispatched to Europe by the Japan Karate Association. Later in 1956, the JKA started a system for nurturing professional instructors. Those who completed their training were sent abroad to teach. Kanazawa Hirokazu focused on Europe, but Nishiyama Hidetaka (who was also from Takushoku) was asked by Ohshima in 1965 to take charge of the US organisation he had established for a year while he toured the world. Nishiyama ended up heading the organisation himself, which led to a bitter feud between the two.

As Nishiyama's organisation grew, he set up the International Amateur Karate Federation (IAKF) separate from the World Union of Karatedo Organisations (WUKO) and applied to the International Olympic Committee to be recognised as the representative body for karate in the world. Consequently, the WUKO and the IAKF applications for IOC affiliation overlapped, leading the IOC to determine that karate was not unified. This prevented it from being contested at the Olympic Games until now. In 1980, the WUKO became the only karate organisation recognised by the IOC, and the IAKF was dissolved.

In Wado-Ryu's case, senior practitioners under Otsuka Hironori—Suzuki Tatsuo and Kono Teruo—visited Europe to disseminate their style from the 1960s. Presently, Goju-ryu and Shito-ryu are also making efforts internationally, but

Shotokan, the first of the schools to establish a worldwide base, is undeniably the mainstream of karate found outside Japan.

3. Overseas Expeditions by Students

The All Japan Student Karatedo Federation wanted to create a tournament system and to take competitive karate to the world. In November 1966, Takushoku alumnus Fukui Isao led a delegation of five students with Keio's Takagi Fusajiro as assistant. They visited Nishiyama Hidetaka, who was teaching karate in Los Angeles, and engineered the Japan-US Student Karate Friendship Tournament. This was the first international karate tournament in which Japanese representatives participated, and it contributed to the popularisation of karate in the USA.

The 2nd Japan-US Student Karate Friendship Tournament was held in July 1967 at the Nippon Budokan (Tokyo) and the Osaka Prefectural Gymnasium. In the first five-man team match at the Nippon Budokan, Takushoku's Ishikawa Tadashi (runner-up in the All Japan Student Championships) beat second generation Japanese American Fujikawa. The second match saw Ono Yasunori of Waseda (winner of the All Japan Student Championships) draw with his opponent. Kokugakuin University's Kurozumi defeated J. Smith, captain of the US team, with a kick to the midsection. After a good start to the tournament (2–0 after three bouts), Japan's vice-captain Iwatake Dai of Kansai University was beaten by P. White, a retired police officer and boxer with seven years of karate experience. In the final match, Ritsumeikan's Shin Yasuo's fist caught Equinor in the face. The judges ruled that it had hit him too hard and ended up losing by *ippon* due to foul play. As a result, the US team won the match, although the score was 2–2. Unfortunately, we have been unable to find any records of the matches in Osaka.

The 3rd Japan–US Student Karate Friendship Tournament was held from November 12 to December 1, 1969, and the Japanese team was captained by Takushoku's Osaka Yoshiharu, who won the All Japan Student Karate Championship that year. Other members included Kato Azuma from Toyo University, Seki Ichiro and Azuma Shin from Hosei, Hino Kazuaki from Seinan Gakuin, Hamasaki Minoru from Kyushu Sangyo, and me (Keio). This time, the tournament took place in the United States. I was the only second-year student at the time. The other six were all fourth-years. I was a little nervous, but the others treated me kindly, to my pleasant surprise (Photo 4–7).

Photo 4-7 Returning from the 3rd US-Japan Student Karate Friend-ship Tournament. (Courtesy of Wada Koji)

Travelling to Los Angeles via Vancouver, we stayed in Los Angeles for a week, then flew to Philadelphia for another week, and returned to Honolulu for four days. We fought many matches and participated in joint training sessions, and felt that karate was truly becoming international.

I was introduced to Mr. Kubota, who taught karate at the Los Angeles Police Department. Thanks to him we were allowed to shoot handguns at the LAPD firing range. This would have been unthinkable in Japan. I could sense the reverence the police officers had for Mr. Kubota, and the sincerity of their feelings for karate. Mr. Kubota was kind enough to point out some flaws in my stance for *shiai kumite*. I retorted that "it was easier this way"—a cheeky response that I am still embarrassed about to this day.

This was the year that Neil Armstrong and his team landed on the moon. When we arrived in Washington, we met with Japan's Prime Minister Sato Eisaku, who was also visiting the United States at the same time. He encouraged us to do our best "to raise Japan's national prestige". I do not remember the details of the six matches we fought, but I do remember that my own results were not great. Osaka, the captain of our team, won all of his matches in the team competition by finishing with a *chudan gyaku-tsuki* (middle reverse punch).

The following year in 1970, a 25-member student team was sent to Europe from June 2–24. This was just before the All Japan Student Championships in July. Although I do not recall the selection criteria for this tour, the team consisted of 17 *karateka* from the Kanto Student Federation, and 8 from the Kansai Student Federation. Specifically, Kitamura

Naomichi of Tokyo University of Agriculture; Naito Takeshi of Komazawa University; Kono Shoji and me from Keio; Kaneko Kiyotaka and Kasuya Hitoshi of Hosei; Yoshioka Satoru of Nihon University; Horiuchi Izumi and Aizawa Yujiro of Meiji; Nakamura Kozaburo and Nagao Seita of Takushoku; Yaguchi Kunio and Shiozawa Kazunori of Kokugakuin University; Kurata Kazuiku and Mifuji Yoshio of Waseda; Tasaka Jun'ichi and Kakuno Kazuaki of Shibaura Institute of Technology; Tomihara Masami of Tenri University; Nakahara Masami of the University of Kitakyushu; Ikari Masaomi of Seinan Gakuin University; Akahoshi Kokichi of Kyushu Sangyo University; Nozaki Hiromichi of Kumamoto University of Commerce; Kamikawa Yasuaki of Okayama University; Sawa Masakatsu of Osaka Institute of Technology; and Ishihara Koichiro of Fukuoka University. Again, I was the youngest in the group.

The first round began with a 7–4 win over Yugoslavia on June 4, followed by a hard-fought 5–4 victory over Italy's student selection on June 8. Then we won 8–3 against the All-Italy team on the same day, took a 2–0 win over Germany's student selection on June 13, and a 7–3 win over the All-Germany team. On June 15, the Japan team defeated the Dutch student team 5–0 and then All-Netherlands 11–4. On June 17, we defeated the French team led by Kase 7–3. On June 18, we beat the French team led by Mr. Jacques Delcourt (2nd president of WUKO) 5–3. The final match was fought on June 20 against the British A and B teams. Japan won 6–3 against the A team, and 10–3 against the B team. I fought in 9 matches and recorded 7 wins, 1 loss and 1 draw. My only defeat was in the first bout against Yugoslavia. One of the things that struck me during the trip was the difference in cultural norms. Most of the matches were fought in the evening. Afterwards there was usually a party that went on into the early hours of the morning. We would always sleep on the bus the next day during the sightseeing tours. I thought it was such a waste not to take in the sights when world travel was still so uncommon in Japan, but drowsiness always won out in the end.

Participants in this expedition, such as Kitamura, Naito, Kasuya, Yoshioka, and Horiuchi, continued their involvement with karate overseas after graduation. Internationalisation of karate was greatly advanced by Japanese college students and the connections they made on these trips.

The cost of both the US and European expeditions was around 400,000 yen—a considerable amount of money in those days— so it is likely that some people declined to participate even if they had ability in karate. The All Japan Student Karatedo Federation and the Nippon Budokan provided blazers and uniforms with Japanese flags attached. The All Japan Student Karatedo Federation's overseas expeditions were excellent preparatory activities for the ensuing amalgamation of karate worldwide. There was also talk of an expedition to Mexico in 1971, but for some reason it was abandoned, and my hopes of being able to attend as a senior were dashed.

4. The World Championships

With karate taking root around the world, WUKO was formed in 1970 and the 1st Karate World Championships were held in Japan in October of that year. There were 33 participating countries with just about 200 athletes in total. There were team and individual competitions, but no weight categories. Matches were decided by *ippon-shobu*.

5. Breaking the Cycle of Retaliation

The world is a dangerous place. The brutality seen in the world is appalling. Throughout history, there has been an unbreakable cycle of violence and retaliation. Japan has seen its fair share of violence in the past. In the final days of the Second World War, 100,000 people lost their lives in the Tokyo air raids, and hundreds of thousands more in the atomic bombings of Hiroshima and Nagasaki. Okinawa, however, was the only island in Japan that became a battleground. One third of the islanders lost their lives in the conflict.

Despite the humiliation of defeat, Japanese did not seek to exact revenge on American and Allied soldiers who occupied Japan in the aftermath. On the contrary, as we have seen with students who willingly taught karate to military personnel, the cycle of revenge was broken very early on.

Karate was born in Okinawa and evolved there for about 500 years. Once arriving on the mainland, in the span of one century it has become a worldwide phenomenon with more than 100-million followers. The introduction of the match system led to an explosion in karate numbers, but it also led to a divergence from the type of karate that originated in Okinawa. Okinawa considers karate to be a cultural asset of the islands, and is sparing no effort to help popularise it even further while protecting its cultural lifeblood. To this end, the Karate Kaikan was constructed in the prefecture to promote and protect the legacy of karate, and its dogma of peace.

I feel indebted to the magnanimous efforts made by those young karate instructors immediately after the war. If people around the world embrace the essence of karatedo—"*karate ni sente nashi*" (there is no first strike in karate)—then surely it can contribute in some way to mutual understanding and a more peaceful world.

||||||||||||||||||||||||||||||||||||||||||||||||||||||||||||||||||||||||||||||||||||||||||||||||||||||||||||||||||||||||||||||||||||||||||||||||||||||||||||||||

Wada Essay 5

Height of the Student Movement —A Discussion with Wako Haruo

Wada Koji

Wako Haruo shook the world by brandishing dynamite at a Singapore industrial complex in 1974, followed by the seizure of the French embassy in the Hague, and the Kuala Lumpur incident in 1975. These acts of terrorism forced the Japanese government into taking extra-judicial measures to release six political prisoners. He was also involved with the PLO where he carried out guerrilla activities. He left the Japanese Red Army in 1979 to work as a commando in southern Lebanon. He was arrested in Lebanon in 1997 on charges of forging travel documents, and was subsequently deported to Japan. He was sentenced to life in prison by a Japanese court and is currently in Tokushima Prison.

Wako was born in Shiogama, Miyagi prefecture, and entered the Faculty of Letters at Keio in 1968. This was at a time when the student movement began protesting against Keio's medical school receiving research funds from the US military. In 1969, the student movement heated up and confrontations with authorities and class boycotts followed. Wako was inspired by the student movement, and became a central figure within it.

I, too, entered the Faculty of Economics at Keio University in 1968, but remained ideologically neutral. My karate classmates varied considerably in this regard. Some sympathised with the student movement, and others resented it. This was problematic for the club. As class boycotts continued, Yamazaki, a karate club member who had been a rival of Wako's in prep school and was now his classmate in the Faculty of Letters, arranged a meeting between us. The meeting took place at Wako's lodgings near Keio's Hiyoshi Campus.

In his dimly lit six-*tatami* room there were triangular cones, flashing lights etc., which he had brought home from his part-time job on the roadworks. It left a deep impression on me. I was in a good mood because the negotiation that was about to take place reminded me of the fateful meeting between Meiji period heroes Katsu Kaishu and Saigo Takamori to avert more violence during the Meiji Restoration. We exchanged views on the student movement, but reached an impasse as it became clear that differences in opinion on blockade tactics, general thoughts on social issues, trust in the government, and so on could not be reconciled. Still, we respected each other as people.

A few days after our meeting, I was walking through campus as it was being blocked by activists. I came across a group of people marching in a zigzag pattern, holding pikes in front of them and shouting "No!" As I walked straight ahead, one of the guys at the end of the line bumped into me. He shouted at me to get out of his way. I told him to shut up, and he made a show of coming at me. None of his fellow protesters stopped to help, so he rushed back to his position in line.

A little further on I was met by a protester who insisted that the school building was off limits. "What authority do you have to stop from me entering?" I inquired. When I tried to go through, he brandished a pike at me and shouted, "You're breaking the strike!" Immediately, five or six others surrounded me. I figured that if I could get the stick off the man in front of me and get behind him, I would be able to escape from the enclosure and nullify any adversaries behind me. I decided that if I acted in a more intimidating manner, I would be able to take them out one by one if necessary.

It was midday and there were lots of students around. If a brawl broke out, I supposed that my friends would also come to assist. Just as I was finishing the simulation in my head, a voice called out. "Don't touch that person." It was Wako. He turned to me and said, "Come in," and let me pass. I raised one hand to greet him and he waved back. I did not have any real business to attend to. I just wanted to pass through the school building. The incident made me realise just how much sway he had in the movement.

I also had other friends in the student movement—twin brothers who belonged to Keio's judo club. They were unable to come to terms with our ideological differences. "You clearly don't study enough" they would rebuke me. About ten years after graduation, I bumped into the younger brother somewhere in Shibuya. "Wada, you were right. My brother is still being hunted by the police…"

According to Yamazaki, a friend of mine who met with Wako in prison, he said that he has no regrets for the acts of terrorism he committed. He does push-ups and sit-ups in his cell to maintain his physical strength and is still defiant. Ironically, however, he is a harsh critic of terrorist activities that are currently taking place around the world.

Acting on one's beliefs can be noble, but it is necessary to consider whether those beliefs are based on correct knowledge and information. It would be a blessing if, through the practice of karatedo, people could come to a common belief in the sanctity of life, rather than be so quick to resort to violence to resolve their differences.

SECTION 3

The 1st Karate World Championships

(Wada Koji)

The 1st Karate World Championships were held in Japan for five days starting from October 9, 1970. With His Imperial Highness Prince Takamatsu as honorary president, the tournament was attended by 193 athletes from 33 countries. Japan fielded 30 representatives Japan. I also participated. I was a member of the second-placed team in the team competition held at the Nippon Budokan, and won the individual competition at the Osaka Prefectural Gymnasium.

Also, on October 11, the World Union of Karate-do Organisations (WUKO) Launch Conference was held at the Tokyo Prince Hotel. Representatives of the participating countries unanimously resolved to create a new organisation for the global development of karatedo.

1. Winning the 1st KWC Individual Competition

On October 9, 1970, the 1st Karate World Championships' opening ceremony was held. The team matches were contested on October 10, Physical Education Day, at the Nippon Budokan. There were no *kata* matches, women's *kumite*, or men's *kumite* weight categories. There were only team and individual *kumite* matches for men. Twenty-nine teams from 22 countries took part in the team competition, with five teams from Japan. It was difficult for foreign teams to field more than three competitors who could match their Japanese counterparts, so Guatemala and Chile formed a coalition team. In the end, however, they decided not to participate.

The remaining teams in the top eight included USA B, France, Great Britain, and Japan. Due to nature of the draw, only Japan E did not have to fight other Japanese teams. Japan B beat Japan A 2–1, and Japan C beat Japan D 4–0 to reach the semi-finals. Japan E went on to beat Great Britain 4–0, and USA B beat France 2–1 to also advance to the semi-finals. In the semi-finals, Japan C defeated Japan B 3–0, and Japan E beat USA B 2–1. Thus, the final was between the Japanese teams. In the third-place match, Japan B defeated USA B 3–1, so the top three places were dominated by Japan. Japan E won the tournament, and my team, Japan C, was the runner-up.

The fact that Japan dominated the team competition was a great honour for us, but it was not so encouraging for the international teams. After the competition, representatives of each country asked tournament officials to limit the number of participants to two in the individual matches to be held at the Osaka Prefectural Gymnasium on October 13. Japan had no choice but to accept this request.

The Japanese team initially planned to field around ten representatives to account for the various karate factions. The task of whittling down the number of competitors to two in a single day proved to be a daunting task: even if Japan was sure to win the team event with five players, there were no guarantees when it came to the individual competition. Even the victorious Japanese E team did not win all of their matches 5–0 against the foreign teams—they barely won in the semifinals with a hard fought 2–1 victory over the USA B team. The fact that the foreign fighters were stronger than expected, made the those representing the various Japanese factions less confident, and even reluctant to fight for the national team.

It was against this background that the youngest representatives of the All Japan Student Karatedo Federation, both 21 years old, Takada Shigeru (a third-year student at Toyo University) and myself, Wada Koji (a third-year student at Keio), were chosen to represent Japan. On the bullet train from Tokyo to Osaka the day before the match, we were told of this decision by Takagi Fusajiro (secretary general of WUKO from 1980). "There is only a pair of fighters representing Japan, and you two are it." Needless to say, I felt the weight of the responsibility more acutely than the joy of being selected.

In those days, matches were *ippon-shobu*, one-point-winner, not the 8-point matches of today. The winner was decided by whoever scored two *waza-ari* techniques or a single *ippon* first. In addition, there were no padded gloves. The matches were fought with bare hands, which made for a very tense atmosphere. There were no weight divisions either, so some of our foreign opponents were monstrous in size compared to us. This amounted to a lot of responsibility for those 'lucky' enough to be selected.

The opening ceremony for the individual competition commenced at 6pm, which was a highly irregular time for tournaments in Japan. Forty-eight players from 27 countries gathered to battle it out. Takada won the first round by default, the second round by two *chudan-tsuki* techniques against Kelvin of the Philippines. He took the third round by decision against Garcia of Argentina. In the quarter-final, he was caught off guard by the American Tulleners, who knocked him down with a foot sweep and then defeated him with a *seiken-tsuki*. The crowd, who were cheering enthusiastically for the Japanese fighter, let out a collective groan. I was fighting against Scheler from Germany on the next court when this happened.

I won my first-round match against Orozco of Guatemala with two *chudan-tsuki*. I defeated Schubert from Austria in the second round with another two *chudan-tsuki*, and won the third round match against Braenecke of the USA with *jodan-tsuki* and *chudan-geri*. During my quarter-final match against German Scheler, I heard the loud groan that reverberated through the gymnasium. When I realised that Takada had been eliminated from the tournament on the next court, I stiffened up. At that instant, Scheler's fist swung down over my head and he was awarded *waza-ari*. The whole gymnasium was buzzing. I could see the newspaper headlines in my mind. "All Japanese fighters eliminated in the quarter-finals!"

With less than 30 seconds to go, a Yugoslavian player cheering from the side called out to me. "Wada, kick, kick!" With all my might, I executed *chudan-geri* to win back the *waza-ari* and managed to take the match into overtime. Then I scored my signature *jodan-tsuki* to advance to the semi-final. The Yugoslavian who was cheering me on was someone I met during the student trip to Europe. It made me appreciate the old maxim that yesterday's foe can become today's best friend!

As there was no 3rd place playoff match, I already knew I had a bronze medal at least, and was quite relieved at that. In the semi-final, I won against Valerer of France with a *jodan-tsuki*. In the final, I was pitted against Carnio of Canada and managed to win with two *jodan-tsuki*.

Photo 4-8 The 1st World Karatedo Championship, Individual Championship October 13, 1970, Osaka Prefectural Gymnasium. (Courtesy of Wada Koji)

I was happy that Japan saved face that day. My victory was also widely reported in the *Sankei Shimbun* and *Sankei Sports* newspapers. I was asked to appear on NTV's "11PM" show, but Obata Isao (Keio University *Shihan*) suggested that I not appear on a show that featured half-naked women. The JKF wanted to maintain a good relationship with the media, and convinced NTV to not reveal my face. I appeared on the show with Takada and the American Tulleners. As agreed, my face was barely visible during the interview, and Takada, who performed a mock *kumite* match with Tulleners, looked as if he was the winner! Although Takada won the *kumite* match on the TV programme, Tulleners' strength was genuine, and the tournament revealed for all to see that the level of karate overseas was rapidly improving.

Looking back on my matches, the American fighter I met in the third round was over 2m tall and weighed over 100kg. I was 173cm and weigh 68kg, which made me quite small by world standards. My fist barely reached his nostrils when I tried my specialty *jodan-tsuki*. As I was pondering how I should tackle him, he kicked me with his left leg. I drew my right foot back and scooped up his kick with my left arm. I was right in front of his face, so I made a *jodan-tsuki* and was awarded *waza-ari*. Then he became even trickier, but I was able to win with *chudan-geri* as he unleashed a thrust.

On December 21, 2010, Takamiyagi Shigeru arranged a visit to the Mita Karate Kai by Higaonna-sensei and leading masters of various Okinawan styles. Higaonna-sensei told me that he had taught my American opponent. Apparently, he told Higaonna-sensei that he "wasn't surprised to lose to a Japanese fighter". That was probably just lip service to his Japanese master!

I also had a hard time with the German fighter in the quarter-final match. It was partly because I was shocked by Takada's defeat, but more so because I was flummoxed by the *jodan ken-tsukiuchi* technique that he unleashed when in close. Back then, no Japanese fighters could use this technique. Referees would not award it even if they could. Nowadays, techniques such as *sasori-geri* and *ura mawashi-geri* are seen often, but these were unthinkable at the time. I see nothing wrong with broadening one's horizons and studying various technical possibilities.

The French fighter I competed with in the semi-final was a student of Ohshima Tsutomu, who now lives in the USA and has 100,000 followers around the world. When I visited Ohshima in Santa Barbara in March 2011, I found out about this connection. The orthodox style of Ohshima's teachings meant that although I did not find the match awkward, I was unable to score an *ippon* against him. This experience made me reflect on the incredible efforts Japanese instructors abroad have made over the years to promote karate to such a high level.

In the final, I felt very comfortable and light on my feet because I knew I at least had a silver medal. I stepped in just as Carnio was about to kick with his right foot, blocked it with my left arm, and scored with a right front *kizami-tsuki*. This is my most effective attack pattern. My opponent did not seem to know how he had been taken

Photo 4-9 The 1st World Karatedo Championship, Individual semi-final. Author is on the right. (Courtesy of Wada Koji)

and before long he did the same move. As if it was *déjà vu*, the same scenario unfolded, and I won the match with *jodan-tsuki*. I was able to deal with him without much difficulty. If he had he lost in the semi-final to the mighty Tulleners, I doubt that I would have won the tournament. Whatever the case, the result went my way that day.

Photo 4-10 The 1st World Karatedo Championship, Individual final. Author is on the right. (Courtesy of *Sankei Shimbun*)

The 1st World Karatedo Championship was a resounding success, and karate had made a great leap forward as a world sport. Who could have imagined that an ancient art from Okinawa would gain such a worldwide following ? It was the 1st KWC that had the biggest impact on my life. My success at the KWC can be attributed to my experiences going on the student federation's trips to the USA and Europe. Those experiences helped me to learn how to fight against non-Japanese *karateka*.

2. Subsequent KWCs Where Japan Struggled

Two years later, the 2nd KWC was held in France in 1972. I had just started working for Ajinomoto and could not participate in the training sessions, so did not make the national team. Although I did not witness it first-hand, apparently it was a very rough tournament. It seems that officials and referees from various countries did not want Japan to win. When a Japanese fighter punched or kicked first, the opponent was awarded with a later counter technique. In addition, Japanese fighters were hit so hard that the strikes would have been called fouls in Japan.

After their early defeat in the team competition, the Japanese team lodged protests against the referees' judgements and expressed concern for the safety of its competitors. The officials responded that the calls were correct. Japanese competitors withdrew from the individual competition as their safety could not be guaranteed. As a result, Japan did not win any medals in the second edition of the tournament.

The 3rd KWC was held in the USA. The Japanese team dominated the individual competition with Murakami Kunio winning and Hamaguchi Junichiro as the runner-up. Japan lost to Great Britain in the team competition and finished in second place. The 4th KWC was in Japan again, but the host country failed to finish with any medals in both the individual and team competitions. The growth of non-Japanese karate athletes after the 1st World Championship was nothing short of spectacular.

3. Competitors Selected for the World Championships

As mentioned above, after winning the 14th All Japan Student Karatedo Championship in July 1970, I was selected to go to Europe just as I had been selected to go the USA the year prior. I was one of the 30 athletes selected for the KWC to be held later that year. Five of the other team members were current students who trained daily, and the rest were company employees. A training camp was held at Lake Motosu for three nights and four days to prepare for the championships. I was told by my senior before going to the camp, "Wada, if students get too big for their boots the other guys will just go in and destroy you. Try not to get killed." I took him at his word, cleaned up my room, and, feeling like a soldier on his way to the front, bid farewell to my parents politely before heading to the camp venue.

I was very nervous during the training camp. So as not to be "destroyed", I made sure all my *jodan-tsuki* techniques only made light contact. I had to keep good control of my fists, but punched to the extent that contact on skin was made with a fleeting "pish" sound. I also made sure I was not counterattacked. In the end, I survived the camp without too many bruises. Ultimately all the members were total gentlemen, and I was the only one whose punches made contact.

When I returned safely from the training camp, the senior who had warned me beforehand dangled a carrot in front of my nose. "If you win, I'll rent a restaurant in Akasaka to celebrate." I hadn't thought about winning, so listened without really taking much notice. When I did end up winning, I waited in anticipation, wondering when he was going to take me out. It seems he forgot and all I got was a hearty "Congratulations!"

It gave me a lot of confidence to win practice bouts against Tabata Yukichi and Tanaka Masahiko at the camp. They were the absolute best at that time. I met Tanaka Masahiko again more than 30 years later when I attended a training session run by the JKA. I was surprised that he remembered our match.

||||||||||||||||||||||||||||||||||||||||||||||||||||||||||||||||||||||||||||||||||||||||||||||||||||||||||||||||||||||||||||||||||||||||||||||||||||||||||||||||||||||||

Wada Essay 6

Weakness of Mind
Wada Koji

In 1969, I participated in the 13th All Japan Student Karate Tournament as a second-year student. In the second round I faced Osaka Yoshiharu of Takushoku. I lost by decision after three extra rounds with no points being scored between us. He went on to win the tournament, which gave me no small amount of confidence.

After that, I was selected to represent the students for the Expedition Team to the United States and Europe. After returning from the European expedition in July, I won the 14th All Japan Student Karate Championship, where I fought Takada Shigeru of Toyo University (also a third-year student) in the semi-final. Takada held his left fist in front of him and jumped in with *kizami-tsuki*. As I was in *gyakutai* (right fist in front), I planned to counter Takada's thrust with my right hand and nail him with a left *chudan-tsuki*. Shortly after the start of the match, Takada came at me from a distance with a left *kizami-tsuki*. I blocked it perfectly and countered with *chudan-tsuki*, but the flags went up for Takada's technique. "This is ridiculous!" I thought, but I had no right to protest. As the match resumed I closed the distance between us, but Takada fell back. It was obvious that his plan was to hold on to victory with his single *waza-ari*.

In those days, there were no penalties for stepping out of bounds. No matter how many times he stepped out, we were simply sent back to the starting line. With time running out, I tried to close the gap but Takada kept retreating. Time ran out and the referee blew his whistle for a decision. Two assistant judges ruled that Takada had won, and the remaining two called for a draw. In this case it should have been a victory for Takada, but the referee called the judges together for a discussion. Then they made their decision again. The result was a draw.

Stepping out and running away were not fouls back then, but clearly his actions were too blatant for the judges to let slide. I was thrown a lifeline and was able to advance to the final match by scoring with a *chudan* kick at the start of overtime.

In the final, I met Nozaki Hiromichi, a fourth-year student at Kumamoto Shodai. Since he was also a member of the European delegation, I knew what I was up against. Nozaki had already fought three extra rounds in the semi-final and seemed to have used up a lot of stamina. I did not feel like losing, and scored a *waza-ari* kick to the mid-section, and then won by decision to take the cup.

I met Takada again in the quarter-final of the Student Championships on November 23. We were the starting fighters of our respective teams. Takada was keen to make amends after his KWC result in October. I was expecting Takada to strike *jodan kizami-tsuki*. If I countered with *chudan-tsuki*, I knew the referees would award him the point. He was well known for his skill in this technique. Instead, I raised my right fist high in a defensive stance against *jodan kizami-tsuki*, but Takada still tried to strike high. There was no way the judges were going to award him a point against my defence, and I won the match with a counter *jodan-tsuki*. The next fighter in my team, Iwasaki Shinji, was also victorious, and it looked as though we would go through to the semi-final.

Alas, we were defeated in succession by the third, fourth, and fifth fighters. Toyo University won the East Japan, Kanto, and All Japan titles that year.

The 15th Student Championship was held at the Osaka Prefectural Gymnasium in July, 1971. Everyone in the Keio club believed that I would win. This was to be expected as I was triumphant at the same tournament and the KWC as a third-year. But, there was no guarantee. The fear of losing made me nervous. The only saving grace was that the event was to be held in Osaka, so there would be fewer people watching if I did lose. Or so I thought.

One of my classmates, Konishi Shun'ichi, bet on and won big at the Japan Derby, and took home a hefty 600,000-yen. He said that his father told him to go and have fun with his newly acquired fortune. He took all our classmates to Osaka to cheer me on. They stayed in a beautiful hotel and painted the town red in Dotonbori. I was invited to join them, but turned the offer down because I was not feeling well. I spent the night in a Japanese inn designated by the All Japan Student Karatedo Federation. I felt feverish when I woke up. I took my temperature and found it was over 39 degrees Celsius.

My coach, Nagura Toshihisa, helped me in the pre-match warm up, but I felt unsteady so he asked me to stop. We had never won the Students Championship back-to-back before, so there would be no shame if it was not to be. Notwithstanding, losing in the first or second round would not do at all. Fortunately, I was seeded in the first round. I managed to get through to the quarter-final by beating Omori of Daisho University in the second round, Yamashita of

Waseda in the third round, and Hashimoto of Kansai University in the fourth round. In the quarter-final match I found my rhythm by scoring two thrusts against Takesako of Komazawa University. In the semifinal I defeated Matsuzaki of Takushoku with a *chudan-geri*. In the final, I faced my nemesis once again, Takada of Toyo University. In the end, it turned out that victory for the second year in a row was meant to be after all, thanks to *chudan-tsuki*.

By the end of the final, I was feeling great, and as I was receiving my certificate and cup at the awards ceremony, I suddenly remembered that I had a fever that morning.

After being hired by Ajinomoto following graduation, I was taught about the term *"shippei-ritoku"* (the benefits and advantages that a person receives as a result of having a disease) during our employee training. It is recognised that people who study hard and attain good grades often fall ill at critical times such as entrance exams. They suddenly develop a fever, or suffer from severe diarrhoea because there is a big gap between the world's expectations and one's own confidence. The fear of not living up to peoples' hopes can be mitigated by claiming that you are ill and off your game. You will be viewed with sympathy. Perhaps this belief is what really made me feel ill on the day of the tournament. My weak mind was looking for an excuse to explain away failure.

SECTION 4

The Internationalisation of Karate —From its Place of Birth, Okinawa

(Kadekaru Toru)

1. Appellations of Okinawan Karate

Chinese martial arts introduced into the Ryukyu Kingdom are described in literature from the 1860s as having been localised and known as *todi* (唐手), Okinawan dialect for "Chinese hand". As Japan modernised, Okinawa prefecture was established in 1879, and from around 1900 onwards, karate was performed

Photo 4-11 *Okinawa Taiwa*, 1880. (*History of Okinawa prefecture [Modern]* Volume 5, 2011)

as Okinawan's "unique martial art" in schools and at local events. It was increasingly featured as such in newspapers and magazines, where it was written as 唐手 in standard Japanese (Photo 4–11).

The integration of Okinawa by the Meiji government was promoted by the governors, officials, teachers and military personnel who came from other prefectures, and by policies issued by the prefectural government. Frequent visits to Okinawa were made by the imperial family and other dignitaries, and this helped karate's reputation grow. In 1922, Funakoshi

Gichin went to Tokyo with the aim of propagating karate, and the subsequent establishment of university study groups in the Kanto and Kansai regions by Okinawan instructors led to an increase in karate's renown.

From around 1930, schools such as Goju-ryu, Shito-ryu, Shotokan, and Wado-ryu were founded along the model of traditional Japanese martial arts schools (Photo 4–12). During the turbulent 1930s, Japan's worsening relationship with China led to the official name change to empty-hand karate with the suffix -*do* to establish its status as a Japanese budo (Funakoshi Gichin had already adopted this *kanji* a decade earlier). While karate was being modernised in this sense, the traditional Okinawan weapon-based arts such as the *bo, sai, tonfa, nunchaku,* etc., took a different route for survival (Photo 4–13).

Photo 4-12 Manuscript of Miyagi Chojun's *Goju-ryu Kempo.* (Courtesy of Tokumura Masatami)

In 2017, Okinawa prefecture established the Karate Kaikan. The tentative name at the time of planning was "Okinawa Karatedo Kaikan". A committee was convened to investigate what the appropriate name for the facility should be. Participants included the vice governor, officers of the Okinawa Traditional Karatedo Promotion Association, which is made up of four major karatedo organisations in Okinawa prefecture, plus other stakeholders. They studied the options until they came to a consensus of what was most suitable. Eventually, it was decided

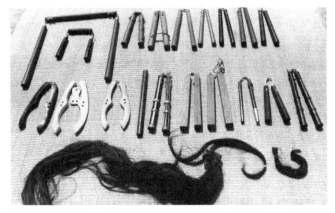

Photo 4-13 Types of *nunchaku*. (Nakamoto Masahiro, *Okinawa no Dento Kobudo: Sono Rekishi to Tamashii*, 1983)

that Okinawan karate included both karatedo and Okinawan *kobudo* (weapon arts).

2. Okinawan Karate Conveyed Through Kata

An important aspect of Okinawan karate's history is the fact that it was conveyed through *kata*. Most of the *kata* passed down from the royal period to modern times have Chinese names and can be regarded as having originated from Chinese *quanfa*. As was covered in Chapter 1, due to the tributary relationship between the Ryukyu Kingdom and China, Ming and Qing Dynasty Chinese martial arts spread to the islands, and Ryukyuan martial arts formed through cultural exchanges (Illustration 4–1).

3. International Recognition of Ryukyuan Martial Arts

What did people think of the Ryukyuan martial arts ? Let us review some of the historical documents dealt with so far.

Illustration 4-1 Investiture ceremony for the King of Chuzan. (Jo Hoko, *Chuzan Denshin-roku*, 1721)

In the *Satsuyu-kiko*, a travelogue written by a samurai of the Higo clan (name unknown) in 1801, a warrior of the Satsuma clan named Mizuno Kumajiro witnessed a Ryukyuan man smash roof tiles with his bare hands. He commented that the Ryukyuan command of swordsmanship and jujutsu was weak, but that their fists and fingertips were more than capable of killing. Nagoya Sagenta, a Satsuma samurai who was sent to Amami Oshima, described with text and illustrations in *Nanto Zatsuwa* (1855) various scenes of men training their fists.

The martial arts of the Ryukyuan people were not practised in secret as is often claimed. The Satsuma clansmen who witnessed the Ryukyuan martial arts recorded their characteristics and introduced them to fellow clansmen on the mainland.

In 1816, Basil Hall, captain of a British sloop, visited the Ryukyu Islands. On his return to Britain, he wrote an account of his voyage to Korea and the Ryukyus (1818) in which he described a peculiar martial art stance adopted by a royal official towards his sailors.

Ernest M. Satow, a British diplomat who stayed in Japan from the end of the Tokugawa Shogunate to the Meiji period, wrote a paper on the Ryukyus in 1873. In it, he records the martial skills of the Ryukyuan people and their ability to smash tiles and kill with a single blow of the fist. Satow toured many parts of Japan during his tenure, but did not actually visit the Ryukyus. As a diplomat, he probably wrote about the martial arts of the Ryukyu Islands based on information he collected from Hall and others.

In 1854, Commodore Matthew Perry of the United States Navy visited the Ryukyus and concluded the Ryukyu-US Treaty. Perry had visited the Ryukyu Islands several times before and gathered a great deal of information about the islands which he wrote about in his report. Perry knew that arms were strictly controlled by the Satsuma clan, and that the Ryukyuans had been essentially disarmed.

From the Ryukyu early-modern period to the end of the Tokugawa shogunate, Japan, China and the Western countries were well aware of Ryukyu's armaments and martial culture. There is no indication that the Ryukyuans were particularly secretive about their martial arts.

4. Modern Karate

In March 1902, karate was performed as entertainment at a graduation party at the Okinawa Prefectural Normal School. The alumni magazine of the school, *Ryutan* (1902), describes the performance as something unique to the prefecture, which could not be imitated by anyone else. The following year at the same party, karate featured once again. In *Ryutan* (1903), the "inimitable nature of karate" was touted again as the exclusive art of the Okinawan people.

The Meiji government changed the official language from Ryukyuan to standard Japanese, and did away with the traditional hairstyle and Ryukyuan clothes. This was an attempt to assimilate Okinawa into mainstream culture as the country sought to modernise. Amidst these trying times for Ryukyuan cultural practices, karate was still performed as part of Okinawan heritage, albeit as a sideshow. The people of Okinawa insisted that karate was their time-honoured legacy.

A reporter wrote in 1905 of how karate was recognised as physical education in Okinawan schools. As it was introduced into middle schools as a regular course of study this year, he boasted that although jujutsu was already known in Europe it was not being taught in Japanese schools, karate was already being taught in Okinawan schools ahead of mainland martial arts before foreigners had even heard of it.

In 1908, Itosu Anko was commissioned by middle schools and teachers' training colleges (normal schools) to teach karate. As he pointed out in "Ten Articles on Karate", he hoped that the initiative would eventually lead to it being taught throughout Japan. Many of his direct students became teachers in and outside the prefecture.

On a school trip to Tokyo in 1911, students of the Okinawa Normal School karate club were accompanied by their judo teacher to the Kodokan, where they met Kano Jigoro. In *Ryutan* (1911), the students wrote of the praise they received from the judo master and how the meeting inspired them to promote karate as an "excellent form of physical education."

The book *Nanto no Shizen to Hito*, published in Okinawa in 1916, includes a section on the "distinctive local martial arts of karate and sumo". The author wrote that as karate was adopted by the navy, it would be regarded as a world-class martial art in the future. Thus, from the 1910s onwards, karate gained a reputation as the representative athletic culture of Okinawa. This status was officially confirmed a little earlier in 1905 when it was introduced into the prefectural school system. Following exchanges with and endorsements from leading Japanese martial artists such as Kano, along with its adoption into the Navy, karate did indeed spread globally.

5. Internationalisation of Karate

Japanese immigration abroad began around 1885. Okinawa first sent 26 immigrants to Hawaii in 1899, 14 years after the first immigrants ventured there from the mainland. The number of migrants increased rapidly after 1904, reaching 4,670 in 1906, and this continued until 1941. By the Second World War, the number of migrants leaving from Okinawa prefecture was

72,227, or 11% of the nation's total of 655,661. Migrants from Japan settled in 21 countries, mainly in the Americas.

After Japan's defeat in the war, Okinawa was separated from Japan and placed under US rule according to conditions stipulated in the 1951 San Francisco Peace Treaty. It remained a US protectorate for 27 years until 1972. Okinawan migration resumed in 1948. Since then until 1993, 17,726 people left Okinawa for Brazil, Argentina, Bolivia, Peru, and other countries. Social and economic factors from both before and after the war forced people to go abroad to make a living.

Expat Okinawans retained their traditional culture and identity, despite the challenging conditions of life abroad. Karate, too, became rooted in their lives in the places they immigrated to. Although research into this area is in its infancy, I will give some examples of karate leaders from Okinawa who visited China, the US mainland, Hawaii and Argentina (Table 4–1).

Year	Name	Country
1915	Miyagi Chojun	China (Fuzhou)
1917	Miyagi Chojun	China (Fuzhou)
1919	Yabu Kentsu	USA (California)
1927	Yabu Kentsu	Hawaii
1932	Motobu Choki	Hawaii
1933	Higaonna Kamesuke, Mutsu Mizuho	Hawaii
1934	Miyagi Chojun	Hawaii
1936	Miyagi Chojun	China (Shanghai)
1937	Asato Kameei, Kamenaga	Argentina

Table 4-1 Early international expeditions by karate teachers

Miyagi Chojun travelled to Fuzhou, China in 1915 and 1917 to investigate Chinese martial arts. Fuzhou had been closely associated with Okinawa since the days of the Ming Dynasty, and Miyagi relied on friends and acquaintances to conduct his field study.

In 1919, retired army lieutenant Yabu Kentsu visited California on a physical education study tour. He stayed in the USA for eight years and worked on farms and in orchards in California while inspecting various schools and facilities. Details of this extended visit are not known, but as Yabu's visa application states "sports visit" it is likely that he had some interaction with locals through karate. On his way back to Japan in 1927, Yabu visited Hawaii at the request of Okinawan immigrants. He stayed there for nine months, visiting the four main Hawaiian islands, and gave lectures and demonstrations of karate (Photo 4–14).

Photo 4-14 Yabu Kentsu (front row, third from left) commemorative photo of his visit to Hawaii. (From *Okinawa Karate Kobudo Jiten*, 2008)

Yabu became the first Okinawan volunteer to join the Japanese Imperial Army Cadet Corps and served in both the Sino-Japanese War and the Russo-Japanese War. He was ordered to visit the United States to inspect physical education practices. It was reported that "Lieutenant Yabu, the karate master who broke through boards with his fist, arrived on the SS President Taft this morning."

His lectures covered the history of karate, the current utilisation of the art in the Imperial Japanese Army and Navy, and a comparison between *kata* and boxing. Karate had already become popular, especially among people of Okinawan descent living in Hawaii. An "Okinawa Karate Tournament" was held there, and *kata* including *Naihanchi*, *Sanchin*, *Pin'an*, *Passai*, *Gojushiho*, and *Kushanku* were broken down and explained.

In March 1932, Motobu Choki also travelled to Hawaii to teach karate. Due to inadequate procedures he was detained in an immigration facility, but even gave instruction there.

In August the following year, Toyo University student Higaonna Kamesuke and Mutsu Mizuho, vice president of Tokyo Imperial University Karate Kenkyu Kai, travelled to Hawaii to promote karate. Higaonna was from Okinawa prefecture, but his mother resided in Hawaii. He and his colleagues sometimes attracted crowds of 1,200 people due to prior publicity campaigns. Demonstrations were also held by expat Okinawans.

In May 1934, Miyagi Chojun visited Hawaii at the invitation of the Yoen Jiho Company, run by a prefectural official named Kinjo Chinyei, and stayed there for ten months giving talks and karate demonstrations. Miyagi had many friends and acquaintances in Hawaii and his main purposes for going there were to teach karate to the Nisei, and conduct research on boxing. Miyagi held important positions, such as director of Karate Division of Okinawa prefecture, and was a prominent member of the Dai-Nippon Butokukai. He also taught at various schools and universities. The name Goju-ryu was already in use at this time, which was when he compiled the book *Karatedo Gaisetsu*.

In February 1936, Miyagi went to Shanghai to observe martial arts. On this occasion he was accompanied by Go Kenki, a master of White Crane Style from Fuzhou who had

Photo 4-15 Brothers Asato Kameei and Kamenaga demonstrating with *bo* and *sai*. (*Aruzenchin no Uchinanchu 80 Nen-shi*, 1994)

emigrated to Okinawa, and his student Aniya Seisho. Miyagi's exchange with local martial artists has been corroborated on a commemorative strip of paper, which reads "Friendship between Japan and China" and bears the signatures of Miyagi, Aniya, Zhao Lianhe, and others.

In the same year, at a picnic event attended by Okinawan settlers in Argentina, a demonstration of *sai* and *bo kumite* was performed (Photo 4–15) by the immigrant brothers Asato Kameei and Kamenaga. In addition to running a laundry business, the Asato brothers also taught karate.

The spread of karate abroad shows that it was closely linked with Okinawan immigrants and involved exchanges with the Chinese martial arts world.

6. Post-war Internationalisation

Okinawa was burnt to the ground in the Battle of Okinawa and took many years to rebuild. The United States commandeered land for the construction of bases, and life was hard for the locals. Despite these harsh conditions, karate practitioners began to train once again. Post-war karate was centred in humble community dojos, and in the central part of the main island where the bases were located. Classes attracted servicemen who worked at the bases. It is useful to look at the cases of Uechi-ryu and Goju-ryu to see what kind of international promotion activities they engaged in.

Uechi Kambun was born in 1877 and visited Fuzhou in 1897, where he practised Southern Shaolin Kung Fu for 13 years.

After returning to Japan, he moved to Wakayama prefecture in search of employment. In 1932 he opened the Pangai Noon-ryu Karatejutsu Kenkyujo. He returned to Okinawa after the war but died soon after in 1948. His eldest son Kan'ei and his students moved to central Okinawa and resumed teaching in Naha. Many Americans, both military and civilian, came to learn karate from them. When these non-Japanese karate students eventually returned to their home country, they opened dojos in America, and in other parts of the world.

The international dissemination of karate can be traced in the book *Seisetsu Okinawa no Karatedo* (1977), supervised and published by Kan'ei. At the time of publication, Uechi-ryu branch dojos had expanded to 10 countries including Canada, Great Britain, France, Australia, New Zealand, Saudi Arabia, former Yugoslavia, Bulgaria, Mexico, Argentina, Brazil and Bolivia. Exchanges between Okinawan instructors and local dojos in these countries continue to this day.

The first Okinawan karate instructor to go abroad to teach officially in the post-war era was Higaonna Morio of Goju-ryu. Born in Naha in 1938, Higaonna started learning Shorin-ryu from his father Seiichi when he was 15 years old. The following year, he began training under Miyagi An'ichi and Miyazato Eiichi of Goju-ryu, and this is what he taught overseas.

Higaonna's first overseas teaching experience was in Spokane, Washington in 1968. He taught Goju-ryu mainly to university students (Photo 4-16). According to Higaonna's *Okinawa Goju-ryu Karatedo* (1983), there were 19 overseas branch dojos in the

Photo 4-16 Teaching in Spokane, Washington. (1968, photo courtesy of Higaonna Morio)

United States, Canada, Great Britain, Spain, Sweden, Belgium, France, West Germany, Greece, Portugal, South Africa, Peru, Chile, Venezuela, New Zealand, India, Hong Kong, Australia and Malaysia.

The efforts of Uechi Kan'ei and Higaonna Morio are a stand-out example of karate's international promotion until the 1980s. The internationalisation of Okinawan karate began with its development into a Japanese budo. Okinawan immigrants took this modernised form of karate to different parts of the world from the 1900s. In this way, the popularity of karate in the post-war period was part of an ongoing process that had already started in the early years of the twentieth century.

7. International Exchanges through Okinawa Karate

In 1990, Okinawa prefecture held the First Worldwide Uchinanchu Festival for people of Okinawan descent. Uchinanchu is a local term for Okinawans. The number of participants from overseas amounted to 3,700, with over 450,000 people in total participating. As one of the main events, the "Okinawa Karate and Kobudo World Exchange Festival" proved to be extremely popular.

The Okinawa Karate & Kobudo World Tournament was convened to mark the 50th anniversary of the Battle of Okinawa in 1995. Over 200 people from 19 countries participated in the competition, which was held in as a lead-up to the establishment of the Okinawa Prefectural Budokan two years later. When the Budokan was completed, another tournament was held with 1,700 participants from 50 countries in attendance.

The Uchinanchu convention has been held 6 times since, and related events such as the Okinawa Karate International Embukai have been held as a part of the festival. Furthermore, Okinawa prefecture has held other international karate events annually since 2013.

In 2016, the prefecture established a new Karate Promotion Section. As part of this policy, the prefecture invested 6.3 billion yen in 2017 to establish the Okinawa Karate Kaikan, which serves as a base for Okinawa karate and the dissemination of related information. Many Okinawan karate enthusiasts from Japan and abroad visit every year as it represents the birthplace of karate. In 2018, the 1st Okinawa Karate International Tournament was held with 1,223 participants from 49 countries attending the competition, and a total of 2,344 people attending seminars and other events. The magnificent Okinawa Karate Kaikan was built with the aim of promoting the art, and it is expected that the facility will continue to be the hub of Okinawan karate activities for the people of Okinawa and karate enthusiasts around the world.

The international dissemination of karate reached a pinnacle of sorts when it was adopted as an official sport for the 2020 Tokyo Olympics. Although the games were postponed until 2021, karate's inclusion has inspired even more people to take it up. It is also taught in schools more than ever before with budo being made a compulsory subject for junior high school students from 2012. It has come an incredibly long way nationally and globally over the last century, but it is important to reiterate its traditional Okinawan origins.

SECTION 5

National Sports Festival of Japan
(Koyama Masashi)

Okinawa came under US military rule after the war. The Butokukai was disbanded, and Okinawan instructors such as Miyagi Chojun no longer came to the mainland to teach. Mabuni Kenwa was in Osaka at the end of the war, and Funakoshi Gichin returned to Tokyo in 1947 after being evacuated from Oita.

1. Sportification
In 1946, the karate club at Waseda University resumed its activities, and from 1948 onwards there was a push to establish new university karate clubs with considerable cooperation being seen among students from different colleges. Shotokan's Japan Karate Association (Nihon Karate Kyokai), Wado-ryu's All Japan Karate Federation (Zen-Nihon Karate Renmei), Goju-ryu's All Japan Karatedo Goju-kai, and so on were also established around this time as the Butokukai was no longer around as a centralised entity to oversee budo activities.

In a *ryuha*, the first step is to choose a person who will run the organisation and create a solid relationship between master and disciples. University karate graduates had considerable experience in administrative activities, and it was they who took up the mantle of responsibility for the various organisations that were launched in the post-war era.

As the theory of modern karatedo evolved, the question of where *kumite* should be positioned became a major issue. Even before the war, some organisations were already experimenting with the use of protective gear for matches. The most notable example being the JKF Renbukai, which held a national championship in 1954. In 1959, the Federation of All Japan Karatedo Organizations (predecessor to the JKF) formulated a system of matches which utilised protective equipment.[1]

The Student Federation (Gakuren) continued with the "no protective gear—bare face, bare hands" method. Although the frequency of *kumite* matches throughout the country increased along with the number of clubs, students held back on adopting protective equipment. As such, the Gakuren system had to overcome various obstacles as it pushed the competitive aspects such as ensuring safety and establishing easy-to-understand rules. At the same time, they deepened their relationship of friendly rivalry through inter-college joint trainings where *jiyu kumite* became mainstream.

Of course, rivalry meant that they wanted to beat each other come what may. While *ryuha* maintained vertical hierarchical relations, university clubs traditionally preferred horizontal relationships. With the proliferation of *kumite*, their strong sense of rivalry gradually surpassed matters of friendship. Although it was referred to as "friendly rivalry", it was much more an intense struggle for supremacy.

(1) From Violent Battles to Organised Competition

There are many articles in commemoration books relating the ferocity of inter-college training sessions in the early days. For example, in Ritsumeikan karate's 40th anniversary publication, *Ichigeki*:

> "Since 1947, we travelled to train together with Kanto universities every two years. Kanto students would come to Kyoto every other year. When with Meiji, we were able to control the intensity because we had known each other since before the war. With other universities, however, we had some brutal battles. We had to cancel the match against Waseda in 1951 because it became too violent. Matches with Chuo and Hosei were also cancelled in 1953 when we put some of them in hospital."

In Toyo University's 70th anniversary publication, Hisatomi Tokio wrote of an exchange training with Kwansei Gakuin and other groups in June 1952. "Even though we were members of the same Shito-ryu school, there was a sense of rivalry between the universities which was quite intense. It was a matter of who could withstand the most pain."

In Keio's 75th anniversary book.

> "On November 21, 1954, the All Japan Student Karate Federation held a demonstration at the Nakanoshima Public Hall in Osaka... The next day, Waseda's club, which happened to be on a tour of the Kansai region, held a joint session with a combined team of Doshisha

and Ritsumeikan. When Mashimo and his team saw how the Kansai team had the upper hand, they immediately asked Ritsumeikan and Doshisha for a joint practice which finally took place at Doshisha on November 24. It was not really exchange training, but rather a marathon duel of 4 versus 80—white belts followed by black belts."

In Meiji University's 40th anniversary book, Iwai Susumu wrote the following:

"When I was in my second year, there was a joint training with Chuo at the dojo in Surugadai. Joint sessions were no more than brawls in the name of exchange training, unless the universities already had an amicable relationship. After the training with Chuo, some of us were taken to Nihon University Hospital on stretchers. The dojo was surrounded by a huge crowd of students curious to see what the commotion was about."

Toning down these rivalries was becoming a matter of great urgency. An effort was made to formulate appropriate rules for friendly competition. It required proper organisation and consensus between stakeholders. In April 1952, alumni of the Kanto universities and the *Shihan* from the various styles began to meet once a week at the Ginza Tsubame Restaurant to try and forge an agreement. The main topic of discussion was the unification of karate in Japan. Nevertheless, the *Shihan* from each *ryuha* could not meet eye-to-eye and the discussions were eventually called off.

It was a time of growth and expansion for the schools. It was also a time when people felt the need to prove to the world that our school and training methods were superior to others. In the democratic atmosphere of the post-war period it was difficult to coordinate the various opinions. "Concerned about the status quo, alumni from various universities in the Kanto region representing various *ryuha* congregated at a noodle shop called Asadaken in Hatchobori in April 1956. They met there every Wednesday. This was the start of the Suiyo-Kai."

"In the beginning, it was mainly Sato, Horiguchi (Meiji); Fukui, Takahashi (Takushoku); Obata, Ito, Takagi (Keio). As time went by, more alumni from each university joined... We discussed the formation of a student federation—which seemed like a dream at the time. We wanted to break away from the situation where university clubs were the private domains of the *ryuha Shihan*. We somehow wanted to contribute to the establishment of an amateur system where students could study freely and improve their skills in a way that transcended school affiliation."

Kinjo Hiroshi's *Gekkan Karatedo* magazine reported on this in an article titled "All Japan Amateur Karate Federation Preparatory Committee Inaugurated". "From Keio were Ito Shuntaro, Takagi Fusajiro, Iwamoto Akiyoshi, Suzuki Hiroo, and Obata Isao; Tokyo University—Ota Yoshihito, Ishizuka Akira, Kojima Tetsuya; Takushoku University—Fukui Isao, Irie Toshio; Meiji University—Sato Yajuo, Horiguchi Ken'ichi, Hada Yoshitaka; Nihon University—Wakabayashi Eiichi,

Tanabe Yoshimitsu; Rikkyo University—Hirai Masana; Tokyo University of Agriculture—Ito Kimio; Kanagawa University—Kimura Kazuo; Toyo University—Ito Shiro".[2] One of their points of discussion was the question of competition. In Keio's 75th anniversary book, the discussions that took place were described as follows:

"In 1955, the Student Federation established a karate tournament system, and the idea of holding tournaments on a national scale began to take shape. Wakabayashi, an alumnus of Nihon University (later executive director of the JKF), Ishizuka, an alumnus of the University of Tokyo (current vice president of the University of Tokyo Alumni Association), and Mochizuki of Keio met several times at Wakabayashi's house to draw up a match system and referee regulations. There would be one referee, four judges, and one match auditor. Match duration would be 2-minutes, five members per team, match court area measuring 7.28 × 7.28-metres (later double these dimensions). The starting distance between the fighters was increased to 3-meters to start the match properly. Basically, it was much the same as the rules formulated by Waseda in 1952. After that, alumni from each university held frequent meetings at the Tsubame Grill in Ginza, and current student members of Takushoku, Meiji, Nihon University and other dojos were mobilised to test the rules out."

Iwai Susumu of Meiji University wrote the following:

"Karate could not continue on this way. Although it was budo, what we were doing was no different to gangster fights… I returned to Wakayama and expressed my intentions to Ujita-sensei (alumnus of Ritsumeikan). At that time, Sekimoto (Wakayama University) had already done a lot of research into methods for holding matches. I took his ideas back to Tokyo and asked alumni from our university as well as those from Takushoku, Keio, Tokyo University and Nihon University for their opinions. At the time, Takushoku seniors Fukui and Nishiyama were researching match rules, and a Takku Cup competition was going to be held between Takushoku alumni and current members. We also tried matches several times during training sessions at Meiji."

Students rejected the brawling *kumite*, and throughout the country there was a movement to devise proper match rules.[3]

"In October 1955, Takushoku, Keio and Meiji held a match at Meiji's dojo. In 1957, a Wado-ryu Student Championship was held at Meiji's gymnasium. Thanks to these two events, alumni from various universities came together in support. At last, the All Japan Student Karatedo Federation's banner was about to be raised."

(2) The 1st All Japan University Karate Championship

Although Waseda and Ritsumeikan were not going to participate, the first student All Japan Championships were about to become a reality.

It was held on November 30, 1957, at the Ryogoku International Stadium (formerly known as the Kokugikan). Originally, 32 universities entered but only 29 universities ended up competing. Iwai's account of the lead up to the tournament is interesting. Iwai was the captain of the winning team and he won his fight with *tettsui-uchi* (hammer fist strike) in the final match (Photo 4–17).[4] Two months before the tournament, Iwai was diagnosed with a serious lung infection. He was unable to train from two months before the match.

Photo 4-17 Iwai (right) scoring with a "*tettsui*" technique in the final. This photo was published in Kinjo's *Gekkan Karatedo*. (Courtesy of Goto Takashi of Meiji University)

"I had met the main fighters of each university in several joint training sessions and competed with each of them in my mind beforehand. How should I attack in the first 30 seconds? What should I do if I got a *waza-ari* scored against me and there are only 10 seconds left? I thought of every possible scenario. I had to think about my stamina and somehow win within the allotted time of two minutes to make sure the match did not go into extra time. I went over all of this in my mind…. I also closed my eyes and put myself in my opponent's shoes, trying to identify my own weak points. Like a computer, I calculated every possible move. I was not worried at all about my lack of practice."

The commitment and care with which they prepared for this inaugural tournament was something to behold. The day before the match, however, something unexpected happened.

"When I was about to go home to get ready for the early start the next day, two or three students from Chuo club asked to meet with me. I asked them to enter the clubroom and they suddenly started reading a statement. They said: 'Karate is not a sport, it is budo, a martial art, so we can't have matches. If we are going to hold matches, we should do it until one or the other collapses. We do not recognise the legitimacy of tomorrow's tournament as the 1st All Japan Student Championship if making contact in an attack is considered a foul.' It was 20 years ago, but I remember clearly that's exactly what they said. I replied to them: 'I'm sure that's not what you guys actually think. Go back and pass on this message to the person who ordered you to come here. After tomorrow's tournament, we will take on any number of people at any time under any rules. Please come to Meiji's dojo."

This anecdote reveals the highly competitive nature of karate. What is karate? Budo, martial art, sport, physical education...? For the students who competed in karate, the court was not just for matches, but was in many ways a battlefield for their lives. They put their heart and souls into it. Iwai concluded with the following statement.

"After the match, I was happy that I had won. But more than that, I was happy that an official karate tournament had finally been organised. After coming back to Surugadai from Ryogoku, we had a celebration party at the dojo where I drank *sake* against doctor's orders. I hugged Suzuki Saburo and couldn't stop crying. I still remember it as if it was yesterday"

2. Founding and Activities of the Japan Karatedo Federation

On October 1, 1964, the day of the Tokyo Olympic Games, the Japan Karatedo Federation (JKF) was launched to unite the karate world and effectively promote it. The first president was also the president of the Student Federation, Ohama Nobumoto (also the Chancellor of Waseda University). Sasakawa Ryoichi (chairman of the Japan Shipbuilding Industry Foundation) made the federation into a foundation. In *Gekkan Karatedo* (July 1972) Eriguchi Eiichi (executive director of the Japan Karatedo Federation) relayed the process of the federation's creation.

"In brief, the Japan Karatedo Federation was created as follows: In the year of the 1964 Olympic Games, the Ministry of Education took the initiative to get things started with help from the Diet Member's Karatedo

Federation. Karate had been introduced to Japan half a century earlier. But it was now divided into several schools and associations, each competing for supremacy. It had reached the stage where it had to be pulled together. At the time of its inauguration, the JKF was formed by people who had previously held leadership positions, but they were unable to do anything of consequence. After a year and a half, a move was made to improve the structure and the board was replaced. From that point on… although I had just been a board member, the others recommended that I be appointed chairman, an honour, albeit an unpopular position. When I first took charge, the JKF was still not officially registered in any of the prefectures, our membership fees were almost non-existent, and as a voluntary organisation we were struggling both financially and in terms of configuration. However, we knew that we had to get on with it, so the nine organisations that existed at the time took the lead, and the implementation of new initiatives started to gather pace… In October of the year before last (1970), we were able to hold the 1st World Championships in Tokyo, where 33 countries gathered in what was a pleasant atmosphere. We were able to inaugurate the first global organisation—the World Union of Karatedo Organisations (WUKO). Of course, there are still a handful of people who don't understand the ideals of the WUKO and insist that they are the best in Japan, but I think that time will tell."

The nine organisations were the Student Federation, Company Federation, Wadokai, Karate Kyokai, Gojukai, Shitokai, Renbukai, Rengokai, and the Self-Defence Forces. Incidentally, for the 1st All Japan Championships mentioned in the text, the steering committee members came from these organisations, and the Tokyo Metropolitan Federation also joined them to help.

An article in the *Karate Shimbun* (1969), published by the Karate Publication Association, ran the news "All Japan Championships opening on October 10—Individual and Inter-prefectural team competitions to decide Japan's best." Out of the 47 prefectures, there were 26 teams (one team from prefectural federations, two teams from Osaka and Tokyo), and 44 individuals (one representative from each prefectural federation, two from Tokyo and Osaka, and two from each of the nine cooperating organisations). This means that 24 of the 47 prefectures participated in the tournament. Okinawa, the birthplace of karate, had not yet been returned to Japan, so it was unable to participate.

(1) Article from *Karate Shimbun* in 1969
—"Current Situation of the Okinawan Karate World"

On July 4, 1969, just before the 1st All Japan Tournament organised by the JKF took place, an article says that Kaneshima Shinsuke, president of the All Okinawa Karatedo Federation, and vice president Yagi Meitoku flew to Tokyo and met with the leaders of the JKF. Their goal was to discuss Okinawa's reversion to Japan and its place in the federation. The article states that the Okinawan karate community, which formed a federation before it was returned to Japan, wished to eventually be affiliated with the mainland. However, they expressed their opposition to the idea of turning *kumite* into a competition.

"Kaneshima: The Okinawa Karatedo Federation was formed in 1956. Our motivation for inauguration was to tidy things up. In the midst of the post-war confusion, people with no ability in karate became dojo owners, and those with no qualifications were given unauthorised Dan grades and titles.

Yagi: A special feature of authentic Okinawan karate is that there is no *kumite*. Therefore, there are no championships, and all demonstrations are based on the performance of *kata*.

Kaneshima: It is almost impossible to stop a *waza* before it touches any part of the body, even if that is the premise. You just cannot stop the momentum. When we talk about free *kumite*, we are talking about offence and defence, which is, after all, a form. The only time we call it a 'match' is when it is a serious contest [of life and death]… The biggest problem is the forthcoming return to the motherland, and our task is to unite with the local karate community by this time."

What then, is karate? The question of Okinawa prefecture's participation in the National Sports Festival (*Kokutai*), and the contemporary problem of the juxtaposition of traditional karate and competition karate can be seen in these statements.

Also, the question of karatedo as an Olympic sport and what karatedo should be as a martial art are linked to these issues.

(2) National Sports Festival
—Japan Karate Association and Kyokushinkai

In 1972, the Japan Sports Association approved the Japan Karatedo Federation as an authorised member. The initial goal of the JKF was to become an official event of the National Sports Festival of Japan (hereafter referred to as *Kokutai*). The *Kokutai* was first held in 1946 in Kansai as a national athletic festival for all citizens.

By the late 1960s, the number of JKF tournaments each year totalled around 20. Recognition of karatedo as a competition event at the *Kokutai* was a way of raising its appeal and status. *Kokutai* is seen as a wonderful opportunity by athletes in all sporting disciplines to represent one's home prefecture. Karate began its journey to becoming an official event as a "demonstration sport" at the Nagano *Kokutai* in September 1978.

The first tournament as a *Kokutai* event was at the Shiga *Kokutai*, held from September 13 to 16, 1981. To select the representative athletes from each prefecture, the JKF consulted with all the organisations that referred to themselves as karatedo even if they followed a different path to the norm. The intention was to make it a true National Sports Festival that united the karate world.

The Japan Karate Association withdrew from the All Japan Karatedo Federation in 1975, and the founder of Kyokushin

Kaikan, Oyama Masutatsu, had his own ideas about how karate should be practised and created a genre later known as "full contact karate". Oyama's karate was popular in boys' magazines and had many devotees. Although the organisation split up after his death, it still retains a significant number of members. Just before karate was made an official event of the *Kokutai*, a record of discussions between the JKF, the JKA and Kyokushin Kaikan regarding participation in the festival was serialised from the February 1981 issue of the *Gekkan Budo* magazine published by the Nippon Budokan.

> "On December 25, 1980, at 10:00am in the special guest room of the Nippon Budokan, Sasakawa Ryoichi (president of the JKF), Kosaka Zentaro (president of the JKA), and Mori Matsuhei (president of Kyokushinkai) met to discuss uniting the karate world in a 'Karatedo Summit Discussion'... The meeting was moderated by Yamanaka Goro (executive director of the Nippon Budokan). Mr. Yamanaka said, 'As karate will be an official event at next year's Shiga *Kokutai*, and as all three presidents are board members of the Nippon Budokan, the Budokan will mediate discussions to bring the various karate groups closer together.'"

Yamanaka continued,

> "If all karate practitioners were to participate in the *Kokutai*, the same rules would apply. The rules of the three organisations are different as it stands, so I would like you to consider making compromises on this point

at a practical level."

All three appeared to be very much in favour and agreed to discuss the details and various issues at a working level. Yamanaka added,

> "From the point of view of safety, it is also necessary to focus on developing protective gear, so the Nippon Budokan has set up a committee to research protective gear for karate along the lines of kendo and naginata… This will be followed up by working-level meetings between the three organisations, to be attended by Eriguchi Eiichi (Japanese Budo Association standing director), Takagi Fusajiro (JKF), Ito Kimio (JKA executive director), and Oyama Masutatsu (Kancho of Kyokushinkai)."

They met six times from January 25 to July 7, 1981.

First meeting (January 22, 1981):

"Correspondence from the 1st Working-level Meeting (Budokan Special Guest Room—All locations below are the same."

"Moderator (Budokan) Yamanaka Goro: Today I would like to ask you, Mr. Eriguchi, in your capacity as an officer of the Japanese Budo Association, and the three representatives from the respective groups to have open and productive talks…"

"Takagi (JKF): The *Kokutai* is a national festival governed by the Japan Sport Association (JSA) as the parent body and the prefectures as the contact points. Through the JKF and JSA, the public will be invited to participate in the planned tournament which will be held under the rules of the JKF (Explanation of the rules for *kumite* and *kata*)."

"Ito (JKA): I think that some of our athletes will participate in the tournament in their own right. I hope that they will not be marginalised or disadvantaged because of their absence from the sport to date."

"Oyama (Kyokushin): … There are many young people who see karate as a fighting art and want to dedicate their energy to competition. I think it is important to think about karate in a way that will be supported by the general public."

(Budokan): I would like to say that karatedo has been recognised as a national sport and that we are very happy that it has been made an official event in the *Kokutai*. We are all very much in favour of this and will do our best to ensure its success. Let us now have a frank discussion for the sake of mutual understanding, and to make sure we are all on the same page…"

The first meeting seemed amicable and all parties were in agreement on the main topics of discussion.

Second meeting (February 17, 1981):

More concrete discussions concerning details were held. The JKF suggested that the two organisations convene a steering committee for tournament officials as cooperating organisations. The JKA calls for new rules. Kyokushinkai argues that it is not too late to decide on the rules. Eriguchi, who attended the meeting in his capacity as a member of the Japan Budo Association, said that karatedo is not only about the *Kokutai*. He suggested that the principles of each organisation should be respected and not so much emphasis placed on uniting everybody. He suggests that the groups could collaborate just for the National Sports Meet.

Third meeting (March 17, 1981):

JKF states, "Changes to our organisation's statutes were approved at the meeting of the JKF's Board of Directors and Trustees held on March 14. Because the federation was founded on the basis of *ryuha*, in addition to prefectural and regional bodies, individual groups have also been affiliated with us. However, we have decided to make them supporting groups and to work within the framework of prefectural units. If JKA and Kyokushinkai are added to the five existing organisations, we will be able to create a cooperative system of the major groups in Japan, and Japanese karate will be able to work as one."

Fourth meeting (April 21, 1981):

The JKF reported that preparations for the *Kokutai* were proceeding well. The JKA reported, "We are willing to cooperate for the National Sports Meet, but we will have to wait until we have coordinated our internal opinions." Kyokushin added, "We have had several meetings about this in Kyokushinkai. To put it bluntly, there are many people who say that we are being 'too amicable' in going along with these proposals, but I say that we should cooperate. Taekwondo in Korea is growing fast and is aiming to become an Olympic sport. Japan is lagging. It is important that we work together as a team."

Fifth meeting (May 7, 1981):

On the matter of how to collaborate the JKF proposed, "We want a system of cooperation that is not limited to *Kokutai*. What do you think about a 'gentleman's agreement' for collaboration without coercion or any obligation? Just an agreement where we cooperate with each other and talk in a friendly manner?" Kyokushinkai: "If JKF and Kyokushinkai, which have not communicated with each other until now, suddenly became 'cooperating organisations', our affiliates will be left confused. I think it is better to document and cooperate with each other as a 'supporting organisation' even if what we are essentially doing is 'cooperation'." "It was confirmed that the JKA will nominate Ito Kimio and Kyokushinkai will nominate Gouda Yuji as members of the *Kokutai* Steering Committee".

Sixth meeting (July 7, 1981):

JKA: "I think the purpose of the cooperation protocols is fine. But I am not sure about talk of the Olympic Games at this juncture. I think it is important to solve our domestic problems first. There is a conflict between WUKO and

IAKF (International Amateur Karate Federation). As for the question of whether we should come under the auspices of the JKF, we have been reborn as a prefecture-based organisation and think that it is better to work together on equal footing."

JKF: "I agree with Mr. Ito. Let's deal with the Olympic issue after the *Kokutai.*"

Kyokushinkai: "Many followers have asked me whether Kyokushinkai is under the umbrella of the JKF. I will cooperate, but I don't remember agreeing to become an affiliate. In order to discuss these matters on an equal footing, I think it would be better if the JSA and the Budokan take the lead in guiding the discussion."

Budokan: "We believe a good result has been achieved in confirming that we can all cooperate with regard to the *Kokutai.* As for future aspirations of the Olympic Games, whether we like it or not the time will come when we need to seriously discuss the issue of 'under which umbrella' in order to proceed. For the meantime, we have decided to suspend these discussions after confirming cooperation for the *Kokutai.* We hope that everyone will continue to work together for unity in karatedo."

The article concludes, "After this, Mr. Takagi of the JKF handed over a 'Request for Approval as Supporting Organisations' to Mr. Ito and Mr. Oyama." The article then goes on to state that "Kyokushinkai, Goju-kai, Shitokai, JKA, Rengokai, Renbukai, and Wadokai" all agreed to unify as a national league in line with the JKF's proposal. Thus, karatedo became an official event from the 36th Shiga National Sports Meet.

Photo 4-18 The handshake. From right to left—Eriguchi, Takagi, Ito and Oyama. (*Gekkan Budo*, February 1981)

誤記事抹消公告

本年八月、当連盟発行役員名簿記載の左記記事は、誤記事のため抹消致します。

お詫び申し上げます。

お二方にご迷惑をおかけしたことを

なお、登記致しておりませんので、念のため申し添えます。

記

一、副会長　毛利　松平殿

一、理　事　郷田　勇三殿

昭和五十六年十月十五日

財団法人　全日本空手道連盟

専務理事　高木房次郎

以上

Photo 4-19 Public notice of apology for publicising incorrect information. (*Gekkan Budo*, December 1981)

This photograph of Eriguchi, Takagi, Ito and Oyama shaking hands (Photo 4–18) was widely circulated. The JKF registered Kyokushinkai's chairman Mori Shohei as "JKF vice chairman" and Goda Yuzo as a JKF director without either's consent. In the December 1981, an apology was published in the *Gekkan Budo* (Photo 4–19) in the name of Takagi Fusajiro (executive director of the JKF). If this system of cooperation between the three karate organisations had been maintained, karatedo's participation in the Olympics would surely have been much faster.

Notes:

(1) After the establishment of Japan Karatedo Federation, Renbukai was changed in name to JKF Renbukai and it was positioned as a "cooperating organisation".

(2) Kinjo, *Gekkan Karatedo*, December 1, 1957, p.16. In the text, it is stated that Ito Kimio represented Tokyo Agricultural University, but it was a mistake. Ito belonged to Hosei. In the 50th anniversary book for Tokyo University of Agriculture's club, there is no mention of Ito, but the name appears as a representative of the JKA. If it is the same person, it should have been recorded as Hosei University.

(3) 40th anniversary book for Meiji, p.39. Tsujikawa Sadachika wrote in *Yukyu no Ken*, p.76, that after the war he worked with the students of Kansai University and Kobe Municipal University of Foreign Studies to create and test rules for *kumite* matches.

(4) Iwai Tatsu passed away in November 2017. At a meeting held in his memory (July 7, 2018), WKF Secretary General Nagura Toshihisa said that he had seen this match when he was in primary school and wondered whether it was an "*ura-uchi* or *tettsui-uchi*". The moment Manabe slipped, he took the opportunity to strike. The *tettsui-uchi* which appears in section 4 of this chapter, is not part of any of today's standard techniques. *Ura-uchi* was often used by Ritsumeikan students, but it is rare in karate now. *Ura-uchi* is a more advanced technique, difficult to control, and hard to judge because of its close proximity.

SECTION 6

Kumite and Kata Competitions

(Koyama Masashi)

I have written about karate competitions focusing on the history of karate up to the 1st World Championships and its official inclusion in the National Sports Festival of Japan. I would now like to look at *kumite* and *kata* events in which I participated as a competitor, and from the perspective of an instructor and referee based on my own experiences.

1. Kumite Competition
(1) Changes in Rules and Techniques in Kumite Competitions (Table 4–2) lists the changes in techniques used in *kumite* matches over the past 40 years.[1] I have included this table to give the reader an idea of the changes in the rules and techniques used over time. Recent changes in the rules and their application have led to a sharp decrease in *chudan-tsuki*, and an increase in *jodan-tsuki*.

Wada Koji and I competed in *kumite* competitions in the early 70s when competitions were mainly decided by *ippon-shobu*.

Suzuki Ryoichi of Ritsumeikan, who won the 4th All Japan Student Individual Championship (1960), kicked himself to victory in almost all his bouts with *chudan-geri*. This was Suzuki's signature technique, and Photo 4–20 is a rare shot of his opponent responding with a *morote-uke*. Ritsumeikan

	1976	1989	2014, 2015
Tournaments Surveyed	All Japan Student Championships (Ind.), East Japan (Teams), Wadokai Nationals	3rd World Games, World Cup, Spain International	All Japan Championships
Results Presented	1976—Budogaku Kenkyu Vol. 9, No. 1~	1990—*Nice Karate Life*	2017—Presentation at the Japanese Academy of Budo
Investigators	Tanabe Hideo (Nihon University karate coach), Professor Tanaka Shizuo	JKF National Team Manager Yanagita Shunsuke	Mimura Yuki, Koyama Masashi
Winning Point	Ippon-shobu, 2 x waza-ari = ippon	Sanbon-shobu. In reality 6-points as 2-points = 1 ippon. Waza-ari = 1-point.	Eight-points. Ippon=3-points. Waza-ari=2-points. Yuko = 1-point.
Referees & Judges (Shimpan)	Four judges (one Fukushin in each corner). Referee (Shushin) takes the leading role. Matches often halted for Shimpan consultation.	Sanbon-shobu further divided into ippon and waza-ari, thus increasing the number of points to be scored. The match duration increased to three minutes. Points for foul play awarded to opponent.	Jodan-geri kick is worth 3-points and chudan-geri 2-points. All thrusts are worth 1-point. Referee must award point if two or more judges' flags are raised.
Notes	Many losses due to fouls by knocking opponent down with a thrust.	9.5% of points are awarded to the opponent for infringements.	A foul does not count as a point for the opponent; after four fouls are committed, the player is declared to have lost the match.

Percentage breakdown (combined / split):

		1976 combined	1976	1989 combined	1989	2014, 2015 combined	2014, 2015
Jodan-waza	Tsuki	57%	57%	32%	32%		75%
	Keri		0%		0%		5%
Chudan-waza	Tsuki	43%	30%	58%	55%	15%	7-13%
	Keri		13%		3%		4-6%

Table 4-2 Changes in Points Scored in Kumite Matches

Photo 4-20 An opponent responds to Suzuki's *chudan-geri* with a double-cross (*morote*) block. (Courtesy of Nakamura Yuji, Ritsumeikan)

Photo 4-21 Suzuki's opponent is trying to block his *chudan-geri* attack. Each university devised countermeasures against Ritsumeikan's kicking techniques. (Courtesy of Nakamura Yuji)

students were very skilled at this particular kick. Suzuki's kick was strong, and few people now could block it in this way. As the level of competition has improved, the study of counterattacking techniques has advanced, and the number of competitors who stay put and brace themselves (as shown in Photo 4–21) has decreased. In my competitive days, a simple middle *mae-geri* was already often being met with counter-strikes and blocks, and more often a combination of the two, or a spinning middle kick was used to score a *waza-ari*. This when the *jodan* kick was still rarely seen in competition.

When it became an official event of the National Sports Festival, the JKF adopted the *sanbon-shobu* system. Thrusts and kicks were both counted as *ippon*, and there were times when it was the first person to get two *ippon*, or three would be the winner. Both thrusts and kicks had the same value, but the value of more difficult kicks later increased. Unfortunately, I have not been able to find any records of research into the period of *sanbon-shobu* matches. The protective equipment which Yamanaka of the Nippon Budokan said was under consideration was called *anzen-gu* (safety gear). This included a protective mask called a *menho*, gloves and a body protector to safeguard the torso. In the National Sports Meet, *kumite* competitions were for different ranks wearing this safety equipment.

To be honest, as a competitor from the *ippon* era I felt uncomfortable wearing gloves and the *menho*. The slight change in distance by wearing gloves and the *menho* meant that there were times when referee flags were raised for a technique that could normally have been avoided. It was necessary to carefully calibrate distancing for blocks. In later years, the *menho* was removed from the All Japan Championships, and it was decided that they would not be used in the Olympics.

The move to 6-point matches brought about a major change in tactics. As more points need to be taken in a match, more stamina is required. To reach the finals, it is better to get two points up and save energy after that. The 1989 data shows that the percentage of Japanese athletes who scored with *jodan-geri* was 0%. The kick was not employed much. Also, it is difficult to control the *jodan* kick itself, and referees often judge it as a foul. At that time, domestic and international rules were different. There was a period in which JKF's 3-point and WUKO's 6-point rule coexisted. This made it challenging for competitors and referees to adapt to each competition.

Now, in the 8-point era *jodan-geri* is judged as a 3-point technique, making it beneficial to get ahead or make up points quickly. *Chudan-geri* is only worth 2-points. In the days of *ippon-shobu*, losing was unpleasant enough. Being knocked down or crawling on the floor, however, was even more embarrassing. *Jodan-geri* often resulted in a loss of balance, and as the groin was left exposed; it is also a dangerous technique in martial arts terms. It was not worth the risk to try in a match. In the current rules, however, it has become a valuable technique for competitive *kumite*.

(2) The Importance of Shimpan in Kumite

As an athlete you are not only fighting against your opponent in a *kumite* match. You are also fighting against the judgement of the referees and judges (*Shimpan*). If the *Shimpan*'s flag does not go up, no points are scored. If no points are scored, victory is not possible. I have served as both a coach and a referee, so I know how difficult it is to adjudicate *kumite*. Karate differs from kendo and fencing in that the weapons are the hands and feet of the fighter. Karate *kumite* is not like sumo or judo, where you also make use of the belt or *mawashi*.

The players attack from a distance using mainly thrusts and kicks, while defending themselves and competing to score points. Attacks to the eyes and other dangerous targets are forbidden. Attacks must be controlled carefully to not make full contact. Although the term usually used is *sundome* (stopping just before impact), I believe that control is really the key word. This is what makes karate such an exciting sport. Two well-trained athletes attack and defend against each other with absolute control of powerful blows to "skin touch" level. If you have a strong core and a stable lower body, it is possible to control your thrusts, strikes, and kicks.

The history of *jiyu kumite* (*choppaa* or *tegumi* in the case of Ritsumeikan) has fostered this ability. There is no doubt that height, length of arms and legs are important factors in karate, but speed, sense of timing, and fighting spirit are also crucial.

In the early days of *kumite*, referees had to make difficult judgments about whether a technique was accurate and powerful enough. Scores were often given even though the opponent had blocked the attack, or not given because a technique was deemed too far away or insufficient. Referee calls must be obeyed, but sometimes one is tempted to say, "open your eyes". Having extensive experience as a competitor, I was acutely aware of this conundrum as a referee later on.

There is a saying in karate, "One integrity, two eyes, three legs, four knowledge". In *kumite*, as an individual or team player for your school, prefecture or country, you cannot take a single point for granted. It is no exaggeration to say that one decision can influence a competitor's entire life thereafter. The *Shimpan* must be able to take the right position, make the right decision, and use his or her wits to win the trust of the players, assistant referees, spectators, and all others involved.

(3) The Spectator Element

During the maturation of karate as a sport, venues, especially in Europe, are often packed with spectators. Tournaments are bigger and widely televised, and now that it has been included in the Olympic Games, momentum seems to be doubling.

Now we have the 8-point system for deciding matches. To prevent favouritism or arbitrary judgements by referees, if two flags of the judges (*Fukushin*) are raised the referee (*Shushin*) must acknowledge the technique. The referee is responsible for calling penalties and must work together with the judges to adjudicate the match.

In the 6-point era, the so-called "mirror method" was once utilised. The referee and judges would manoeuvre to the closest position on either side to view the exchange of techniques between players. The theory was that with their extensive experience, the closer they were to the action the more likely correct decisions would be made. The system was changed because it obscured the view when televised. Only one referee could move freely, while the three judges observed and raised their flags at courtside. Now, as was the case in the *ippon-shobu* 1-point era, four judges sit in the corners and raise their red and blue flags to indicate their decisions.

In competitions, *Shimpan* must correctly and instantaneously judge thrusts and kicks of swift-moving fighters. This requires a great deal of skill on the part of the referee. As the sport progresses from regional to national, then to the international stage, the *Shimpan* are selected for their trustworthiness, good eyesight, and excellent powers of judgment. With the introduction of video judging, there has to be an environment where players, coaches and referees can interrelate with peace of mind. A sense of mutual trust needs to be fostered so that as the level of karate competition is raised spectators can understand what is going on. *Shimpan* experience, competence, and understanding is crucial for this to happen.

2. Kata Competition
(1) The Introduction of Kata Matches
The following exchange took place in a roundtable discussion entitled "The History of Karatedo and the Prospects of WUKO", which appeared in the first issue of *Karatedo* (published by Sozo Co., Ltd. on March 15, 1977).

> Fujiwara: "Mr. Eriguchi, have there been any requests from WUKO members to introduce *kata* matches into international competition?"
> Eriguchi: "I've heard about it from some of our members as something to aspire to in the future. But it is not a concrete proposal yet. Technical ability has to reach a

very high level before it will be accepted internationally."

Fujiwara: "Mr. Eriguchi, it will be difficult to introduce *kata* competition into international matches.

Eriguchi: "It is a question of organising the *kata*."

In Japan, women's *kata* was performed for the first time at the 3rd All Japan Championships (1973) where Saito Toshiko won. In the 4th Championship (1975), Yamaguchi Wakako, daughter of Yamaguchi Gogen, was victorious. Although *kata* competitions were being tried in Japan, the concept was still considered premature internationally. Two pages before this article in the same magazine a notice appeared for the 4th Karate World Championships, and in the tournament schedule, along with (A) team competitions and (B) individual competitions to be held on December 3 and 4, (C) *kata* competitions were also included. It is likely that the roundtable meeting was held before the decision was made to introduce *kata* competitions, but we are unsure how and when it was decided to include *kata* at the World Championships.

At the 5th All Japan Championships in 1976, Miyano Hiromasa became the first Japanese champion in men's *kata*. At the 4th World Championships held in Tokyo, only a men's *kata* competition was held, and two members of the Shito-ryu team, Miyano and Okada, were selected to represent Japan. The young Okada, a high school student, won the championship and became the first men's *kata* world champion.

(2) Shitei Kata (Standardised Forms)

In anticipation of karate becoming an official event of the National Sports Festival, *kata* from each *ryuha* were designated as *Shitei Kata*. Two *kata* from each of the four major schools that make up the JKF were chosen, and in the opening round of the tournament, all competitors were required to demonstrate one of the eight *kata*. The designated *kata* are listed in the notes.[2] The *kata* were judged by a points-scoring system, in which the highest and lowest scores given by five judges were cut, and the total points of three remaining judges were used to determine the result. It has been an official event since the Shiga *Kokutai* in 1981, but did appear as a demonstration event two tournaments before at the Miyazaki *Kokutai*.

The *kata* were chosen from the four major schools to maintain balance. However, there was a big problem. The *kata* judges—instructors of their respective schools—were only familiar with the *kata* of their own *ryuha*. They had insufficient understanding of the *kata* of other schools. For this reason, the order of the *embu* was important for the competitors and swayed the results. There was a noticeable tendency for the first performers to be awarded lower scores, and later performers getting higher totals.

As competition experience progressed, the JKF made it compulsory to train in *kata* from other schools at *Shitei Kata* seminars and other events. With this, the overall understanding of *kata* among practitioners deepened and the problems associated with *kata* competition were gradually mitigated.

(3) Pre-Kokutai Tournament in Miyazaki

I competed in the first *kata* selection trials for the World Championships but did not get a place in the national team. Later, when I became a teacher and my life became more stable, I was selected to represent Japan in *kumite*. I competed at the Asian Championships and in France, and I was often asked to give *kata* demonstrations between *kumite* matches.

I always believed that the *kata* should reflect the space (*maai*) and breathing of *kumite*, and that there should be no gaps between the techniques. Moreover, I was aware that the gaze, *zanshin* and *kiai* that I expressed as a *kumite* competitor were different from those of someone who only specialised in *kata*. Of course, *kata* performed by *kata* specialists is very beautiful.

An opportunity arose to show the power and potential of *kata* at the Miyazaki Pre-*Kokutai* Tournament. The men's *kata* final was a match against Okada Keiji, winner of the individual *kata* at the 4th World Championships. The final was judged a draw. In the rematch, the scores were the same again. There was an uproar in the hall. From the spectator seats, I could hear Tomoyori Ryuichiro cheering me on. He was the eldest son of Tomoyori Ryusei of Kenyu-ryu, the 3rd All Japan Student Individual Champion who is mentioned in Chapter 3. He shouted, "Koyama, show them your *kumite*!"

I chose to do *Seisan*, a traditional *kata* that both Miyagi Chojun and Shinzato Jin'an excelled at. It is the only *kata* in Goju-ryu where you stamp loudly on the floor and do "*hakkei*" (outpouring of force) and let out *kiai* a little longer than usual.

I do not remember all the details, but I cannot forget the moment when I felt total control over my breathing and my *ki* had settled in my lower abdomen (*tanden*) as I stood in *musubi-dachi*. That was when I overtook Okada.

(4) 5th Karate World Championship (1980)—Women

The 5th KWC, held in Madrid, Spain, was a memorable event in which women made their debut on the world stage. The 4th World Championships marked the debut of the men's *kata* competition. At the following World Championships, women's *kata* was also adopted as one of the events. The Japanese representatives were Nakayama Mie and Okamura Suzuko. Nakayama is a member of Shito-ryu and Okamura of Goju-ryu. This was the first time that Okamura performed *Suparinpei*. Together with Okada, the winner of the 4th Championship, I represented Japan in the men's *kata* team. I also aspired to represent Japan in *kumite* (70kg), but I had to limit myself to *kata*.

From this tournament, the men's *kumite* competition introduced the *sanbon-shobu* 3-point system and weight categories. Winner (gold medal)—65kg Maeda Toshiaki and 75kg Tajima Sadao; 2nd place (silver medal)—65kg Ono Zen'ichi, 75kg Imamatsu Sadanori, 80kg Takakuwa Naomi; 3rd place (bronze medal)—60kg Sugiyama Jun'ichi. *Ippon-Shobu* (for a while there was an event called "*Ippon-Shobu*" from this tournament)—Murase Hisao. Japan was unable to take the title in the men's team *kumite*.

(5) The 36th National Sports Festival in Shiga

After that, I attempted to win both *kumite* and *kata* at the *Kokutai*. I represented Kyoto at the first official karate event in Shiga (the neighbouring prefecture) and was cheered on vociferously by many supporters who came to watch.

In the men's *kumite* open category, I defeated a few of the young guns: Nishiuchi Shigeo (Miyazaki), Suzuki Yuichi (Kanagawa), and Tajima Sadao (Gunma). In the quarter-final against Wadokai world champion Ono Yoshikazu, I was the first person at the *Kokutai* to successfully execute *furi-uchi* (swinging strike) for the win.[3] This technique is seen in *kata* but is rarely used as a technique in *kumite*. It was my intention to somehow employ a *kata* technique in my matches.

In the semi-final I took the first point from Hyogo's Sasaki Masaki. However, a momentary lapse in concentration, perhaps through relief of just about reaching the final, left me open for Sasaki to score the winning blow. My hopes of winning two events at the *Kokutai* were crushed. In any case, thanks to performing *kata* with the same feeling as *kumite*, I was able to retain the national *Kokutai kata* title for three consecutive tournaments.

(6) Suparinpei and Nipaipo

A *kata* which has been demonstrated since the early days of competition and which still often features in semi-finals and finals is *Suparinpei*. The first person to perform this *kata* in competition in Japan was Okamura Suzuko (I happen to be the first male competitor.) It is the same *kata* performed by

Tomimura Pechin in 1867 when the last envoy from China visited the Ryukyu Kingdom. It is said that there are three versions of *Suparinpei*: *jo* (upper), *chu* (middle), and *ge* (lower), but it is unclear whether the composition and content of the techniques performed today is exactly the same as in the early days. Even if they are not the same, one can still feel the profundity and depth in *Suparinpei* as a form deemed worthy of performing in front of the royal family and officials of the Qing Dynasty. It has been handed down through generations in Naha-te. It combines the characteristic Naha-te breathing techniques, circular movements, and the internal strength based on *Sanchin*.

After seeing and being impressed by Okamura's *Suparinpei* at the 5th World Championships, Nakayama worked on a new *kata*, a form called *Nipaipo* (probably written in Chinese as 二十八步 = "28 steps".) Nakayama's *Nipaipo* was an old form which had been handed down in Shito-ryu. It became very popular once adapted for competition.

Nipaipo is said to have been taught in Okinawa by Go Kenki.[4] Miyagi Chojun's senior, Kyoda Juhatsu, taught the *kata* as *Nepai* in To'on-ryu. It can be assumed that Mabuni was also taught by Go, and that *Nipaipo* is connected to him. As competition evolved, forms such as *Ahnan* and *Chatan Yara Kusanku* also became popular. These *kata* had been neglected during the years of so-called friendly rivalry in *kumite* competition. This *kata* revival has all come to pass over the last three decades.

(7) The Ryuei-ryu and Sakumoto Tsuguo

At the 5th WUKO tournament in Spain, the champion Okada amassed too many points for me to beat him. I won the 6th WUKO championship in Taiwan as well, and was confident I would take the 7th WUKO competition as well. Unfortunately, I was involved in a car accident that left me with a 28-stitch laceration near my left eye and two windscreen fragments in my left eyeball. As a result, I had to stop training for a year. Then came Sakumoto Tsuguo and his signature *kata Ahnan* to the world stage.

"What on earth is Ryuei-ryu ?" This was the question on many people's lips. I was in awe of what I witnessed. When I visited Okinawa to find out more about the history of karatedo, I went to Nago City to meet Nakaima Kenko, third generation headmaster of Ryuei-ryu. The school was not well known at the time. Although I had the opportunity to interview him, he did not talk much of Ryuei-ryu, but more about kendo and martial arts in general. On my way home, Nakaima mentioned, "There is a teacher at Naha High School called Sakumoto. I have told him about you. Please go and chat with him."

I planned on visiting many places in the prefecture from a guest house near Naha High School, but in the end, I did not have a chance to meet with Sakumoto. I had no idea that I was destined to meet him five years later at a tournament, let alone that I would lose the championship to him. Sakumoto went on to compete in subsequent world championships and continues to train champions as an instructor in Okinawa to this day.

(8) Mimura Yuki vs. Yokoyama Hisami

I was asked to coach the national team when Takagi Fusajiro (JKF executive director and WUKO secretary general) and Mano Koichi (JKF general manager) retired. For *kumite*, the coaching team was rejuvenated by Maeda Toshiaki and Murase Hisao. I ended up coaching both *kumite* and *kata*, but with a focus on the latter. It was around this time that Mimura Yuki emerged, a third-year student at Matsumoto Fukashi High School. She performed the *kata Unsu* in competition finals, as did most competitors from the JKA. This *kata* requires precise basics, sharpness in body movement, and a certain amount of weight in the thrusts.

After the training camp and the first selection round, without Nakayama in the team, I sensed that she was the only one who could win on the world stage even though she was only 18 years old. On the train back from the training camp, I had a conversation about her "X-factor" with Mano, chairman of the Strengthening Committee.

As predicted, Mimura was destined to become the champion in Egypt. She went on to win the tournament a total of four times, but it was Yokoyama Hisami who stood in her way. The older Yokoyama (now Inoue) captained the women's *kata* team (women's team *kata* competition had just started) and was also hoping to represent Japan in the individual event. Just as Nakayama challenged with *Nipaipo*, she performed *Unshu* (Shito-ryu form of Mimura's *Unsu*) but without any success. After much toing and froing, we decided on *Chatan Yara Kushanku*.

Up to now, the longest form was *Suparinpei*. The number of moves totals about 50, but in *Chatan Yara Kushanku* there are over 70. It is long, and like *Unsu*, it involves a leap which Yokoyama found difficult. Nevertheless, Yokoyama dared to perform this challenging *kata*. Although she was always behind Mimura in the national team fitness tests, Yokoyama made a determined effort to catch up and overtake her. She did the team *kata* and followed Mimura's lead as an individual competitor. Yokoyama won. She competed with *Chatan Yara Kushanku* triumphantly at the *Kokutai* and the Asian Games. Many competitors still perform *Chatan Yara Kushanku* in finals thanks to the precedent she set.

One of the most memorable moments of my *kata* coaching days was when Aihara Tomoyuki, a student at my first school as a teacher, won the Mexico tournament after Sakumoto retired. His tooth flew out in the last *kiai* (we were practising together in high school when I accidentally cracked his tooth). Aihara later went on to win the Hokkaido National Sports Meet in *kumite*.

Another fond memory was the emergence of group *kata* competitions (*dantai kata*). The men's group *kata* was pioneered by Hasegawa Shin'ichi, the Yukimitsu brothers, and Higawa Koji. In the women's group *kata*, Yokoyama Hisami, Kamino Mari and Watanabe Keiko were the first champions, and when *bunkai kumite* was introduced, Hasegawa, who was also a champion in *kumite*, and others performed magnificently, conveying the allure of *kata* to the audience in an easily understandable way. The group *kata* was a new event for competition, but it also had wonderful potential as a teaching material for budo classes in schools.

Notes

(1) There are shortcomings in this table in that there are no records from the *sanbon-shobu* era. In addition, the level of the competitors is different (university students, world level, All-Japan level). And, it is not always useful to compare techniques used by the competitors in Japan and abroad.

(2) Name of the *Seitei* forms: Goju – *Sepai*, *Saifa*; Shoto – *Jion*, *Kankudai*; Shito – *Passai Dai*, *Seienchin*; Wado – *Seishan*, *Chinto*.

(3) *"Furi-uchi"* = "Swinging strike" or "long inverted hook" is a technique in which the opponent's forearm in a stance or while thrusting is held down, and a strike is made to the open upper body region. At the time, there was a wrestling technique called "Western Lariat", which was regarded as being very similar. If the arm is swung, it will hit the opponent and be judged as a foul. I used a variety of techniques as attacks and counter moves. As my opponent's level increased it became more difficult to get into the right distance to strike. I had more success with counter moves. In the fight with Ono, I scooped up his left-front kick with my right hand and scored with a left *furi-uchi*. It was a spur-of-the-moment move, and one that I had never used in training.

(4) A man who taught karate while running a tea business in Naha before the war. He was a close friend of Miyagi Chojun and other Okinawan masters and is said to have been skilled at White Crane.

||||||||||||||||||||||||||||||||||||||||||||||||||||||||||||||||||||||||||||||||||||||||||||||||||||||||||||||||||||||||||||||||||||||||||||||||||||||

Koyama Essay 2

Kata

Koyama Masashi

In his detailed article "*Okinawa no Karate to 'Kata' ni tsuite*" (Okinawan karate and *kata*), Shinzato Katsuhiko writes, "In Okinawa, karate training has traditionally been based on the practice of *kata*. Training begins and ends with *kata*. It is hard to believe that a martial art can be mastered only by practising *kata* repeatedly. At any rate, karate takes *kata* more seriously than any other budo." (p. 93).

In Chapter 4, Section 6, I mentioned that before the 1st All Japan Championships, the president and vice president of the Okinawa Karatedo Federation met with the leaders of the JKF to discuss their relationship with the mainland after Okinawa was returned to Japan. I also reported that there were some differences in the way *kumite* and kata were perceived between Okinawa and the mainland. Since then, *kata* has become a competition event on the mainland, and the kanji used to write word was changed from 型 to 形.

At a symposium held in March 2017 to celebrate the opening of the Okinawa Karate Kaikan, local instructors said that reconciling the juxtaposition of traditional karate and competition karate will be a challenge for post-Olympic karatedo. This same observation is also very relevant to *kata*. From here, I will introduce my thoughts on *kata* along with Shinzato's theories.

Shinzato is also co-author with Takamiyagi Shigeru of *Okinawa Karate Kobudo Jiten*, and the aforementioned article is a special contribution to the *Okinawa Karatedo Gaisetsu—Budo Karate no Shoso* (ed. Takamiyagi, August 30, 1996). Born in 1939, Shinzato is a practitioner of Shorin-ryu and is a professor at Okinawa International University. He translated Nagamine Shoshin's book *The Essence of Okinawan Karate-Do* from Japanese into English.

① Shinzato Katsuhiko's Article "Okinawan Karate and Kata"

"Offensive and defensive techniques on vital points of the human body are acquired through the practice of *kata*. *Kata* represents the path to the mastery of the martial arts and is the medium for learning. The various *kata* and their martial qualities have been tested over time and generations... There is a depth to traditional Okinawan *kata* that cannot be attained in a single generation... *Kata* has many faces depending on how it is done. Sometimes *kata* are graceful. Sometimes they show a wild face. Sometimes even, it is the face of a demon. Notwithstanding, if *kata* is practised properly, it will reveal the martial outlook, humanity, and values of the practitioner." (p. 94)

1. From the "Karate and Kata" Manuscript

"*Kata* exist as models or as the norms for the various disciplines which incorporate them. *Kata* are found in all the arts. In the world of Kabuki and Noh, they dictate strict traditions on how to perform. In the world of calligraphy, they are models to imitate in order to achieve the aesthetics of brushwork. The main martial arts with *kata* are kendo, judo, aikido and naginata. All of them have different concepts and different ways of dealing with *kata*. Perhaps this is why the ideograph 形 is used instead of 型 in modern budo."

In other words, there is more personal expression in 形. This is followed by some ideas on how the two interpretations of *kata* are different.

"The *kata* of karate exist solely as a method for building the body, generating techniques, developing the mind, and improving one's overall combat skills. It is also a method which enables the study of martial arts alone... This is why *kata* in karate requires going through a process of trial and error. Logic and reasoning are necessary to extract specific techniques from the sequences of abstract movements. Of course, this reasoning is not contemplative, but is the result of analysis and synthesis through the body. A karate *kata* cannot become a martial art simply by training according to the *kata* form. There must be a way of extracting the martial art *from* the *kata*." (p. 95)

2. In "Karate and Kata" and Other Points of Interest

"In the case of karate, the traditional understanding is that 'hand' (*te* or *tii*) = 'martial art'." "'*Tii* is both a martial art and a *kata*." "The forefathers of karate bequeathed knowledge on how to create, acquire, and retain techniques. These are the *kata* of karate." "The *kata* are the greatest common denominator of myriad techniques." These are just a few of the expressions Shinzato used that fascinate me.

Other interesting sections follow: "3. Kata and Keiko; 4. Kata Functions; 5. Kata Structure; 6. Kata Interpretation". From *kata*, a medium for learning martial techniques, we find ways of extracting *waza* which can then be applied to practical combat situations. Or, they serve to strengthen body and mind, so that if a critical situation is encountered, the practitioner will be mentally and physically prepared. *Kata* are sequences of dozens of techniques seamlessly linked together, and they are inspiring to watch. Athletes in competitive karate can gain a deeper understanding of *waza* through *kata*. Shinzato's article is an excellent reminder that we are all undergoing a process of never-ending learning.

② Zeami's Teachings

Zeami's *Kakyo* is a collection sublime wisdom regarding the art of performing. It is said that the artistic Ways exist because there are audiences who appreciate them. Karate must also win the hearts and minds of the judges and spectators and is in this sense a performance art. Let us now look at the concept of *kata* from the purview of Zeami's teachings.

"First, the tonality; second, the activating force; third, the voice..." (*iccho-niki-sansei*). In *Kakyo*, Zeami states that these form the essentials of vocal technique. How does this relate to *kata* competition? "At the perfect moment, close your eyes, draw in your breath, and speak out..." urges Zeami. In the case of *kata*, the athlete answers the call to commence, steps forward, bows, and stands at the starting line. At this point, there is a quiet, short period of meditation. Then, the performer announces the name of the *kata* to the judges and spectators. Next, "The voice comes out from the tonality first." Zeami said that the "first voice" is the most important, and that it decides the outcome of the performance.

This is precisely the part of the *kata* in which you vocalise its title, inform the judges and spectators, and then begin the first movement in your own time. Stepping forward with all the attention of the judges and spectators on you, vocalise the name of the *kata* from your gut, and begin the first movement in sync with the breath. I try to synchronise cadence with those who are watching. If you can "pull your breath in" and synchronise your breathing with that of the spectators, then a connection is created. In a *kata* demonstration it is possible to assess the skill of the performer just by observing the first movement.

In the old days when the points system was used to decide *kata* matches, referees gauged the approximate score level of a *kata* by the first move. Then judgements were made on each successive movement. If it was the first time for a referee to see a particular competitor in action, his or her rating might increase as the performance progressed. On the other hand, if an unknown competitor showed signs of inexperience, their rating would go down. If it was a top-level competitor, or somebody the referees had seen many times, they automatically assessed whether he or she was having a good day or not. From the very first movement to the last breath, the judges observed with a cold eye to see if the performance was living up to expectations.

Zeami said, "operating the body only seven-tenths while operating the mind ten-tenths…" He also asserted: "An interval of inactivity is interesting." In the case of karate *kata*, the intervals of inactivity are exactly where one needs to reveal one's understanding of the *kata*. This is the part of the *kata* that Zeami refers to as "performing with vigilance". And, this is where the "pleasantness of the aesthetic effects of physical expression" and the "subtle charm" emanates from.

When you transition from one technique to the next, you must visualise the opponent's position and movements. In other words, the *kata* performer must draw an image of the opponent's presence. Imagination guides movement, as does breath, and *ki*. "When we are in the right frame of mind to move to the place of seeing", one's inner senses peak. It is then that the moment must be seized, and the maximum energy is focussed on the point of attack.

Since the days of So Neiju at Ritsumeikan, "stones" was always a part of our training routine. Before training, first and second-year students started with bench presses lifting the stone weights, while the senior students kicked sandbags. After preliminary exercises, basic drills involved a long period of *shiko-dachi*, and left and right *neko-dachi*. All we did was strengthen our bodies and repeat the basics. *Kata* were added on top of this physical and mental foundation. As Shinzato states, "Unearth the martial techniques and discover the intention of the *kata* to draw out the *waza* from the sequence of movements" is the traditional approach in the eternal search for the unity of mind, body and technique. Traditional *kata* are the gateway to karate, and a treasure trove for practise and reflection.

||||||||||||||||||||||||||||||||||||||||||||||||||||||||||||||||||||||||||||||||||||||||||||||||||||||||||||||||||||||||||||||||

SECTION 7

Compulsory Budo
in Junior High Schools,
and the Road to the Olympics

Karate in school education was first introduced in Okinawa in the Meiji period. The spread of karate to the mainland led to the Okinawan martial art becoming a Japanese budo. Consequently, people throughout the country became aware of its educational potential. As a competitive event, karate is now only one of two budo, the other being judo, that is an Olympic sport. In this section Koyama Masashi will outline how budo was made a compulsory subject in Japanese junior high schools. WKF Secretary General, Nagura Toshihisa, will explain how the decision was made to adopt karate into the 2020 Tokyo Olympics.

1. Compulsory Budo in Junior High Schools

(1) Historical Connection Between Karatedo and Education
① Meiji Period in Okinawa
During the Meiji period (1868–1912), Ryukyu-era *todi* underwent a major transformation into modern karate. In 1901, Ogawa Gintaro, principal of Okinawa prefecture Normal School, attended a meeting of district supervisors and school principals in October, and gave a speech on physical education. The following year, in March 1902, karate was performed at the

farewell party for graduates of the Normal School. In August the same year, karate was included in local athletic events, and was becoming widely respected in the field of education. It was becoming the pride of Okinawa.

In December 1904, staff at the Okinawa prefecture Middle School set up a study group for karate. The following year, karate was implemented as part of the department's curriculum. From 1906, karate was also taught at the Normal School, almost on the same standing as a regular course. At the same time, the Ministry of Education revised the national curriculum for middle schools to promote the ideal of "*Fukoku Kyohei*" (wealthy country, strong army). This culminated in the inclusion of bujutsu (kendo and judo) as a part of the callisthenics regular course in 1911. In this sense, it can be said that Okinawa was one step ahead of mainland Japan in its promotion of martial arts as regular subjects.

② From Club Activities to Regular Classes

"After receiving his *shodan* grade in April 1924, Kasuya gathered a group of students at Keio Gijuku University. On October 15 that year he established the Karate Kenkyu Kai…" As we have seen, it was the university clubs that played a central role in the spread of karate on the mainland. Before and after the war, karate became a club activity at many colleges. In the post-war period karate evolved into a competitive sport, and this contributed to its further propagation. University championships, Japanese championships, and world championships were contested fiercely. Karate also became an official event of the National Sports Festival. From this time, the sport became increasingly popular among high school students, and it also marks the time when girls became pro-actively involved. Recognition of karate as a club activity recognised by the High School Athletic Federation facilitated further dissemination and depth of its coaching base.

In this way, karatedo followed the same path that other budo (judo and kendo) took in the Meiji period: from extracurricular club activities to regular classes. Budo was banned after Japan's defeat in the war. Kendo and judo were later resurrected in schools for PE classes in the 1950s under the category of *Kakugi* (fighting sports), not as *Budo*. The Japan Karatedo Federation became a member of the Japan Budo Association and waited in anticipation for the time when budo would once again become an integral part of the school curriculum.

(2) School Budo
① From Kakugi to Budo

With the revision of National Curriculum Guidelines in 1989, the term *Kakugi* was changed back to *Budo*. On the mainland, Kusaka Shuji (current secretary general of the Japan Karate Federation) produced a karatedo textbook for use in junior high schools. In Okinawa, a local version of the textbook was produced, and *Fukyu Kata* I & II created before the war by Miyagi Chojun and Nagamine Shoshin were adopted as the main teaching material. Instructors from the four major Okinawan karate styles were invited to give lessons at Okinawa schools, and the teaching of karate in regular classes commenced. In 1990, I started teaching karate in regular classes at Osaka Prefectural Horticultural High School.

② The Japanese Academy of Budo

In August 2009, at the 42nd annual gathering of the Japanese Academy of Budo held at Osaka University, there was a symposium on the topic of making budo compulsory in junior high schools. I participated as a panellist. In the other sessions, participants were able to witness an actual karatedo lesson taken by an active physical education teacher with no karatedo experience. From 2012, budo became a compulsory subject in the over 10,000 junior high schools in Japan. Compulsory means that all junior high school students, regardless of gender, must learn a budo discipline during PE. Schools could choose what budo they would teach to pupils. The fact that it was made compulsory meant that teachers with government certification for teaching Health and Physical Education had to somehow convey the value of karatedo (or other budo) in what was only an extremely limited period of time in the curriculum. Experts focused on organising theory and practical skills that could be taught and learned easily by beginners.

③ Cooperation and Commencement

Preparations were made at the JKF in collaboration with the Junior High School Karatedo Federation (Chukoren), led by Kono Masahiro (JKF executive director) and Oinuma Tsuyoshi (JKF secretary general), Kono (vice president of the Chukoren), and Iwashiro Koji (president). Nakamura Takeshi, Nonaka Fumiko, Chiba Kaneko, Matsuda Ken and Sakae Yoko from the Chukoren, and Toyoshima Takehiro, Inoshita Kaori and myself from the Japanese Academy of Budo organised an event at the Nippon Budokan Training Centre (Katsuura City, Chiba prefecture) to investigate the best way to teach junior high school students. The test classes lasted for three days and two nights. With support from the Nippon Budokan, a textbook for teaching karate in junior high school compulsory budo classes was completed in August 2010, just before a national seminar for instructors was scheduled.

(3) The Challenges Making Content Suitable for Schools
① Technical Refinement

Our challenge was to find a method for effectively conveying the essence of karatedo in 10 lessons of 50 minutes. Fortunately, our task was helped by the fact that karatedo needs no equipment, and there is an emphasis on using the right and left sides of the body equally. We thought that if we could make the most of these characteristics, then karatedo would most certainly be a valuable educational tool on par with the other budo disciplines. The main teaching points of the textbook are as follows:

A. Standing (*Tachi*)—*Ki wo tsuke* (Attention) = *Musubi-dachi*. *Yoi* (Ready) = *Heiko-dachi* (or *Soto hachiji-dachi*). By basing our teaching on the *Heian* form as conveyed by Itosu Anko and Funakoshi Gichin, we could construct movements using only *zenkutsu-dachi* (forward stance). By adding movement in the teaching of basic techniques the all-important sense of the centre of gravity can be felt. Three commands are sufficient: Attention, Ready and *Kamaete* (take your stance). If you add *Hajime*, this makes four.

B. Blocks (*Uke*)—Once students can stand properly, the next step is to teach *uke*. To make it easier for beginners to

下段受け 受けの構え 上段受け 受けの構え

拳を捻り終えたところ。「極め」（きめ）の状態。

受けの構え。両手で拳を握り、胸の前で手首を交差させる。受ける方の手が外側になる。

拳を捻り終えたところ。「極め」（きめ）の状態。

受けの構え。両手で拳を握り、胸の前で手首を交差させる。受ける方の手が外側になる。

JKF Ayumi Vol. 4

understand, the basic stance taken involves crossing both left and right arms to protect the centreline. From this position, the left and right arms move upwards and downwards to block, thereby accentuating "*karate ni sente nashi*" (no first attack in karate). From the very outset, students are taught that the purpose of the fighting stance is for self-defence only. The movements of *jodan-uke* for face protection and *gedan-uke* for protecting the lower body, are combined with *uke-te* and *hiki-te* on both the left and right sides.

C. Thrust (Tsuki)—Even though it is taught that there is "no first attack in karate", there is no point if you do not learn the basic attacking techniques. The only attacking *waza* taught is the thrust—"*seiken-tsuki*". The *hiki-te* automatically becomes self-defence (*hiji-uchi*). This is a system in which both sides of the body complement each other in generating power, and in which strength from the whole body is concentrated in the fist.

D. Tachi, Uke, Tsuki in Kata and Kumite

These three elements, or four basic movements in terms of the number of techniques, are all that is needed to engage in *kata* and *kumite*. Karatedo is a system of self-study. Both arms and legs are used in different ways: up, down, left and right, but centred on the body's axis. In *kumite*, two students are taught to attack, dodge, catch, counterattack and perform *zanshin*.

The distance between the two people, the timing of the attack, the distance and angle of the counterattack, the *zanshin* after the attack, and so on, are all elements of budo that can be experienced in a short period of study. Through karate junior high school students become aware of the need to protect themselves. Self-protection is the essence of crisis management, and an important lesson to learn at a young age.

E. Kihon Kata 1, 2, 3, Bunkai Kumite 2–8

In the last 6 years, the number of schools that have adopted karatedo for PE classes has doubled from 126 to about 260. Furthermore, the number of schools that continue to teach karatedo to 2nd- and 3rd-year students has also increased. Therefore, in 2015, the JKF Secretary General Kusaka Shuji took the initiative to increase the number of *kata* taught by two, and the number of *kumite* patterns by six. *Kihon Kata* 2 (which includes a kick), *Kihon Kata* 3 (which includes a mid-level uke and a reverse thrust), and eight *yakusoku kumite* patterns which include more variations of *uke*. All of these forms are easy to learn after memorising *Kihon Kata* 1, and they are designed to help learn other basic elements such as kicks and *gyaku-tsuki*. The kicks are effective for developing a sense of balance and strengthening the lower body and seem to be of great interest to young students. The use of kicks outside of class is strictly forbidden, so students look forward to the karate classes where they are allowed to try the techniques out in a controlled environment. At this more advanced stage, the importance of respect for each other and the practice of *rei* is taught. *Kumite* is a wonderful opportunity to experience the invisible but important sensations of distance, timing, and *zanshin*, which can be applied in some way to everyday relationships and activities.

F. Instructor Training

To improve the compulsory junior high school budo classes, the Nippon Budokan and the JKA co-host a national training seminar for three days each year for junior high school physical education teachers. In addition, people from primary, senior high schools, universities, as well as government and federation officials also attend to learn or help with seminar classes.

We have taught over 600 teachers since the first session in 2010. Karate has the advantage that it can be taught in any location, without the need for equipment, and with many or few students. There are also many facets of karate that can be taught, such as self-defence, competition, and budo as lifelong pursuit. The number of schools adopting karatedo is constantly increasing as its educational potential is becoming widely acknowledged.

G. New Discoveries and the Road Ahead

In the ten years since budo classes were made compulsory in junior high schools, we have discovered how enormous the educational power of group *kata* is. In the past, the order of instruction was typically structured as basics, individual *kata*, *yakusoku kumite*, and then group *kata*. We have come to realise that the process of moving from basics to *kata* allows students to work in teams. This in turn encourages them to learn from each other, and to develop communication, coordination, and independent thinking skills. The group *kata* contains elements that meet all the objectives outlined in the National Curriculum Guidelines, such as fostering expressive ability, cooperation and planning, and students enjoy competing in group form competitions. Discovering and developing effective teaching content for classes in schools is an ongoing process.[1]

Photo 4-22 The 1st National Karatedo Instructors' Training Seminar hosted by the Nippon Budokan and JKF in August, 2010 at the Nippon Karatedo Kaikan.

Notes
(1)   JKF 2018 Plan—Characteristics of Junior High School Karate Classes
1.   By teaching the principle of "no first attack in karate", pupils can develop high ethical standards through budo.
2.   By learning the concept and methods of self-defence, students develop skills for crisis management.
3.   Because there is no direct contact, it is possible for both girls and boys to learn together with low risk of injury.
4.   Pupils who are not good at sports, or who have disabilities, can take part in classes with their peers.

5. There is no need to prepare *tatami* mats or put on protective gear, thereby allowing more class time.
6. There is no need for a martial arts hall or other facilities. Classes can be held in any sized venue.
7. To reduce the financial burden on the parents, classes can be carried out in normal sportswear.
8. It is possible to hold group demonstrations at sports days and cultural festivals to show the fruits of the classes.
9. Active learning can be introduced in group *kata* and *yakusoku kumite* team competitions.

2. Karatedo's Road to the Olympics

Special Contribution by Nagura Toshihisa

(1) The WKF and its History of Hardship

The JKF was created in 1964, the year of the first Tokyo Olympics. Only six years later, in 1970, the World Karate Federation (WKF) was created in Tokyo, and the first World Championships were held at the Nippon Budokan. (At that time, the world body was called WUKO but was later renamed WKF.) This was the moment when karatedo became world-renowned KARATE.

It was not until 1999 that the WKF was recognised by the IOC as the governing body for karate. It took a further 20 years for the WKF to be included in the Olympic Games. This was despite the fact that the WKF stated in its statutes it aims to be an Olympic sport, and that it has a comparatively large number of enthusiasts around the world compared to other sports. Nevertheless, overcoming various fundamental problems was the only way the WKF could make Olympic status a realistic goal.

There were three formal presentations made to the IOC in 2005, 2009 and 2013 (London, Rio and Tokyo respectively). In all three cases, karate was selected as a finalist, but never made it through to selection as an Olympic event. What were the reasons for this? The truth is, there is no established reason for karate's failure to convince the IOC of its worthiness as an official event. In November 2013, I became an officer of the organisation for the first time as a president-appointed director of the WKF. Shortly afterwards I had a meeting with President Espinós at the WKF headquarters in Madrid.

Our meeting lasted five hours. The president analysed various factors that needed to be addressed if we were to succeed. In summary, he said that during the 16 years since becoming president, communication between the main karate nations had been insufficient. This, he concluded, was a major reason why karate would not become an Olympic sport. He even went so far as to say he felt karate's cause was a hopeless one. Thus, I think it is fair to say that karate's inclusion in the Olympic Games before 2013 would have been premature.

(2) Meeting with IOC President Bach and the Proposal for Additional Events by the Host City

In 2014, rumours of a possible event addition to the Tokyo Olympic Games began to surface. After four months of planning at the behest of JKF President Sasagawa to meet with IOC President Bach, we finally managed to make an appointment July 28 at the IOC headquarters in Lausanne. The meeting lasted for 15-minutes, or 7-minutes if you include the interpreter.

"Mr. Bach, I want to see karate at the 2020 Olympics in Tokyo, whatever it takes."

"Mr. Sasagawa, that is not for me to decide. It is for you, the Tokyo side, to decide."

At the time, his comment seemed like a Zen *koan*.

This moment marked the beginning of the story that would see karate included in the 2020 Tokyo Olympic and Paralympic Games as an additional host city event for the first time. It later revealed that the Olympic reform plan "Agenda 2020, Item 10" states that host cities have the right to propose additional events. This was announced in December of that year and had been decided in secret at a sub-committee meeting at the end of June. It is possible that President Bach waited for this decision before meeting with us.

Photo 4-23 Visit to see President Bach at the IOC Headquarters in 2014. From left to right: Nagura Toshihisa, JKF President Sasagawa, IOC President Bach, WKF President Espinós, WKF Director Weigert, IOC Sports Director McConnell. (Courtesy of Nagura Toshihisa, WKF Secretary General)

(3) Opening the WKF Tokyo Office and Final Approval

In December 2014, when the right for host cities to propose additional events was announced, it seemed like an early Christmas gift. What was discussed at the June sub-committee meeting was completely unknown to us. Not only the WKF and JKF, but also to the members of national sports federations, and media all over the world. In fact, even in the IOC and the Tokyo Organising Committee for the Olympic Games, most people had no idea that this would happen.

The WKF opened its General Secretariat office in Tokyo around the end of 2014, and began a full-scale campaign to gain the understanding, support and cooperation of the JKF and other stakeholders. We were given until the end of September in 2015. To make our bid a success, we had already implemented a corporate project approach since our meeting with President Bach.

The application and proposal to TOCOG stated that karate fully satisfies all of the conditions expected by the IOC, i.e. popularity among young people, safety, gender equality, etc., and also emphasised that karate could add new value to the Olympic Games as a "universal sport" that retains educational values and traditional Japanese values of civility.

In addition, to encourage TOCOG to decide in our favour, we engaged in frantic lobbying to the Tokyo Metropolitan Assembly and House of Representatives. We made presentations to the top management of major companies including Keidanren (Japan Business Federation), and we sought the support of various academic experts, and engaged in media activities on an unprecedented scale. In addition, we organised a petition with 720,000 signatures from karate enthusiasts in Japan and around the world. The fact that the Nippon Budokan had agreed to host the event was also a great advantage.

The difficulties we faced by entering this challenging, unknown world were not easily overcome. There were many misunderstandings, conflicts of interest, and setbacks. In the end, the patience and wisdom demonstrated by those involved allowed us to overcome all obstacles and achieve our dream of making karatedo an official Olympic sport.

In August 2015, eight finalists made their final presentations to the TOCOG. In addition to the standard presentation, karate included a *kata* and *kumite* demonstration by Japan's top athletes. All of the presentations for the eight sports were to be delivered in English, but President Espinós requested, and TOCOG agreed, that karate's session should be given in Japanese except for the opening speech. On September 28, TOCOG proposed to the IOC that karate be added as an additional sport, along with four others. We had finally conquered the biggest hurdle.

On August 3, 2016, the IOC General Assembly in Rio de Janeiro unanimously approved the inclusion of the five additional events in the Tokyo Olympics. In addition, the venue for the karate matches was decided as the Nippon Budokan, the hallowed hall for karate practitioners around the world. Fifty years after the first karate match was held at the Nippon Budokan in 1970, karate was finally going to debut as an Olympic event.

(4) WKF's Current Situation and Challenges
—Budo or Sport?

Now that karate has made it to the Olympic Games, there are many new challenges ahead of us. Triumphalism, commercialisation, doping, and organisational compliance are all things that the WKF had to address urgently. The IOC and international sports federations have provided us with advice, and we must move forward with a broad perspective that recognises needs of the times while preserving traditions of the past.

I would like to conclude by addressing a question that I am sure many readers of this book are no doubt concerned about: "Will karate ever degenerate from a budo discipline into a mere competitive sport?" I would like to conclude by expressing the WKF's view on this question.

Photo 4-24 At the IOC General Assembly in 2016 when it was decided that karate would be officially adopted as an additional sport in Tokyo 2020. With WKF President Espinós. (Courtesy of Nagura Toshihisa)

- Karate enthusiasts ranging in age from 5 to 90 years old from all parts of the world work hard at karate for a variety of reasons: health, enjoyment, training in budo with the aim of building character, learning techniques that one may never use against an opponent, and competition. Karate is now an Olympic sport for top athletes, while retaining its strong martial arts character. In this sense, karate is broad and boundless, and each practitioner finds their own reason for studying it.

- *Kata* includes an astonishing variety of traditional techniques. These are impressive to watch, and make people understand that karate is more than just a competition in which contestants vie to strike each other. It becomes apparent that karate is a "Way". *Kumite* is highly competitive but limits dangerous techniques, and has rules too protect competitors from injury. *Kata* and *kumite* are the two wheels of karate, and together they can become an Olympic sport that preserves the essence of traditional budo.

- WKF ensures that the spirit of *rei* and *setsu* (respect and courtesy) are instilled in the rules of competition from which this spirit is injected into the forms, while new *kumite* techniques are sought and developed. In other words, WKF aims to become an Olympic sport that seeks a "perfect harmony between tradition and innovation".

As long as those involved in karate have the determination and ambition to improve Olympic Karate, we are confident that karate will not degenerate from a budo discipline into a mere sport. This is what we intend to diligently uphold.

ııı

Special Essay

Nagura Toshihisa

The following is a memo I wrote immediately after returning from the IOC General Assembly in Rio de Janeiro, Brazil, on August 3, 2016. I was reflecting on the joy of realising my dream, and the 20 months we endured at the WKF to make karate an Olympic sport.

The eight that made it to the first round were all wonderful sports, and any one of them was worthy of being proposed to the IOC. I am so happy to have been present at the historic moment when karate was proposed and accepted. There are no other words to describe it. I felt as if the trinity of "Heaven, Earth, and Humankind" brought this day to fruition.

- I think of the incredible efforts of Funakoshi Gichin, the great man who introduced karate from Okinawa to the mainland in the 1920s. I think of our predecessors who promoted karate from the mainland and Okinawa to the world from the 1950s onwards. I think of those who have passed away, and those who continue to teach karate today.

- I think of the All Japan Student Karatedo Federation and how it is to be congratulated for the wisdom and enterprising spirit it showed to organise *jiyu kumite*, transforming karate from a mysterious art of self-defence and fighting into a healthy sport that transcends differences between schools.

- I think of karate practitioners from all over the world, who cross the seas and come to Japan to study and develop their spirit, style and technique in budo.

- I think of the wisdom and hard work of past WKF officials who succeeded in developing KARATE into a universal sport and manage it on a global scale without losing the spirit of *"rei* and *setsu"*.

- And, I accept the fact that we tried three times for Olympic inclusion beforehand, and lost three times.

Without these contributions we would not be where we are today... In just two years, especially in the last year, many things happened and then we heard of "Agenda 2020", the proposal for additional host city events. We were approved by the IOC as hoped. It is a miraculous turn of events that can only be explained by that trinity "Heaven, Earth, and Humankind".

I would like to thank WKF President Espinós for his persistence, JKF President Sasagawa for his exceptional leadership, the WKF and JKF for their unprecedented mutual understanding and cooperation, and more than 700,000 karate practitioners and fans around the world who signed the petition. We are indebted to the Tokyo Metropolitan Assembly, the House of Representatives, the Nippon Budokan, the JOC and all other related organisations, not to mention the future Olympians who continue to work tirelessly to make this event a reality. Everybody came together for this.

Karate is still a rough diamond. Today, the mysterious power of the trinity "Heaven, Earth, and Humankind" will polish this diamond for the Olympic stage.

Whenever I was about to give up, I was given strength by a single line in an essay written by a primary school student at one of our dojos. "Nagura-sensei, please do your best to get karate into the Olympics."

SECTION 8

JKF & WKF
Organisation and Activities

Koyama Masashi

1. The Organisations and Activities
(1) JKF

We have written at length about the Japan Karatedo Federation in this book. The following is quoted from a lecture given by Kurihara Shigeo, vice president of the JKF, at the 9th Japan Karatedo Instructors Training Seminar.

> "The purpose of the JKF is to <u>coordinate and represent amateur karate in Japan.</u> We aim to promote the sound development and spread of karatedo and contribute to the development of body and mind among its practitioners.

First of all, it is important to note that the JKF represents amateur karatedo in Japan. When the Student Federation was formed in 1957, it stated that it was an amateur organisation responsible for the promotion of karate in Japan irrespective of *ryuha* in order to accomplish the sound development and spread of karate. As a member of the Japan Budo Association, which was launched to facilitate the "promotion and dissemination of the spirit of budo to the people to enrich their lives", one of the main achievements of the JKF's activities was to make budo compulsory for junior high school students.

JKF History 1964–2016

- October 1, 1964—All Japan Karatedo Federation (JKF) established
- January 13, 1969—Approved as an incorporated foundation by the Ministry of Education
- October 10, 1969—The 1st All Japan Karatedo Tournament is held at the Nippon Budokan
- October 9, 1970—Joined WUKO
- October 10 and 13, 1970—1st Karate World Championships held at Nippon Budokan and Osaka Prefectural Gymnasium
- March 29, 1972—Joined the Japan Sports Association
- September 23 and 24, 1978—Demonstration of karatedo at Nagano National Sports Festival (*Kokutai*)
- September 13-16, 1981—Karatedo became an official event of the Shiga *Kokutai*
- October 3, 1999—The World Karate Federation (WKF) is recognised by the IOC
- August 5, 2001—1st All Japan Boys and Girls Karatedo Tournament at Komazawa Gymnasium
- September 22-25, 2001—Participated in Japan Sports Masters at Miyazaki Prefectural Budokan
- September 22, 2005—The 1st All Japan Karatedo Tournament for the Disabled at Toyama City General Gymnasium
- November 13-16, 2008—19th Karate World Championships - 888 athletes from 99 countries at the Nippon Budokan
- June 5, 2010—Establishment of the "Japan Karatedo Federation Karate Charter" and the "Children's Karate Charter"
- November 2011—Completion of the Nippon Karatedo Kaikan (JKF headquarters)
- April 1, 2012—Approved by the Cabinet Office to became a Public Interest Incorporated Foundation

- August 3, 2016—Karate was approved by the IOC as an additional sport for the Tokyo Olympics
- December 11, 2016—The Emperor's Cup and Empress's Cup presented to the JKF

Organisation

What of the organisational structure and national and international competitions supported by JKF? Domestically, the organisation consists of nine regional councils (47 prefectural federations), four sports organisations, seven partner organisations, and one friendship organisation.

Participation in and Hosting of Competitions

The number and variety of national and international karate tournaments have increased dramatically in the last few decades. This culminated in karatedo becoming an Olympic sport. The future of karatedo depends on how all those involved and appreciate the multi-faceted nature of the discipline, and how they wish to remain involved in its activities.

Domestic Tournaments

- Emperor's Cup and Empress's Cup All Japan Karatedo Tournament
- National Sports Festival of Japan (*Kokutai*)
- Japan Sports Masters Karatedo Competition
- All Japan Karatedo Tournament for the Disabled
- National Junior High School Karatedo Tournament
- All Japan Junior High School Karatedo Tournament
- All Japan Youth Rensei Karatedo Tournament

International Competitions
- Olympic Games
- World Games
- SportAccord Combat Games
- Asian Games
- Karate World Championships
- World Junior Cadet-21 Karatedo Championships
- Asian Karatedo Championships
- Asian Junior Cadet-21 Karatedo Championships
- East Asia Karatedo Championships
- Karate 1 Premier League
- Asian Championships (Okinawa) and Premier League (Tokyo)

(2) The World Karate Federation
—Organisation and Activities

The WKF has what is called *The Book* (available online) as its official publication. I will quote from the president's preface and *The Book* to provide an overview of how the organisation changed from WUKO to WKF.

"Sport Karate has become a massive phenomenon across the globe involving millions of families spanning countries within all five continents, and thus is deeply entrenched in global society.

The WKF is the only organization to have achieved consensus among innumerable visions, styles and cultures of Karate. It is now the focal point for National Federations, supporters, referees, coaches, athletes and recreational practitioners. The WKF has driven the evolution of karate from an esoteric Asian martial art into a captivating and dynamic sport with global appeal.

Through four decades of diligent investment in the safety of karate athletes, standardized coaching and refereeing competence, as well as contemporary media promotion, the WKF has brought real-time, world-class karate into the lives and living rooms of anyone, anywhere on the planet. The WKF has thus provided a way for citizens of all countries to improve their lives by participation in any aspect of karate—from recreational activity to high-performance competition—and form enduring relationships that transcend boundaries and promote inter-cultural understanding.

After almost half a century of innovative success, the WKF looks forward to continuing the multifaceted development of karate for the benefit of humankind." (WKF President Antonio Espinós, *The Book*)

WUKO to WKF

"After several decades of rapid worldwide growth, competitions started to attract karate athletes from several countries during the 1960s.

The different styles of karate, diversity of the rules and lack of unified protocols that govern any type of competition indicated a need to create an international governing body comprising united national karate federations that could start to address these issues from a unified global perspective.

Ryoichi Sasakawa, President of the JKF and Jacques Delcourt, President of the European Karate Union (EKU) jointly proposed a series of meetings that would produce not only the first amalgamated international rules for sport karate, but also the establishment of the World Union of Karate Do Organisations (WUKO) on October 10, 1970." (*The Book*)

The Birth of WUKO

"Tokyo was the site where WUKO was inaugurated and where the first WUKO World Championships were held. Portland, Oregon hosted the first meeting of the fledgling WUKO Directing Committee, the objective of which was to lay the foundation for the future of unified sport karate. National karate federations recognised by their national Olympic committees and highest sport authorities soon became members and thus WUKO became the most important world governing body for karate. In this way, the national karate federations of the WUKO were recognised by their national Olympic committees and the highest sports authorities, and the WUKO quickly became the most important global governing body in karate." (*The Book*)

Change to WKF

"The integration of several new organizations during the 1990s saw WUKO membership increase to 150 National Federations. Therefore, a new name that would more accurately reflect the size and scope of the organization was needed. The name of the first international organization representing sport karate was thus changed to World Karate Federation (WKF) on December 20, 1992." (*The Book*)

Evolution of WKF Competition

The first World Karate Championship in Tokyo was a breakthrough, which led to a remarkable development of international karatedo competitions in the following years. At the first Congress, there were only men's team and individual *kumite* divisions. It was not until 12 years later, at the 1980 World Championships in Madrid, that *kata* divisions were introduced, and women began to participate. It is also worth noting that the 2014 World Championships introduced a category for people with disabilities. There was overwhelming public support for the inclusion of disabled competitors in the World Championships. It was born in Okinawa became world KARATE. (Capitals are used here to accentuate the fact that international karate has taken on a life of its own.)

WKF's Status as an International Federation

In the 1980s and 1990s the WKF grew in leaps and bounds and developed competitive karate at an international level. Its international status was established in 1999 when the IOC officially recognised the WKF as the sole governing body for sport karate in the world. The World Karate Federation is a member of the following major international organisations: The Association of IOC Recognised International Sports Federations (ARISF), The International World Games Association

(IWGA), SportAccord.

Membership

The WKF now has 196 affiliated regional and country members on countries on five continents. The five colours in the WKF logo represent the five continents, symbolising karatedo as a sport, and the universal spirit of the organisation that oversees it.

2. About Kara, Te, and Do

The terms karate and karatedo are used in various ways by different organisations and groups such as the Japan "Karatedo" Federation, the World Karate Federation, the Nippon Karatedo Kaikan, the Okinawa Karate Kaikan, etc.

Should it be karate or karatedo? The transition from jujutsu to judo was driven by pioneering instructor Kano Jigoro. The move from kenjutsu to kendo was driven by the Dai-Nippon Butokukai. It is also "KARATE" to people involved in the Olympic games. What is the best way for Okinawan, Japanese, and international karate enthusiasts to understand karatedo? I would like to conclude this chapter by providing my own views on the "Kara", "Te", and "Do".

(1) Kara—Universe, Freedom

In 1929, Shimokawa Goro, a member of Keio's karate club when it was celebrating its fifth anniversary, visited Furukawa Gyodo, the head priest of Engakuji Temple in Kamakura. He asked on behalf of Funakoshi Gichin to think of an appropriate *kanji* for karate. The character that came to mind was *kara* or *kuu* (空) which means sky, or empty in the Zen teaching "Form is empty, emptiness is form" (*shiki-zoku-ze-ku* = 色即是空). Funakoshi was satisfied with this reasoning and changed the *kanji* to empty hand.

This new character for karate was subsequently used in the titles of Funakoshi's and Mabuni's books. In Chapter 1, Section 7, Kadekaru points out that in 1936, there was a discussion in Okinawa about the adoption of this character for "*kara*". Kinjo Hiroshi wrote that many participated in these discussions. "The participation of the prefectural director of academic affairs, government officials, journalists and the people (karate experts) was unusual, and has an extremely important meaning for the history of karate." At the meetings, they also discussed the drastic changes seen in the karate environment since Funakoshi's relocation to Tokyo. As the birthplace of karate, the Okinawan participants agreed to discuss not only changing the *kanji* to 空, but also to decide on the creation of a unified model of karate for its dissemination and the establishment of a promotion association.[1]

"*Kenzen-itchi*" (the fist and Zen as one) is a term that has been used in Buddhism for thousands of years, and has been interpreted in many different ways by Buddhists in India, China, and Japan. It is a difficult concept to explain, but it is profound, and leads to questioning ourselves about views of life and death. The shift from China (唐) to empty (空) can be said to have introduced the philosophical depth of "the void" (emptiness) to karate. It was accepted by karate practitioners in Japan, a country where Buddhism is deeply rooted, and this led to fusion of Okinawan karate with mainland karate. There is a verse in the "Heart Sutra" that says: "Seeing the five skandhas are all empty." (The five skandhas (aggregates) are form, sensation, perception, mental formations, and consciousness.) There is another interpretation of the void that suggests, "The one character for 'sky' contains the profound meaning of ten-million immeasurable things."

As Miyagi Chojun said to his students, "Karate is the universe." It extends throughout the whole world. The universalistic world-view intrinsic to the notion of *kara* is what has enabled it to become a global martial art. The freedom of the empty- hand transcends boundaries of race and nationality and crystallises the wisdom of Okinawan and mainland karate.

(2) Te—Technique and Method

In an earlier discussion (*Ryukyu Shimpo*, October 27, 1936), Hanashiro Chomo wrote: "In the old days, the term 'karate' did not exist. It was called *todi* or simply *tii* (*te*). It means to fight with empty hands". Miyagi Chojun also said, "When people come to me to learn karate, they ask me to teach *tii*."

Kinjo wrote, "There is a theory that Okinawa had a unique style of *kempo* called *tii* since ancient times." He also explains how *kempo* was brought to Okinawa from China and it was "Okinawan-ised". Kadekaru mentioned earlier in this book that there are very few early-modern documents that reveal the true history of karatedo in its ancient form. It seems that after the modern period when the history of karatedo began to be written down, the summations of the martial art's development could only be inferred from a handful of historical documents of which the content was difficult to verify. There has been a tendency to believe anything that was written in the early-modern period at face value.

Screeds of historical documents from the Kingdom of Ryukyu era were destroyed during the Battle of Okinawa. There are only a few surviving specimens to draw from. Japanese martial arts can be roughly divided into two categories: the bare-handed kind such as judo, sumo and karatedo, and the weapon arts such as kendo, kyudo and naginata. Karatedo, or "empty handed fist", is one of the most popular of these martial arts and has a worldwide following.

The hand functions as a tool for human activity. Everything, from agriculture to the construction of today's complex information society, and the invention and use of letters is the work of the human hand. Okinawan *tii*, Japanese karatedo, and world KARATE are all based on techniques performed by the human hand. *Tii* is also a method or a Way to improve the self and to connect the world. The hands of karatedo, the "empty-handed" art, transform into the hands of the "thousand-armed Kannon"; that is, the hands enable independence and freedom. "When we see and hear the suffering of others and respond to that suffering, we are the heads and arms of the thousand-armed Kannon." That is what the hand stands for in karatedo.

(3) The Way—Inheritance and Creation
In Chapter 3, I quoted the meaning of the Way as explained by Suzuki Daisetz. It is difficult to grasp exactly what he means,

but anybody with years of experience in karatedo or other budo will be able to understand at some level the profundity of the "Way". Karatedo developed into a modern Japanese budo Way and has spread far beyond Japan's shores.

It has the potential to keep developing as society's needs change. The path that the ancients tread leads to the future and is open to all who seek it. There is no instant "karate Way" for beginners. It is only for those who seek it that karate as a Way that it truly becomes karatedo. All things called Ways are only so when people pass through them. Karatedo is no exception. Now millions practise karate as they seek the Way. This is karatedo, and it is now one of the great paths of the world.

The Way is both inherited and created. It is from the past and extends into the future. The path of karatedo may not be smooth, but it is full of potential. Those who are involved in karatedo should be cognisant of what its Way is. This is how practitioners are able to improve themselves and aspire to be someone who can contribute to society. It is our hope that the values of karatedo will remain steadfast and not succumb to the pitfalls and temptations that come with overt commercialisation as karate enters a new era as an Olympic event.

I interviewed JKF National Team Coach Hayashi Ko at the 46th All Japan Championships held at the Nippon Budokan on December 9, 2018. I re-read the "National Team Strength Plan" for 2018 and asked him about the national team's philosophy shared by the members.

"I was born into this world and encountered karatedo. With a sense of gratitude for all things, I recognise that it is most important to accept and overcome adversity no matter how hard it may be, and to improve my strength as a person. Through karatedo, I will aim to live a life without regret and with a rich heart."

In the interview, coach Hayashi also talks about the current state of the national team players and their determination for 2020 (2021). What he is seeking is a style of karatedo that represents the sentiments contained in the national team philosophy. No matter how the form of karatedo changes, the life of a karate person must never waver. This was his straightforward message: "Karatedo is budo".

More than 100 years have passed since Kano Jigoro founded judo, and the Dai-Nippon Butokukai modified bujutsu into budo. It is our duty to nurture people who can contribute to society through karatedo. We must cherish the culture of the "Way". This will in no small way contribute to world peace and will help people live their lives without regret through karatedo. Funakoshi left us a famous teaching—there is no first attack in karate. We all have a responsibility to take the spirit of karatedo bequeathed by our forebears such as Itosu Anko and Miyagi Chojun, and continue to find and create new value in karatedo.

Note
(1) In March 2005, the Okinawa prefecture Assembly passed a resolution to designate October 25, the day of the roundtable discussion, as "Karate Day". Various events have been held since then.

CHAPTER 5

SPECIAL ROUNDTABLE DISCUSSION

Mifuji Yoshio
Koyama Masashi
Wada Koji
Kadekaru Toru

Starting with the April 2017 issue of *Gekkan Budo*, the 26-part series "Karate: Its History and Techniques" ran for just over two years. To finish the series off, the Budokan convened a special roundtable discussion moderated by Mifuji Yoshio, executive director of the Nippon Budokan. All three authors, Koyama Masashi, Wada Koji, and Kadekaru Toru gathered at the Nippon Budokan on February 25, 2019.

Moderator   **Mifuji Yoshio**
(Standing Director & Secretary General of the Nippon Budokan)

Attendees   **Koyama Masashi**
(authors)   (Specially Appointed Professor, Morinomiya University of Medical Sciences)

Wada Koji
(Standing Director of the All Japan Karatedo Shotokan)

Kadekaru Toru
(Part-time Lecturer, University of the Ryukyus and Okinawa University)

How the Series Began

Mifuji: First, I would like to relate the background of this series. Since 2010, the Nippon Budokan's monthly magazine,

Gekkan Budo, has published a series of articles on the history and practice of the four budo disciplines of kyudo, judo, sumo, and kendo. Six years ago, when we started the series "Karate: Its History and Practice", we discussed at length what the overall concept would be. The idea was presented to Nagura Toshihisa (secretary general of the World Karate Federation, and graduate of Keio University's karate club) and Koyama Masashi (Goju-ryu, and alumnus of Ritsumeikan University). We talked about the purpose of the series, and who would make up the best team of authors to present a comprehensive picture of karatedo.

Koyama: That's right.

Mifuji: Initially, we were planning to ask Mr. Nagura and Mr. Koyama to write the articles. You agreed to do it but Mr. Nagura recommended that Wada Koji, his junior at Keio, co-author the arictles instead because the WKF was extremely busy getting ready for their bid to be accepted as a sport at the Tokyo Olympics. Mr. Koyama also recommended "a great karate researcher in Okinawa", the birthplace of karate, named Kadekaru Toru. He suggested that Mr. Kadekaru could write about Okinawa, and make the series of articles even better.

Koyama: Indeed, I remember that discussion well.

Mifuji: Karate originated in the Ryukyus, or Okinawa as it is known today, based on Chinese *kempo*. It was introduced into Japan and developed in its own unique way to become the karate that is now popular all around the world. However, there is a distinct lack of historical documents and reliable commentaries on karate that plot out its evolution. As Mr. Koyama and Mr. Wada are former world champions in *kata* and *kumite*, and as Mr. Kadekaru is a renowned instructor of Okinawan karate, we decided to base the book's content on their experiences. We started with the idea that Kadekaru-sensei would write about the history and transmission of karate to Japan by introducing rare historical documents uncovered in Okinawa. Koyama-sensei and Wada-sensei would then write about training methods, the history of *kumite* and *kata* competitions, and the internationalisation of karatedo based on their personal involvement. To conclude the series, we decided to hold a special roundtable discussion, which is where we are now.

Mifuji: Koyama-sensei, please tell us how you feel now that the series is completed and the book is out.

Koyama
—"One of the definitive works on the history of karate"

Koyama: I remember you asked me and Mr. Nagura to write a series of articles exactly six years ago during the reception for the Japanese Academy of Budo's annual general meeting. The Budokan had already published a book on the history of karatedo, *Karate kara Karate e* by Kinjo Hiroshi. If my memory serves, you recommended that we ask Mr. Kinjo to contribute as co-author, but sadly he had passed away. Mr. Nagura and I visited his home and saw his incredible collection of books. We spoke to his daughters Makiko and Mayumi to get as much information as we could, as we were determined to make this one of the definitive works on the history of karate. As for the historical side of things, Kadekaru Toru's research is well known for its thoroughness, so we approached you with the idea, and you agreed that Mr. Kadekaru should be brought on-board.

In Kinjo Hiroshi's study (From left to right: Kinjo Mayumi, WKF Secretary General Nagura Toshihisa, and Kinjo Makiko).

Mifuji: It was a great idea to ask Mr. Kadekaru.

Koyama: The first thing the three of us did was compare our views and understanding of the history of karate. Karate started in Okinawa and went through many changes. The modernised art was popularised in Okinawa by Itosu Anko. It was then spread to the mainland, predominantly in the Kanto and Kansai regions by Funakoshi Gichin and Miyagi Chojun. This flow of events is known by most people already. In Kinjo Hiroshi's book there was very little mention of student activities, so I felt that it was important to address this subject in our articles. There were some details that we couldn't figure out, but the three of us had enough specialised knowledge in different areas to fill in most of the gaps. I am very satisfied with what we were able to achieve.

Mifuji: Thank you very much for your excellent work. Next, I would like to ask Mr. Wada about his thoughts.

Wada
— "I came to realise that karate is for the benefit of all the people in the world"

Wada: It was a wonderful opportunity for me to contribute, and I learned a lot in the process of putting my articles together. It gave me a chance to reassess what karate is all about. I have been practising karate only to train myself, but through writing the articles I came to realise that karate is for the benefit of all people. Many things have become clear to me. I would like to continue to promote karate with new-found confidence and knowledge of what karate is meant to be.

Mifuji: Thank you for sharing your own experiences through your truly wonderful articles. Next, Mr. Kadekaru.

Kadekaru
— "Shedding some new light on various important points in the history of karate in Okinawa."

Kadekaru: In the course of writing the articles, I discovered many things from the historical materials I managed to dig up in Okinawa. Unfortunately, the history of karate in Okinawa is not well documented, and countless primary sources were destroyed by fire during the Battle of Okinawa. As such, there were many aspects of karate's history that were difficult to verify. Nevertheless, I hope our articles will shed some new light on various important events in its history in Okinawa. I believe that we managed to clear up some issues, but at the same time, some things have become more problematic. Many new questions have popped up. In any case, it was a valuable experience.

Mifuji: Thank you for uncovering so many historical records from Okinawa and sharing them with us.

History of Karatedo

Mifuji: Now, I would like to ask you all to share your views on the history of karatedo from the regions you represent.

The History of Okinawa
— Karate was adopted into Okinawan schools before judo and kendo were introduced into mainland schools

Kadekaru: When considering the history of karate, we should first try to understand the history of Okinawa. After all, it is the birthplace of karate. In modern Okinawa, karate spread thanks to its role in school education. On the mainland, Funakoshi Gichin popularised karate in university clubs. At the time, university students were known as the elites of Japanese society. They essentially took charge of karate and studied it very diligently. Our articles covered this trend in considerable detail. I tried to collate as many historical documents as possible in Okinawa to compose my articles. It took quite a while to write it all up as a complete history, but I hope that I have managed to convey the facts despite the various challenges in piecing it all together.

Mifuji: You explained the relationship and continuity of karate in Okinawa from "Chinese hand" karate, or *todi*, to "empty hand" karate by sourcing articles from local newspapers in Okinawa, posthumously published manuscripts, and various historical manuscripts. As with any budo, there is a lack of certainty regarding historical accuracy as many things were written down by later generations and are based on hearsay.

Koyama: Mr. Kadekaru used to be a vice principal at a primary school. After he retired, he started working in an editorial office that was compiling the history of Okinawa prefecture. It was through access to the archives that he discovered valuable source materials, many of which I referenced in my own articles.

Kadekaru: I taught karate when I was a schoolteacher. Then I entered graduate school at the University of the Ryukyus mid-career. When I was wondering what I wanted to research, it suddenly occurred to me that not much reliable work had been done on karate itself. I decided to look into the characteristics of karate *kata* from the perspective of exercise physiology. After that, I was transferred to the archive editorial office, where I had the chance to meet Kinjo Hiroshi. He had already written a lot about karate and was contemplating how to pass on to future generations the vast amount of historical materials he had amassed. He said he would like to donate his collection to an archive located in Okinawa so that they could be of use to many people.

Mifuji: I remember being consulted on that matter.

Kadekaru: Some people thought it would be better to donate the materials to an institution somewhere in Tokyo so that even more people would have access. Mr. Kinjo expressed his explicit desire that the materials go to Okinawa, to a place like the Okinawa Prefectural Library. Even though some of the documents he had collected over the years were old and tattered, they were of immense historical value, and he was adamant that their new home be the birthplace of karate. I was very fortunate to have free access to his collection, and it really opened my eyes to many aspects of karate history that I had not considered before. I noticed how karate spread in Okinawa through its schools, and on mainland Japan through universities. I also realised the immense cultural significance of karate in the Ryukyu Kingdom when it was simultaneously under Japan's shogunate system and in a tributary relationship with China. Pre-modern karate was not only a martial art, but was also a way for educating members of the warrior class.

Although subordinate to Japan, the Ryukyu Kingdom was its own country, and the martial arts, culture and entertainment of the Ryukyu Islands therefore evolved independently of Japan. During the Meiji period, Okinawa was incorporated into Japan. As a result, many aspects of Okinawan culture were lost, and karate was scorned for representing the culture and customs of the old royal government. However, when Japan started touting the motto *Fukoku Kyohei* (wealthy nation and strong military), karate's value was reassessed, and it came to be seen as a useful tool for strengthening the nation. That is why karate was adopted into the school system early on.

Mifuji: Indeed, the change in times amplified the value of karate in Okinawa. Karate was introduced into schools earlier than judo and kendo were in mainland Japan.

Kadekaru: Yes, karate was introduced in Okinawan schools in 1905 as a component of regular physical education. From the beginning, karate practitioners supported the spread of Okinawan culture in the mainland to "make Okinawan culture and identity known throughout the nation". When karate did make its way to the mainland, university students took a liking to it, and before long it was integrated as a part of Japanese culture. This was the beginning of the development of karatedo as a budo. It was also during this period that karate received the support of the so-called "father of modern budo and sports" in Japan, Kano Jigoro. Karatedo developed into a martial art that was on par with other Japanese budo, and then it spread throughout the world.

On the history of Kanto
— The spread of karate in the university setting, starting with Funakoshi Gichin

Mifuji: Kano systematised jujutsu into judo as a vehicle for learning. This process was completed in the Meiji period. Funakoshi Gichin came to Tokyo in the early 1920s. During the Meiji period, the government sought to foster national wealth and strength, so karatedo's rise was in large part a product of the times. Now, I would like to ask Mr. Wada to tell us about Funakoshi Gichin and his story.

Wada: Within the larger theme of "Karate: Its History and Practice", I was put in charge of the period from when Funakoshi introduced karate to the mainland up to when I became world champion. The Keio Gijuku University Athletic Association Karate Club was the first to be established under the instruction of Funakoshi-sensei. Some senior members of Keio Mita Karate Kai were directly taught by Funakoshi himself. I accepted the offer to co-author the articles that make up this section of the book because I knew I could get plenty of information from old karate practitioners in my network who were actually there in the early days. I referred to various documents in circulation and also found out about universities that did not study Shotokan. Those included for example, the University of Tokyo, which studies Wado-ryu, and Toyo University, which studies Shito-ryu. All of the people I asked to provide me with relevant information were very responsive, but the information itself was very piecemeal.

In December 2010, well before the series of articles was published, more than 10 teachers from Okinawa came to Tokyo and held an exchange demonstration with the Keio Mita Karate Kai. At the time, I was told that one of Higaonna Morio-sensei's students competed

Commemorative photo at the exchange demonstration (Kadekaru Toru is on the far right of the first row, and Wada Koji is seventh from the left in the second row).

against me at the World Championships. Also, during my trip to the USA, I had an opportunity to meet Oshima Tsutomu, an alumnus of Waseda University. I was also informed that one of Oshima-sensei's students had competed against me at the KWC. I realised that karatedo is all about connections between people.

Mifuji: As we travel the path, we have many different encounters with all sorts of people. What kind of people do you meet along the way? What do you see? What do you think about? How do you pass it on? It is through these connections that the Japanese budo disciplines have developed over a thousand years of history. Mr. Wada, you seem to have discovered much about Funakoshi Gichin through writing these articles, and the same can be said of Mr. Koyama with Miyagi Chojun. Mr. Kadekaru compiled manuscripts and historical documents concerning all the pioneer teachers in

Okinawa. In other sports, such as athletics and the like, the connection with ancestors is not valued as much as it is in budo. The main concern is about winning and losing in the present. In budo, however, this link with the past is crucial. It is up to the individual to find out and think about why it is important. Without thinking about one's connection to the masters of the past, the only thing left is the relationship between the current teacher and student, or the current senior and junior.

The purpose of this series was to identify the history and techniques of karatedo, to ascertain how the traditions have been taught and conveyed to successive generations, and to understand what was considered important in this process. In other "History and Practice" serialisations of different budo, such as judo and kendo, we asked one expert to write the articles. For karatedo, however, we asked three experts to co-author the book. The aim was to give a multifaceted view of karate, since it has many *ryuha* and factions. The diversity of karate makes it all the more difficult for a single person to summarise the issues confronting each of the different schools and the various problems of transmission. We also asked each author to write about his own experiences. I think this is a unique aspect of this series. Mr. Wada, you wrote a number of interesting personal essays, which I know readers will enjoy.

The History of Karate in Kansai
— Weaving together a narrative with recently uncovered historical materials

Koyama: When I was in high school, I had the opportunity to meet Mr. Kasao, an alumnus of Waseda University's karate club. I read his books and learned his *kata*. This was the foundation of my karate for when I joined the club at Ritsumeikan, and when I ended up winning the All Japan Student Championship. I was unsure about what to do after graduating from Ritsumeikan. I thought long and hard about whether I should continue with karate or not. I decided to become a teacher and entered Kyoto University of Education to study budo history. My main research theme was concerned with the history of karatedo. Ritsumeikan's karate club was the first one founded by Miyagi Chojun. Most people do not know much about Miyagi Chojun, so I decided to focus on him and visited Okinawa to conduct research on his life. I met many of his disciples who were still alive then, including his second daughter Kojo Yasuko, his fourth son Ken, and master Miyagi An'ichi. I wrote about Miyagi Chojun when I was in my twenties, but there were many aspects of his life which I was unable to work out. I have long continued researching him and have had opportunities to present the results of my research while also studying the history of Okinawa. I believe I was very lucky to have been given the opportunity to write a series of articles on this topic.

Mifuji: You've been studying Miyagi Chojun for over 40 years now haven't you.

Koyama: While writing the series of articles, Mr. Kadekaru unearthed some valuable materials. It has long been said that Miyagi Chojun studied in Fujian Province in China for two years, starting from 1915. But his second daughter, Yasuko, told me that it was only for two months in 1915. This was the year Higaonna Kanryo died. I thought that Miyagi Chojun went to Fujian Province for two years after the death of Higaonna Kanryo, because Miyagi is thought to have stayed in Japan until Kanryo's condition deteriorated. Over the course of his research, Mr. Kadekaru discovered Miyagi's travel records, which showed that the period was from April to June in 1915. Since Kanryo died in October, this means that Miyagi went to Fujian for two months before his master's death, and proved that Yasuko's memory was correct.

Incidentally, it was also Mr. Kadekaru who found the *Kyoto University Newspaper* article about Miyagi Chojun's karate seminar. He procured for me the list of Kyoto University Judo Club members who invited Miyagi, and I was able to confirm the names in the article. In the course of my writing, I was also able to find records that pointed to a demonstration held in the Butokuden in October, 1928, and found obscure records that show Konishi Yasuhiro, Ueshima Sannosuke, and Miyagi Chojun, who would later become the first three men in the karate world to receive their *Kyoshi* titles, demonstrated at the 1929 Dai-Nippon Butokukai *Butokusai* festival. This was a lucky find. In addition, I found records about Yamaguchi Gogen, the founder of the Ritsumeikan club, and the club's other early members. Also, I came across interesting information about the Gihokai dojo, which was built by the prominent judo master Fukushima Seisaburo. Fukushima was a devotee of Ishiwara Kanji, who was both the mastermind of the Manchurian Incident and an ardent critic of Tojo Hideki. Many famous martial artists such as Ushijima Tatsukuma, Kimura Masahiko, and Oyama Masutatsu frequented the dojo. Preparing the articles really was a journey of discovery.

Mifuji: The Butokukai was based in Kyoto, making the city a mecca for budo in the first half of the twentieth century. The discovery of hitherto unknown materials was indeed a wonderful achievement. Each of the authors painstakingly wrote their articles, and we have collated them all for this book. In the case of co-authorship, there is always the problem of how to make the content consistent. In the case of these articles, this was not a problem. The editors at the Nippon Budokan did not need to make any changes to the text to keep the stories coherent. The authors wrote on the "three trunks" (Okinawa, Shuri lineage in Kanto and Naha lineage in Kansai) based on their experiences. Of course, there is some repetition in some places, but this can't be helped. The text is quite dynamic overall, and a joy to read.

The personal essays by the authors also made the series more attractive. There was an episode at the World Championships when Mr. Wada was cheered on by a Yugoslavian athlete he met before on a school federation trip to Europe: "Wada! Kick, kick!" Unthinkable as it may seem now, he won a rematch in the final of the All Japan Student Championships after the decision was redrawn. Then there was Mr. Koyama's final in the *kata* division of the *Kokutai* (National Sports Festival). He also wrote a additional essay about the young karate competitors during his tenure as the coach of the national team. These are all first-hand accounts that portray the intense atmosphere of national and world championships by people who were in the thick of it all. They will also become a valuable source of information in the future.

Current Status and Challenges of Karatedo

Mifuji: Now, based on your own experiences, I would like you to address the second theme: the current situation and challenges of karatedo. Wada-sensei, please start us off.

"The essence of karate is self-defence
— It is important that the benefits of competition karate and of karate as self-defence complement each other as two wheels of a cart"

Wada: As I was writing my articles, I spent a lot of time reconsidering the essence of karatedo. I came to the realisation that the essence of karate is as a martial art of self-defence. I believe that karate is about developing the ability and skills to defend yourself. When aiming to increase our capacity as individuals to defend ourselves, the first thing we need to do is to train our fists. Karate does mean empty hand after all. The second thing we need to do, after training our fists, is to understand how to use our fists—how to manipulate them. This is the art of karate. Of course, it is best if you do not have to resort to violence in the first place.

Mifuji: That is just like the old saying "There is no first strike in karate".

Wada: That's right! One does not attack first in karate. These words are connected to everything. The same goes for Funakoshi Gichin's teachings, "Make everything into karate" and "Don't think about winning. One must think about how to not lose". The goal of karate is not to become strong per se, but instead to have the power not to be defeated by others, no matter what. Karate is about defending yourself. In order to protect yourself, you need both strength and wisdom. That is why we are taught to think of everything *as* karate. Karate is the empty-handed art of self-defence that is relevant to everything.

On February 24, 2019, the Okinawan Karate Grand Demonstration Embukai was held at the JP Tower in Tokyo. Okinawan *kobudo*, which uses weapons, was also demonstrated. Some of the *kata* practised at Keio still use weapons. Actually, you can use anything you find around you as a weapon. Still, I found that karate as a form of self-defence is about how to defend yourself when you are in the weakest position, i.e., when you are empty-handed. This leads me to Funakoshi-sensei's teachings in *Karatedo Nijuka-jo*. "Karate begins and ends with courtesy". A sense of respect and courtesy is the key to not making enemies. In the end, I feel that the teaching "karate has no first strike" can contribute to peaceful relations around the world.

Mifuji: It is wonderful that karate has developed from an indigenous Okinawan martial art passed down from generation to generation, and has grown to be respected around the world as a form of self-defence that stresses non-violence.

Kadekaru: Karate was originally the domain of the warrior class in the Ryukyu Kingdom. Now it is widely practised by the general public. Many Okinawans immigrated abroad at the turn of the last century and they took karate with them. As we have shown in this book, Okinawans used karate as a source of strength to overcome adversity they faced when they left Japan. The relationship between Okinawan immigrants and those who established themselves abroad as instructors is not clear, but there is most certainly a connection.

Mifuji: In the Meiji era, karate was taught at Naha's normal school as part of the physical education curriculum and this phenomenon continues today. Budo is now a compulsory unit in physical education classes for all junior high schools in Japan, and in Okinawa about 80% of schools offer karate. Of the nine budo disciplines, karate has the largest number of community dojos in Japan, with about 400 in Okinawa alone. Okinawa is the birthplace of karate, and the tradition is being kept alive in all echelons of society. As you say Mr. Wada, Funakoshi Gichin stated the spirit of karate in his twenty maxims. I think you have inherited these teachings. This is the reason why budo is a Way. The past and future are connected by an ongoing chain of wisdom. Those who respect the wisdom of our predecessors will find the Way, and they in turn will pass it on. It is through this tradition and unbroken link that we can learn the value of life, the importance of respect for each other, and many other things that make us better human beings. It is not just a world of competition where you are a winner or a loser. I think it's wonderful that you have rediscovered this through writing your articles. Mr. Wada, what challenges does the karate world face at this moment in time?

Wada: Unfortunately, karate will not be included in the 2024 Olympics in Paris. We must not forget the value of karate as a sport, and as a traditional self-defence system. Both of these aspects are a part of karate's legacy. We must take care not to drift too far in one direction or the other. I think the three of us shared this idea, and touched on it in many of our respective sections.

Mifuji: Fusing together karate as a Way and karate as a sport to create a greater force for the good of the world and its people. We need to make this a reality. Next, I would like to ask Mr. Kadekaru for his opinion.

Introducing Okinawan karate to the world
— Study the old literature

Kadekaru: Since the 1990s, Okinawa has started to hold its own world conventions. The aforementioned World Uchinanchu Tournament, to which Okinawans living abroad were invited, was the start of a series of events aimed at promoting Okinawan identity and culture and building stronger networks. One of the major events is the karate demonstration. In the course of writing, I noticed that in recent years, these events have become ever more popular. The prefectural government took notice of this and established the Karate Promotion Division as an administrative body and also built the Okinawa Karate Kaikan. This is now the centre of dissemination for information on karate. It also aims to

The Okinawa Karate Kaikan opened in 2017.

promote the Okinawan karate brand. However, there is still a lot of work to be done, and we are searching for ways to meet the needs of Okinawan karate enthusiasts. For example, there is a lack of information about the characteristics and philosophy of Okinawan karate in comparison to other Japanese budo. Similarly, in terms of Japanese karatedo (as opposed to Okinawan karate), what is the philosophy that makes it distinctive among the various budo disciplines? The obvious characteristic of karatedo is the use of bare hands to attack and defend vital points. It is also a sport where attacks are stopped just short of the target (*sundome*). This act of pulling back before contact is not only a rule for competition, but also represents a profound philosophical principle.

Mifuji: Peaceful co-existence!

Kadekaru: If you read publications from the pre-war period, you find that Itosu Anko and Funakoshi Gichin wrote a lot about their ideas and teachings. These have not lost their lustre and are still quoted today. More than a century has passed since Itosu Anko's day. Today, it is incumbent on us to build on that philosophy so that it will guide the future of karatedo.

Mifuji: Our predecessors in Okinawa were keen on research. They had the will to convey their ideas succinctly. Itosu-sensei, Funakoshi-sensei, and Miyagi Chojun-sensei devoted themselves to study. Miyagi-sensei used to buy books on budo and its philosophy in Kanda whenever he went to Tokyo. This anecdote is not widely known, but there are many such fascinating insights in this book.

Kadekaru: I think we need to re-read those old books now. As there are different styles of karate, we tend to restrict ourselves to the *ryuha* to which we belong. We really should broaden our horizons and study the ways of different styles. What I mean by this is to study the founder of each school, read the writings of the pre-war masters, and to try to understand the background of the times in which they wrote.

Mifuji: As you wrote, Funakoshi Gichin connected with Kano Jigoro, which ultimately led to the establishment of karate clubs at universities. Students industriously spread the word, and even devised ways to make it a competitive sport. Although Funakoshi-sensei was against the idea of competition, students carried on with their experimentation while abiding by the teachings of their master. You have all iterated your hope that traditional and competitive karate can be fused to improve karate as a whole. There are many different styles of karate, but the ideas that there is no first strike, and that the training of the body as a weapon for self-defence is where control is cultivated permeates them all. That's why we should be grateful that the old Okinawan masters recorded their thoughts on the higher principles of what karate should be as a Way of life. In this sense I think it was meaningful that you all wrote about your own travels down the path of karate in this book. Mr. Koyama, how about you?

Karate is Passed on from Person to Person
—the Kara, Te, and Do of Karatedo

Koyama: When I wrote the first article in the series, I began from the year 1872. This year was the beginning of the Ryukyu Disposition. It was also a big turning point for karate. The process from then until the late 1890s, when Itosu Anko created the *Heian* (*Pin'an*) *kata*, is a very interesting story. From the early decades of the twentieth century, seeds were sown in Japan for the promotion of karate by teachers such as Funakoshi Gichin and Miyagi Chojun. It is significant that those who sowed the seeds were and still are respected masters. Whatever form we take for conveying karate teachings in the future, it will always be from person to person. We must not forget that. How we think about karatedo and how we pass it on is an important theme that we always need to keep in mind.

Mifuji: You are absolutely right.

Koyama: In order to do this, we need to know how history transpired, and how people made decisions that have led to what we have today. The main purpose of this book is to share the results of our multifaceted historical investigation driven by this objective.

Mifuji: Indeed.

Koyama: We all had the same mindset in this regard, and this helped us get through the massive task of writing the book. I was allowed to write pretty much whatever I wanted (laughs).

Mifuji: You've pretty much written everything!

Koyama: No, no, there is still much more that needs to be said (laughs). In Chapter 4, Section 7 of this book I wrote about compulsory junior high school budo classes and the Tokyo Olympics. Karate will not be an Olympic sport contested in 2024. Notwithstanding, how will those involved in karatedo in Japan react from now? What are we going to do about it? We must not give up on karatedo. I believe that the turning point will be when we finally manage to combine the competition and the art of karatedo, rather than having one or the other, as is often the case.

In Chapter 4, Section 8, I wrote about my personal views on *Kara*, *Te* and *Do*. Initially, we were thinking of making a chapter for each of these topics. In the end I put them all together as the last part of the book. "*Kara*" (*ku* = empty) is originally a Buddhist term. In the world, there are people of various religions such as Christianity and Islam. People from all over the world may not know the meaning or implications behind the Buddhist concept of *ku*, but as their training progresses, they start to explore its meaning. When karate was changed from "Chinese hand" to "empty hand", karate made its own version of *ku* that is distinct from Buddhism. This is an important point to remember. It is a universal concept for all of humanity.

Mifuji: That was a big leap forward.

Koyama: Still, there is still a lot of work to be done from now to examine various aspects that are not in the historical record.

Karatedo
—Its Potential for Physical Education in Schools

Mifuji: In 2015, Mr. Koyama was asked to be a researcher for a project conducted by the Nippon Budokan and the Japan Karatedo Federation to study how to teach budo in junior high schools. The junior high schools in Fukushima, whose gymnasiums were washed away in the Great East Japan Earthquake, have adopted karate as part of their physical education classes. At the school festival, in the schoolyard where the gymnasium used

Karate is seen as having high value as a teaching tool.

to stand, all of the students performed a group *kata* in front of their parents and teachers. The spectators were moved to tears. The group *kata* united everyone's feelings towards the recovery of their hometown. Karate is more than a sport. The sky's the limit in its power to bring people together.

Koyama: When we started our research into making a karate curriculum for schools, we discovered the educational benefits of group *kata*. You can increase the educational effect making by putting the pupil in teams. Karate classes help pupils develop their ability to think, and other skills mentioned in the new national curriculum guidelines. It is a great way for junior high school pupils to get to know themselves and others. Karate really is an incredible teaching tool.

Mifuji: More than 100 years ago, students of the Okinawa Normal School performed a group demonstration at Shuri Castle. Now it is happening in junior high schools in Japan. Competitions usually only involve a few participants at a time, but in schools, events can be held by classes, or even by the whole school at the same time. The bigger the group, the greater the educational power of karate. In today's world, people are less connected to each other. But you can't do group *kata* without making a connection first. The fact that Mr. Koyama, who won the world championship in individual *kata*, discovered the merits of group *kata* is more than mere coincidence. Karatedo as a teaching tool has many possibilities and is truly "empty". It is not fixed, and it will continue to improve.

During the past two years, I have learned a lot about karate through the authors' manuscripts. The "empty" in karatedo points to freedom. Just as people benefit from karate and become better human beings through its practice, there is still much potential for karate to become even better as well. Budo has always been able to adapt to the changes and needs of the times. Japan's karatedo, which originated in Okinawa, has also kept up with the times and has become a truly global martial art. We hope that this book will in some way contribute to the future development of karatedo and facilitate a greater understanding of its profound culture. It has been a great pleasure for the Nippon Budokan to be able to conclude this series of articles and publish them as a book. Hopefully this volume will be used as a basis for educational and cultural activities in which karate can benefit people and the world. Thank you all very much.

From the left: Kadekaru Toru, Wada Koji, Mifuji Yoshio, and Koyama Masashi.

REFERENCES

Ahagon Chokusei, *Yoshu: Soritsu Hachiju Shunen Kinen*, Yoshu Dosokai, 1961
(阿波根直成『養秀　創立80周年記念誌』養秀同窓会 1961)

Aka Chokushiki, "Aka Chokushiki Yuigonsho", 1778. Higaonna Kanjun, *Higaonna Kanjun Zenshu* Vol. 5, Daiichi Shobo, 1978
(阿嘉直識「阿嘉直識遺言書」1778. 東恩納寛惇『東恩納寛惇全集』5 第一書房 1978)

Akamine Mamoru, *Ryukyu O-koku: Higashi Ajia no Koonaa-sutoon*, Kodansha, 2004
(赤嶺守『琉球王国　東アジアのコーナーストーン』講談社 2004)

Aruzenchin Nouchinaanchu Hachiju Shunen-shi Henshu Iinkai, *Aruzenchin Nouchinaanchu Hachiju Shunen-shi*, Zaia Okinawa-kenjin Rengokai, 1994
(アルゼンチンのうちなーんちゅ80年史編集委員会編『アルゼンチンのうちなーんちゅ80年史』在亜沖縄県人連合会 1994)

Asato Genshu, *Ryutan Hyaku-nen*, Ryutan Dosokai, 1981
(安里源秀『龍潭百年』龍潭同窓会 1981)

Cho Gakurei, *Chuzan Kiraku*, in Harada Nobuki, *Cho Gakurei Shi Ryukyu-ki—Chuzan Kiryaku*, Yoju Shorin, 1998
(張学礼『中山紀略』1663年。原田禹雄『張学礼　使琉球紀・中山紀略』榕樹書林 1998)

Dai-Nippon Butokukai (ed.), *Butoku Kaishi*, Dai-Nippon Butokukai Hombu, 1910-12 (Reprint) Yushodo Shuppan, 1985
(大日本武徳会編『武徳会誌』大日本武徳本部、1910～1912年 (復刻版) 雄松堂出版 1985)

Dai-Nippon Butokukai (ed.), *Butoku Kaishi*, Dai-Nippon Butokukai Hombu, 1906-09 (Reprint) Yushodo Shuppan, 1985
(大日本武徳会編『武徳誌』大日本武徳本部、1906～1909年　(復刻版) 雄松(堂出版 1985)

Doshisha University Karate Club, *Doshisha Daigaku Karatedo-bu 60 Shunen Kinen-shi*, 1997
(同志社大学空手道部『同志社大学空手道部60周年記念誌』1997)

Doshisha University Karate Club, *Doshisha Daigaku Karatedo-bu Enkaku*, 1997
(同志社大学空手道部『同志社大学空手道部沿革』1997)

E. M. Satow, "Notes on Loochoo", *The Phoenix*, James Summers, 1873

Funakoshi Gichin (Shoto), "Karate wa bugei no kozui nari", *Ryukyu Shimpo*, January 9, 1913
(松濤（富名腰義珍）「唐手は武藝の骨髄なり」『琉球新報』琉球新報社 1913年1月9日)

Funakoshi Gichin, *Ryukyu Kempo Karate*, Bukyosha, 1922
(富名腰義珍『琉球拳法唐手』武侠社、1922)

Funakakoshi Gichin, "Karate monogatari", *Gekkan Bunka Okinawa* (May), Gekkan Bunka Okinawa Sha, 1941
(富名腰義珍「空手物語」『月刊文化沖縄』5月号 月刊文化沖縄社 1941)

Funakoshi Gichin, *Zoho Karatedo Kyohan*, Kobundo Shoten, 1941
(富名腰義珍『増補 空手道教範』廣文堂書店 1941)

Funakoshi Gichin, *Ryukyu Kempo Karate*, Bukyosha, 1922
(富名腰義珍『琉球拳法 唐手』武侠社、1922)

Funakoshi Gichin, *Karatedo Kyohan*, Kobundo Shoten, 1935. Reprinted by Kazusa in 1990
(富名腰義珍『空手道教範』廣文堂書店、1935年。富名腰義珍『空手道教範』復刻版 カズサ、1990)

Funakoshi Gichin, *Rentan Goshin Karatejutsu*, Okura Kobundo, 1925. Reprinted by Yojusha in 1996
(富名腰義珍『錬膽護身 唐手術』大倉廣文堂、1925年。富名腰義珍『錬膽護身 唐手術』復刻版榕樹社 1996)

Funakakoshi Gichin, *Karatedo Ichiro*, Kodansha, 1981
(船越義珍『空手道一路』講談社 1981)

Gima Shinkin, Fujiwara Ryuzo, *Taidan Kindai Karatedo no Rekishi wo Kataru*, Baseball Magazine-sha, 1986
(儀間真謹・藤原稜三『対談 近代空手道の歴史を語る』ベースボール・マガジン社 1986)

Hall, Basil, (Trans. Haruna Tetsu), *Chosen Ryukyu Kokai-ki*, Iwanami Shoten, 1991
ベイジル・ホール（春名徹訳）『朝鮮・琉球航海記』岩波書店、1991年。

Hanashiro Chomo, "Karate kumite", in Nakasone Genwa (ed.), *Karatedo Taikan*, 1938
(花城長茂「空手組手」『空手道大観』1938年。仲宗根源和編著)

Hayase Toshiyuki, *Ishiwara Kanji – Makkasa ga Ichiban Osoreta Nihonjin*, Futaba Shinsho, 2013
(早瀬利之『石原莞爾 マッカーサーが一番恐れた日本人』双葉新書 2013)

Higaonna Morio, *Okinawa Goju-ryu Karatedo*, Keibunsha, 1981
(東恩納盛男『沖縄剛柔流空手道』主文社 1981)

Higaonna Morio, *Okinawa Gojuryu Karatedo II*, Keibunsha, 1983
(東恩納盛男『沖縄剛柔流空手道・II』主文社 1983)

Higaonna Morio, *Goju-ryu Karatedo-shi*, Champpu, 2001
(東恩納盛男著『剛柔流空手道史　二大拳聖東恩納寛量宮城長順』チャンプ 2001)

Higashionna Kanjun, *Higashionna Kanjun Zenshu*, Ryukyu Shimposha, 1979
(東恩納寛惇『東恩納寛惇全集』琉球新報社 1979)

Iha Fuyu, *Iha Fuyu Zenshu* Vol. 1–11, Heibonsha, 1974–1976
(伊波普猷『伊波普猷全集』第1〜11巻　平凡社、1974〜1976)

Ikemiya Masaharu, Odo Kiyotaka, Dana Masayuki (ed.), *Kumemura Rekishi to Jinbutsu*, Hirugi-sha, 1993
(池宮正治・小渡清孝・田名真之編『久米村抱―歴史と人物―』ひるぎ社 1993)

Ikemiya Masaharu, Oshiro Manabu, *Okansen Odori: Kumi-odori, Buyo*, Kaiyo Hakurankai Kinen Koen Kanri Zaidan, 2000
(池宮正治・大城學『御冠船踊―組踊・舞踊―』財団法人海洋博覧会記念公園管理財団 2000)

International Budo University, *Budo no Rekishi to Sono Seishin*, IBU Budo Sports Research Centre, 2010
(国際武道大学『武道の歴史とその精神』国際武道大学武道・スポーツ研究所 2010)

Iokibe Makoto, "Toa renmei-ron no kihon-teki seikaku", *Asia Kenkyu* Vol. 22 No.1, 1975
(五百旗頭眞「東亜連盟論の基本的性格」『アジア研究』第22巻1号 1975)

Ishikawa Yuki, "Sengo Okinawa-ken ni okeru kaigai imin no rekishi to jittai", *Imin Kenkyu* 6, Ryukyu University, 2010
(石川友紀「戦後沖縄県における海外移民の歴史と実態」『移民研究』6　琉球大学 2010)

Ishino Ei, "Dokutoku no bugi karate to sumo", *Minami-shima no Shizen to Hito*, Sanshodo Shoten, 1916
(石野瑛「独特の武技唐手と相撲」『南島の自然と人』三笑堂書店 1916)

Itosu Anko, "Karate jukka-jo", in Nakasone Genwa (ed.), *Karatedo Taikan*, 1938
(糸洲安恒「唐手十カ条」『空手道大観』1938年。仲宗根源和編著)

JKF Shito-kai, *Yukyu no Ken*, 1995
(全日本空手道連盟糸東会発行『悠久之拳』1995)

JKF, *Karatedo Kyohan*, (Reprint) 2015
(全日本空手道連盟『空手道教範』改訂版 2015)

Kabe Masaaki, Miyagi Tamotsu (ed.), *Meiji Taisho Showa—Okinawa-ken Gakko Shashin-cho*, Naha Shuppansha, 1987
(我部政男・宮城保編『明治・大正・昭和　沖縄県学校写真帳』那覇出版社 1987)

Kabushiki-gaisha Sozo, *Karatedo – Hozon-ban*, 1977]
(株式会社創造『空手道　保存版』1977)

Kadekaru Toru, "Kenkyu Nooto: Kindai karate-shi wo kenkyu suru ni atatte", *Karatedo Kenkyu*, Karatedo Kenkyukai No.14–15, 2012
(嘉手苅徹「〈研究ノート〉近代空手史を研究するにあたって」『空手道研究』空手道研究会、第14・15号 2012)

Kadekaru Toru, "Te kara Tii e", Shimamura Koichi (ed.), *Ryukyu – Kosa Suru Rekishi to Bunka*, Bensei Shuppan, 2014
(嘉手苅徹「『手』から『唐手』へ」島村幸一編『琉球　交差する歴史と文化』勉誠出版 2014)

Kadekaru Toru, Toyoshima Tatehiro, Inoshita Kaori, "Ryukyu shobun iko ni tenkanki no karate ni kansuru kosatsu", *Reitaku Gakusai Journal*, Reitaku Daigaku Keizai Gakkai, 2016
(嘉手苅徹・豊嶋建広・井下佳織「琉球処分以降における転換期の唐手に関する一考察」『麗澤学際ジャーナル』麗澤大学経済学会 2016)

Kadena Sotoku, "Bubi", *Okinawa Dai Hyakka Jiten* Vol. 2, Okinawa Times-sha, 1983
(嘉手納宗徳「武備」『沖縄大百科事典』下巻 沖縄タイムス社 1983)

Kaku Kozo, *Butoden*, Mainichi Shimbunsha, 1996
(加来耕三『武闘伝』毎日新聞社 1996)

Kano Jigoro, "Seiryoku Zen'yo Kokumin Taiiku", *Kano Jigoro Taikei* Vol. 8, Kodokan, 1988
(嘉納治五郎「精力善用国民体育」講道館『嘉納治五郎大系』第8巻 1988)

Kansai Student Karatedo Federation, *Yakushin* (60th Anniversary), 2017
(関西学生空手道連盟60周年記念誌『躍進』2017)

Kasao Kyoji, *Chugoku Bujutsu-shi Taikan*, Fukushodo, 1994
(笠尾恭二『中国武術史大観』福昌堂 1994)

Kawazu Rie, "Nanto Zatsuwa no kosei to seiritsu haikei ni kansuru kosatsu", *Shiryo Henshushitsu Kiyo* No. 29, Okinawa Pref. Board of Education, 2004
(河津梨絵「『南島雑話』の構成と成立背景に関する一考察」『史料編集室紀要』第29号、沖縄県教育委員会、2004)

Kinjo Hiroshi, "Heian no kenkyu", *Gekkan Karatedo* Vol. 1 No. 2, June 1956 (Reprint) Yoju Shorin 1-10, 1977
(金城裕「平安の研究」『月刊空手道』第1巻第2号、1956年6月号 (榕樹書林『月刊空手道 合本復刻版 (創刊号〜第10号)』1977)

Kinjo Hiroshi, *Karate kara Karate e*, Nippon Budokan, 2011
(金城裕『唐手から空手へ』日本武道館 2011)

Kinjo Seitoku (et al.), *Okinawa-ken no Hyaku-nen*, Yamakawa Shuppansha, 2005
(金城正篤・上原兼善・秋山勝・仲地哲夫・大城将保『沖縄県の百年』山川出版社 2005)

Kinoshita Hideaki, "Jutsu kara michi e", *Taiiku no Kagaku* Vol. 48, Kyorin Shoten, 1998
(木下秀明「術から道へ」『体育の科学』48巻 杏林書院 1998)

Kodokan, *Kano Jigoro Taikei* Vol. 8, Hon no Tomosha, 1988
(講道館『嘉納治五郎大系』第8巻 本の友社 1988)

Kodokan, *Kano Jigoro Taikei* Vol. 8, Hon no Tomosha, 1988
(講道館『嘉納治五郎大系』第9巻、本の友社、1988年)

Kokawa Tsuneo (ed.), *Yoku Wakaru Supotsu Jinrui-gaku*, Mineruva Shobo, 2017
(寒川恒夫編『よくわかるスポーツ人類学』ミネルヴァ書房 2017)

Kokawa Tsuneo, *Nihon Budo to Toyo Shiso*, Heibonsha, 2014
(寒川恒夫『日本の武道と東洋思想』平凡社 2014)

Kokubu Naoichi, *Nanto Zatsuwa (2)*, Heibonsha, 1996
(國分直一『南島雑話』2、平凡社、1996)

Kondo Ken'ichiro, "Kindai kyoiku no donyu", *Okinawa-ken Shi* Vol. 5 *Kindai-hen*, Okinawa Prefecture Board of Education, 2011
(近藤健一郎「近代教育の導入」『沖縄県史　第5巻　近代編』沖縄県教育委員会 2011)

Konno Bin, *Gichin no Ken*, Shueisha, 2005
(今野敏『義珍の拳』集英社 2005)

Konuma Tamotsu, *Motobu Choki to Yamada Tatsuo Kenkyu*, Sojin-sha, 1994
(小沼保『本部朝基と山田辰雄研究』壮神社 1994)

Koyama Masashi, "Waga Miyagi Chojun", *Gekkan Karatedo*, Fukushodo, May 1981
(小山正辰「我が宮城長順」『月刊空手道』福昌堂 1981年5月号)

Kyoto University Karate Club, *Kyoto Daigaku Karatedo-bu 80-Shunen Kinen-shi*, 2017
(京都大学空手道部『京都大学空手道部80周年記念誌』2017)

Mabuni Ken'ei, *Budo Karate e no Shotai*, Sankosha Hakkosho, 2001
(摩文仁賢榮『武道空手への招待』株式会社三交社発行所 2001)

Mabuni Kenwa, "Nihon bushido no ichibunha toshite kakuritsu saseru karatedo", *Gekkan Bunka Okinawa* (June), Gekkan Bunka Okinawa-sha, 1941
(摩文仁賢和「日本武士道の一分派として確立せる空手道」『月刊文化沖縄』6月号　月刊文化沖縄社 1941)

Mabuni Kenwa, "Budo soku seikatsu", *Gekkan Bunka Okinawa* (March), Gekkan Bunka Okinawasha, 1941
(摩文仁賢和「武道即生活」『月刊文化沖縄』3月号　月刊文化沖縄社 1941)

Mabuni Kenwa, *Kobo Jizai Karate Kempo – Juuhachi no Kenkyu*, Karate Kenkyusha Kobukan, 1934 (Reprinted by Yoju Shorin in 2006)
(摩文仁賢和『功防自在・空手拳法　十八の研究』空手研究社興武館1934年。摩文仁賢和『攻防自在空手拳法　十八手の研究』復刻版 榕樹書林 2006)

Mabuni Kenwa, *Kobo Jizai Goshinjutsu Karate Kempo*, Tainan Yosha, 1934 (Reprinted by Yoju Shorin in 2006)
(摩文仁賢和『攻防自在護身術　空手拳法』大南洋社　1934年。摩文仁賢和『攻防自在　空手拳法』復刻版 榕樹書林 2006)

Mabuni Kenwa, Nakasone Genwa, *Kobo Jizai Goshin Kempo Karatedo Nyumon*, Karate Kenkyusha Kobukan, 1935 (Reprinted by Yojusha in 1996)
(摩文仁賢和・仲宗根源和著『攻防自在護身拳法　空手道入門—別名・空手獨習—』空手研究社興武館 1935年。摩文仁賢和・仲宗根源和『攻防拳法　空手道入門』復刻版　榕樹社 1996)

Maeshiro Tsutomu, "Meiji-ki no Okinawa ni okeru undokai ni kansuru rekishi-teki kenkyu", *Ryukyu Daigaku Kyoiku Gakubu Kiyo* No. 42, University of the Ryukyus, 1992
(真栄城勉「明治期の沖縄県における運動会に関する歴史的研究」『琉球大学教育学部紀要』第42号　琉球大学 1992)

Majikina Anko, *Majikina Anko Zenshu* Vol. 1-4, Ryukyu Shimposha, 1993
(真境名安興『真境名安興全集』第1〜4巻　琉球新報社 1993)

Matsuda Toshihiko, "So Neiju to Kyoto ni okeru toa renmei undo – Toa renmei undo to Chosen - Chosen-jin (2)", *Sekai Jinken MOndai Kenkyu Senta Kenkyu Kiyo* No. 3, 1998
(松田利彦「曹寧柱と京都における東亜連盟運動——東亜連盟運動と朝鮮・朝鮮人 (2)」『世界人権問題研究センター研究紀要』第3号 1998)

Matsuzaki Horyu, *Jinsei wo Shobu Suru Kushin-ryu Karatedo Gokui*, Gurafusha, 2005
(松崎寶龍『人生を勝負する　空眞流空手道極意』株式会社グラフ社 2005)

Meigenro Shujin, "Nikudan aiutsu karate kento dai-shiai, *King* (Sept.), 1925
(鳴絃楼主人「肉弾相打つ唐手拳闘大試合」『キング』9月号　大日本雄弁会講談社 1925)

Meiji University Karate Club, *Karate-bu Shi – Soritsu 40-Shunen Kinen Tokushu-go Showa 52-nendo*, Meiji Daigaku Surugadai Karate Kai, 1977
(明治大学空手部『空手部誌 創立40周年記念特集号 昭和52年度』明治大学駿台空手会 1977)

Miki Jisaburo, Mutsu Mizuho, *Kempo Gaisetsu*, Tokyo Imperial University Karate Kenkyu Kai, 1930 (Reprinted by Yoju Shorin in 2002)
(三木二三郎・陸奥瑞穂編『拳法概説』東京帝國大學唐手研究會 1930年。三木二三郎・高田瑞穂『拳法概説』復刻版 榕樹書林 2002)

Mita Karate Kai, *Keio Gijuku Taiikukai Karate-bu 75-Nenshi*, 1999
(三田空手会『慶應義塾体育会空手部75年史』1999)

Miyagi Chojun, "Karatedo gaisetsu", *Toka* No. 2, Osaka Togyo Club, 1936
(宮城長順「唐手道概説 (琉球拳法唐手道沿革概要)」『糖華』第2号 大阪糖業倶楽部 1936)

Miyagi Chojun, "Ho goju donto – karate nanakusagayu", Gekkan Bunka Okinawa (Aug.), Gekkan Bunka Okinawasha, 1942
(宮城長順「法剛柔呑吐―空手雑藁―」『月刊文化沖縄』8月号 月刊文化沖縄社 1942)

Miyagi Chojun, *Goju-ryu Kempo*, 1932
(宮城長順『剛柔流拳法』1932)

Miyagi Chojun, *Karatedo Gaisetsu*, 1934
(宮城長順『唐手道概説 (琉球拳法唐手道沿革概要)』1934)

Miyagi Tokumasa, *Karate no Rekishi*, Hirugisha, 1987
(宮城篤正『空手の歴史』ひるぎ社 1987)

Motobu Choki, *Watashi no Karatejutsu*, Tokyo Karate Fukyukai, 1932
(本部朝基『私の唐手術』東京唐手普及會 1932)

Motobu Choki, *Okinawa Kempo Karatejutsu Kumite-hen*, Karate Fukyukai, 1926
(本部朝基『沖縄拳法唐手術 組手編』唐手術普及会 1926)

Murata Naoki, *Kano Jigoroo Shihan ni Manabu*, Nippon Budokan, 2001
(村田直樹『嘉納治五郎師範に学ぶ』日本武道館 2001)

Murayama Terushi, "Budo no bunkasei – budo to shingon mikkyo-no menkyo", *Kanoya Taiiku Daigaku Kenkyu Kiyo* Vol. 5, 1990
(村山輝志「武道の文化性─武道と真言密教の免許─」『鹿屋体育大学研究紀要』第5号 1990)

Mutsu Mizuho, *Karate Kempo – Zen*, Todai Karate Kenkyu Kai, 1933 (Reprinted by Yoju Shorin in 1999)
(陸奥瑞穂『唐手拳法　全』東大唐手研究會、1933年。陸奥瑞穂『唐手拳法　全』復刻版　榕樹書林 1999)

Nagai Ryuichi (ed.), *Nanto Zatsuwa Hoi-hen*, Kagoshima Prefectural Library, 1933
(永井竜一編『南島雑話　補遺編』鹿児島県立図書館 1933)

Nagamine Shoshin, *Shijitsu to Dento wo Mamoru Okinwa no Karate-edo*, Shinjinbutsu Oraisha, 1983
(長嶺将真『史実と伝統を守る 沖縄の空手道』新人物往来社 1983)

Nagamine Shoshin, *Shijitsu wo Kuden ni yoru Okinawa no Karate Kakuryoku Meijin-den*, Shinjinbutsu Oraisha, 1986
(長嶺将真『史実を口伝による 沖縄の空手・角力名人伝』新人物往来社 1986)

Naha City Planning Division History Project, *Gekido no Kiroku – Naha Hyaku-nen no Ayumi*, Naha City, 1980
(那覇市企画部市史編集室『激動の記録　那覇百年のあゆみ』那覇市 1980)

Nakabayashi Shinji, "Budo ni okeru menkyo dan'i-sei", *Taiyo* (Sept.), Heibonsha, 1980
(中林信二「武道における免許段位制」『太陽』1980年9月号 平凡社)

Nakahara Zenchu, *Nakahara Zenchu Zenshu* Vols. 1-4, Okinawa Taimususha, 1978
(仲原善忠『仲原善忠全集』第1～4巻　沖縄タイムス社 1978)

Nakamoto Masahiro, *Okinawa Dento Kobudo Sono Rekishi to Tamashii*, Bunbukan, 1983
(仲本政博『沖縄伝統古武道　その歴史と魂』文武館 1983)

Nakasone Genwa (ed.), Karatedo Taikan, Tokyo Tosho Co. 1938 (Reprinted by Rokurindo Shoten in 1991)
(仲宗根源和編『空手道大觀』東京圖書株式會社　1938年 仲宗根源和編『空手道大観』復刻版緑林堂書店 1991)

Nomura Otojiro, *Toa Renmei-ki Ishiwara Kanji Shiryo*, Doesisha, 2007
(野村乙二朗『東亜連盟期の石原莞爾資料』同成社 2007)

Nonomura Takashi, *Natsukashiki Okinawa*, Ryukyu Shimposha, 2000
(野々村孝『懐かしき沖縄』琉球新報社 2000)

Okinawa Culture Promotion Society, *Okinawa-ken Shi* – Vol. 3 *Ko-Ryukyu*, Okinawa Prefecture Board of Education, 2010
(財団法人沖縄県文化振興会『沖縄県史 各論編 第3巻 古琉球』沖縄県教育委員会 2010)

Okinawa Culture Promotion Society, *Okinawa-ken Shi* – Vol. *4 Kinsei*, Okinawa Prefecture Board of Education, 2010
(財団法人沖縄県文化振興会『沖縄県史 各論編 第4巻 近世』沖縄県教育委員会 2003)

Okinawa Goju-ryu Karatedo Kyokai, *Miyazato Eiichi Sensei Sankai Kitsuizen Kinenshi—Ho Goju Donto*, Okinawa Goju-ryu Karatedo Kyokai, 2001
(沖縄剛柔流空手道協会『宮里栄一先生三回忌追善記念誌 法剛柔呑吐』沖縄剛柔流空手道協会 2001)

Okinawa Prefecture Education Council, *Okinawa Kyoiku* Vols. 1–39, 1906–1944 (Reprinted by Fuji Shuppan 2009–15)
(沖縄県教育会/沖縄教育会『沖縄教育』第1～39巻、1906～1944年。復刻版 不二出版 2009～2015)

Okinawa Prefecture Shiritsu Kyoiku Kai, *Okinawa Kyoiku* Vols. 1–12, 1896-1906 (Reprinted by Hongo Shoseki in 1980)
(沖縄県私立教育会事務所『琉球教育』第1～12巻、1896～1906年。ハワイ大学 復刻版 本邦書籍 1980)

Okinawa Times Dai Hyakka Jiten Kanko Jimukyoku, *Okinawa Dai Hyakka Jiten* Vols. 1–3, Okinawa Taimususha, 1983
(沖縄タイムス大百科事典刊行事務局『沖縄大百科事典』（上）（中）（下）沖縄タイムス社 1983)

Okinawa-ken Bunka Kanko Supootsu-bu Karate Shinkoka (ed.), *Okinawa Karate Ryuha Kenkyu Jigyo—Uechi-ryu Kaisetsu-sho*, Okinawa Prefecture Board of Education, 2018
(沖縄県文化観光スポーツ部空手振興課編『沖縄空手流派研究事業 上地流解説書』沖縄県教育委員会 2018)

Okinawa-ken Bunka Kanko Supootsu-bu Karate Shinkoka (ed.), *Okinawa Karate Ryuha Kenkyu Jigyo—Goju-ryu Kaisetsu-sho*, Okinawa Prefecture Board of Education, 2019
(沖縄県文化観光スポーツ部空手振興課編『沖縄空手流派研究事業　剛柔流解説書』沖縄県教育委員会 2019)

Okinawa-ken Kyoiku-cho Bunkaka (ed.), *Gakko Taiiku ni Okeru Karatedo Shido no Tebiki* Vol. 2, Okinawa-ken Kyoiku-cho, 1995
(沖縄県教育庁保健体育課編『学校体育における空手道指導の手引』第2集　沖縄県教育庁 1995)

Okinawa-ken Kyoiku-cho Bunkaka (ed.), *Gakko Taiiku ni Okeru Karatedo Shido no Tebiki* Vol. 3, Okinawa-ken Kyoiku-cho, 1996
(沖縄県教育庁保健体育課編『学校体育における空手道指導の手引』第3集　沖縄県教育委員会 1996)

Okinawa-ken Kyoiku-cho Bunkaka (ed.), *Karatedo-Kobudo Kihon Chosa Hokoku*, Gajumarusha, 1994
(沖縄県教育庁文化課編『空手道・古武道基本調査報告書』榕樹社 1994)

Okinawa-ken Kyoiku-cho Bunkaka (ed.), *Karatedo-Kobudo Kihon Chosa Hokoku II*, Okinawa Prefecture Board of Education, 1995
(沖縄県教育庁文化課編『空手道・古武道基本調査報告書・Ⅱ』沖縄県教育委員会 1995)

Okinawa Prefecture Normal School Gakuyukai, "Honkai kiji", *Ryutan* No.1, 1902
(沖縄県師範学校内学友会「本会記事」『龍潭』第1号　沖縄県師範学校内学友会1 902)

Okinawa Prefecture Normal School Gakuyukai, "Ko Yabu-sensei wo itamu", *Ryutan* No.33, 1938
(沖縄県師範学校学友会「故屋部先生を悼む」『龍潭』第33号　沖縄県師範学校学友会 1938)

Okinawa Prefecture Normal School Gakuyukai, "Sobetsukai", *Ryutan* No.2, 1903
(沖縄県師範学校内学友会「送別会」『龍潭』第2号　沖縄県師範学校内学友会 1903)

Okinawa-ken Taiiku Kyokai-shi Iinkai-shu, *Okinawa-ken Taiiku Kyokai-shi*, Okinawa-ken Taiiku Kyokai, 1995
(沖縄県体育協会史編集委員会編『沖縄県体育協会史』沖縄県体育協会 1995)

Ono Masako (et al.), "Shiryo shokai—Kishi Akimasa Bunko Satsuyu-kiko", *Shiryo Henshu-shitsu Kiyo* Vol. 31, Okinawa Prefecture Board of Education, 2006
(小野まさ子・漢那敬子　田口恵・冨田千夏「資料紹介　岸秋正文庫　薩遊紀行」『史料編集室紀要』第31号　沖縄県教育委員会 2006)

Otsuki Fumihiko, *Genkai*, Rokugokan, 1931 (Reprint by Chikuma Shobo, 2012)
(大槻文彦『言海』六号館、1931年。大槻文彦、復刻版、筑摩書房、2012)

Pao-kuang Hsu, *Chuzan Denshin-roku*, (1721) in　Harada Nobuo, *Chuzan Denshin-roku Shinyaku-chu-ban*, Yoju Shorin, 1999
(徐葆光『中山伝信録』1721年。原田禹雄『中山伝信録　新訳注版』榕樹書林 1999)

Rin Hakugen, *Chugoku Bujutsu-shi*, Gigeisha, 2015
(林伯原『中国武術史』技藝社)

Ritsumeikan University Karatedo Club, *Ritsumeikan Daigaku Karatedo-bu Enkaku-shi* (60th Anniversary), 1998
(立命館大学空手道部『立命館大学空手道部沿革史 (60周年記念誌)』)

Sawayama Muneochi, *Nippon Kempo*, Mainichi Shimbunsha 1964
(澤山宗海『日本拳法』毎日新聞社 1964)

Shiitada Atsushi, *Ryukyu Kyukoku Undo*, Mugen, 2010
(後多田敦『琉球救国運動』出版者Mugen 2010)

Shimabukuro Zempatsu Iko Kankokai, *Shimabukuro Zempatsu Zenshu*, Okinawasha, 1956
(島袋全発遺稿刊行会『島袋全発著作集』おきなわ社 1956)

Shimabukuro Zempatsu, *Taafaaku*, 1867
(島袋全発「三六九並書芸番組」『打花鼓』1867)
Shimabukuro Zempatsu, *Shimabukuro Zempatsu Chosakushu*, Okinawasha, 1953
(島袋全発『島袋全発著作集』おきなわ社、1953)

Shimamura Koichi, "Ryukyu fune, Tosa hyochaku shiryo ni miru Nihon bungei no kyoju", *Rissho Daigaku Kokugo Kokubun* Vol. 46, Rissho University Bungaku-bu Kokugo Kokubun Bungaku-kai, 2008
島村幸一「琉球船、土佐漂着史料にみる日本文芸の享受」『立正大学國語國文』第46号　立正大学文学部國語國文学会、2008)

Shimamura Koichi, *Oshima Hikki* related materials in *Rissho Daigaku Bungaku-bu Ronso* Vol. 134, Rissho University Bungaku-bu, 2012
(島村幸一『大島筆記』に関連する資料『立正大学文学部論叢』第134号　立正大学文学部、2012)

Shishida Fumiaki, "Budoka Fukushima Seizaburo to Ishihara Kanji", *Waseda Daigaku Ningen Kagaku Kenkyu* Vol. 7.1, 1994
(志々田文明「武道家福島清三郎と石原莞爾」『早稲田大学人間科学研究』第7巻第1号、1994)

Shishida Fumiaki, *Kano Jigoro no Judo-kan to Sono Tenkai*, Masters Thesis (University of Tsukuba), 1979
(志々田文明『嘉納治五郎の柔道観とその展開』修士論文 (筑波大学)、1979)

Shogakkan, *Dijitaru Daijisen* 3rd ed., Shogakkan, 2018
(小学館『デジタル大辞泉　第三版』小学館、2018)

Sugimoto Yoshiro, *Butoku-shi* Vol. 3.8, Butoku-shi Hakkojo, 1908. Dai-Nihon Butokukai, *Butoku-shi* (reprint), Yushodo, 1985
(杉本善郎『武徳誌』第3編第8号　武徳誌発行所、1908年。大日本武徳会編『武徳誌　復刻版』雄松堂、1985)

Sugimoto Yoshiro, *Butoku-shi* Vol. 4.10, Butoku-shi Hakkojo, 1909. Dai-Nihon Butokukai, *Butoku-shi* (reprint), Yushodo, 1985
(杉本善郎『武徳誌』第4編第10号　武徳誌発行所、1909年。大日本武徳会編『武徳誌　復刻版』雄松堂、1985)

Takamiya Shigeru (et. al), *Okinawa karate kobudo jiten*, Kashiwashobo, 2008
(高宮城繁・新里勝彦・仲本政博『沖縄空手古武道事典』柏書房、2008)

Takushoku University Karate Club, "Takushoko daigaku karate-bu monogatari" No. 1, *Kinjo-ban Gekkan Karatedo* Vol. 1, Yojushorin, 1956
(拓殖大学空手部「拓殖大学空手部物語」第1回『金城版月刊空手道』第1号、榕樹書林)

Takushoku University Karate Club, "Takushoko daigaku karate-bu monogatari" No. 3, *Kinjo-ban Gekkan Karatedo* Vol. 1, Yojushorin, July/August 1956
(拓殖大学空手部「拓殖大学空手部物語」第3回『金城版月刊空手道』昭和31年7・8月合併号)

Tanaka Akira, *Karatedo*, Sozo, 1977
(田中晶『空手道』創造、1977)

Tei Heitetsu, *Kyuyo*, 1524, in Kyuyo Kenyu-kai (ed.), *Kyuyo*, Kadokawa Shoten, 1965
(鄭秉哲『球陽』1524年。球陽研究会『球陽』角川書店)

Tobe Yoshihiro, *Oshima Hikki*, 1762
(戸部良熙『大島筆記』1762)
Miyamoto Tsuneichi (et. al), *Nihon Shomin Seikatsu Shiryo Shusei—Tanken, Kiko, Chishi (Minamishima-hen)* Vol. 1, Daiichi Shobo, 1968
(宮本常一・原口虎雄・比嘉春潮『日本庶民生活史料集成　探検・紀行・地誌（南島編）』第1巻　第一書房、1968)

Todo Yoshiaki, *Gakko Budo no Rekishi wo Tadoru*, Nippon Budokan, 2018
(藤堂良明『学校武道の歴史を辿る』日本武道館、2018)

Todo Yoshiaki, *Judo—Sono Rekishi to Giho*, Nippon Budokan, 2014
(藤堂良明『柔道　その歴史と技法』日本武道館、2014)

Tokuda Antei, "Karate", *Kyuyo* Vol. 18, Okinawa Kenritsu Chugakko Gakuyu-kai, 1909
(徳田安貞「唐手」『球陽』第18号　沖縄県立中学校学友会、1909)

Tokyo University of Agriculture Karate Club, *Tokyo Nogyo Daigaku Karate-bu 50 Nenshi*, Midori Kukai, 1985
(東京農業大学空手部『東京農業大学空手部50年史』緑空会、1985)

Uechi Kan'ei ed., *Seisetsu Okinawa Karatedo—Sono Rekishi to Giho*, Uechi Kan'ei Karatedo Kyokai, 1977
(上地完英監修『精説　沖縄空手道―その歴史と技法』上地流空手道協会、1977)

Yamauchi Seihin, Moromizato Choho, "Karate-bu kiroku", *Ryutan*, Okinawa Prefecture Normal School Gakuyukai, 1911
(山内盛彬・諸見里朝保「唐手部記録」『龍潭』沖縄県師範学校学友会、1911)

Yokoyama Manabu, "Horeki 20-nen Ryukyu koku fune hyochaku kiryoku 'Oshima Hikki' shohon ni tsuite", *Seikatsu Bunka Kenkyu-sho Nenpo* Vol. 11, Notre Dame Seishin University Seikatsu Bunka Kenkyu-jo, 1997
(横山学「宝暦十二年琉球国船漂着記録「大島筆記」諸本について」『生活文化研究所年報』第11集　ノートルダム清心女子大学生活文化研究所、1997)

Yokoyama Shinpei, *Hitsuroku Ishiwara Kanji*, Fuyoshobo, 1971
(横山臣平『秘録　石原莞爾』芙蓉書房、1971)

Yoshimura Jinsai, "Jiden budo-ki", *Gekkan Bunka Okinawa*, Gekkan Bunka Okinawa Sha, 1941
(義村仁齋「自傳武道記」『月刊文化沖縄』月刊文化沖縄社)

NEWSPAPER ARTICLES

"Akada no miroku", *Ryukyu Shimpo*, August 19, 1899
(「赤田の弥勒」『琉球新報』1899年8月19日)

"Ayajo tsunahiki-go dai shinbokukai", *Ryukyu Shimpo*, August 19, 1898
(「綾門大綱引後の大親睦会」『琉球新報』1898年8月19日)

"Botokyokusha no undo-kai hyo", *Ryukyu Shimpo*, May 21, 1902
(「某当局者の運動会評」『琉球新報』1902年5月21日)

"Bunki kenkyu kunai undokai no keikyo", *Ryukyu Shimpo*, May 31, 1907
(「文喜研究区内運動会の景況」『琉球新報』1907年5月31日)

"Bushi Motobu Choki ogina ni 'jissen Dan' wo kiku (1)", *Ryukyu Shimpo*, November 9, 1936
(「武士・本部朝基翁に「実践談」を聴く」(1)『琉球新報』1936年11月9日)

"Bushi Motobu Choki ogina ni 'jissen Dan' wo kiku (2)", *Ryukyu Shimpo*, November 10, 1936
(「武士・本部朝基翁に「実践談」を聴く」(2)『琉球新報』1936年11月10日)

"Bushi Motobu Choki ogina ni 'jissen Dan' wo kiku (3)", *Ryukyu Shimpo*, November 11, 1936
(「武士・本部朝基翁に「実践談」を聴く」(3)『琉球新報』1936年11月11日)

"Butokukai seinen taikai (mikka gogo)", *Kyoto Hinode Shimbun*, August 7, 1908
(「武徳会青年大会 (3日午後)」『京都日出新聞』1908年8月7日)

"Chugakko judo gekiken taikai", *Ryukyu Shimpo,* February 6, 1907
(「中学校の柔道撃剣大会」『琉球新報』1907年2月6日)

"Chugakko no dojo-biraki", *Ryukyu Shimpo,* November 2, 1906
(「中学校の道場開き」『琉球新報』1906年11月2日)

"Chugakko no dosokai", *Ryukyu Shimpo*, Agust 13, 1907
(「中学の同窓会」『琉球新報』1907年8月13日)

"Chugakko shokuin no karate", *Ryukyu Shimpo,* February 5, 1905
(「中学校職員の唐手」『琉球新報』1905年2月5日)

"Chugaku doso shinbokukai", Ryukyu Shimpo, August 19, 1905
(「中学の同窓親睦会」『琉球新報』1905年8月19日)

"Chugaku yoshu rengotai undokai", Ryukyu Shimpo, December 1,
1905
(「中学養秀連合大運動会」『琉球新報』1905年12月1日)

"Chugaku yoshu rengotai undokai", *Ryukyu Shimpo*, November 25,
1907
(「中学養秀連合運動会」『琉球新報』1907年11月25日)

"Fusoku shogakko no gakugei-kai", *Ryukyu Shimpo*, February 3,
1907
(「附属小学校の学芸会」『琉球新報』1907年2月3日)

"Ganko no jido kyoiku", *Ryukyu Shimpo*, June 13, 1898
(「頑固の児童教育」『琉球新報』1898年6月13日)

"Gekiken taikai", *Ryukyu Shimpo*, March 21, 1906
(「撃剣大会」『琉球新報』1906年3月21日)

"Genkotsu-ron", *Ryukyu Shimpo*, April 10, 1907
(「拳骨論」『琉球新報』1907年4月10日)

"Ginowanko no sotsugyo-shiki", *Ryukyu Shimpo*, March 27, 1907
「宜野湾校の卒業式」『琉球新報』1907年3月27日)

"Hojo jiju juraiken to sougo undo-kai", *Ryukyu Shimpo*, February
27, 1905
(「北條侍従来県と総合運動会」『琉球新報』1905年2月27日)

"Hojo jiju no gakko junshi", *Ryukyu Shimpo*, February 3, 1907
(「北條侍従の学校巡視」『琉球新報』1907年2月3日)

"Honbuko no gakugei-kai", *Ryukyu Shimpo,* March 30, 1907
(「本部校の学芸会」　『琉球新報』1907年3月30日)

"Honbuko no gakugei-kai", *Ryukyu Shimpo*, November 5, 1907
(「本部校の学芸会」 『琉球新報』1907年11月5日)

"Itosu buyu-den—Shorei-ryu no meijin" (1), *Ryukyu Shimpo*, March 15, 1915
(「糸洲武勇傳　昭霊流の名人」(一)『琉球新報』1915年3月15日)

"Itosu buyu-den—Shorei-ryu no meijin" (2), *Ryukyu Shimpo*, March 16, 1915
「糸洲武勇傳　昭霊流の名人」(二)『琉球新報』1915年3月16日

"Itosu buyu-den—Shorei-ryu no meijin" (3), *Ryukyu Shimpo*, March 17, 1915
「糸洲武勇傳　昭霊流の名人」(三)『琉球新報』1915年3月17日

"Itosu buyu-den—Shorei-ryu no meijin" (4), *Ryukyu Shimpo*, March 18, 1915
「糸洲武勇傳　昭霊流の名人」(四)『琉球新報』1915年3月18日

"Itosu buyu-den—Shorei-ryu no meijin" (5), *Ryukyu Shimpo*, March 19, 1915
「糸洲武勇傳　昭霊流の名人」(五)『琉球新報』1915年3月19日

"Itosu buyu-den—Shorei-ryu no meijin" (6), *Ryukyu Shimpo*, March 20, 1915
「糸洲武勇傳　昭霊流の名人」(六)『琉球新報』1915年3月20日

"Itosu buyu-den—Shorei-ryu no meijin" (7), *Ryukyu Shimpo*, March 22, 1915
「糸洲武勇傳　昭霊流の名人」(七)『琉球新報』1915年3月22日

"Itosu buyu-den—Shorei-ryu no meijin" (8), *Ryukyu Shimpo*, March 28, 1915
「糸洲武勇傳　昭霊流の名人」(八)『琉球新報』1915年3月28日

"Jiko boei toshite no karate no myomi wo hakki—Kanju nisen ni fukaki kanmei", *Hawai Hochi*, September 11, 1933
(「自己防衛としての唐手の妙味を発揮　観衆二千に深き感銘」『布哇報知』1933年9月11日)

"Karate honba no nanba-wan—Okinawa taikyo no miyagi-shi—Kaku-chi de　Koen Oyobi Koshu", *Nippu Jiji*, May 7, 1934
(「唐手本場のナンバワン　沖縄体協の宮城氏　各地で講演及講習」『日布時事』1934年5月7日)

"Karate koenkai—Karate kempo no taika Miyagi Chojun sensei no 'Goju-ryu Karate Kempo ni Tsuite'", *Hawai Hochi*, May 10, 1934
(「唐手後援会　唐手拳法の大家宮城長順先生の「剛柔流唐手拳法に就いて」」『布哇報知』1934年 5月10日)

"Karate zadankai" (1), *Ryukyu Shimpo*, October 27, 1936
(「空手座談会」(1)『琉球新報』1936年10月27日)

"Karate zadankai" (2), *Ryukyu Shimpo*, October 30, 1936
(「空手座談会」(2)『琉球新報』1936年10月30日)

"Karate zadankai" (3), *Ryukyu Shimpo*, October 31, 1936
(「空手座談会」(3)『琉球新報』1936年10月31日)

"Karate zadankai" (4), *Ryukyu Shimpo*, November 1, 1936
(「空手座談会」(4)『琉球新報』1936年11月1日)

"Karate zadankai" (5), *Ryukyu Shimpo*, November 2, 1936
(「空手座談会」(5)『琉球新報』1936年11月2日)

"Karate zadankai" (6), *Ryukyu Shimpo*, November 6, 1936
(「空手座談会」(6)『琉球新報』1936年11月6日)

"Karate zadankai" (7), *Ryukyu Shimpo*, November 7, 1936
「空手座談会」(7)『琉球新報』1936年11月7日)

"Karate zadankai" (8), *Ryukyu Shimpo*, November 8, 1936
「空手座談会」(8)『琉球新報』1936年11月8日)

"Karate shoreikai", *Ryukyu Shimpo*, February 10, 1908
(「唐手奨励会」『琉球新報』1908年2月10日)

"Karate no denrai", No.1, *Okinawa Times*, April 25, 1922
(「唐手の伝来」(上)『沖縄タイムス』1922年4月25日)

"Karate no denrai", No.2, *Okinawa Times*, April 27, 1922
「唐手の伝来」(下)『沖縄タイムス』1922年4月27日

"Karate no tatsujin tachi ga ichido ni atsumatta kino no shihan gakko bujutsu kenkyu-kai", *Ryukyu Shimpo*, March 21, 1918
(「唐手の達人達が一同に集まった昨日の師範学校武術研究会」『琉球新報』1918年3月21日)

"Karate wa bugei no kotsuzui nari", *Ryukyu Shimpo*, January 9, 1913
(「唐手は武芸の骨髄なり」『琉球新報』1913年1月9日)

"Katabaru no ryoku kakuko undokai", *Ryukyu Shimpo*, October 6, 1906
(「潟原の両区各校運動会」『琉球新報』1906年10月6日)

"Kempo taika iku", *Ryukyu Shimpo*, March 13, 1915
「拳法大家逝く」『琉球新報』1915年3月13日)

"Kenka no taiiku dantai wo morashite—Okinawa-ken taiiku kyokai umaru", *Okinawa Asahi Shimbun*, November 22, 1930
「県下の体育団体を網羅して　沖縄県体育協会生まる」『沖縄朝日新聞』1930年11月22日

"Kotetsu gotoki ken: roren jukutatsu no meijin", *Ryukyu Shimpo*, 14/3/1915.
(「鋼鉄の如き拳　老練熟達の名人」『琉球新報』1915年3月14日)

"Kumejima tsushin", *Ryukyu Shimpo*, December 5, 1905
(「久米島通信」『琉球新報』1905年12月5日)

"Kumejima tsushin", *Ryukyu Shimpo*, February 14, 1907
「久米島通信」『琉球新報』1907年2月14日)

"Kumejima tsushin", *Ryukyu Shimpo*, October 3, 1907
(「久米島通信」（下）『琉球新報』1907年10月3日)

"Manjo no kansen wo kanpuku saseta—karatejutsu no iroku", *Okinawa Asahi Shimbun*, November 11, 1930
(「満場の観衆を感服させた　唐手術の偉力」『沖縄朝日新聞』1930年11月11日)

"Meisho wo 'karate' ni toitsu shi shinkokai wo kessei!", *Ryukyu Shimpo*, 26/10, 1936
(「名称を〝空手〟に統一し　振興会を結成！」『琉球新報』1936年10月26日)

"Naha Shuri rinji rengo undokai", *Ryukyu Shimpo*, March 9, 1905
(「那覇首里臨時連合運動会」『琉球新報』1905年3月9日)

"Ogawa shigakukan shisatsu-dan", *Ryukyu Shimpo*, May 5, 1905
(「小川視学官の九州視察談」『琉球新報』1901年5月5日)

"Okinawa kara sensei nyuraku—Karatejutsu no koshu", *Ryukyu Shimpo*, October 1, 1928
(「沖縄から先生入洛　唐手術の講習」『京都帝国大学新聞』1928年10月1日)

"Okinawa no bugi No.1—Asato Anko-shi dan (Shoto)", *Ryukyu Shimpo*, January 17, 1914
(「沖縄の武技」（上）安里安恒氏談（松濤）『琉球新報』1914年1月17日)

"Okinawa no bugi No.2—Asato Anko-shi dan (Shoto)", *Ryukyu Shimpo*, January 18, 1914
「沖縄の武技」(中) 安里安恒氏談 (松濤)『琉球新報』1914年1月18日

"Okinawa no bugi No.3—Asato Anko-shi san (Shoto)", *Ryukyu Shimpo*, January 19, 1914
「沖縄の武技」(下) 安里安恒氏談 (松濤)『琉球新報』1914年1月19日

"Osato magiri shokonsai to kangei-kai", *Ryukyu Shimpo*, June 20, 1906
(「大里間切招魂祭と歓迎会」『琉球新報』1906年6月20日)

"Ranbokan no yose-ijo", *Ryukyu Shimpo*, January 15, 1899
(「乱暴漢の養成所」『琉球新報』1899年1月15日)

"Rengo undokai", *Ryukyu Shimpo*, November 11, 1905
「連合運動会」『琉球新報』1905年11月11日)

"Ryukyu bujutsu no fukyu wo hakaru—Okinawa Budo Kyokai", *Okinawa Asahi Shimbun*, May 23, 1925
(「琉球武術の普及を計る　沖縄武道協会」『沖縄朝日新聞』1925年5月23日)

"Ryukyu denrai kempo—karate no meishu raifu", *Nippu Jiji*, March 17, 1927
(「琉球伝来拳法　唐手の名手来布」『日布時事』1927年3月17日)

"Ryukyu no mutekatsu-ryu", *Osaka Jiji Shimpo*, August 9, 1908
「琉球の無手勝流」『大阪時事新報』1908年8月9日)

"Seinen embu taikai (futsuka-me)", *Osaka Jiji Shimpo*, August 7, 1908
(「青年演武大会 (2日目)」『大阪時事新報』1908年8月7日)

"Shichibu ita wo tsukiyabutta—Karate no meijin Yabe Chui", *Hawai Hochi*, March 25, 1927
(「七分板を突き破った　唐手の名人屋部中尉」『日布時事』1927年3月25日)

"Shihan gakko enkaku hobo" (3), *Ryukyu Shimpo*, June 27, 1906
(「師範学校沿革略」(3)『琉球新報』1906年6月27日)

"Shihan gakko karate taikai", *Ryukyu Shimpo*, January 25, 1911
(「師範学校唐手大会」『琉球新報』1911年1月25日)

"Shihan gakko kinenkai yoko", *Ryukyu Shimpo*, June 19, 1907
(「師範学校記念会余興」『琉球新報』1907年6月19日)

"Shihan gakko soritsu kinenkai", *Ryukyu Shimpo*, June 22, 1907
(「師範学校創立記念会」『琉球新報』1907年6月22日)

"Shihan gakko soritsu kinenshiki", *Ryukyu Shimpo*, June 22, 1906
「師範学校の創立記念式」『琉球新報』1906年6月22日)

"Shihan gakko no sotsugyoshiki", *Ryukyu Shimpo*, March 26, 1911
「師範校の卒業式」『琉球新報』1911年3月26日

"Shihan gakko no sotsugyoshiki", *Ryukyu Shimpo*, March 27, 1907
「師範学校の卒業式」　『琉球新報』1907年3月27日)

"Shihan gakko - kaiko kinen-shi", *Ryukyu Shimpo*, June 16, 1906
「師範学校　開校記念式」『琉球新報』1906年6月16日)

"Shihan karate taikai", *Ryukyu Shimpo*, February 22, 1915
「師範唐手大会」『琉球新報』1915年2月22日)

"Shihan kojo ryoko no gakugeikai", *Ryukyu Shimpo*, December 21, 1905
(「師範高女両校の学芸会」『琉球新報』1905年12月21日)

"Shihan kojo no rengo dai undokai", *Ryukyu Shimpo*, October 28, 1906
(「師範高女の連合大運動会」『琉球新報』1906年10月28日)

"Shihan koto jogakko shosho juyoshiki", *Ryukyu Shimpo*, March 29, 1905
「師範高等女学校証書授与式」『琉球新報』1905年3月29日)

"Shinkoku jihen", *Ryukyu Shimpo*, July 9, 1900
(「清国事変」『琉球新報』1900年7月9日)

"Shinpi-teki na bujutsu Ryukyu no 'karate'", *Tokyo Nichinichi Shimbun*, June 3, 1922
(「神秘的な武術琉球の「唐手」」『東京日日新聞』1922年6月3日)

"Shuri-ku shokonsai", *Ryukyu Shimpo*, April 6, 1906
「首里区招魂祭」『琉球新報』1906年4月6日)

"Shussei gunjin oyobi kazoku dai-ikkai kenbu taikai", *Ryukyu Shimpo*, April 15, 1904
(「出征軍人及家族救護第一回剣舞大会」『琉球新報』1904年4月15日)

"Tokubetsu kokoku: Dai- Nippon Butokukai Okinawa-ken chiho iincho Naharaha danshaku", *Ryukyu Shimpo*, May 11, 1902
(「特別広告　大日本武徳会沖縄県地方委員長奈良原男爵」『琉球新報』1902年5月11日)

"Tomari no shukushokai", *Ryukyu Shimpo*, August 23, 1900
「泊の祝捷会」『琉球新報』1900年8月23日)

"Undo-kai Zakkan", *Ryukyu Shimpo*, November 13, 1905
(「運動会雑感」『琉球新報』1905年11月13日)

"Yagi socho no kangei-kai", *Ryukyu Shimpo*, October 21, 1899
「屋宜曹長の歓迎会」『琉球新報』1899年10月21日)

"Yamada Butokukai kanji-cho no taiwa", *Ryukyu Shimpo*, May 9, 1902
(「山田武徳会幹事長の談話」『琉球新報』1902年5月9日)

"Yoshu gakko no kaiko-shiki", *Ryukyu Shimpo*, May 15, 1905
(「養秀学校の開校式」『琉球新報』1905年5月15日)

"Yuntan denshinkyoku kaishi-shiki", *Ryukyu Shimpo*, March 29, 1907
(「読谷山電信局開始式」『琉球新報』1907年3月29日)

TIMELINE

Year	Todi and Karate Events in Okinawa	Budo and Karatedo Events in Japan
1187	King Shunten assumes the throne.	
1260	King Eiso assumes the throne.	
1350	King Satto assumes the throne.	
1392	The so-called "Thirty-six Families" from China settle in Kumemura near Naha. Thirty-six is a figurative number for many families.	
1404	The Ming Emperor sends the first ambassadorial delegation to Ryukyu.	Zeami writes *Fushi Kaden* in 1400.
1406	The Sho dynasty begins with the ascendance of Sho Shisho.	
1429	Sho Hashi unifies the Three Kingdoms.	
1458	The "Bridge of Nations Bell" is cast and hung in the main hall of Shuri Castle. Gozamaru-Amawari Rebellion.	
1469	Ryukyu Pavilion established in Fuzhou.	
1479	Record of a king's armed procession (*Richo Jitsuroku*). Sho Shin becomes king of Chuzan.	
1500	Oyake Akahachi rebellion.	
1531	*Omoro Soshi* compiled.	
1534	*Shi Ryukyu-ki*.	
1537	Sho Shin's conquest of Oshima.	
1554	Yaraza Mori Castle completed.	
1605	*Ryukyu Shinto-ki*.	
1609	Satsuma Shimazu's invasion of Ryukyu.	
1611	Satsuma decrees the "Fifteen Articles of Law" for governing Ryukyu.	
1612	Establishment of the Ryukyu Kan in Satsuma.	
1613	The possession of guns in Ryukyu is prohibited in principle.	

Year	Todi and Karate Events in Okinawa	Budo and Karatedo Events in Japan
1623	*Omoro Soshi* Vol. 3.	1621 Mao Yuanyi writes *Wubei Zhi* (*Bubishi*) published in 240 volumes. Satsuma Jigen-ryu named. Genpin Chin is said to have introduced jujutsu in this period. Takuan writes *Fudochi Shin-myo-roku.*
1631	Satsuma sends a magistrate to Naha.	1632 Yagyu Munenori writes *Heiho Kadensho.*
1646	Satsuma bans the export of weapons and armour.	
1650	Haneji Choshu writes *Chuzan Seikan.*	
1667	*Haneji Directives* promulgated.	
1683	Wang Ji writes *Shi Ryukyu Zatsuroku.*	
1701	*Chuzan Seifu* written by Sai Taku.	*Gekiken* (full-contact swordsmanship) begins in the Jikishinkage-ryu.
1718	Tamagusuku Ueekata Chokun appointed as master of ceremonies (entertainment) for royal ceremony.	
1721	Pao-kuang Hsü writes *Chuzan Denshin-roku.*	
1762	Tobe Genzan writes *Oshima Hikki.*	
1778	Aka Chokushiki writes *Aka Chokushiki Yuigonsho.*	
1801	*Satsuyu-kiko* written by a samurai from Higo.	
1816	Basil Hall visits the Ryukyus is an English sloop.	
1818	Basil Hall publishes *Account of a Voyage of Discovery to the West Coast of Corea and the Great Loo-Choo Island in the Japan Sea.*	
1840	Three British ships visit Ryukyu.	
1850	Nagoya Sagenta writes *Nanto Zatsuwa.*	
1853	Perry visits with the US fleet.	Tokugawa Nariaki writes *Kaibo Gunson Jukka-jo.*
1854	Perry visits again and signs the Ryukyu-US Treaty of Amity.	

Year	Todi and Karate Events in Okinawa	Budo and Karatedo Events in Japan
1855	French ship arrives in Ryukyu, signing of the Treaty of Amity between Ryukyu and France.	
1858		The Bakufu builds the Kobusho military academy.
1859	Signing of the Treaty of Peace between the Ryukyus and the Netherlands, and the Makishi-Onga Incident.	
1866	Final investiture mission confirms Sho Tai as King of Ryukyu.	
1867	Record of *todi* performance at end of investiture mission.	
1870	Dispatch of tribute envoys to the Qing Dynasty.	
1871	Botansha Incident.	
1872	Establishment of Ryukyu domain.	
1873	Matsumura Sokon presents Kuwae Ryosei with a secret document on martial arts.	
1875	Meiji Government decides to ban trade with Qing Empire. Adoption of the Japanese (solar) calendar in Ryukyu.	
1877	The Ryukyu issue reappears as a diplomatic problem between Japan and China. Around this time, Yoshimura Choza receives instruction in karate.	Kano Jigoro starts Tenjin Shin'yo-ryu.
1878	The issue of ceding Miyako and Yaeyama to the Qing government emerges.	
1879	March 27, Ryukyu Disposition. Meiji Government establishes Okinawa prefecture.	
1880	Funakoshi Gichin is taught by Asato Anko. Shuri Middle School and Okinawa Normal School established.	
1882	Matsumura Sokon presents Kuwae Ryosei with scrolls.	Kano Jigoro founds Kodokan Judo.

Year	Todi and Karate Events in Okinawa	Budo and Karatedo Events in Japan
1883	Yoshimura Chogi receives instruction from Matsumura Sokon. Many Okinawans defect to the Qing Empire.	
1889	Higaonna Kanryo receives instruction from Yoshimura Chogi.	
1890	Yabu Kentsu and Hanashiro Chomo join the Army Training Corp.	
1893	Launch of *Ryukyu Shimbun*.	
1895		Establishment of the Dai-Nippon Butokukai.
1898	Conscription Order enforced in Okinawa.	
1899		The Butokuden in Kyoto is constructed. The *Butokusai* festival is held on May 4. Nitobe Inazo publishes Bushido: The Soul of Japan.
1900	Reports of karate related to the Boxer Rebellion.	Match rules for kenjutsu and jujutsu established by the Butokukai.
1901	Around this time, karate classes began at Shuri Primary School (Miyagi Chojun, *Karatedo Gaisetsu*).	
1902	Karate demonstration at the graduation ceremony of Okinawa Prefectural Normal School. Mutekatsu-ryu perfromed at the "Northern Union Sports Festival".	
1903	Jinruikan Incident. Okinawan display at the 5th International Industrial Exhibition.	Dai-Nippon Butokukai adopts the titles of *Hanshi* and *Kyoshi*. *Seirensho* certificate becomes subordinate to the title of *Kyoshi*.
1904	Okinawan Middle School staff trained in karate (taught by Asato Anko and Higaonna Kanryo).	
1905	Karate is taught as a regular class in most middle and normal schools in Okinawa under the guidance of Hanashiro and Yabu.	Establishment of a martial arts teacher training college in Kyoto.
1906	Higaonna Kanryo teaches karate at the Fisheries School and Naha Industrial School. Yabu becomes teacher at the Normal School.	Dai-Nippon Butokukai formulates standardised kenjutsu and jujutsu *kata*.

Year	Todi and Karate Events in Okinawa	Budo and Karatedo Events in Japan
1907	Tokuda Antei and others demonstrate at the Butokuden.	
1908	Okinawa Prefectural Middle School students perform karate at the 10th Youth Demonstration, hosted by the Butokukai. Kano is there to observe. Submission of "Ten Articles of Itosu" to the prefectural school affairs division (October). Yabu teaches karate at the Normal School as a club activity.	
1909		Butokukai becomes an incorporated foundation. Kano becomes the first Asian member of the IOC.
1910	Petty officers in the Naval Training Fleet (Rear Admiral Yashiro) study *Naihanchi* at the Normal School.	
1911	Certificate of promotion awarded at the graduation ceremony of Okinawa Normal School.	Establishment of the Japan Sports Association (Chairman: Jigoro Kano).
1912	Officers from the First Naval Fleet teach karate at the First Middle School during a port stop at Nakagusuku Bay.	Japan's first participation in the 5th Olympic Games in Stockholm (delegate leader: Jigoro Kano).
1913	Funakoshi's "bone marrow" article in *Ryukyu Shimpo*.	
1914	Article in Ryukyu Shimpo on Asato Anko. Under the pseudonym of Shoto, Funakoshi Gichin pens "Okinawa no bugi".	
1915	March—Itosu Anko dies. The *Ryukyu Shimpo* publishes an article entitled "Itosu buyuden Shorei-ryu no meijin". Miyagi Chojun goes to Fuzhou (April-June). Higaonna dies in October.	Butokukai match and refereeing rules for jujutsu established.
1916	Demonstration in Butokuden by Funakoshi and Matayoshi.	Takano Sasaburo (Professor at the Tokyo Higher Normal School) publishes *Kendo*.
1917	Miyagi Chojun revisits Fuzhou.	
1918	Inauguration of the Karate Kenkyu Kai by Funakoshi and Mabuni et al.	

Year	Todi and Karate Events in Okinawa	Budo and Karatedo Events in Japan
1919	Funakoshi succeeds Yabu as karate *Shihan* of the Normal School.	Dai-Nippon Butokukai changes terminology from *bujutsu* to *budo*. Bujutsu Senmon Gakko (Bujutsu Vocational School) also changes its name to Budo Senmon Gakko.
1921	The Crown Prince (later Emperor Showa), watches a karate demonstration in the main hall of Shuri Castle on his way to Europe.	
1922		Kano founds the Kodokan Cultural Association and the Yudansha Kai Association. Funakoshi Gichin (54 years old) performs karate at the 1st Exhibition of Sport and Physical Education. Demonstrates karate at the Kodokan, and starts teaching at the Meishojuku. Publishes *Ryukyu Kempo Karate*. Motobu Choki (age 52) wins a prize fight against a foreign boxer in Kyoto. Kano Jigoro announces his ideals of *seiryoku-zen'yo* and *jita-kyoei* (*Sakko* Vol.4 No. 12).
1923		
1924		Konishi Yasuhiro receives *Seirensho* certificate in kendo. Funakoshi Gichin adopts the Dan promotion system. Funakoshi publishes *Ryukyu Kempo Karate*. Keio University's Karate Kenkyu Kai launched.
1925	Inauguration of Okinawa Karate Kenkyu Club (Chairman: Motobu Choyu).	Funakoshi Gichin publishes *Rentai Goshin Karatejutsu*. September issue of *King* runs article, "Fist-fighting karate match".
1926	Miyagi Chojun commissioned to teach karate at the first martial arts seminar held by the Okinawa branch of the Dai-Nippon Butokukai.	Motobu Choki publishes *Okinawa Kenpo Karatejutsu*.
1927	Visit by Kano Jigoro at the invitation of the Okinawa Judo Yudansha Association. Karate demonstration held as part of the welcome event (January).	Kano gives a lecture on "offensive and defensive national physical education" at the Ministry of Education (February). *Sakko* Vol. 6 No. 4.

Year	Todi and Karate Events in Okinawa	Budo and Karatedo Events in Japan
1928		Funakoshi demonstrates at Saineikan. Miyagi demonstrates at Butokuden. Miyagi Chojun holds a karate workshop at Kyoto Imperial University.
1929	Karate is adopted by the Okinawa Prefectural Police Training Center, and Miyagi Chojun becomes the *Shihan*. Miki Jisaburo goes to Okinawa.	Mabuni Kenwa moves to Osaka. Miyagi Chojun, Konishi Yasuhiro and Ueshima Sannosuke perform at *Butokusai* festival (listed in the judo section of the 33rd *Butokusai* Grand Demonstration Programme).
1930	Establishment of the Okinawa Prefecture Sports Association and Karate Division. Miyagi Chojun is appointed as manager. The Karate Club is absorbed into the division.	*Kempo Gaisetsu* written by Miki Jisaburo and Takada Mizuho. Ueshima Sannosuke is awarded *Seirensho* title in judo. Kano publicises *Seiryoku Zen'yo Kokumin Taiiku* (Kodokan Bunka-kai). Record of Konishi Yasuhiro's demonstration. Shinzato Jin'an participates in the Meiji Jingu budo demonstration in place of Miyagi, and was asked about the name of his *ryuha*. Keio Karate Kenkyu Kai publishes first issue of *Ken*.
1931	Miyagi Chojun declares his school as Goju-ryu.	Funakoshi establishes the Dai-Nippon Karatedo Kenkyu Kai
1930	Miyagi Chojun writes *Goju-ryu Kempo*.	Motobu Choki writes *Watashi no Karatejutsu*. Miyagi demonstrates at the Saineikan Budo Tournament. Uechi Kambun starts Pangi Noon-ryu Karatejutsu in Wakayama.
1933	Butokukai establishes branch in Okinawa. Chibana Choshin calls his school Shorin-ryu.	Ueshima Sannosuke is awarded *Kyoshi* for judo. Mutsu Mizuho writes *Karate Kempo*.
1934	Miyagi Chojun becomes a councillor of the Okinawa branch of the Butokukai. Publishes *Ryukyu Kempo Karatedo Enkaku Gaiyo* (*Karatedo Gaisetsu*). Awarded by the MOE for services to sport. Goes to Hawaii (February 1935).	Mabuni Kenwa publishes *Kobojizai Goshinjutsu Karate Kempo*. Mabuni's (Goju-ryu at this stage) *Seirensho* is replaced with the title of *Renshi*. Publishes *Kobojizai Karate Kempo - Sepai no Kenkyu* (Karate Kenkyusha, *Karate Kenkyu* No.1.
1935		Ueshima Sannosuke performs at the *Butokusai* Festival with his daughter. Demonstrates with Miyagi Chojun and Yogi Jitsuei. Funakoshi Gichin publishes *Karatedo Kyohan*.

Year	Todi and Karate Events in Okinawa	Budo and Karatedo Events in Japan
1936	Miyagi Chojun goes to Shanghai (February). Okinawa karate master roundtable discussion "From karate (Chinese hand) to karate (empty hand) (October 25). Okinawa Karatedo Promotion Association formed (November).	Miyagi Chojun gives a lecture in Osaka based on *Ryukyu Kempo Karatedo Enkaku Gaisetsu*.
1937	*Karatedo Kihon Kata Juni-Dan* formulated.	Butokukai *Kyoshi* titles for Miyagi, Konishi and Ueshima. Miyagi Chojun commissioned as a member of the Okinawa Butokuden construction committee.
1938		Otsuka appears in *Butokusai* and becomes *Renshi*. Mabuni Kenwa and Nakasone Genwa's *Kobo Kempo Karatedo Nyumon* published. Mabuni calls his school Shito-ryu. Kano Jigoro dies on board the Hikawa-Maru. Nakasone Genwa publishes *Karatedo Taikan*.
1939	Ujita Shozo (Ritsumeikan) and others study for two months with Miyagi.	Wado-ryu registered with the Butokukai. Eto Takehiko (Meiji University) and Kihara Hidejiro (Tokyo University of Agriculture) pass the *Renshi* examination. Mabuni is awarded *Renshi* in karatejutsu (July).
1940	Miyagi formulates *Gekisai Dai-ichi*.	Ueshima Sannosuke, commissioned as a Butokukai judge (1940–41). Funakoshi, appears in the *Butokusai* demonstration and was awarded *Renshi* (was upgraded to *Tasshi* in 1942).
1941	*Fukyu Kata* 1 (Nagamine Shoshin); *Fukyu Kata* 2 (Miyagi Chojun) formulated.	Many records of karate demonstrations. In summer, Matsuzaki and 3 others from Keio go to Okinawa. Fukui. Students from Takushoku University also go to Okinawa and receive instruction from Miyagi and other masters. Autumn, Meiji University Karate Club holds a commemoration All Japan Student Karatedo Demonstration to celebrate registration with the school's Athletic Association.

Year	Todi and Karate Events in Okinawa	Budo and Karatedo Events in Japan
1942		Dai-Nippon Butokukai reorganised into a government-run entity. Headquarters moved from Butokuden in Kyoto to the Ministry of Health and Welfare. Miyagi Chojun teaches at Ritsumeikan University.
1943		*Butokusai* festival cancelled due to worsening war situation.
1944	Most of Naha is destroyed by fire in the Okinawa Air Raid (also known as the 10/10 Air Raid). Motobu Choki dies.	
1945	Commander Ushijima Mitsuru commits suicide on June 22 in Okinawa.	Butokukai is disbanded by GHQ.
1947	Nagamine Shoshin calls his school Shorin-ryu.	Funakoshi returns to Tokyo.
1948	Chibana Choshin forms the Okinawa Shorin-ryu Karatedo Kyokai.	All Japan Student Federation is formed by Keio, Waseda, Chuo, Hosei, Senshu and Takushoku universities. However, it does not become a nationwide organisation.
1950	The Okinawa Gunto Government is formed. University of the Ryukyus opened.	Students from 20 universities form the Student Karate Federation. Japan Karate Association formed (Saigo Kichinosuke). Japan Karatedo Gojukai started (Yamaguchi Gogen).
1952	Ryukyu Government Founding Ceremony. Establishment of the Karatedo Goju-ryu Promotion Association founded (Nakaima Genkai appointed as chairman).	Mabuni Kenwa dies.
1953	Miyagi Chojun dies.	Obata, Kamata, Nishiyama go to the USA and give workshops.
1954		Shotokan JKA reorganised.
1955		All Japan Student Karatedo Federation is established and starts activities.
1956	Okinawa Karate Federation established (Okinawa Four Schools united, Chibana Choshin is president). Okinawa Karatedo Gojukai formed (Yagi Meitoku).	Funakoshi Gichin publishes *Karatedo Ichiro.*

Year	Todi and Karate Events in Okinawa	Budo and Karatedo Events in Japan
1957		Funakoshi Gichin dies (4/26). All Japan Student Karate Embukai (7/4). 1st All Japan Student Championships (Winner: Meiji University).
1958		6/10 1st All Kansai Student Championships (Ritsumeikan wins). 1st All Japan Individuals Championships (Mimoto Hitoshi wins). *Kakugi* (combat sports) introduced into the Junior High School National Curriculum.
1959	Statutes and regulations of Okinawa Karate Federation Dan-Kyu examinations established. Karate and *kobujutsu* introduced in the teaching materials of junior high schools.	
1960	Okinawa Prefecture Homeland Reversion Conference convened. The International Karate and Kobudo Federation is established (Higa Seko is president). Okinawa Karate Federation petitions for the adoption of karate into the physical education curriculum of primary, junior, and senior high schools.	
1962		All Japan Student Karatedo Federation reorganised.
1963	Shorin-ryu Karatedo Kyokai withdraws from Okikawa Karate Federation. 50th anniversary of Itosu Anko's death. Miyagi Chojun's 10th anniversary.	
1964	A monument in honour of Itosu Anko is erected. Karate stamp series (*Naifanchi*) released.	Nippon Budokan constructed. The Japan Karatedo Federation is formed (Ohama Nobumoto). Establishment of Kyokushinkan by Oyama Masutatsu.
1965		All Japan Student Karatedo Federation, 1st US-Japanese Student Goodwill Match.
1966		Formation of the European Karate Union (EK) and the 1st European Championships.

Year	Todi and Karate Events in Okinawa	Budo and Karatedo Events in Japan
1967	Okinawa Karate Federation is dissolved, and All Okinawa Karatedo Federation is established with Nagamine Shoshin as chairman.	2nd US-Japanese Student Goodwill Match.
1968		Japan Karatedo Federation with Sasakawa Ryoichi as chairman. Mexico Olympic Invitational International Karatedo Championship (Winner: Takeshi Oishi). 19th Mexico Olympic Memorial International Karatedo Championship (first official international tournament).
1969		Inauguration of the Japan Karatedo Federation as an incorporated foundation (Chairman Sasakawa Ryoichi). 3rd US-Japanese Students Goodwill Match. 1st FAJKO All Japan Championship (Iida Norihiko wins. Uechi Kan'ei demonstrates *kata*). Death of Kasuya Shinyo (80).
1970		1st European-Japanese Student Goodwill Tournament. WUKO is launched with Sasakawa Ryoichi as chairman and Eriguchi Eiichi as secretary general. 1st WUKO World Karatedo Championship (Wada Koji wins the individual competition).
1971	Okinawa Reversion Agreement.	Formation of the All Japan Company Federation.
1972	5/15 Return of administration for Okinawa to Okinawa prefecture.	The Japan Sport Association approves membership of the JKF. 2nd WUKO World Karatedo Championship (Paris). Asian Pacific Union of Karatedo Organizations gets under way.
1973	Special National Sports Festival (*Kokutai*) held to commemorate the return of Okinawa to Japan (Wakakusa National Sports Festival Meet).	1st Asia Pacific Karatedo Championships (Singapore).
1974	Okinawa High School Athletic Federation establishes a karate division (first tournament was held).	

Year	Todi and Karate Events in Okinawa	Budo and Karatedo Events in Japan
1975	Nagamine Shoshin's *Shijitsu to Den-to wo Mamoru Karatedo* published.	3rd WUKO World Karatedo Championship (Long Beach, USA, won by Murakami Kunio). Pan-American Karatedo Union formed. JKA withdraws from JKF.
1976		Ohama Nobumoto dies (84).
1977	Uechi Kan'ei's *Seisetsu Okinawa Karatedo–Sono Rekishi to Giho* is published.	4th WUKO Karate World Championships in Tokyo. Official men's *kata* event (Okada wins). Inauguration of the Japanese Budo Association.
1978		Pre-*Kokutai* (Nagano), 3 height classes for *kumite* (LMS).
1979		Pre-*Kokutai* (Miyazaki), 3 weight classes for *kumite* (light, middle, heavy), men's *kata*.
1980	Okinawa prefecture Board of Education considers introducing karate into schools.	Pre-*Kokutai* (Tochigi). 5th WUKO Karate World Championships (Madrid); 6 weight categories for men, and *kata* events for women. JKF, JKA and Kyokushinkai consider reorganising (amalgamating).
1981	Okinawa Karatedo Federation established with Nagamine Shoshin as president.	Karate becomes official event of National Sports Festival (Shiga), 4 divisions in *kumite* (open weight added); women's *kata*.
1982	Okinawa Karate and Kobudo Federation established.	6th WUKO Karate World Championships in Taipei; women's *kumite* event.
1983	Matsumora Kosaku monument erected (Naha City).	1st World Games, Santa Clara, USA.
1984	Prefectural Board of Education "Instructions for Karate in Schools".	7th WUKO Karate World Championships in Maastricht, the Netherlands.
1986		The 8th WUKO Karate World Championships (Sydney). Gima Shinkin and Fujiwara Ryozo's *Kindai Karate wo Kataru* is published.
1987	Monument erected in honour of Miyagi Chojun and Higaonna Kanryo (Matsuyama Park, Naha City). 42nd National Sports Festival (Kaiho *Kokutai*) held in Okinawa.	

Year	Todi and Karate Events in Okinawa	Budo and Karatedo Events in Japan
1988	Okinawa and Fuzhou Martial Arts Association exchange.	9th WUKO Karate World Championships in Cairo, Egypt.
1989		PE subject "Kakugi" changed to "Budo" in the National Curriculum.
1990	First Uchinanchu Tournament (Karatedo Kobudo World Exchange Festival) held in cooperation with three federations. Monument erected in honour of Kanryo in Fujian.	10th WUKO Karate World Championships in Mexico City.
1991		
1992		11th WUKO Karate World Championships in Granada, Spain.
1993	Okinawa Karate Federation established.	World Union of Karate Organizations, WUKO changes name to World Karate Federation.
1994	Okinawa prefecture Board of Education publish *Karatedo Kobudo Kihon Chosasho I.*	Karatedo becomes official event at the Hiroshima Asian Games. 12th WKF Karate World Championships in Kota Kinabalu, Malaysia.
1995	Okinawa prefecture Board of Education publish *Karatedo Kobudo Kihon Chosasho II.* 50th anniversary of the Battle of Okinawa. Okinawa Karate and Kobudo World Tournament Pre-Convention. 2nd Uchinanchu Tournament (Okinawa Convention Centre).	1st Tokyo World Women's Karatedo Championship.
1996	Okinawa prefecture Board of Education, Culture Division publishes *Gakko Kyoiku ni okeru Karatedo Shido Tebiki Vol.2.*	13th WKF Karate World Championships in Sun City, South Africa.
1997	Inauguration of the Okinawa Prefectural Budokan.	
1998		14th WKF Karate World Championships in Rio de Janeiro, Brazil.
1999	Monument erected in honour of Kyan Chotoku (Kadena Town). Kinjo Akio's *Karate Den-shin-roku—Denraishi no Genryu-ga-ta* published.	WKF recognised by the IOC.
2000		15th WKF World Karatedo Championship in Munich, Germany.

Year	Todi and Karate Events in Okinawa	Budo and Karatedo Events in Japan
2001	3rd Worldwide Uchinanchu Festival Tournament (Okinawa Convention Centre).	First karate participation in Japan Masters. The 1st All Japan Boys and Girls Championships (Nippon Budokan).
2002		16th WKF Karate World Championships in Madrid, Spain.
2004		17th WKF World Karatedo Championship in Mondelez, Mexico. Japanese Budo Association create the "Children's Budo Charter".
2005	Okinawa prefecture designates October 25 as Karate Day. The Proposal at "Conference on Human Resource Development for Independence" to unify the four karate organisations in Okinawa.	
2006	The missing section of the *Karate Zadankai* discussion of 1936 is found. The 4th Uchinanchu Tournament (Okinawa Convention Centre).	18th WKF World Karatedo Championship (Tamperej, Finland).
2007	Funakoshi's "No first move in karate" monument erected in Onoyama Park.	
2008	Okinawa Traditional Karatedo Promotion Association is established (Governor Nakaima Hirokazu is the first chairman). Unity of the four Okinawan organisations: All Okinawa Karate Federation (Chairman: Senaga Yoshitsune), Prefectural Federation (Chairman: Hijiya Yoshio), Prefectural Union (Chairman: Goya Hidenobu), and Karate and Kobudo Federation (Chairman: Shima Isao).	19th WKF Karate World Championships (Tokyo, Japan). Revision of National Curriculum to make budo compulsory in all junior high schools.
2009	2009 Okinawa Traditional Karatedo World Tournament.	
2010		Distribution of the Junior High School "Guide to Karatedo Instruction" at the 1st National Instructors Training Seminar. 20th WKF World Karatedo Championship in Belgrade, Serbia.

Year	Todi and Karate Events in Okinawa	Budo and Karatedo Events in Japan
2011	The 5th Worldwide Uchinanchu Festival Tournament (Okinawa Convention Centre).	
2012		In April, Junior high school budo compulsory classes. Karate is the adopted budo in about 126 schools. 21st WKF Karate World Championships (Paris, France).
2014		Revised version of the junior high school "Guide to Karatedo Instruction" is distributed at the 5th National Instructors Training Seminar. 22nd WKF World Karatedo Championship in Bremen, Germany.
2016	Karate Promotion Section established in Okinawa prefecture. 6th Worldwide Uchinanchu Festival Tournament (Okinawa Convention Centre and other venues).	23rd WKF World Karatedo Championship in Linz, Austria.
2017	Opening of Okinawa Karate Kaikan.	Nine budo arts (including judo, kendo and sumo) are specified in the revised National Curriculum.
2018	The 1st World Okinawa Karate International Tournament.	
2020		Karate to debut as Olympic sport in Tokyo. Event to be conducted at the Nippon Budokan. Postponed to 2021.

INDEX

Y

PROFILE

Koyama Masashi

Born in 1952 in Kagawa prefecture. Currently specially appointed professor at Morinomiya Academy of Medical Sciences; part-time lecturer at Osaka University; member of the Japan Karatedo Federation's School Budo Development Committee; JKF certified 6th Dan.

Wada Koji

Born in Kanagawa prefecture in 1949. Currently a standing director of Shotokan's JKA; director of Mita Karate Kai and chairman of the Promotion Committee. JKF certified 6th Dan.

Kadekaru Toru

Born in Okinawa prefecture in 1956. Currently a part-time lecturer at the University of the Ryukyus and Okinawa University (Exercise and Sports Science - Karate); standing director of Okinawa Goju-ryu Karatedo Kyokai; committee member of the Okinawa prefecture Culture and Arts Promotion Council. *Kyoshi* 8th Dan of Okinawa Goju-ryu Karatedo Kyokai.

Translator—Alex Bennett

Born in New Zealand in 1970. Professor of Japanese history and budo at Kansai University. Director of the New Zealand Kendo Federation; All Japan Kendo Federation International Committee; All Japan Jukendo Federation International Committee; vice president of the International Naginata Federation. Kendo *Kyoshi* 7th Dan.

Karate
Its History and Practice

（空手道—その歴史と技法 英語版）

（定価はカバーに明記してあります）

令和 3 年 8 月 1 日　初版第 1 刷　印刷
令和 3 年 8 月 1 日　初版第 1 刷　発行

著　者　小山 正辰・和田 光二・嘉手苅 徹
訳　者　アレキサンダー ベネット
発行者　臼井 日出男
発行所　公益財団法人 日本武道館
　　　　〒 102-8321 東京都千代田区北の丸公園 2 番 3 号
　　　　電　話　03-3216-5100　/　FAX　03-3216-5158

《不許複製・禁転載》

ISBN978-4-583-11401-9　C0075